D1714784

Entrepreneurship as Experience

Entrepreneurship as Experience

How Events Create Ventures and Ventures Create Entrepreneurs

Michael H. Morris

Oklahoma State University, USA

Christopher G. Pryor

Oklahoma State University, USA

Minet Schindehutte

Syracuse University, USA

with

Donald F. Kuratko

Indiana University, USA

Edward Elgar
Cheltenham, UK • Northampton, MA, USA

Published by
Edward Elgar Publishing Limited
The Lypiatts
15 Lansdown Road
Cheltenham
Glos GL50 2JA
UK

Edward Elgar Publishing, Inc.
William Pratt House
9 Dewey Court
Northampton
Massachusetts 01060
USA

A catalogue record for this book
is available from the British Library

Library of Congress Control Number: 2011942536

MIX
Paper from
responsible sources
FSC® C018575

ISBN 978 1 84844 048 7

Typeset by Servis Filmsetting Ltd, Stockport, Cheshire
Printed and bound by MPG Books Group, UK

Contents

Figures

Tables

Boxes

Foreword: Why readers in search of new ideas should make *Entrepreneurship as Experience* part of *their* experience

At the entrance of the gym where I regularly work out stands a bulletin board containing the following message: "Experience is not what happens to a man/woman; it is what that person *does* with what happens to him/her." I don't know why this particular quotation (unattributed) was chosen for display, but it is very hard for me to imagine a statement that better captures the essence of this provocative and creative book. Although the book has many themes – all of which might well be worthy of comment here – the central one is that although, in a very real sense, entrepreneurs create their new companies, they, in turn, are shaped, formed, and changed by the experiences they have en route, while attempting to convert ideas generated by their own creativity into something tangible – a product, service, process, raw material, whatever – that is both new and useful, and also creates economic or social value. This, as the authors aptly and carefully note, is at the heart of the process. And as they eloquently put it, this complex journey – from ideas to reality – is "Largely unscripted, unpredictable and uncontrollable" and is *personally* experienced by the entrepreneur. Having been an entrepreneur myself, I could not agree more: in many ways, I *was* a different person after moving through all the steps in the process – formation of the idea, seeking intellectual property protection for it, obtaining required resources (financial, technical, social), and then, finally, founding and running the company. And it was indeed a rich and absorbing experience or, more accurately, set of experiences.

Interestingly, the idea that we are shaped by our experiences – and, more importantly, what we *do* with these events as they unfold – was central to the field of psychology when it emerged more than 100 years ago. Learning was viewed as *the* central process, and it was – and still is – defined as *relatively permanent changes in behavior* resulting from experience (with the term "behavior" meaning everything we do, feel, or think). Moreover, these experienced-generated changes are distinct from one produced by factors such as physical maturation, and temporary causes such as illness, fatigue or, even, the effects of several glasses of wine! So powerful was the faith of early psychologists in the central importance of this "change through experience" idea, that by the 1920s, John B. Watson, one of the key founders of the scientific side of psychology made the following claim: "Give me a dozen healthy infants, well-formed, and my own specified world to bring them up in, and I'll guarantee to take any one at random and train him to become any type of specialist I might select – doctor, lawyer, artist, merchant-chief and, yes, even beggar-man and thief, regardless of his talents, penchants, tendencies, abilities, vocations, and race of his ancestors" (Watson, 1924/25, *Behaviorism*). In his view, then, experience clearly trumped everything else in forming human behavior.

This somewhat extreme view has, of course, been called into serious question by growing evidence that even complex forms of human behavior are, in fact, influenced by genetic factors. Indeed, some researchers in entrepreneurship (especially Scott Shane and his colleagues) even propose, and find evidence for the view, that genetic factors underlie even the decision to become an entrepreneur. Such claims remain controversial, but regardless of their ultimate fate, they do not in any way detract from or contradict the primary logic developed in *Entrepreneurship as Experience*. Even if genetic factors do somewhat restrict the impact of what happens to us during life, there can be no doubt that to a large degree, we *are* a product of this intricate web of events, and – of course – our interpretations of and reactions to it.

This raises an intriguing question that, in a sense, might be viewed as a subtext of this book. Are entrepreneurs really different from other persons, and, if so, *why*? Several branches of management (e.g., human resources management, organizational behavior) would answer: "Of course," they would argue, "entrepreneurs *must* be different for the same reasons that the members of any given, highly-selected occupation or career group are different from those in other occupation or career groups." Are emergency room physicians different from accountants in their personal characteristics and preferences? Of course. Are professional politicians different from, for instance, scientists? Again, the answer is "almost certainly." How, in fact, could it be otherwise? Each of these groups has contrasting motives, different goals, and are attracted to distinct kinds of work and situations. As expressed clearly in the well-known attraction-selection-attrition model, various occupational or career groups are indeed different from one another because (1) only some individuals are attracted to a given profession or activity, (2) only some find that they actually enjoy or are suitable for these careers or activities, and (3) only some of *these* succeed and remain in their chosen field. Entrepreneurs can hardly be different in this respect, but as the authors of this book note, entrepreneurship itself *is* different. Unlike dentists, military officers, or even CEOs, entrepreneurs, at least during early stages of the process, must perform a hugely varied array of tasks and activities. Moreover, unlike fields such as medicine, accounting, architecture, or engineering, there are no firmly established principles or rules they must acquire and follow as they proceed. This virtually assures that entrepreneurs' experiences will be incredibly varied – much more diverse than those of persons in other fields or professions. In a very basic sense, entrepreneurs are "mavericks" when they start, and as a result of their enormously varied experiences, almost certainly become more so – more unique, more varied – as the entrepreneurial process unfolds.

And so I come to a final key question: what can we learn from adopting the experience-focused perspective recommended in this book? Like the authors, I believe that the answer is "many valuable things." First, the field of entrepreneurship itself may finally learn to stop treating or viewing entrepreneurs as a homogeneous group. On the contrary, entrepreneurs probably show greater variability along almost any chosen dimension than any other group. (Although perhaps there are a few exceptions to this general principle: entrepreneurs may actually be somewhat less varied with respect to creativity, the capacity to persevere, and passion for what they do – basic requirements for starting and completing the journey). As the authors note, however, great variability among entrepreneurs in terms of many other dimensions is reflected in the kinds of ventures they start. These do not all fit the "high-growth, high-profit" model that is widely accepted in the media and even in our own entrepreneurship courses. Rather, while many new ventures do fit this model, others involve many different approaches, for instance "survival or extra income" ventures – ones in which the entrepreneurs simply want to earn extra income or merely enough to maintain their current lifestyle; "cocktail party" ventures – in which entrepreneurs don't expect to generate significant profits, but enjoy living the lifestyle of an entrepreneur, and telling others (e.g., other guests at cocktail parties) that this is what they do; and "start-sell-and-get-out" ventures, where entrepreneurs who enjoy the process itself start with the intention of an early sell so that they can repeat the process! In a sense, entrepreneurs who adopt these different models for their new ventures are doing what the authors of this book suggest – they are not merely being changed by their experiences, they are also actively selecting or creating these experiences.

Similarly, the experience-based approach recommended in this book directs attention to the key point that human beings are truly *active*-information processors: they are involved in constant efforts to understand and interpret what happens to them so that they can make sense out of it, adapt to it, and move on from there as stronger and more competent persons than before. Such "sense-making" activities are important for everyone, but may be especially important for entrepreneurs, who often find themselves facing highly uncertain and unpredictable environments in which accurate interpretations of their experiences are essential. Perhaps this is one reason why entrepreneurs are often strong supporters of the view that "what doesn't kill you makes you stronger." They, even more than most other persons, recognize the need for, and benefits of, accurate understanding of their own experience.

In sum, this is indeed a thought-provoking book and one that provides the proverbial "breath of fresh air" to a field that, by its very nature, views creativity, flexibility, and adaptability as very close to the top of any list of desirable human attributes. Readers who perform the hard cognitive work necessary to integrate this volume's many intriguing ideas into their own thinking, will, I'm sure, find that they themselves have been are changed, in constructive ways, by *that* set of experiences.

Robert A. Baron
Stillwater, Oklahoma
November, 2011

About the authors

Michael H. Morris, Ph.D. holds the N. Malone Mitchell Chair in Entrepreneurship at Oklahoma State University and is the Head of the School of Entrepreneurship at OSU. He has built nationally recognized entrepreneurship programs at three universities, and is a pioneer in curricular innovation and high impact experiential engagement with the entrepreneurial community. Morris founded and annually runs the Experiential Classroom, the leading forum on best practices in entrepreneurship education. He also annually leads the Entrepreneurship Empowerment in South Africa (EESA) Program, working with historically disadvantaged entrepreneurs. A widely published author and researcher, Morris has written nine books and over 130 peer-reviewed academic articles in the *Journal of Business Venturing*, *Journal of Management*, *Entrepreneurship Theory and Practice*, *Journal of Business Ethics*, *Journal of International Business Studies*, and *Journal of the Academy of Marketing Science*, among others. He is the co-editor of the Entrepreneurship Series published by Prentice-Hall, and a former editor of the *Journal of Developmental Entrepreneurship*. Morris is a past president of the United States Association for Small Business & Entrepreneurship. In addition, he has been a principal in three entrepreneurial start-ups. He has received the Edwin M. and Gloria W. Appel Prize for contributions to the field of entrepreneurship, and is a recipient of the regional Ernst and Young Entrepreneur of the Year Award. He is a former Fulbright Scholar (South Africa, 1993), was selected as one of the top 20 entrepreneurship professors in the United States by *Fortune Small Business*, and has been inducted as a "21st Century Entrepreneurship Research Fellow" by the Global Consortium of Entrepreneurship Centers. In 2011 he received the Leavey Award from the Freedoms Foundation for affecting private enterprise education.

Minet Schindehutte, Ph.D. is Associate Professor of Entrepreneurship in the Martin J. Whitman School of Management, Syracuse University, New York. A South African national, she has worked both in academia and the private sector, and her professional background includes technical marketing, brand management and entrepreneurship-related activities.

Following completion of her Ph.D. in Chemistry at the University of Pretoria in South Africa, she spent a number of years with Shell Oil, where she was responsible for brand management, new business generation, technical customer consulting, strategic planning, price negotiation, development of new customer service programs, designing and implementing an innovative team-selling system, and production optimization. She subsequently was the founder and managing director of two entrepreneurial start-ups, Proxi Business Resource Centers and PenteVision, Ltd. She has served as a strategic marketing consultant to a number of major companies in South Africa and the United States. Her current research interests center on interfaces between entrepreneurship, innovation, marketing and strategy.

Christopher G. Pryor is currently a Ph.D. candidate in the School of Entrepreneurship at Oklahoma State University. He obtained his MBA from OSU in 2009, and has been active in the School of Entrepreneurship at various levels since the school's inception in 2008. Pryor's current research interests include institutional entrepreneurship and opportunity exploitation. Prior to returning for his Ph.D., Pryor worked as a reporter and editor at several newspapers, including *The Dallas Morning News*, and led several magazine and tabloid start-ups.

Donald F. Kuratko, Ph.D. is the Jack M. Gill Chair of Entrepreneurship, Professor of Entrepreneurship and Executive Director, Johnson Center for Entrepreneurship & Innovation, Kelley School of Business, Indiana University – Bloomington. He has published over 180 articles on aspects of entrepreneurship. His work has appeared in journals such as the *Journal of Business Venturing, Entrepreneurship Theory & Practice, Strategic Management Journal, Journal of Operations Management, Academy of Management Executive, Journal of Small Business Management, Family Business Review*, and the *Journal of Business Ethics*. Professor Kuratko has authored 24 books, including the leading entrepreneurship books in the world today, *Entrepreneurship: Theory, Process, Practice*, 8th edn (2009), as well as *Corporate Entrepreneurship & Innovation*, 3rd edn (2011), and *New Venture Management* (2009). In addition, Kuratko has been a consultant on corporate entrepreneurship and innovation to a number of major Fortune 100 corporations. Kuratko also serves as the Executive Director of the Global Consortium of Entrepreneurship Centers. His honors include earning the Entrepreneur of the Year award for the state of Indiana and induction into the Institute of American Entrepreneurs Hall of Fame. He has been honored with The George Washington Medal of Honor; the Leavey Foundation Award for Excellence in Private

Enterprise; and the NFIB Entrepreneurship Excellence Award. In addition, he was named the National Outstanding Entrepreneurship Educator by the US Association for Small Business and Entrepreneurship and he was named one of the Top 50 Entrepreneurship Scholars over the last ten years. Kuratko was honored by *Entrepreneur* magazine as the Number 1 Entrepreneurship Program Director in the US.

1. Entrepreneurship as experience

> Philosophy does not raise questions and does not provide answers that would
> little by little fill in the blanks. The questions are within our life, within our
> history; they are born there, they die there . . . It is a past of experience that
> one day ends up at this open wondering.
> (Maurice Merleau-Ponty, 1960)

INTRODUCTION

The dominant perspective among contemporary entrepreneurship scholars is that the creation of a venture involves a process, or an evolving
set of steps, that happen over time (Carter et al., 1996; Stevenson et al.,
1989). What starts as recognition of an opportunity and development of a
business concept evolves through identification and acquisition of needed
resources, implementation or start-up of the venture, adjustment or modification of the concept, achievement of a sustainable business model, management of growth, and eventually some sort of exit. For the individual
entrepreneur, then, the movement through these steps or stages represents
an emerging, temporal experience. In a very real sense, it is a journey
where both the destination and the path to that destination are uncertain.

We know strikingly little about how this journey unfolds. Yet, as a
venture is launched, takes form, and either becomes sustainable or fails,
we do know that hundreds if not thousands of salient activities, events,
and developments take place. The range of these events is considerable,
entailing everything from rejection of a loan request by multiple banks to
the company's first big sale, and from winning a patent to the loss of a key
employee. Box 1.1 provides further examples of such events. Many of these
events are novel, unexpected, and represent significant highs and lows in
the evolution of the business. A key question concerns how the entrepreneur experiences these developments, how they impact him or her, how
she or he reacts to them, and how they impact ongoing decision-making.

As it is largely unscripted, unpredictable, and uncontrollable, we
argue in this book that the richness of the entrepreneurial journey lies in
how it is personally experienced. Borrowing from Dilthey (1976), there
is a pulsating, rhythmical aspect to the venture creation experience.

1

BOX 1.1   SAMPLE EVENTS AND DEVELOPMENTS AS A VENTURE EVOLVES

Opening day
Significant criticism of your
 business idea
Rejection of loan request by
 multiple banks
First time seeing your
 signage on the building
First sale or first deposit of
 customer check
Closing a major customer
 deal
Hiring first employee
Hours or days with no
 customers
Inability to make payroll
Failure to fulfill a major order
Move from home base to
 own premises
Receipt of major loan from
 bank
Employee theft
Winning a patent
Divorce because business is
 so absorbing
Bounced check from
 customer
Need to sell or mortgage
 personal asset to keep
 business going
Bad publicity of your
 business in media
Hiring your tenth or one
 hundredth employee
Competitor directly copies
 something unique you are
 doing

Purchase of defective goods
 for the business
Testimonial from major
 customer
Major unexpected tax bill
Write up of business in news
 paper
First long-term client contract
Insufficient funds notice from
 your bank
Loss of key account
First period of profit
Supplier cuts you off
Distributor agrees to carry
 your product
Partner disagreement and
 departure
Major commitment from
 customer not honored
Loss of key employee
Bank calls a loan
Purchase of major piece of
 equipment
Angel investor agrees to
 invest
Fine or regulatory restriction
 imposed by government
Significant employee
 accomplishment
Offer from someone to buy
 your business
Technology you have spent
 money developing fails to
 work properly in key test
Employee strike
Robbery

Major piece of equipment is
defective
Weather, flood or fire
disaster
Business wins award
Firing an employee
Landlord forces you to move
Addition of new product or
service to your line
Expansion of facilities
Purchasing your own
building
Customer fails to pay
Personal injury to or death of
an employee
Business is able to give back
to community
Elimination of key product or
service or withdrawal from
a particular market
New competitor enters with
serious advantage
Paying off business debt
First major exhibition of your
product at a trade show

Lawsuit from a customer or
competitor
Asking family member to
leave business
Major insurance claim against
your company
Opening an additional
location
Bank grants you line of credit
First time that demand
exceeds your capacity
Books do not balance
Bribe demand from key
customer or regulator
First time you advertise in
major medium
Contractual commitment
from supplier, customer or
distributor is not honored
Inventory is damaged or
becomes obsolete
Company goes public
Failure of your product in the
field
Employee leaves to start
competing business

Entrepreneurship has a vitality not captured by simply examining aspects of the entrepreneur, opportunity, venture, network or other traditional foci. As a result, we propose that the experienced event should be a principal focus in attempts to understand entrepreneurship. Further, we argue that these experiences are richly affective in nature, meaning they give rise to emotions and feelings as they are processed by the individual. In addition, we suggest that a better understanding of the ways in which events are processed and acted upon holds great promise in addressing a number of critical questions surrounding the entrepreneurial process.

If entrepreneurship is fundamentally experiential, much remains to be learned about the nature of the experience. What is it like to be "in the moment" as a venture takes form? What are the implications of experiencing an inability to meet payroll for weeks on end, acquisition of a customer contract that seemed unattainable, the successful launch of a revolutionary product, or alienation of one's family as a venture becomes all-consuming? These sorts of events represent the fabric of the entrepreneurial experience and, while it is generally acknowledged that they occur, their significance has not been explored (Gartner, 1993).

Extant work in entrepreneurship emphasizes the impact of previous professional and personal experiences on venture management and performance (e.g., Cliff et al., 2006; Corbett, 2007; Krueger, 2007). Experience is an asset one brings to the venture. Just as important, however, is the ongoing, real-time experiencing of events as a venture unfolds. As Bird and West (1997, p. 5) have noted, "temporal dynamics are at the heart of entrepreneurship." The unfolding experience is replete with mundane and momentous events, changes in pace as things slow down or speed up, developments that represent emotional highs and lows, and periodic turning and tipping points that punctuate attempts at establishing repetition and rhythm in the business (Dew and Sarasvathy, 2007; Lichtenstein et al., 2007).

This book explores entrepreneurship as a phenomenon experienced uniquely by each individual. The entrepreneur is, in effect, constructing their own reality as they experience a temporal series of salient, interacting events. These events give rise to a wide range of feelings and emotions. A critical question concerns how such events are processed. We argue that this processing involves the dynamic interplay between cognitive, affective, and physiological elements.

We will argue that individuals "experience" venture creation just as they do other dominant aspects of life, and that positive and negative emotions and feelings are at the core of human experiencing. Cumulative exposure and reaction to a wide array of novel, idiosyncratic events surrounding the entrepreneurial process serve to form the entrepreneur and influence development of an entrepreneurial mindset. As with a painting that emerges based on the individual interacting with, feeling, and agonizing over his or her creation, the entrepreneur is a work in progress.

The manner in which events are processed also has implications for the type of venture that emerges. The venture an individual sets out to create typically differs meaningfully from what is actually created (Drucker, 1985). Mistakes are common, changes are emergent, and many actions are unplanned. Ongoing goal-setting, risk-taking, and decision-making are heavily impacted by the occurrence of salient events and the manner in which they are processed. As a by-product of this processing, the entrepreneur's affective state (e.g., exhilarated, exhausted, depressed) at a given moment can result in actions that are more bold or conservative, novel or predictable, aggressive or passive. Hence, what started out as a family-owned, lifestyle venture operating in a niche market might emerge as a privately-held, high-growth firm serving global markets. An experiential view also moves us past a static "snapshot" perspective and approaches entrepreneurship as a dynamic, socially-situated process driven by unfolding events. Our focus becomes the emergent and temporal nature of a venture. Further, it allows for the fact that the many events occurring as a venture unfolds are experienced and responded to by different actors in different ways (Politis, 2005).

Our purpose, then, is to introduce a new lens through which to view entrepreneurship – the first-person perspective of the individual's multi-dimensional experience. We start in this opening chapter by defining the terms "experience" and "experiencing." We then look at how the venture creation experience can be captured as a sequence of events and event streams that vary in volume, velocity, and volatility. An overview of how experiences are processed is then provided. Attention is devoted to an examination of why an experiential perspective is needed in entrepreneurship. Finally, we explore 11 unique characteristics of entrepreneurship as an experience.

DEFINING EXPERIENCE AND EXPERIENCING

Experience is an elusive construct. Laing (1967, p. 18) notes, "I cannot experience your experience. You cannot experience my experience . . . Experience is man's invisibility to man." How individuals experience the world around them is a topic that scholars have wrestled with for hundreds of years. The universal nature of experiencing has attracted researchers from an array of disciplines. A number of theoretical perspectives have been employed to examine such diverse experiences as being poor in the inner city, participating in extreme sports, having cancer, consuming a product, and being an undergraduate student (see Table 1.1 for examples). Regardless of their perspective, scholars uniformly agree on the ambiguous yet complex nature of experience as a subject of inquiry (e.g., Throop, 2003). As such, in this book we employ a cross-theoretic perspective for understanding the experiential nature of entrepreneurship.

What is an *experience*? In Table 1.2, we provide a range of definitional perspectives on this construct. Synthesizing this work, we define an experience as a lived-through event, where the individual is "in the moment" (Cantor et al., 1991). It is the content of consciousness, synonymous with "what it is like," in our case when creating a new venture (Bruner, 1986; Throop, 2003). Experiences can include fairly discrete events, sets of

Table 1.1 Disciplinary perspectives on experiencing

Author(s)	Type of Experience	Discipline [Theory]	Characteristics of experience	Dimensions [Methodology]
Mano and Oliver (1993)	Post-consumption experience	Marketing [expectancy theory]	Interrelationships between judgment, affective responses evoked and evaluation of high and low involvement products	Product evaluation, elicited affect, satisfaction [survey]
Taylor (1994)	Wait experience of delayed airline passengers	Marketing [attribution theory]	Negative affective reactions (anger, frustration) mediate the relationship between delay and service attribute evaluation	Affective (uncertainty and anger) [surveys with interviews]
Gersick et al. (2000)	Professional relationships experience	Management [network theory]	Roles of workplace relationships in professional career logics of men and women	Helpfulness, harmfulness, and emotional support of relationships [in-depth interviews]
Kotha et al. (2004)	Online purchasing experience	Marketing [resource-based theory]	Internet experience	Quality ratings, Tobin's Q
Birnbaum et al. (2001)	Sexual experience	Psychology [phenomenology]	Feelings, thoughts, and motives regarding the relationship, self-awareness, and the experience itself	Emotional, cognitive, motivational [in-depth interviews]

Tarrant et al. (1994)	Outdoor recreation experiences	Psychology [arousal theory]	Physiological and psychological responses to recalled experiences (active, passive, and distressful)	Arousal, clarity of thought, and pleasure [repeated measures design]
Csikszentmihalyi and Larson (1996)	Optimal experience in work or leisure	Psychology [flow theory]	Impact of flow on the quality of experience	Affect, potency, concentration, creativity, motivation, relaxation, satisfaction [experience sampling method]
Taylor et al. (2001)	Lived experiences of battered women	Psychology [eidetic phenomenology]	Issues, motivations, fears, and hopes of abused women from different cultures	Colaizzi's themes and sub-themes [unstructured interviews]
Russell (1999)	Experience in the intensive care unit	Nursing [bio-psycho-socio perspective]	Causes of psychological problems after discharge	Thematic analysis of patients' memories [survey and interviews]
Moch (1990)	Breast cancer experience	Nursing [Newman's theory]	Newman's theory of illness as expanding consciousness supported by crisis and developmental theory	Emergent themes extracted from person–environment interactions [open-ended interviews]

Table 1.2   Definitions of experience

Author(s)	Definition
Turner (1986)	Mere experience is simply the passive endurance and acceptance of events
Desjarlais (1997)	An "inwardly reflexive, hermeneutically rich process that coheres through time by way of narrative"
Kant ([1781] 1990)	A priorist rendering of experience as arising out of the categorical structuring of what is otherwise an undifferentiated sensory flux
Locke ([1689] 1979)	A synthesis of active reflection and passive sensation
Gadamer (1975)	A fluctuating "immediacy that precedes all interpretation" and a mediated coherence that "makes a special impression that gives . . . lasting importance"
Levinas (1998)	Experience is simultaneously understood as an intentionally structured "presence" and a "temporal flux of a sensuous matter"
Husserl ([1948] 1997)	Every lived experience, every consciousness, is subject to the original law of flow. It undergoes a continuity of alterations that cannot be indifferent to its intentionality and that must, therefore, come to light in its intentional correlate. Every concrete lived experience is a unity of becoming and is constituted as an object in internal time consciousness in the form of temporality
Geertz (1986)	An "interpretive replay [of an event] as we recollect it to ourselves and recount it to others"
James ([1912] 1996)	A non-reflexive, non-verbal, pre-conceptual "feeling" that grasps the "immediate flux of life" in terms of its undifferentiated unfolding in the field of sensory immediacy, prior to its organization into distinctive contents, forms, and structures
Gorcia-Prieto et al. (2003)	We define the individual experience of a diversity category as the subjective importance that a team member gives to a particular social identity, at a particular moment, in a particular context

events over longer time frames, and events that entail multiple stages over a few years. For an individual, experiences are authentic, transparent, immediate, visible, and subjectively interpreted (Desjarlais, 1997).

"Experiencing" is the active participation in the events surrounding a particular activity or phenomenon (Csikszentmihalyi and Larson, 1996). It involves the individual receiving these events into one's consciousness and can include sensing, feeling, unconscious reacting, reflecting, interpreting, and linking to other experiences (Bruner, 1986; Mano and Oliver, 1993). Hence, experiencing something implies being conscious of something; being conscious of something implies experiencing something.

The act of experiencing is complex and occurs simultaneously at different levels. Experiences can be perceptual (e.g., touching, seeing), bodily sensational (e.g., pain, nervousness, loss of appetite), imaginative (e.g., regarding one's own actions and perceptions), and streams of thought, as in the experience of thinking "in words" or "in images" (Czikszentmihalyi, 1990). The individual processes and encodes these layers in sensorial, affective, and motor ways rich in implicit meaning (Tuan, 1977).

Jackson (1996, p.42) suggests that there are "significant differences between the way the world appears to our consciousness when we are fully engaged in activity and the way it appears to us when we subject it to reflection and retrospective analysis." Consequently, at least two modes of experiencing (two rather different selves) can be identified on the basis of how brain systems coordinate with consciousness: (1) an "objective me" (distinguishable from "objective others") uniquely experiences the contents or objects of the event as they occur, and (2) a "monitoring, narrative I" that subsequently re-constructs the experience in the form of a self-composed narrative, where interpretations of episodes or events are moderated by attention, intention, and thinking (Pribram, 1999). The content may well change between these two modes.

As we attempt to grasp the complex nature of "lived experience" in the chapters ahead, three distinct philosophies guide our efforts. The first of these, phenomenology, is concerned with how lived-through events are internalized and manifested by an individual's consciousness. Phenomenology grew out of the early twentieth-century work of Edmund Husserl and his followers, such as Martin Heidegger, Alfred Schütz, and Maurice Merleau-Ponty. Today phenomenology has broadened to include perspectives such as existentialism and social constructionism. The second philosophy, pragmatism, is concerned with how meaning is constituted through social experiences, or individuals' interactions with each other. Pragmatism developed from the philosophical works of William James and John Dewey in the late nineteenth and early twentieth centuries and was expanded by later scholars, especially in the sociology of George Herbert Mead and Herbert Blumer. The third philosophy, critical theory, is concerned with the interaction between social structures and individuals. Based on Bourdieu's theory of practice, this perspective suggests that through practical lived-through experience with social structures, individuals develop *habitus*, which are acquired schemas that influence their thought and action with relation to their social context (Bourdieu, 1977).

TEMPORAL STRUCTURES: EVENTS, STREAMS, AND STOCKS

Experiences are temporal, occurring at points in time and over time. Hence, experience has been examined as a short-lived consumer purchase (Mano and Oliver, 1993), and the more cumulative experience of living as a battered wife (Buchbinder and Eisikovits, 2003). Experiences produce "information" in the form of "bundles of explanations," which is characterized in neuro-psychological terms as categorization, while "processing" is characterized as constructive operations by which multi-modal categories are physically and temporally related (Edelman, 1987). Since information processing is tied to experience and experience is embedded in time, experience can also be subdivided into finer units of measure.

The conclusion that experience has a temporal structure is well-substantiated in the literature. Turner (1986), for instance, posits that there are moments of experience that represent component parts of an emerging structure of experience. Throop (2003) concludes that the structure of experience derives from a combination of temporal succession, fragmentary disjunction, and meaningful coherence. For our purposes, experience at a particular slice in time, or operating within a relatively narrow time expanse, can be considered an action-relevant episode, significant instance, or *event* (Bruner, 1986; Magnusson, 1981). One's life involves thousands of events, many of which are not meaningfully different from the homeostatic state, resulting in little attention paid to that moment in time. A fraction of these are considered significant by the individual (Bruner, 1986). An example of such an event might be the moment an entrepreneur sees the amount on their first check from an angel investor.

When multiple instances over time are related, the resultant accumulated picture can be referred to as a *stream of experience* (Magnusson, 1981 uses the term "sequence"). The metaphor of a stream is expanded upon by Throop (2003, p. 228), who explains that a stream "comes into being and passes away, moment by moment," and that it "ebbs and flows continually forward while retaining residues . . . of past experience(s)." This stream can vary in duration depending on the definitive bounds being arbitrarily assigned to an experience (Reuber and Fischer, 1999). Given its idiosyncratic nature, the way in which each person delineates the parameters of the same type of experience depends upon their conscious analysis and decision as to what streams and instances should be included. Using the receipt of angel funds in the example presented above, the stream of experience in which this instance is embedded might encompass the experience of determining financial needs, searching for venture financing, a number of rejections, deferring the payment of bills, and various daily aspects of being an entrepreneur. In each of these examples, there is a path-dependent quality to the stream, such that each instance interacts with the next in the creation of the stream.

To be meaningful, the events that constitute an experience do not have to be contiguous in time and space. Further, the form of constructed experiences does not depend on then–now causal relations, but on a complex interaction of present with past and past with present – and anticipation of the future (Bradley, 2005). In processing events, much may be filtered out and forgotten almost as soon as it has registered, while other aspects are the focus of attention, and still others are peripheral and get processed if not immediately attended to (Bradley, 2005; Magnusson, 1981). Entrepreneurs also differ in their "temporal depth," or the time distances they consider when contemplating streams of events that have occurred (Bluedorn and Martin, 2008). What emerges, then, is entrepreneurship as a rich mosaic of interwoven events that are unevenly processed. Entrepreneurial experiencing is an immediate, inwardly reflexive, and interpretatively rich process that coheres through time (Desjarlais, 1997).

When referring to one's cumulative experience of a given type, all the instances and streams of that type are melded to become what might be termed a *stock* (Reuber and Fischer, 1999). When a person is asked how much entrepreneurial experience they have, they are being asked to add up the various temporal streams of experience they have been part of. When asked how they feel about being an entrepreneur, the individual again combines these streams, but in his or her own personal way, either conjunctively or disjunctively, to arrive at their stock assessment. These bouts of entrepreneurial experiences may not necessarily be temporally juxtaposed, yet a person collects and merges them to define their stock of experience. It is the stock quality of experience that is most frequently referred to by entrepreneurship scholars (Westhead et al., 2005). As we have noted, this stock often appears as the antecedent within research studies (e.g., Eckhardt and Shane, 2003).

Does the venture creation experience have a definable beginning and end? As with many experiences, it may be difficult to identify discrete points of start and stop. Cope and Watts (2000) suggest that it can prove difficult to define the perpetual boundaries of particular experiences. A pregnancy experience, for instance, may arguably end with the birth of a child, but there may be lingering physical and psychological aspects that remain highly relevant for one's ongoing functioning and experiencing. Turner (1986, p. 35) argues that the structure of experience "does not have an arbitrary beginning and ending, cut out of the stream of chronological temporality, but has what Dewey called 'an initiation and a consummation'." Clearly subjective, little guidance exists for how to define relevant time parameters. Magnusson (1981) proposes the use of generative rules that dominate the context (e.g., venture sustainability not yet established), such that the experience lasts as long as the generative rule prevails. Where such rules are not apparent, he emphasizes achievement of the end the individual was pursuing when entering the objective situation. Thus, we might conclude that the venture creation experience represents the time frame from the decision to start the venture to the point where a sustainable business model is in place and ostensibly working.

VOLUME, VELOCITY, AND VOLATILITY

If we think about the venture creation experience in terms of stocks and streams of events, then what are the properties of these stocks and streams? There are at least three key properties, which we can label volume, velocity, and volatility.

Volume refers to the number of salient events that are processed as the experience unfolds. This total can vary significantly as it is the individual entrepreneur who attaches some level of saliency to a given development. Any two individuals who start the same type of venture and encounter some of the same events are likely to process those events differently. Thinking back to the events in Box 1.1, a given entrepreneur may or may not attach saliency to some of these developments. Variables such as the relative novelty of the event, the entrepreneur's knowledge base, and previous entrepreneurial experience might be expected to influence the number of events that are included in one's streams and overall stock. High volumes of events create distinct challenges in terms of information processing, sense-making, emotional reactions, and the entrepreneur's sense of control.

We define velocity as the rate at which these events are processed. It concerns how rapidly events come at the entrepreneur. Higher volumes of events generally mean higher velocity, although the pace at which events are encountered likely varies over time. Thus, there could be periods of extremely high velocity and periods of relatively low velocity. Planning becomes more problematic when the pace at which salient events are encountered is high. Moreover, the abilities to properly interpret a given event, understand its meaning, emotionally adjust, and behaviorally respond can be compromised by high levels of event velocity. Alternatively, high velocity may find the entrepreneur performing at high levels, where he or she achieves peak experiences and flow, or is "in the zone." This is a topic to which we will return in Chapter 8.

The third property underlying stocks and streams is volatility, or the extent to which events vary in their degree of intensity. Events can be more positively or negatively intense. Volatility captures the degree of variance, and hence the peaks and valleys (highs and lows) associated with the events being experienced over time. As with velocity, volatility likely varies over time, and one would expect it to lessen as a sustainable business model takes root and the venture stabilizes. However, high rates of venture growth, ongoing innovation, and new market entry are examples of factors that would likely contribute to greater velocity and volatility. The wide swings associated with a more volatile venture creation experience are likely to result in stronger affect, and thus stronger emotional swings. These ups and downs can contribute to dysfunctional behaviors, such as employee abuse, alcoholism, and poor eating and sleeping habits.

Increased volume, velocity, and volatility can produce a more interesting, engaging, challenging, and fulfilling entrepreneurial experience. Similarly, all three can contribute to the levels of stress, anxiety, and physical exhaustion in a venture. Importantly, as we shall see in the chapters to come, they have implications for the entrepreneur's behavior and decision-making, and ultimately for the type of venture that emerges.

EXPERIENTIAL PROCESSING

What happens as a founder experiences a continuous stream of new and novel events? Each event is unique, with any two individuals experiencing the same event differently. In fact, the event is not the same to the extent that a person becomes part of the experience as it occurs – there is reciprocal interaction between the entrepreneur and context. To the individual, there is directionality to an experience, with a center and periphery of attention (Bruner, 1986). He or she is in the moment, a participant in a performance, responding to cues as they occur. The individual attempts to impose structure on events as they are received into consciousness, in the process making them intelligible. It is a gestalt structure, more complex than the sum of its component parts (Weick, 1979).

The processing of experiences entails more than rational thought. The complex demands associated with the entrepreneurial context go beyond rational assessment, hypothesis testing, pre-defined goals, and planning. Venture creation is riddled with unexpected obstacles, interrupted plans, conflicting goals, and unattainable aspirations. These realities force ongoing reconstruction and renegotiation of thought–feeling–action repertoires to ensure continued progress in venture development.

Beyond rational thought processes, then, experiential processing includes emotions, impulses, and physiological responses as individuals react to a diverse, multi-faceted, and imposing array of activities and developments (Cardon et al., 2009). Further, outcomes of ongoing processing impact the entrepreneur's emotional or affective state (e.g., the experience as positive/negative, or as intense/passive), which in turn influences decision-making (Baron, 2008). This perspective is consistent with recent interest in a situated view of entrepreneurial action (Berglund, 2007), emphasizing the interface between inner and outer environments "in the mud of common human experience" (Sarasvathy, 2004, p. 289).

We argue that the entrepreneurial experience involves an interplay of cognition, affect, and physiological responses as events are "lived through" (Barrett, 2006). Bi-directional links exist among all three (Forgas, 1999; Stein and Levine, 1999). Thus, Pessoa et al. (2002) have found attenuation of an emotional response during increasing levels of cognitive load, while Abercrombie et al. (1998) demonstrate that higher levels of dispositional negative affect are associated with a greater metabolic rate. Consider the entrepreneur who realizes a key order is not coming through, only $3000 remains in the bank, a large payment is due, and a major investor is arguing that the business model is flawed. This temporal event produces physiological reactions such as loss of appetite and nervousness that interact with affective responses such as frustration and panic, which simultaneously result in cognitive reactions, such as heightened awareness, biases in information processing, and some sort of decision about cutting prices.

WHY AN EXPERIENTIAL PERSPECTIVE IS NEEDED IN ENTREPRENEURSHIP

Entrepreneurship as an experience has long been implied in the literature. For instance, Baumol (2001) talks of a gambling experience, and others allude to an adaptive experience (Stoica and Schindehutte, 1999), learning experience (Cope and Watts, 2000), evolutionary experience (Andren et al., 2003), self-discovery experience (Gibb, 1993), peak experience (Schindehutte et al., 2006), social experience (Aldrich and Zimmer, 1986), grieving experience (Shepherd, 2003), and passionate experience (Cardon et al., 2009).

While the experiential nature of entrepreneurship is acknowledged by scholars (e.g., Cope and Watts, 2000), its implications are underdeveloped. Entrepreneurship has generally been conceptualized as a process involving multiple stages over time (Shane and Khurana, 2003). Others have gone further, noting the dynamic, multi-level, intertwined, non-linear and emergent nature of the process (Schindehutte and Morris, 2009). Even so, the research tends to be more static, approaching the venture at a moment in time, or measuring variables between two points in time, ignoring what takes place within the day-to-day or between measuring points. Scholars examine the entrepreneur's strategy, network, perceptions, skills, resource slack, and a host of other variables at a particular moment, often associating such variables with various outcomes. They frequently use cross-sectional surveys, with analysis focused on central tendencies. What is ignored are the realities and abnormalities of ongoing experiencing, which can be far removed from the more recognizable patterns, norms, and averages upon which behavioral researchers dwell, or the situational sampling that drives much research. A considerable amount can be missed or filtered out in terms of the hidden richness that lies within the crevices of a temporal experience. That drama is involved in the unfolding of a new venture is made evident by Downing (2005), while the influence of emotions and feelings is demonstrated by various observers (e.g., Baron, 2008; Brundin et al., 2008; Cardon et al., 2009). Yet, the ability to deconstruct the drama and understand the emotions requires that we integrate new building blocks for developing entrepreneurship theory: the experienced event and temporal structure of events, the corresponding volume (number of events), velocity (rate at which they are processed) and volatility (degree or intensity) of these events, and the processing of events over time. These event streams produce the ongoing highs and lows, and intensity and passivity that are the essence of venture creation.

As a lived experience, we highlight the critical role played by idiosyncratic events that are frequently uncontrollable and unpredictable. Lichtenstein et al. (2007) argue that such events are the essence of entrepreneurship, and give rise to patterns and punctuating moments. The ongoing processing of events, interdependencies among them, and cumulative impact they have on affective and cognitive states at any point in time hold significant implications. An experiential perspective offers promising insights into critical questions about which relatively little is known. For instance, how do ongoing experiences foster a willingness to adapt one's initial concept into something quite different? Does experiencing influence an individual's tendencies to become more tolerant of ambiguity, optimistic, or achievement motivated? Do aspects of experiencing become addictive, or result in addictive behaviors? The experiential perspective moves our focus to streams of salient events that not only define what it is like to be an entrepreneur, but are triggers for the emergent nature of a venture. The entrepreneur is being constructed while he or she constructs reality. A portfolio of significant events is accumulating, each contributing to the entrepreneur's emotional fabric and ongoing decision-making.

WHAT IS UNIQUE ABOUT ENTREPRENEURSHIP AS AN EXPERIENCE

Implied in the argument that entrepreneurship should be approached as an experience is the notion that there is something about venture creation that distinguishes it from other life experiences. While there are idiosyncrasies in how any venture unfolds, the entrepreneurial experience does have a number of common characteristics. Let us consider 11 of these characteristics:

1. *Temporal*: Venture creation involves a series of events and activities, many of which are unplanned and unexpected, occurring over a number of months and years. As time unfolds, the entrepreneur processes, responds to, and is also personally affected by these events. Past events affect interpretation of and reactions to current ones, and expectations about future ones. A challenge with examining entrepreneurship as an experience is the difficulty in defining temporal boundaries. Does venture creation begin with the start of the business, with the conception of an idea for a business, or at some other time? Does it conclude when the venture has developed to the point where its business model and profit performance is sustainable, when the entrepreneur exits the venture, or at some other point in time? As with the experience of motherhood or alcoholism, once one is an entrepreneur, is she or he always an entrepreneur?

2. *Purposive and terminable*: Entrepreneurship is a choice. While some are pushed into a venture by necessity and others are pulled by opportunity, the individual chooses to become an entrepreneur. As a purposive action, the individual is motivated by a host of possible considerations (e.g., survive, generate an income, build wealth, be independent, achieve a vision or dream, improve one's community, change the world), and is making some level of commitment. He or she is pursuing a path that is individualistic in nature, even where partners or others are involved, and attempting to take control of their own destiny. Further, while the barriers to exit can sometimes be significant, the individual has the ability to quit the experience if he or she desires.

3. *Idiosyncratic*: Every individual experiences venture creation in their own unique way. A given event is not typically experienced identically by any two individuals. Further, the events given salience, and the amount of salience given to an event, will vary across entrepreneurs. Thus, streams and stocks that define the entrepreneurial experience will differ among individuals, even those pursuing the exact

same type of venture in the same type of context or environment. Further, events have the potential to change the entrepreneur, in turn affecting how future events are interpreted and responded to.

4. *Performative*: The entrepreneur is a performer in an unscripted play. More than simply reacting or being a participant, the individual is expected to produce organizational outcomes (survival, financial growth, loyal customers, etc.) based directly on his or her inputs or contribution. One does not know where the entrepreneurial path will lead, but as it unfolds, the entrepreneur must perform at organizing, staffing, producing, selling, financing, distributing, and much more. Especially in the early stages of a venture, it is a performance that is judged on virtually a daily basis. One can see the relative difference in terms of the performative nature of the entrepreneurial experience in considering someone who acquires a highly-structured franchise versus someone who starts their own venture predicated on a new product or service where a market must be created. In the former case, the franchisee's various roles are fairly tightly scripted. In the latter case, the entrepreneur alternatively finds that success is tied to improvisational performance, especially in the early stages of venture creation.

5. *Transformative*: Entrepreneurship is about change. It involves the individual interacting with the context and environment to produce something novel or new. Elements are being combined in new ways to produce an original outcome. Starbucks created a globally successful venture by combining resources in a unique manner to produce not simply a coffee shop, but a unique customer experience. All ventures create some level of change, whether to a product, a customer market, a competitive context, a technology, a distribution channel, or some other element in the venture's environment. The degree of transformation typically goes up as we move from survival to lifestyle, then to managed growth, and finally to aggressive growth ventures.

6. *Uncertain*: The act of creation takes place in uncertain circumstances where the individual has relatively little control over conditions and outcomes. There is uncertainty regarding customer reactions, responses from competitors, margins one can earn, the veracity of one's technology, regulatory obstacles, and much more. Even with a superior business plan, it is unusual for the entrepreneur to have much certainty regarding the correct price to charge, services to offer, segments to target, employees to hire, location to choose, hours to operate, assets to own, and so forth. Variables beyond the control of the entrepreneur significantly impact what is ultimately created.

7. *Ambiguous*: In the early stages of a venture, the entrepreneur encounters considerable ambiguity surrounding what is to be done and how it should be accomplished. A wide range of needs, opportunities, issues, and challenges remain vague and subject to different interpretations. Ambiguity characterizes the appropriateness of a given course of action. Simple cause-and-effect relationships between actions of the entrepreneur or other stakeholders and both operational and financial outcomes are often not in evidence. It can also be difficult to discern reasons why a given action appears to work and another does not.

8. *Novel*: Venture creation represents an ongoing encounter with novelty. Events occur, perhaps periodically and sometimes frequently, that are in part or wholly unconnected to the entrepreneur's past experiences and expectations. They may be objectively new, or simply perceived to be so. As such, their nature and meaning may be unclear. Novelty is one of the principal reasons that a given event is given saliency by the individual, and hence becomes a defining component of the overall experience.

9. *Diverse*: The performative aspect of the entrepreneurial experience discussed above is complicated by the fact that being an entrepreneur is not a single role, but instead, involves a multiplicity of roles. Diversity is about difference. Many of the roles involved in venture creation require very different skills sets (e.g., creating, negotiating, staffing, planning, organizing, mentoring, allocating, selling). While the entrepreneur sometimes is able to afford and find people with some of these skill sets to whom she or he can delegate particular tasks, she or he is unable to eliminate the considerable diversity that remains with the entrepreneurial role. Moreover, this role is not static. The events encountered as the venture unfolds are themselves diverse, continually placing new demands on the role of the entrepreneur.

10. *Volatile*: The events encountered by the entrepreneur vary both in their intensity and the degree to which they represent positive versus negative developments. For example, it might be expected that the first experience of having one of the company's checks returned by the bank due to insufficient funds is less intense and less negative than, say, losing the company's biggest client. As a sequence of events is encountered over time, the potential exists for wide swings in terms of how intense and positive/negative these developments are perceived to be. The entrepreneurial path can be quite volatile, including any number of emotional peaks and valleys. We can express this volatility as the amount of variance that occurs in the frequency and degree of these highs and lows.

11. *Emergent*: Venture creation is an emergent experience. More than simple evolution, emergence finds new patterns and properties arising over time that are traceable not to a system's properties but to the process of interaction among these properties. Emergence can be found at three levels. The venture is emerging, transforming, and morphing into forms not intended or anticipated when the business was launched. The opportunity on which the venture is predicated is emerging as new facets of market need are discovered and/or created. The entrepreneur is also emerging, for a person does not start as an entrepreneur, but rather, is formed into one. The individual is continually developing an entrepreneurial identity and mindset. The emerging entrepreneurial self is dynamically constructed at the interface between the individual, the environment, and the activities involved in organizational emergence.

Although other experiences demonstrate some of these characteristics, entrepreneurship is unique in the tendency for all 11 to be present, albeit in varying degrees. Importantly, each characteristic described above is core to the fabric of the experience, especially ambiguity and uncertainty. The characteristics also interact with one another. For instance, ambiguity creates uncertainty, and both can be affected by volatility. Novelty can also contribute to uncertainty as well as diversity, and create a need for new forms of performance. The prominence of a given characteristic will likely vary over time. Thus, in a lifestyle-type venture, where size and growth ambitions are limited, one might expect amounts of transformation, volatility, diversity, and novelty to decline relatively early in the venture's life cycle as the founder figures things out.

EXPERIENCE IN THE ENTREPRENEURSHIP LITERATURE

This book introduces a new experiential lens for use in understanding the nature of venture creation. It builds on a rich tradition of research in a number of disciplines, most notably anthropology, psychology, sociology. Yet, there is also an emerging tradition of work on the concept of "experience" in the entrepreneurship literature. Most of this work is quite recent, with some of the earlier work dating to 1985. In Appendix A that follows this chapter, we provide a broad overview of ways in which experience is used within the field of entrepreneurship.

In the Appendix, we organize the extant literature into a set of themes. The diversity of these themes suggest that "entrepreneurial experience" is a complex, multifaceted subject area having an array of foci informed by different disciplines and theories. Hence, there is not one monolithic notion of the "entrepreneurial experience." A number of these themes become relevant as we explore critical issues impacting how entrepreneurs process and respond to the series of events and event streams that make up venture creation. The themes also demonstrate the many interfaces between aspects of experience and leading topics being addressed by contemporary entrepreneurship scholars. These interfaces represent promising new avenues for future research. Importantly, by delineating what has been done on experience, we will demonstrate the distinct contributions of the conceptualization of the entrepreneurial experience provided in the chapters of this book. Moreover, the implications of these differences for future directions in entrepreneurship will be the focus of our closing discussion in Chapter 13.

Fourteen major themes underlie the emerging body of work that addresses experience in entrepreneurship. Overlap exists among these themes, and there is certainly room to classify things into fewer, more or different categories. But the literature here is representative of research efforts to date (we selected a sample of articles in each category). The greatest emphasis in terms of the themes is experience gained in some prior activity or life/career stage, in functional areas of business, and with decision-making and leadership. This perspective centers on human/social capital, where experience is a skill/knowledge/resource that entrepreneurs possess, and these experiences (collectively) have been accumulated in *the past*, and thus are part of the structure of experience (see Chapter 2 on the anthropology of experience). This is quite different from our concern for *the* "experience" in *the present*. Some of the other themes touch on sub-components, outcomes or derivative aspects of our perspective. Thus, expertise is a variable that emerges as events unfold and are processed, and experiential learning and identity formation become important outcomes of experiential processing in our framework. Further, the fact that experiencing has a strong affective component has important implications not only for processing, but for behavioral outcomes of experiencing and for the emergence of the venture.

A critical conclusion from reviewing Appendix A is that what researchers typically do with the word "experience" is very different from the main gist of "experiencing" as we address it in this book. The closest theme to our work is the last one, wherein entrepreneurship as lived experience is the focus. Accordingly, the current work offers promise for new directions and insights from scholars within entrepreneurship. We should also note that a number of articles not included here have "experience" in the title but actually have little to do with the subject area.

CONCLUSIONS

In this opening chapter, we have introduced the concepts of experience and experiencing as they apply to venture creation. As a lived-through phenomenon, entrepreneurship is authentic, transparent, immediate, visible, and subjectively interpreted. Moreover, experience has a temporal structure, such that moments of experience represent component parts of an emerging structure of experience. We have approached the structure of experience in terms of individual events, streams of events, and an overall stock of events. These events and event streams will vary in terms of their volume, velocity, and volatility. As events occur, they are processed by the entrepreneur. This processing is complex and entails more than rational thought. It involves the dynamic interplay between cognition, affect or emotion, and physiological reaction, and produces a range of different outcomes (i.e., emotional states, learning, behaviors, decisions, and ultimately the emergence of the entrepreneur and the venture).

Attention has also been devoted to establishing why an experiential perspective is critical for advancing our understanding of entrepreneurship. It captures the emergent, temporal nature of the venture creation process, and provides a useful way to frame the roles of cognition, affect, and physiology in venture creation. It offers a perspective on such basic questions as "how do individuals develop entrepreneurial mindsets?" and "why does the venture that ultimately results frequently look so different than the venture that was initially intended?"

Life is filled with many experiences that affect and form us as human beings. Sometimes certain of these can serve to define us as human beings, such as the experience of fatherhood, the prison experience, the experience of sexual abuse, the African American experience, or the military experience. Yet, we have argued that the entrepreneurial experience is unique compared to virtually all of life's other experiences, further supporting the importance of approaching entrepreneurship from an experiential perspective. Eleven characteristics contributing to this uniqueness were identified and explored.

In ensuing chapters, we will explore a range of topics surrounding how experiencing can be used to better understand entrepreneurship. We will examine how different disciplines have conceptualized and approached experiencing, and draw implications for entrepreneurship. An integrated model for capturing entrepreneurial experiencing will be introduced. The emotional or affective nature of experiencing will receive extensive attention, including an investigation of how venture creation results in peak experiences, peak performance, and flow. We will explore the implications of experiencing for various facets of entrepreneurship, linking experiencing to some of the other key constructs being focused on by scholars. Most critically, we will look at how experiencing leads to the formation over time of both the entrepreneur and the venture. Attention will also be devoted to reviewing recent empirical work that demonstrates how experiencing can be measured in entrepreneurship. Separately, a chapter will be devoted to discussing the range of issues and approaches to measuring entrepreneurial experiences. The book closes with a discussion of where work on entrepreneurial experiencing goes from here.

REFERENCES

Abercrombie, P. et al. (1998), 'Metabolic rate in the right amygdala predicts negative affect in depressed patients', *Neuroreport*, **9**(14): 3301–7.

Aldrich, H. and C. Zimmer (1986), 'Entrepreneurship through social networks', in D. Sexton and R. Smilor (eds), *The Art and Science of Entrepreneurship*, New York: Ballinger, pp. 23–46.

Andren, L., M. Magnussun and S. Solander (2003), 'Opportunistic adaptation in start-up firms', *International Journal of Entrepreneurship and Innovation Management*, **3**(5): 546–62.

Baron, R.A. (2008), 'The role of affect in the entrepreneurial process', *Academy of Management Review*, **33**(2): 328–40.

Barrett, L.F. (2006), 'Solving the emotion paradox: categorization and the experience of emotion', *Personality and Social Psychology Review*, **10**(1): 20–46.

Baumol, W.J. (2001), 'When is inter-firm coordination beneficial? The case of innovation', *International Journal of Industrial Organization*, **19**(5): 727–37.

Berglund, H. (2007), 'Entrepreneurship and phenomenology', in J. Ulhøi and H. Neergaard (eds), *Handbook of Qualitative Research Methods in Entrepreneurship*, Cheltenham, UK and Northampton, MA, USA: Edward Elgar, pp. 75–96.

Bird, B. and G. West (1997), 'Time and entrepreneurship', *Entrepreneurship Theory and Practice*, **22**(2): 5–9.

Birnbaum, G., H. Glaubman and M. Mikulincer (2001), 'Women's experience of heterosexual intercourse – scale construction, factor structure, and relations to orgasmic disorder', *Journal of Sex Research*, **38**(3): 191–204.

Bluedorn, A.C. and G. Martin (2008), 'The time frames of entrepreneurs', *Journal of Business Venturing*, **23**(1): 1–20.

Bourdieu, P. (1977), *Outline of a Theory of Practice*, Cambridge: Cambridge University Press.

Bradley, B. (2005), *Psychology and Experience*, Cambridge: Cambridge University Press.

Brundin, E., H. Patzelt and D. Shepherd (2008), 'Managers' emotional displays and employees' willingness to act entrepreneurially', *Journal of Business Venturing*, **23**(2): 221–38.

Bruner, E. (1986), 'Experience and its expressions', in V. Turner and E. Bruner (eds), *The Anthropology of Experience*, Urbana, IL: University of Illinois Press, pp. 3–32.

Buchbinder, E. and Z. Eisikovits (2003), 'Battered women's entrapment in shame: a phenomenological study', *American Journal of Orthopsychiatry*, **73**(4): 355–66.

Cantor, N., J. Norem, C. J. Langston, S. Zirkel, W. Fleeson and C. Cook-Flanagan (1991), 'Life tasks and daily life experience', *Journal of Personality*, **59**(3): 425–51.

Cardon, M.S., J. Wincent, J. Singh and M. Drnovsek (2009), 'The nature and experience of entrepreneurial passion', *Academy of Management Review*, **34**(3): 511–32.

Carter, N.M., W.B. Gartner and P.D. Reynolds (1996), 'Exploring start-up event sequences', *Journal of Business Venturing*, **11**(3): 151–66.

Cliff, J., P. Jennings and R. Greenwood (2006), 'New to the game and questioning the rules: experiences and beliefs of founders of imitative vs. innovative firms', *Journal of Business Venturing*, **21**(5): 633–50.

Cope, J. and G. Watts (2000), 'Learning by doing – an exploration of experience, critical incidents and reflection in entrepreneurial learning', *International Journal of Entrepreneurial Behaviour & Research*, **6**(3): 104–19.

Corbett, A.C. (2007), 'Learning asymmetries and discovery of entrepreneurial opportunities', *Journal of Business Venturing*, **22**(1): 97–114.

Csikszentmihalyi, M. (1990), *The Psychology of Optimal Experience*, New York: Harper & Row.

Csikszentmihalyi, M. and R. Larson (1996), 'Experience sampling method applications to communication research questions', *Journal of Communication*, **46**(2): 99–120.

Desjarlais, R. (1997), *Shelter Blues*, Philadelphia, PA: University of Pennsylvania Press.

Dew, N. and S.D. Sarasvathy (2007), 'Innovations, stakeholders & entrepreneurship', *Journal of Business Ethics*, **74**(3): 267–83.

Dilthey, W. (1976), *Selected Writings*, H. Rickman (ed.), Cambridge: Cambridge University Press.

Downing, S. (2005), 'The social construction of entrepreneurship: narrative and dramatic processes in the coproduction of organizations and identities', *Entrepreneurship Theory and Practice*, **29**(2): 185–204.

Drucker, Peter F. (1985), 'The discipline of innovation', *Harvard Business Review*, **63**(3): 67–72.

Eckhardt, J. and S. Shane (2003), 'The importance of opportunities to entrepreneurship', *Journal of Management*, **29**(3): 333–49.

Edelman, G. (1987), *Neural Darwinism*, New York: Basic Books.

Forgas, J.P. (1999), 'On feeling good and being rude: affective influences on language use and request formulations', *Journal of Personality and Social Psychology*, **76**(6): 928–39.

Gadamer, Hans-Georg (1975), *Truth and Method*, New York: Continuum.

Garcia-Prieto, P., E. Bellard and S.C. Schneider (2003), 'Experiencing diversity, conflict, and emotions in teams', *Applied Psychology*, **52**(3): 413–40.

Gartner, W.B. (1993), 'Words lead to deeds: toward an organizational emergence vocabulary', *Journal of Business Venturing*, **8**(3): 231–40.

Geertz, Clifford (1986), 'Making experience, authoring selves', in Victor Turner and Edward Bruner (eds), *The Anthropology of Experience*, Urbana, IL: University of Illinois Press.

Gersick, C., J.M. Bartunek and J.E. Dutton (2000), 'Learning from academia: the importance of relationships in professional life', *The Academy of Management Journal*, **43**(6): 1026–44.

Jackson, F. (1996), 'The primary quality view of color', *Philosophical Perspectives*, **30**(10): 199–219.

James, William ([1912] 1996), *Essays in Radical Empiricism*, Lincoln, NE: University of Nebraska Press.

Kant, Immanuel ([1781] 1990), *Critique of Pure Reason*, (translated by J.M.D. Meiklejohn), New York: Prometheus Books.

Kotha, S., S. Rajgopal and M. Venkatachalam (2004), 'The role of online buying experience as a competitive advantage: evidence from third-party ratings for e-commerce firms', University of Washington Business School working paper.

Krueger, N.F. (2007), 'What lies beneath: the experiential essence of entrepreneurial thinking', *Entrepreneurship Theory and Practice*, **31**(1): 123–42.

Laing, R.D. (1967), *The Politics of Experience*, New York: Ballantine Books, Inc.

Levinas, Emmanuel (1998), 'Intentionality and sensation', in R.A. Cohen and M.B. Smith (translators), *Discovering Existence with Husserl*, Evanston, IL: Northwestern University Press.

Lichtenstein, B., N. Carter, K. Dooley and W. Gartner (2007), 'Complexity dynamics of nascent entrepreneurship', *Journal of Business Venturing*, **22**(2): 236–53.

Locke, John ([1689] 1979), *An Essay Concerning Human Understanding*, Oxford: Clarendon Press.

Magnusson, D. (1981), *Toward a Psychology of Situations*, Hillsdale, NJ: Lawrence Erlbaum.

Mano, H. and R.L. Oliver (1993), 'Assessing the dimensionality and structure of the consumption experience', *Journal of Consumer Research*, **20**(3): 451–66.

Merleau-Ponty, M. ([1960] 1964), *Signs*, translated by R.C. McClearly, Evanston, IL: Northwestern University Press, p. 105.

Moch, S.D. (1990), 'Health within the experience of breast cancer', *Journal of Advanced Nursing*, **15**(12): 1426–35.

Pessoa, L., M. McKenna, E. Gutierrez and L. Ungerleider (2002), 'Neural processing of emotional faces requires attention', *Proceedings*, National Academy of Science, pp. 11458–63.

Politis, D. (2005), 'The process of entrepreneurial learning: a conceptual framework', *Entrepreneurship Theory and Practice*, **29**(4): 399–424.

Pribram, K.H. (1999), 'Brain and the composition of conscious experience', *Journal of Consciousness Studies*, **6**(5): 19–42.

Reuber, A. and E. Fischer (1999), 'Entrepreneurs' experience, expertise, and performance of technology-based firms', *IEEE Transactions on Engineering Management*, **41**(4): 365–84.

Russell, S. (1999), 'An exploratory study of patients' perceptions, memories and experiences of an intensive care unit', *Journal of Advanced Nursing*, **29**(4): 783–91.

Sarasvathy, S. (2004), 'Constructing corridors to economic primitives', in J. Butler (ed.), *Opportunity Identification and Entrepreneurial Behavior*, Greenwich, CT: Information Age Publishing, pp. 291–312.

Schindehutte, M. and M.H. Morris (2009), 'Advancing strategic entrepreneurship research: the role of complexity science in shifting the paradigm', *Entrepreneurship Theory and Practice*, **33**(1): 241–76.

Shane, S. and R. Khurana (2003), 'Bringing individuals back in: the effects of career experience on new firm founding', *Industrial and Corporate Change*, **12**(3): 519–43.

Shepherd, D.A. (2003), 'Learning from business failure: propositions of grief recovery for the self-employed', *Academy of Management Review*, **28**(2): 318–37.

Stein, N. and L.J. Levine (1999), 'Early emergence of emotional understanding and appraisal', in T. Dalgleish and M. Power (ed.), *Handbook of Cognition and Emotion*, New York: John Wiley, pp. 383–408.

Stevenson, H., M.J. Roberts and I. Grousbeck (1989), *New Business Ventures and the Entrepreneur*, 3rd edn, Homewood, IL: Irwin Publishing.

Stoica, M. and M. Schindehutte (1999), 'Understanding adaptation in small firms: links to culture and performance', *Journal of Developmental Entrepreneurship*, **4**(1): 1–18.

Tarrant, M., M. Manfredo and B. Driver (1994), 'Recollections of outdoor recreation experiences: a psychological perspective', *Journal of Leisure Research*, **26**(4): 357–71.

Taylor, S. (1994), 'Waiting for service: the relationship between delays and evaluations of service', *The Journal of Marketing*, **58**(2): 56–69.

Taylor, W., L. Magnussen and M.J. Amundson (2001), 'The lived experience of battered women', *Violence Against Women*, **7**(5): 563–85.

Throop, C.J. (2003), 'Articulating experience', *Anthropological Theory*, **3**(2): 219–41.

Tuan, Y. (1977), *Space and Place: The Perspective of Experience*, Minneapolis, MN: University of Minnesota Press.

Turner, V. (1986), 'Dewey, Dilthey, and drama', in V. Turner and E. Bruner (eds), *The Anthropology of Experience*, Urbana, IL: University of Illinois Press, pp. 33–44.

Weick, K.E. (1979), *The Social Psychology of Organizing*, Reading, MA: Addison-Wesley.

Westhead, P., D. Ucbasaran and M. Wright (2005), 'Decisions, actions, and performance: do novice, serial, and portfolio entrepreneurs differ?', *Journal of Small Business Management*, **43**(4): 393–418.

APPENDIX A

Table 1A.1   Themes underlying research on experience in the entrepreneurship literature

#	Entrepreneurial Experience Is . . .	Perspective Centers On . . .	Entrepreneurial Topics Associated with Themes . . .	Exemplars
1	A set of start-up activities	Organizing activities	Venture creation (Entrepreneurial events)	Gartner (1985) Carter et al. (1996) Gatewood et al. (1995) Lichtenstein et al. (2006) Rotefoss and Kolvereid (2005)
2	Previous preparation that affects an initial start-up	Personal background	Venture capital (Investor assessment of venture viability)	Patzelt et al. (2009) Metzger (2007) Reuber and Fischer (1999) Stuart and Abetti (1990) Walske and Zacharakis (2009)
3	Re-entry experiences	Business ownership	Serial/habitual/portfolio entrepreneurs (New venture formation and mgt. expertise)	Alsos and Kolvereid (1998) Ucbasaran et al. (2003) Westhead and Wright (1998) Westhead et al. (2005) Wiklund and Shepherd (2008)
4	Entrepreneurial expertise	Decision-making	Novice/expert entrepreneurs (Decision-making expertise)	Baron and Ensley (2006) Baron and Henri (2010) Dew et al. (2009) Franke et al. (2008) Sarasvathy (2001)

5	Experiential learning	Learning	Entrepreneurial learning	Cope (2003, 2005, 2010) Corbett (2005) Holcomb et al. (2009) Politis (2005) Ravasi and Turati (2005)
6	Experiential aspects of the entrepreneurial process	Psychology (situational)	Affect, emotion, intuition, passion, resilience, peak experience	Baron (2008) Cardon et al. (2009) Crossan et al. (1999) Foo et al. (2009) Schindehutte et al. (2006)
7	Failure experience	Outcomes	Emotional costs of failure	Politis and Gabrielsson (2009) Shepherd (2003, 2009) Shepherd et al. (2009) Ucbasaran et al. (2003)
8	Self-making experience	Role as a founder	Entrepreneurial self-identity (Entrepreneur's role identity)	Farmer et al. (2011) Hoang and Gimeno (2010) Shepherd and Haynie (2009) Warren (2004)
9	Transition (into) experience	Career	Self-employment (Social structural/pre-dispositional/contextual antecedents)	Haynie and Shepherd (2011) Ozcan (2009) Stuart and Ding (2006) Sorensen (2007)
10	Transition (out) experience	Career	Entrepreneurial exit (Entrepreneurial career transitions)	DeTienne (2010) DeTienne and Cardon (2010) Wennberg et al. (2010)

Table 1A.1 (continued)

#	Entrepreneurial Experience Is . . .	Perspective Centers On . . .	Entrepreneurial Topics Associated with Themes . . .	Exemplars
11	Family experiences	Life course	Family business (Succession experience)	Handler (1992) Klein et al. (2005) Morris et al. (2010) Rutherford et al. (2008)
12	Founding team experience	Team	Entrepreneurial teams (Top management team demography, turnover; composition)	Burton et al. (2002) Beckman and Burton (2007, 2008) Dobrev and Barnett (2006) Dimov et al. (2007) Vanaelst et al. (2006)
13	Entrepreneuring	Relational	Practice perspective (Agency, rituals, and social interactions)	Goss et al. (2011) Hjorth (2007) Johannisson (2011) Steyaert (2007) Terjesen and Elam (2009)
14	Living the experience	Corporeal	Doing entrepreneurship (Lived experiences of the entrepreneur)	Berglund (2007) Bruni and Gherardi (2004) Morris et al. (2010)

BIBLIOGRAPHY FOR APPENDIX A

Alsos, G.A. and L. Kolvereid (1998), 'The business gestation process of novice, serial, and parallel business founders', *Entrepreneurship Theory and Practice*, **22**(2): 101–14.

Aram, J.D. (1989), 'Attitudes and behaviors of informal investors toward early-stage investments, technology-based ventures, and co-investors', *Journal of Business Venturing*, **4**(5): 333–47.

Baron, R.A. (2008), 'The role of affect in the entrepreneurial process', *Academy of Management Review*, **33**(2): 328–40.

Baron, R.A. and M.D. Ensley (2006), 'Opportunity recognition as the detection of meaningful patterns: evidence from comparisons of novice and experienced entrepreneurs', *Management Science*, **52**(9): 1331–44.

Baron, R.A. and R.A. Henry (2010), 'How entrepreneurs acquire the capacity to excel: insights from research on expert performance', *Strategic Entrepreneurship Journal*, **4**(1): 49–65.

Beckman, C.M. and M.D. Burton (2007), 'Early teams: the impact of team demography on VC financing and going public', *Journal of Business Venturing*, **22**(2): 147–73.

Beckman, C.M. and M.D. Burton (2008), 'Founding the future: path dependence in the evolution of top management teams from founding to IPO', *Organization Science*, **19**(1): 3–24.

Berglund, H. (2007), 'Entrepreneurship and phenomenology: researching entrepreneurship as lived experience', in J. Ulhøi and H. Neergaard (eds). *Handbook of Qualitative Research Methods in Entrepreneurship*, Cheltenham, UK and Northampton, MA, USA: Edward Elgar, pp. 75–96.

Biniari, M.G. (2011), 'The emotional embeddedness of corporate entrepreneurship: the case of envy', *Entrepreneurship Theory and Practice*. Early view online at http://www.onlinelibrary.wiley.com/journal/10.1111/(ISSN)1540-6520/early view; accessed 22 November 2011.

Boeker, W. and R. Karichalil (2002), 'Entrepreneurial transitions: factors influencing founder departure', *Academy of Management Journal*, **45**(3): 818–26.

Box, T.M., M.A. White and S.H. Barr (1993), 'A contingency model of new manufacturing firm performance', *Entrepreneurship Theory and Practice*, **18**(2): 31–45.

Brandstätter, H. (1997), 'Becoming an entrepreneur – a question of personality structure?', *Journal of Economic Psychology*, **18**(2–3): 157–77.

Brundin, E., H. Patzelt and D. Shepherd (2008), 'Managers' emotional displays and employees' willingness to act entrepreneurially', *Journal of Business Venturing*, **23**(2): 221–38.

Bruni, A. and S. Gherardi (2004), 'Doing gender, doing entrepreneurship: an ethnographic account of intertwined practices', *Gender, Work & Organization*, **11**(4): 406–30.

Burton, M.D., C. Beckman and J. Sørensen (2002), 'Coming from good stock: career histories and new venture formation', *Research in Sociology of Organizations*, **19**: 229–62.

Cardon, M.S., J. Wincent, J. Singh and M. Drnovsek (2009), 'The nature and experience of entrepreneurial passion', *Academy of Management Review*, **34**(3): 511–32.

Carroll, G.R. and E. Mosakowski (1987), 'The career dynamics of the self-employed', *Administrative Science Quarterly*, **32**(4): 570–90.

Carter, N.M., W.B. Gartner and P.D. Reynolds (1996), 'Exploring start-up event sequences', *Journal of Business Venturing*, **11**(3): 151–66.

Chandler, G.N. (1996), 'Business similarity as a moderator of the relationship between pre-ownership experience and venture performance', *Entrepreneurship Theory and Practice*, **20**(3): 51–65.

Cliff, J.E. and P.D. Jennings (2005), 'Commentary on the multidimensional degree of family influence construct and the F-PEC measurement instrument', *Entrepreneurship Theory and Practice*, **29**(3): 341–7.

Cliff, J., P. Jennings and R. Greenwood (2006), 'New to the game and questioning the rules: experiences and beliefs of founders of imitative vs. innovative firms', *Journal of Business Venturing*, **21**(5): 633–50.

Cooper, A.C., T.B. Folta and C. Woo (1995), 'Entrepreneurial information search', *Journal of Business Venturing*, **10**(2): 107–20.

Cope, J. (2003), 'Entrepreneurial learning and critical reflection: discontinuous events as triggers for higher level learning', *Management Learning*, **34**(4): 429–50.

Cope, J. (2005), 'Toward a dynamic learning perspective of entrepreneurship', *Entrepreneurship Theory and Practice*, **29**(4): 373–97.

Cope, J. (2010), 'Entrepreneurial learning from failure: an interpretative phenomenological analysis', *Journal of Business Venturing*, **6**: 604–23.

Cope, J. and G. Watts (2000), 'Learning by doing: an exploration of experience, critical incidents and reflection in entrepreneurial learning', *International Journal of Entrepreneurial Behaviour & Research*, **6**(3): 104–24.

Cope, J., F. Cave and S. Eccles (2004), 'Attitudes of venture capital investors to entrepreneurs with previous business failure', *Venture Capital: An International Journal of Entrepreneurial Finance*, **6**(2/3): 147–72.

Corbett, A.C. (2005), 'Experiential learning within the process of opportunity identification and exploitation', *Entrepreneurship Theory and Practice*, **29**(4): 473–91.

Crossan, M.M., H.M. Lane and R.E. White (1999), 'An organizational learning framework: from intuition to institution', *Academy of Management Review*, **24**(3): 522–37.

De Clercq, D. and H.J. Sapienza (2005), 'When do venture capital firms learn from their portfolio companies?', *Entrepreneurship Theory and Practice*, **29**(4): 517–35.

DeTienne, D.R. (2010), 'Entrepreneurial exit as a critical component of the entrepreneurial process: theoretical development', *Journal of Business Venturing*, **25**(2): 203–15.

DeTienne, D. and M. Cardon (2010), 'Impact of founder experience on exit intentions', *Small Business Economics*, **36**: 1–24.

Dew, N., S. Read, S. Sarasvathy and R. Wiltbank (2009), 'Effectual versus predictive logics in entrepreneurial decision-making: differences between experts and novices', *Journal of Business Venturing*, **24**(4): 287–309.

Dimov, D. (2010), 'Nascent entrepreneurs and venture emergence: opportunity confidence, human capital, and early planning', *Journal of Management Studies*, **47**(6): 1123–53.

Dimov, D., D.A. Shepherd and K.M. Sutcliff (2007), 'Requisite expertise, firm reputation, and status in venture capital investment allocation decisions', *Journal of Business Venturing*, **22**(4): 481–502.

Dobrev, S.D. and W.P. Barnett (2005), 'Organizational roles and transition to entrepreneurship', *Academy of Management Journal*, **48**(3): 433–49.

Downing, S. (2005), 'The social construction of entrepreneurship: narrative and dramatic processes in the coproduction of organizations and identities', *Entrepreneurship Theory and Practice*, **29**(2): 18.

Dyer, W.G. Jr. (1994), 'Toward a theory of entrepreneurial careers', *Entrepreneurship Theory and Practice*, **19**(2): 7–21.

Dyer, Jr., W. Gibb and W. Handler (1994), 'Entrepreneurship and family business: exploring the connections', *Entrepreneurship Theory and Practice*, **19**(1): 71–83.

Erikson, T. (2003), 'Towards a taxonomy of entrepreneurial learning experiences among potential entrepreneurs', *Journal of Small Business and Enterprise Development*, **10**(1): 106–12.

Farmer, S.M., Y. Xin and K. Kung-Mcintyre (2011), 'The behavioral impact of entrepreneur identity aspiration and prior entrepreneurial experience', *Entrepreneurship Theory and Practice*, **35**(2): 245–73.

Fischer, E.M., R.A. Reuber and L.S. Dyke (1993), 'A theoretical overview and extension of research on sex, gender, and entrepreneurship', *Journal of Business Venturing*, **8**(2): 151–68.

Foo, M.D., M. Uy and R.A. Baron (2009), 'How do feelings influence effort? An empirical study of entrepreneurs' affect and venture effort', *Journal of Applied Psychology*, **94**(4): 1086–94.

Forbes, D.P. (2005), 'Managerial determinants of decision speed in new ventures', *Strategic Management Journal*, **26**(4): 355–66.

Franke, N., M. Gruber, D. Harhoff and J. Henkel (2008), 'Venture capitalists' evaluations of start-up teams: trade-offs, knock-out criteria, and the impact of VC experience', *Entrepreneurship Theory and Practice*, **32**(3): 459–83.

Gartner, W.B., N.M. Carter and P.D. Reynolds (2004), 'Business start-up activities', in W.B. Gartner, K.G. Shaver, N.M. Carter and P.D. Reynolds (eds), *Handbook of Entrepreneurial Dynamics: The Process of Business Creation*, Thousand Oaks, CA: Sage, 285–98.

Gatewood, E.J., K.G. Shaver and W.B. Gartner (1995), 'A longitudinal study of cognitive factors influencing start-up behaviors and success at venture creation', *Journal of Business Venturing*, **10**(5): 371–91.

Goss, D. (2008), 'Enterprise ritual: a theory of entrepreneurial emotion and exchange', *British Journal of Management*, **19**(2): 120–37.

Goss, D., R. Jones, M. Betta and J. Latham (2011), 'Power as practice: a micro-sociological analysis of the dynamics of emancipatory entrepreneurship', *Organization Studies*, **32**(2): 211–29.

Handler, W. (1992), 'The succession experience of the next generation', *Family Business Review*, **5**(3): 283–307.

Harrison, R.T. and C.M. Leitch (2005), 'Entrepreneurial learning: researching the interface between learning and the entrepreneurial context', *Entrepreneurship Theory and Practice*, **29**(4): 351–71.

Haynie, J.M. and D.A. Shepherd (2011), 'Toward a theory of discontinuous career transition: investigating career transitions necessitated by traumatic life events', *Journal of Applied Psychology*, **96**(3): 501–24.

Hayward, M., W. Forster and B. Fredrickson (2009), 'Beyond hubris: how highly confident entrepreneurs rebound to venture again', *Journal of Business Venturing*, **25**(6): 569–78.

Hill, R.C. and M. Levenhagen (1995), 'Metaphors and mental models: sensemaking and sensegiving in innovative and entrepreneurial activities', *Journal of Management*, **21**(6): 1057.

Hjorth, D. (2007), 'Lessons from Iago: narrating the event of entrepreneurship', *Journal of Business Venturing*, **22**(5): 712–32.

Hoang, H. and J. Gimeno (2010), 'Becoming a founder: how founder role identity affects entrepreneurial transitions and persistence in founding', *Journal of Business Venturing*, **25**(1): 41–53.

Holcomb, T.R., R.D. Ireland, R.M. Holmes Jr. and M.A. Hitt (2009), 'Architecture of entrepreneurial learning: exploring the link among heuristics, knowledge, and action', *Entrepreneurship Theory and Practice*, **33**(1): 167–92.

Holland, D.V. and D.A. Shepherd (2011), 'Deciding to persist: adversity, values, and entrepreneurs' decision policies', *Entrepreneurship Theory and Practice*, published online.

Johannisson, B. (2011), 'Towards a practice theory of entrepreneuring', *Small Business Economics*, **36**: 135–50.

Kets de Vries, M.F.R. (1996), 'The anatomy of the entrepreneur: clinical observations', *Human Relations*, **49**: 853–83.

Klein, S.B., J.H. Astrachan and K.X. Smyrnios (2005), 'The F-PEC scale of family influence: construction, validation, and further implication for theory', *Entrepreneurship Theory and Practice*, **29**(3): 321–39.

Krueger, N. (1993), 'The impact of prior entrepreneurial exposure on perceptions of new venture feasibility and desirability', *Entrepreneurship Theory and Practice*, **18**(1): 5–21.

Krueger, N.F. (2007), 'What lies beneath? The experiential essence of entrepreneurial thinking', *Entrepreneurship Theory and Practice*, **31**(1): 123–38.

Lerner, M., C. Brush and R. Hisrich (1997), 'Israeli women entrepreneurs: an examination of factors affecting performance', *Journal of Business Venturing*, **12**(4): 315–39.

Lévesque, M., M. Minniti and D. Shepherd (2009), 'Entrepreneurs' decisions on timing of entry: learning from participation and from the experiences of others', *Entrepreneurship Theory and Practice*, **33**(2): 547–70.

Lichtenstein, B.B., K.J. Dooley and G.T. Lumpkin (2006), 'Measuring emergence in the dynamics of new venture creation', *Journal of Business Venturing*, **21**(2): 15.

Mallon, M. and L. Cohen (2001), 'Time for a change? Women's account of the move from organizational careers to self employment', *British Journal of Management*, **12**(3): 217–30.

Markman, G.D. (2007), 'Entrepreneurs' competencies', in J.R. Baum, M. Frese and R. Baron (eds), *The Psychology of Entrepreneurship*, Mahwah, NJ: Erlbaum, pp. 67–92.

Marvel, M.R. and G.T. Lumpkin (2007), 'Technology entrepreneurs' human capital and its effects on innovation radicalness', *Entrepreneurship Theory and Practice*, **31**(6): 807–28.

McGrath, R.G. and I.C. MacMillan (1992), 'More like each other than anyone else? A cross-cultural study of entrepreneurial perceptions', *Journal of Business Venturing*, **7**(5): 419–29.

Metzger, G. (2007), 'Personal experience: a most vicious and limited circle!? On the role of entrepreneurial experience for firm survival', Centre for European Economic Research Discussion Paper No. 07-046, Mannheim, Germany.

Minguzzi, A. and R. Passaro (2001), 'The network of relationships between the economic environment and the entrepreneurial culture in small firms', *Journal of Business Venturing*, **16**(2): 181–207.

Minniti, M. and W. Bygrave (2001), 'A dynamic model of entrepreneurial learning', *Entrepreneurship Theory and Practice*, **25**(3): 5.

Mitchell, R.K. (1994), 'The composition, classification, and creation of new venture formation expertise', University of Utah School of Business dissertation Salt Lake City.

Morris, M.H., J.A. Allen, D.F. Kuratko and D. Brannon (2010), 'Experiencing family business creation: differences between founders, nonfamily managers, and founders of nonfamily firms', *Entrepreneurship Theory and Practice*, **34**(6): 1057–84.

Mosey, S. and M. Wright (2007), 'From human capital to social capital: a longitudinal study of technology-based academic entrepreneurs', *Entrepreneurship Theory and Practice*, **31**(6): 909–35.

Ozcan, S. (2009), 'Transition to entrepreneurship from the public sector: predispositional and contextual effects', *Management Science*, **55**(4): 604–18.

Patzelt, H., D. zu Knyphausen-Aufsess and H. Fischer (2009), 'Upper echelons and portfolio strategies of venture capital firms', *Journal of Business Venturing*, **24**(6): 558–72.

Phillips, D.J. (2002), 'A genealogical approach to organizational life chances: the parent–progeny transfer among Silicon Valley law firms, 1946–1996', *Administrative Science Quarterly*, **47**(3): 474–506.

Politis, D. (2005), 'The process of entrepreneurial learning: a conceptual framework', *Entrepreneurship Theory and Practice*, **29**(4): 399–424.

Politis, D. (2008), 'Does prior start-up experience matter for entrepreneur's learning? A comparison between novice and habitual entrepreneurs', *Journal of Small Business and Enterprise Development*, **15**(3): 472–89.

Politis, D. and J. Gabrielsson (2009), 'Entrepreneurs' attitudes towards failure: an experiential learning approach', *International Journal of Entrepreneurial Behaviour & Research*, **5**(4): 364–83.

Rae, D. (2000), 'Understanding entrepreneurial learning: a question of how?', *International Journal of Entrepreneurial Behaviour & Research*, **6**(3): 145–59.

Rae, D. (2004), 'Entrepreneurial learning: a practical model from the creative industries', *Education and Training*, **46**(8/9): 492–500.

Rae, (2006), 'Entrepreneurial learning: a conceptual framework for technology-based enterprise', *Technology Analysis & Strategic Management*, **18**(1): 39–56.

Rasmussen, E., S. Mosey and M. Wright (2011), 'The evolution of entrepreneurial competencies: a longitudinal study of university spin-off venture emergence', *Journal of Management Studies*, **48**(6): 1314–45.

Ravasi, D. and C. Turati (2005), 'Exploring entrepreneurial learning: a comparative study of technology development projects', *Journal of Business Venturing*, **20**(1): 137–64.

Rerup, C. (2005), 'Learning from past experience: footnotes on mindfulness and habitual entrepreneurship', *Scandinavian Journal of Management*, **21**: 451–72.

Reuber, A.R. and E. Fischer (1999), 'Understanding the consequences of founders' experience', *Journal of Small Business Management*, **37**(2): 30–45.

Reynolds, P.D. (1991), 'Sociology and entrepreneurship: concepts and contributions', *Entrepreneurship Theory and Practice*, **16**(2): 47–70.

Rindova, V., D. Barry and D.J. Ketchen Jr. (2009), 'Introduction to special topic forum: entrepreneuring as emancipation', *Academy of Management Review*, **34**(3): 477–91.

Rotefoss, B. and L. Kolvereid (2005), 'Aspiring, nascent and fledgling entrepreneurs: an investigation of the business start-up process', *Entrepreneurship and Regional Development*, **17**(2): 109–27.

Rutherford, M.W., D.F. Kuratko and D.T. Holt (2008), 'Examining the link between "familiness" and performance: can the F-PEC untangle the family business theory jungle?', *Entrepreneurship Theory and Practice*, **32**(6): 1089–109.

Sarasvathy, S.D. (2001), 'Causation and effectuation: toward a theoretical shift from economic inevitability to entrepreneurial contingency', *Academy of Management Review*, **26**(2): 243.

Schindehutte, M., M. Morris and J. Allen (2006), 'Beyond achievement: entrepreneurship as extreme experience', *Small Business Economics*, **27**(4): 349–68.

Shepherd, D.A. (2003), 'Learning from business failure: propositions of grief recovery for the self-employed', *Academy of Management Review*, **28**(2): 318–28.

Shepherd, D.A. (2004), 'Educating entrepreneurship students about emotion and learning from failure', *Academy of Management Learning and Education*, **3**(3): 274–87.

Shepherd, D.A. (2009), 'Grief recovery from the loss of a family business: a multi- and meso-level study', *Journal of Business Venturing*, **24**(1): 81–97.

Shepherd, D. and J.M. Haynie (2009), 'Birds of a feather don't always flock together: identity management in entrepreneurship', *Journal of Business Venturing*, **24**(4): 316–37.

Shepherd, D.A., J. Wiklund and M. Haynie (2009), 'Moving forward: balancing the financial and emotional costs of business failure', *Journal of Business Venturing*, **24**(2): 134–48.

Shrader, R. and D.S. Siegel (2007), 'Assessing the relationship between human capital and firm performance: evidence from technology-based new ventures', *Entrepreneurship Theory and Practice*, **31**(6): 893–908.

Singh, S., P. Corner and K. Pavolvich (2007), 'Coping with entrepreneurial failure', *Journal of Management and Organization*, **13**(4): 331–44.

Sørensen, J.B. (2007), 'Bureaucracy and entrepreneurship: workplace effects on entrepreneurial entry', *Administrative Science Quarterly*, **52**(3): 387–412.

Stanley, L.J. (2010), 'Emotions and family business creation: an extension and implications', *Entrepreneurship Theory and Practice*, **34**(6): 1085–92.

Stanworth, J., S. Blythe, B. Granger and C. Stanworth (1989), 'Who becomes an entrepreneur?', *International Small Business Journal*, **8**(1): 11–22.

Starr, J.A. and N. Fondas (1992), 'A model of entrepreneurial socialization and organization formation', *Entrepreneurship Theory and Practice*, **17**(1): 67–76.

Steyaert, C. (2007), '"Entrepreneuring" as a conceptual attractor? A review of process theories in 20 years of entrepreneurship studies', *Entrepreneurship & Regional Development*, **19**(6): 453–77.

Steyaert, C. and J. Katz (2004), 'Reclaiming the space of entrepreneurship in society: geographical, discursive and social dimensions', *Entrepreneurship & Regional Development*, **16**(3): 179–96.

Stuart, R.W. and P.A. Abetti (1990), 'Impact of entrepreneurial and management experience on early performance', *Journal of Business Venturing*, **5**(3): 151–62.

Stuart, T.E. and W.W. Ding (2006), 'When do scientists become entrepreneurs? The social structural antecedents of commercial activity in the life sciences', *American Journal of Sociology*, **112**(1): 97–144.

Taylor, D.W. and R. Thorpe (2004), 'Entrepreneurial learning: a process of co-participation', *Journal of Small Business and Enterprise Development*, **11**(2): 203–11.

Terjesen, S. and A. Elam (2009), 'Transnational entrepreneurs' venture internationalization strategies: a practice theory approach', *Entrepreneurship Theory and Practice*, **33**(5): 1093–120.

Ucbasaran, D., A. Lockett and M. Wright (2003), 'Entrepreneurial founder teams: factors associated with member entry and exit', *Entrepreneurship Theory and Practice*, **28**(2): 107–28.

Ucbasaran, D., P. Westhead and M. Wright (2009), 'The extent and nature of opportunity identification by experienced entrepreneurs', *Journal of Business Venturing*, **24**(2): 99–115.

Ucbasaran, D., P. Westhead, M. Wright and M. Flores (2010), 'The nature of entrepreneurial experience, business failure and comparative optimism', *Journal of Business Venturing*, **25**(6): 541–55.

Ucbasaran, D., M. Wright, P. Westhead and L. Busenitz (2003), 'The impact of entrepreneurial experience on opportunity identification and exploitation: habitual and novice entrepreneurs', in J. Katz and D. Shepherd (eds), *Cognitive Approaches to Entrepreneurship Research. Advances in Entrepreneurship, Firm Emergence and Growth*, vol. 6, New York: Elsevier/JAI, pp. 231–64.

Vanaelst, I., B. Clarysse, M. Wright, A. Lockett, N. Moray and R. S'Jegers (2006), 'Entrepreneurial team development in academic spinouts: an examination of team heterogeneity', *Entrepreneurship Theory and Practice*, **30**(2): 249–71.

Walske, J.M. and A. Zacharakis (2009), 'Genetically engineered: why some venture capital firms are more successful than others', *Entrepreneurship Theory and Practice*, **33**(1): 297–318.

Warren, L. (2004), 'Negotiating entrepreneurial identity: communities of practice and changing discourses', *International Journal of Entrepreneurship and Innovation*, **5**(1): 25–35.

Weinberg, K., J. Wiklund, D.R. DeTienne and M.S. Cardon (2010), 'Reconceptualizing entrepreneurial exit: divergent exit routes and their drivers', *Journal of Business Venturing*, **25**(4): 361–75.

Westhead, P. and M. Wright (1998), 'Novice, portfolio, and serial founders: are they different?', *Journal of Business Venturing*, **13**(3): 173–204.

Westhead, P., D. Ucbasaran and M. Wright (2005), 'Experience and cognition: do novice, serial and portfolio entrepreneurs differ?', *International Small Business Journal*, **23**(1): 72–98.

Westhead, P., D. Ucbasaran, M. Wright and M. Binks (2005), 'Novice, serial and portfolio entrepreneur behavior and contributions', *Small Business Economics*, **25**(2): 109–32.

Wiklund, J. and D.A. Shepherd (2008), 'Portfolio entrepreneurship: habitual and novice founders, new entry, and mode of organizing', *Entrepreneurship Theory and Practice*, **32**(4): 701–25.

2. Anthropology and experience

> [E]very experience has something of an adventure about it. An adventure
> interrupts the customary course of events, but is positively and significantly
> related to the context which it interrupts. Thus an adventure lets life be felt of
> as a whole, in its breadth and in its strength. It ventures out into the uncertain.
> (Hans-Georg Gadamer, 1988)

INTRODUCTION

When William James, nineteenth-century philosopher and psychologist, set out to describe the nature of human consciousness and experience, he compared it to a stream, gushing continually forward, its flow influenced and nudged by the ripples, silt, and currents of past experiences (James, 1890). Just like the water of James's stream, the concept of human experience has permeated every aspect of anthropology theory and research. Anthropology is the study of humanness through the careful observation of actual behavior. Human experience is the basis for these studies because experiences give rise to consciousness, which is the essence of humanness (Turner, 1985). Consciousness "is the awareness of being aware of having experience" (Brereton, 2009, p. 8).

Experience itself has been subject to ebbs and flows within anthropology, finding favor at the end of the nineteenth century in works of William Dilthey, William James, and John Dewey (Throop, 2003a) and again at the end of the twentieth century, culminating in the publication of *The Anthropology of Experience* (Turner and Bruner, 1986). Most recent scholarship has attempted to codify experience as a concept, which, though pervasive within the anthropology discipline, has remained largely ephemeral and undefined (Brereton, 2009; Desjarlais, 1994; Throop, 2002, 2003a).

This chapter will proceed by first offering a current conceptualization of experience within the anthropology perspective. Second, we will discuss the development of the concept and trends that have affected how anthropologists have come to define and use experience in their work. Third, we will discuss some of the major areas within anthropology where the study and application of experience has played a major role. Next, we will describe the methodology anthropologists have developed and used in researching experience. The chapter will close with a discussion about the implications the anthropological perspective might have on the study of entrepreneurship and experience.

HOW EXPERIENCE IS DEFINED IN ANTHROPOLOGY

Experience is composed of two elements. The first of these is the pre-human, objective, describable occurrence – "things that happen to us or others" (Abrahams, 1986, p. 55). These experiences form the building blocks of human consciousness. The second element represents the accrual of lived-through experiences and the construction of a retrospective set of meanings ascribed to the experiences – that is, the structure of experience (Turner, 1985). Individuals use their emergent sets of experiences to define themselves and the culture in which they are embedded (Bruner, 1986).

Objective Experience

Drawing on John Dewey's (1925) work in *Experience and Nature*, Brereton (2009) attempts to refine and delineate a set of dimensions that constitute objective experience (see Box 2.1). They are temporalization, location, matter, energy, personhood, sensation, affect, events, rhythmicity, prolepsis, absence, and culture.

Experiences occupy *temporal* space, especially as considered relative to a sequence of events. Experiences have beginnings and endings. As Turner (1986, p. 35) writes: "An experience, like a rock in a Zen sand garden, stands out from the evenness of passing hours and years . . . it does not have an arbitrary beginning or ending, cut out of the stream of chronological temporality but has what Dewey called 'an initiation and a consummation'." Brereton (2009) notes that although the conceptualization of time itself may differ from culture to culture, sequentiality is ubiquitous and essential to the experience. He writes: "one must first draw the bow before it will propel the arrow; put a hat on before it will provide shade" (p. 14).

Location is essential to the experience. Experiences cannot exist without a place, nor can an experience be reproduced in a different place – two identical performances of a play, performed on different stages, constitute two different experiences, as would repeat performances of the play at different times. Brereton (2009) argues that this location-dependent nature of experience is closely tied to human cognitive and affective processes, which depend on location mapping and help individuals orient themselves in the world.

BOX 2.1   ELEMENTS OF EXPERIENCE IN ANTHROPOLOGY

Temporality: An experience contains a beginning and ending, and thus occupies temporal space.

Location: Experiences are attached to a place; the setting affects an individual's intentionality toward the experience.

Material: Experiences occupy physical space within the experiencer. And as experiences are physical objects, they consist of *energy.*

Personalized: Self-awareness is necessary for a lived-through moment to become an experience. As such, experience is uniquely human.

Sensorial: Experience represents the nexus between the individual and the environment; the individual is dependent on sensory perception to perceive the experience.

Affective: Humans attach positive or negative attributes to their experiences; in other words, experiences are the foundation of emotion.

Events: Experiences are individual events within a broader stream of the lived-through here-and-now.

Rhythm: Individuals' experiences accumulate in patterns, whether spaced out far apart or in clumps; they do not occur at regular intervals, and each individual's pattern of experience is unique from another's.

Prolepsis: Experience constitutes the foundation from which we judge future situations.

Absential: Experiences are exclusive. In other words, while one experience is occurring, another is not occurring.

Cultural: Individuals understand the environment through sensory information and through the context of their lives. Therefore, the individual's culture always affects how a moment is experienced.

Source: Adapted from Brereton (2009).

Experience is *materialized* internally, such as the creation of neural connections and sensual processing, and externally, as an experience is exhibited in the environment. Brereton (ibid.) writes that individuals detect experiences through their senses, which are, in turn, predicated on physical attributes of reality. Likewise as experiences are composed of physical attributes and are material objects, they also possess *energy*.

Brereton (ibid., p. 8) describes consciousness as the meta-cognition of experience – "an awareness of being aware of having experience." Protozoa may have experiences, and so may a primate, but only humans exhibit the self-awareness or consciousness necessary to construct reality from a collection of sensory memories of experiences. Therefore, experiences are *personalized* – they can only exist in so far as an individual human has had sensory interface with an experience's ontic attributes.

The five senses are the nexus between the individual and the environment. While experience is not purely *sensorial*, sensory perception is, nonetheless, the primary mechanism through which individuals experience things (Brereton, 2009). Experience is not purely sensorial because neurological processing of sense stimulation by an experience occurs before an individual has access to the experience. In addition, memory and intention can mediate how individuals experience. Experience is also *affective*. Brereton (ibid.) adopts Dewey's evolutionary model of experience, which is tied to human adaptation. Adaptation implies that individuals place "approach" or "avoid" values on experiences, which depends on whether an experience represents something desirable, ambivalent or harmful. Therefore, all experiences have affective components. Brereton (ibid.) further states that the process of evolutionary selection does not favor those who fail to attach affective states to experiences.

Experiences are always parts of larger *events* – experiences cannot occur unitarily or in isolation. Brereton (ibid.) notes, for example, that the experience of dropping a pot of hot water might occur during the larger event of meal preparation.

While Brereton acknowledges that time itself is an important component of experience, he adds seriality or sequentiality as an essential characteristic of time that also mimics and plays a role in human experience. Experiences do not occur at even intervals through the passage of a human lifetime. Rather, they are lumped together or widely dispersed across individuals, creating a *rhythm* unique to each individual.

Experiences possess *prolepsis*: "Because experience is not only beholden to extant conditions, but also appeals to hypothetically possible ones; because experience is the transformation of past into future in light of meaning" (ibid., p. 16). Individuals draw on experiences to judge future outcomes. Turner (1986) describes experiences as dramatic phenomena – because they possess beginnings, middles, and ends, they have direction and momentum, which individuals interpret or even use to craft favorable outcomes for tomorrow.

Brereton (2009) also describes experiencing as being *absential*. In other words, the experience that occurs implies that other experiences might not be occurring, such as the experience of a drought implying that the experience of a flood is not likely to follow. Moreover, experiences are *cultural*, in that culture shapes both the individual's internal mechanisms for processing experiences as well as giving rise to experiences within the external environment.

Beyond these qualities, anthropologists have discussed other relevant dimensions of experience. Among the most frequently discussed of these is the distinction between experiences in terms of: (1) those that are directly connected to the day-to-day activities of life, relatively disconnected from previous experience, and that are unexpected, and (2) those that might be classified as a "Big Experience" – planned-for and expected moments with preconceived outcomes, such as rites of passage, marriages, vacations or deaths (Abrahams, 1986). Abrahams describes ordinary experiences as unexpected and surprising – they might appear meaningful only in afterthought. In contrast, major experiences are frequently planned or they at least unfold in predictable ways. Major experiences might carry a lesson or have a teaching point; either way, they are usually transformative for the experiencing individual. It is not surprising that a large amount of anthropological research on experience examines ritual and dramatic expressions of experiences, such as dramatic plays or novels – these major experiences and expressions often have explicit lessons embedded within them, and they are often repeated and predictable (Turner and Bruner, 1986). While major experiences can be prepared and stylized – which makes it easier to share them across cultures – this preparation can also tend to decrease the effect or import of the experience (Abrahams, 1986). A ceremony repeatedly performed may lose its ability to create a spirit of collective effervescence; a musical Broadway production dragged out through the years will eventually lose its ability to generate an emotional resonance in its audience.

Structured Experience

Objective experiences represent the particular lived-through moments that individuals accumulate through a lifetime. As individuals accrue experience, they begin to develop a structure of experience, which is the contemplative post-assessment of the set of experiences, which unites them into a common form or unit (Throop, 2003a). Expression, which is the communication or narrative of experiences, such as through storytelling, literature, or drama, is only possible after meaning is assigned to a set of experiences and a structure is thereby erected. This structure, which represents consciousness, is how individuals ultimately come to understand themselves and their role in society and nature (Bruner, 1986; Rickman, 1976).

For anthropologists, the study of humanness and consciousness requires examining and interpreting expressions, the narrative form of human experience. Turner (1982) outlines the processual link between individual objective experiences and the formation of a structure of experience: from a root sensory experience an individual builds recollected images of the experience that give rise to emotional reactions, meanings, and values attached to the memory, which ultimately culminate in the expression or narrative of experience. Current theory about the structure of experience draws heavily on Wilhelm Dilthey's work in descriptive psychology (see Ermarth, 1978; Throop, 2002), and few anthropologists have studied and written more about Dilthey's concept of experience than Victor Turner (1982; 1985), who explains that the retrospective addition of meaning to experiences creates a coherent body of experience. As Throop (2003a, p. 223) suggests that, for Turner, "it is primarily the cognitive category of 'meaning' as mediated through memory that provides the reflexive articulation of what would otherwise be the affectively infused experience of mere temporal succession through value." Individuals create structures of experience to create an ordered, rational consciousness, and yet this structure is in a constant state of flux as new experiences are assigned meaning and assimilated into the flow of the human psyche (Ermarth, 1978).

When anthropologists write about the importance of the structure of experience, they use terms such as "authenticating ourselves" (Abrahams, 1985, p. 40), describe "people as active agents in the historical process who construct their own world" (Bruner, 1986, p. 12), or portray experience as a "unity of becoming" (Husserl, 1997, p. 254). Experiences and the subsequent meaning-laden structures of experiences give humans their only bearing on the unfolding world and are the building blocks of consciousness (Brereton, 2009). Experience, which is the basis for expression and narrative, is crucial for anthropologists, whose research focuses on analyzing, describing, and categorizing expression – that is, the visible manifestation of latent human experience.

DEVELOPMENT OF AN ANTHROPOLOGY OF EXPERIENCE

While the foundational theorists of experience were philosophers such as Dewey, Dilthey, and James, the impetus that drove anthropologists toward conceptualizing experience as a concept at the root of consciousness and reality was the nineteenth-century drive toward empiricism. Experience appeals to empiricists because of its concrete and constant existence across every aspect of human life, and it "confers a truth more exacting than cultural, intellectualist, conceptual, and/or theoretical models can convey" (Desjarlais, 1997, p. 13). Social scientists have come to use experience as a basis for establishing irrefutable fact (Scott, 1991).

Empiricism had already begun to create a division within philosophy by the time the earliest anthropologists began to conduct their own research. Immanuel Kant proposed that consciousness was a priori divided into categories (e.g., time and space) and that concepts of reality were instilled in individuals before experience (Godlove, 1996). Others, such as John Locke and David Hume suggested that these categories could only be understood after individuals accrued a collection of sensual experiences and gained a concrete apprehension of their world – foreshadowing the concept of a structure of experience. Early anthropologists and sociologists similarly placed an emphasis on empiricism. Whereas Hume and Locke were interested in understanding the individual consciousness, empirical social scientists such as Emile Durkheim and Claude Levi-Strauss focused on using empiricism to discover social and cultural phenomena (Throop, 2003b). These early French social scientists are known for their work in anthropology, although they were not always focused on that discipline. Durkheim, for example, is considered one of the founders of sociology; however, his 1912 work, *The Elementary Forms of Religious Life* ([1912] 1995), is anthropological. Talcott Parsons, a foundational sociologist, even advised sociology students to avoid Durkheim's later body of work because of its anthropological bent (Parsons, 1937).

Just as anthropologists today recognize the difference between objective, sensory-based experiences and the meaning-laden structures of experience, Durkheim and Levi-Strauss similarly delineated experience. Where Kant believed that categories of thought existed a priori, Durkheim (taking a stricter sociological stance) argued that these categories can only be developed through collective social experience, such as through participation in a religious ritual (Throop, 2003b). For Durkheim, these experiences constituted two levels: the collection of ontic sense data, which is concrete, authentic, and irreducible, and the individual's broader interpretation of the experience, subjectively translated through memory. This second component of experience is at the heart of Durkheim's concept of collective effervescence. The sights, smells, feelings, and sounds of religious ritual experience are objective, and to this is added collective representation, which refers to the socially instilled cognitive and affective processes for assigning meaning to the experience. According to Durkheim ([1912] 1995, p. 228), consciousness "[adds] to whatever is immediately given through the senses, projecting its own impressions."

Ultimately, Durkheim saw two varieties of experience, split along a line of: (1) perceptual experience, which is the "direct apprehension of the external world," and (2) conceptual experience, which is "mediated by collective representations that serve to impose structure on the fluctuating stream of the senses" (as cited in Throop, 2003b, p. 370). Durkheim's sociologically inspired perspective of experience, and the structure of this experience, differs from the views of contemporary anthropologists. To him, individual cognition and affective states play no role in creating that individual's structure of experience. Instead, the individual relies on collective representations, which are external social phenomena, to process sensory perceptions. In many ways, this might amount to his viewing of Kant's a priori vision from a sociological perspective – while individuals do not have innate, pre-experience categories of consciousness through which they process experiences, they do have a priori collective representations through which they process experiences.

Levi-Strauss (1955) also acknowledged a difference between objective, sensory experience and constructed, meaning-laden experience. However, in contrast to Durkheim and more current theorists such as Bruner and Turner who suggest that individuals independently or collectively can find meaning within a structure of individual or collective experience, Levi-Strauss took a firmer cognitive perspective, similar to Kant's a priori conceptualization of consciousness. Levi-Strauss's chief aim was to "seek the generative source of cultural givens in the universal structures of the human brain" (Throop, 2003b, p. 376). For him, experience is culturally mediated; sensory perception and retrospective meaning attribution is subjective. However, underlying this development of a structure of experience are constant cognitive mechanisms, and these mechanisms are what primarily interested Levi-Strauss. Because of the subjectivity of experience, he was hesitant, even as an anthropologist, to accept natives' perceptions and descriptions of their own experiences within their society or culture. For example, Levi-Strauss would question the efficacy of such an approach to explain non-experiential social phenomena, such as myths (Throop, 2003b). Levi-Strauss believed in the "need to place any emic or indigenous reality in its proper context; not by destroying or mutilating its empirical reality, but by going beyond or behind such phenomenal manifestations" (Scholte, 1973, p. 682). This perspective differs from that of Durkheim in that its emphasis is not on experience as a universal constant of human consciousness, but on the underlying cognitive processes that turn sensory perception into a structure of experience (Throop, 2003b). Levi-Strauss ultimately concluded that experience itself is not worth studying, and he turned instead to using experience as a way of explaining how the Kantian a priori cognitive processes work.

While Durkheim, Levi-Strauss, and others disagreed about the importance and essence of experience, their work still persists in current anthropology. Durkheim's notion of collective representations has informed and influenced anthropologists interested in studying experience, who frequently turn to ritual, dramatic, and literary expressions as a way to empirically study experience. Perhaps more importantly, Durkheim's appeal for greater empiricism in social science has placed experience at the forefront of social science research because of its cross-cultural ubiquity and authenticity (Scott, 1991). And while Levi-Strauss eschewed experience as a subject of empirical study, his skepticism about the efficacy of using experience as an objective fact has perhaps influenced anthropologists to engage in hermeneutics, or the use of interpretation to derive empirical data. Social scientists do not use experience and its subsequent expression prima facie; it is only through understanding experience and the underlying processes that social and cultural reality emerges. Perhaps ironically, Levi-Strauss's concern about the validity of researching pure experience did not diminish experience as an object of study; rather, his arguments enhanced scholars' desire for a vigorous, interpretive methodology to understand the underlying dynamics of experience.

EXPERIENCE AS APPLIED WITHIN ANTHROPOLOGY

Conducting field work and living among foreign or isolated cultures is the essence of the anthropologist's work. Anthropologists themselves experience these settings and create expressions, whether through publishing scholarly journal articles, giving lectures or writing books, in order to communicate their own lived experience.

As Bruner (1986) explains, and as Durkheim and Levi-Strauss suggested, studying experience itself is tricky – experience lies within individuals, and one can never really know the objective facts of another's sensory experiences. In assigning meaning to experiences, individuals can alter, enhance, downplay, obfuscate or even eliminate the actual experience from their consciousness. Moreover, individuals differ in their ability to articulate their experiences, which adds another variable that affects the reliability of others' shared experience (Bruner, 1986). Dilthey provides an answer to this problem: instead of studying experiences, which are difficult to get at, study and interpret the social manifestations, or expressions, of experience (Rickman, 1976). For Dilthey, expressions included "representations, performances, objectifications, or texts" (Bruner, 1986, p. 5). Turner (1982, p. 17) describes expressions as "the crystalized secretions of once living human experience." As Bruner (1986) points out, the wide variety of types of expressions have led to a wide variety of topics studied, from hunting stories, to Broadway plays to pottery.

Bruner makes two important points regarding expression. First, he draws distinctions between *reality*, which is "what is really out there, whatever that may be" (p. 6), *experience*, which is an individual's perception of reality, and *expression*, which is how an experience is retold to others. Importantly, the relationship between experience and expression is recursive. Echoing Durkheim's discussion of how collective representations can alter the way individuals process experiences, Bruner similarly argues that expressions can structure experience. Expressions, whether religious rituals, literary works, or important dramas, can leave indelible impressions that shape the way new experiences are processed. Some works of art are so intense and powerful that they can reveal "everyday experience and thereby enrich and clarify that experience" (ibid.).

The second point Bruner (1986, p. 7) illustrates about expression is that it always implies action, a "processual activity," that is, "A ritual must be enacted, a myth recited, a narrative told, a novel read, a drama performed." Just as experiences require agency – they are constituted as the individual lives through them – expressions also require agency. The teller in each telling of an experience is framing, slanting or emphasizing certain parts of the experience to create or teach meaning to those that receive the expression. This is a crucial notion for anthropologists studying societies and cultures – instead of the anthropologist arriving on a scene with a conceptual frame through which to study and interpret the culture, the anthropologist lets the indigenous people tell their own stories and create their own units of analysis (Bruner, 1986).

Turner (1985, 1986) describes these social expressions of experience as "social drama." Turner saw social drama – those transitions from chaos and disorder to harmony and equilibrium, which can "reach the depth of the experiencer's being" (1986, p. 38) – as a manifestation of the most important experiences. To facilitate the study of experience through expression, Turner (1985) created a four-part framework that constitutes what he meant by social drama: (1) breach; (2) crisis; (3) redress; and (4) reintegration. *Breach* represents the moment a rule, social norm or custom is broken. This breach can be intentional, such as criminal activity or the instigation of war, or it can be accidental, such as a dinner party guest unwittingly violating the rules of etiquette. For Turner, *crisis* occurs in balkanization as individuals and groups line up in opposition to or in solidarity with the rule-breaker. During the crisis stage, old grievances might be redressed, and the true state of order, which had until then existed as an undercurrent, is revealed. Ultimately, leaders, who had drawn their legitimacy through conforming to, and supporting, tradition either win or they lose legitimacy as tradition is overthrown. Should the challenged faction overcome the challenging faction, the social drama moves to *redress*, in which the old social order is reinforced. Here, Turner makes a compelling argument by comparing the nature of law and judicial organizations to a body of collective social experience. Just as an individual remembers a previously lived-through experience within the larger flow of the structure of experience and in doing so, attaches meaning to the experience, judges create justice (or, for Turner, "meaning") in the social drama by recalling relevant pieces of law and applying them to resolve the crisis (Turner, 1985). It is no accident, for Turner, that in most societies, law originated from and is accompanied by a religious component, where a god provides remedies for social breaches. Here, also, Turner is echoing Durkheim (1964) from a century before, who believed crime was a natural part of social structure and served to reinforce normative meanings and social solidarity. Lastly, during *reintegration*, those who challenged the rules and norms of the social system accept the redress and become again conscious conformers. While at the end of a processual social drama the community may appear to have returned to normal, the experience has changed it in some way – traditional forces lose ground to new ideas, individuals shift allegiance to different factions and the hammer has been pulled for a subsequent social drama to take place (Turner, 1985). Turner eschews equilibrium, as it is suggested within structural functionalism, and instead suggests that stability is no more than the consequence of a momentary pause between factional strife inherent in social drama.

Bruner (1986) writes that social drama, or individual experience manifested through collective expression, can be exhibited in all aspects of anthropology – even in the pursuit of anthropology itself, such as in the academic papers scholars write about their own experiences. As such, *interpreting* the meaning of social drama and the underlying cultural experience is the lens through which researchers can examine a topic within anthropology. Turner draws a distinction between anthropologists who study the expression of experience – that is, the "theaters, tales, ballads, epics, operas" (Bruner, 1986, p.13) – and other social scientists who are interested in mere social habit (ibid.). In the next section, we discuss the concept that underlies anthropologists' method for interpreting the expressions they witness and experience.

UNDERSTANDING EXPERIENCE

Anthropology scholars have applied many methodologies to study experience, and we describe in great detail in a later chapter the philosophy underlying an interpretivist approach to understanding experience. In this chapter, we choose to outline a few of the principles of hermeneutics, or interpretation. Hermeneutics arose as a method for interpreting religious scripture but came to be more broadly applied by philosophers and social scientists, not least of whom were the foundational scholars in experience.

For Dilthey, the methods for understanding natural occurrences were insufficient when applied to understanding experiences (Palmer, 1969). As opposed to the natural sciences, where the facts of objective phenomena are studied to understand nature, human sciences have to delve into the inner thoughts and hidden consciousness to understand the subject. While both sciences were employed in developing understanding, Dilthey argued that a positivist approach to studying humanness wasn't enough – that the understanding of humanness can only be found in the meanings humans attached to experience. To discover that meaning, social scientists have to interpret the manifestations of experience, which Dilthey suggested is best found in written or unwritten texts, such as literature or drama. According to Dilthey, hermeneutics, which is the method of interpreting texts, could be applied to the broader purpose of examining meanings and experiences that underlie the texts (Palmer, 1969).

Hermeneutics is the process for understanding the subjectivity that underlies all human expression and creation, whether an economic system, a dramatic play or even a sandwich (Baronov, 2004). Hermeneutics makes four assumptions about human beings. First, humans are intentional creators. Second, the objects people create have meaning, which is a consequence of human subjectivity. A painting, a hospital, and a shoe are all subjective creations in so far as they embody the creators' feelings and emotions. Third, this meaning attribution exists both at an individual level and at the social level. The painting embodies the individual's subjectivity, the city embodies the society's subjectivity; but the painting can come to embody social subjectivity just as a city may possess subjective meaning for an individual. Fourth, these meanings are embedded within, and can only be understood through, the context of the times and society of the creator. This assumption draws on the notion that individuals' perspective and understanding is strongly dependent on history: both the history of the subject and the history of the interpreter (Gadamer, 1975). For example, to understand the meaning of *East of Eden*, the social researcher must also understand John Steinbeck's life and the culture in which he lived (Baronov, 2004).

Hermeneutics developed during the Protestant Reformation and is most commonly understood today as the process for interpreting the Bible. As copies of the Bible were translated from Latin into German, English, and other languages of the laity, individuals consequently took it upon themselves to begin interpreting the Bible on their own. In 1654, the first appearance of the word "hermeneutics" appeared on the cover of a guide to writing exegesis for Protestant ministers, who were no longer able to turn to the Church for scriptural guidance. Today, hermeneutics is more broadly applied but still retains its original meaning as the process of interpretation: "We mean by hermeneutics the theory of rules that govern an exegesis, that is to say, an interpretation of a particular text or collection of signs susceptible of being considered as a text" (Ricoeur, 1965, cited in Palmer, 1969, p. 43).

Hermeneutics has been described as anti-methodological: "method is in reality a form of dogmatism, separating the interpreter from the work, standing between it and him, and barring him from experiencing the work in its fullness. Analytical seeing is blindness to experience; it is analytical blindness" (Palmer, 1969, p. 247). Palmer's attack on method-driven interpretation has perhaps had a deleterious effect on developing or explicating Ricoeur's (1984) guidelines for interpretation. Given hermeneutics' concern with subjective meaning instead of objective reality, strict adherence to method appears to be antithetical to interpretation itself. Nevertheless, some social scientists have established principles to guide an open interpretation of experience (e.g., Butler, 1998; Madison, 1988). Madison (1988) presents nine such principles. Interpretation must:

- be *coherent*, in that the picture it presents of an expression must not be contradictory to itself;
- be *comprehensive*, in that it considers the creator's entire set of thoughts regarding the expression he or she created;
- *penetrate*, in that it must uncover the meaning, hidden or subjective, that lies imbedded in each creation;
- be *thorough*, in that it addresses every question raised by the creation for the researcher or the researcher about the creation.[1]
- be *appropriate*, in that the interpretation must concern itself only with the questions or issues raised within the creation;
- be *contextual*, in that the researcher must be aware of and account for the history and culture in which the creator was embedded;
- *agree* both with the actual content of the creation as well as established interpretations of the creation;
- be *suggestive*, in that it probes forward and raises new research questions; and
- interpretations that meet these requirements can be judged to have *potential*, or truth, if in reaching conclusions, they "unfold themselves harmoniously" (Butler, 1998, p. 292).

IMPLICATIONS FOR ENTREPRENEURSHIP RESEARCH

We turn now to discussing how anthropological perspectives can inform those studying entrepreneurs and venture creation. Anthropology is the study of humanness – in other words, the qualities, whether social or cultural, whether biological or cognitive, that separate humans from other life on earth. In order to understand these qualities, anthropologists examine humans in action and the products of human action, especially through field work. Durkheim's research ([1912] 1995) on tribes in Australia, Desjarlais' portrait (1997) of homelessness in Boston, and Lindholm and Lindholm's work (1982) on present-day life for women living behind the veil in the Middle East, are directed at understanding how people think, behave, and interact, all the while trying to delve closer to what it means to be human. The creation of a new venture is as uniquely human a social context, and as filled with drama, ritual, expression, and artifacts, as these other research contexts. If entrepreneurship is an individual's enactment of their own dreams and aspirations, then certainly it can also prove to be a fruitful field for accessing those intrinsic qualities that make humans distinct.

Drawing from anthropology, four general areas emerge as applicable to studying entrepreneurship. First, what is the nature of an entrepreneurial experience? Second, how do entrepreneurs attach meaning to these experiences? Third, how do entrepreneurs build structures of experience, and how do these constructions affect entrepreneurs' performance? Lastly, what is the nature of expression in entrepreneurship? Do ventures themselves represent interpretable expressions of experience? What about written business plans and business models? And to what extent do these expressions represent a collective, or social, representation of meaning?

Entrepreneurship implies agency. It is the material implementation of creativity and innovation, and it requires behavior. Experience is the self-referential description of that behavior. "It is not customary to say, 'Let me tell you about my behavior'; rather, we tell about experiences, which include not only actions and feelings but also reflections about those actions and feelings" (Bruner, 1986, p. 5). Entrepreneurship is uncertain and ambiguous, and from the outside looking in, the entrepreneur's behavior is to "make it up as they go along" (Baron, 2008, p. 329). On the inside looking out, this behavior-qua-experience might be best described through the framework of effectuation (Dew et al., 2009; Sarasvathy, 2001). Sarasvathy delineates between causal logic and effectual logic – causal logic is focused on arriving at a predetermined end where the prediction of the outcome is possible; effectual logic is focused on the process of creation with an uncertain end. While entrepreneurs engaged in either type of logic can have experiences, effectuation, as it considers the entrepreneur living through the process of creation, lends itself as a frame for studying the actual experiences of entrepreneurs themselves. Further, methodological approaches, such as think-aloud protocols, used in studying effectuation (Dew et al., 2009; Sarasvathy, 2008) capture the entrepreneur in the moment, living through the experience. As we have discussed above, anthropologists have long been concerned with the subjectivity of experience. Effectuation and the methodology employed may be a fruitful way of capturing the experience instantaneously within its temporal setting, absent of the individual's post hoc meaning attributions. Bricolage is another theme running through entrepreneurship scholarship related to agency and which draws directly on an anthropological perspective. Levi-Strauss (1967) described how certain tribes would adopt the symbols of nearby tribes and recombine them to create new meanings. Within entrepreneurship, bricolage means to create outcomes through new combinations of existing resources (Baker and Nelson, 2005) or improvisation (Garud and Karnoe, 2003).

Researchers have begun the process of examining how entrepreneurs attribute meaning to their experiences (Morris et al., 2010) or to themselves as a consequence of venture creation (Morris et al., 2011). Other researchers have examined how entrepreneurs attach meaning to their specific experiences, and how this meaning affects subsequent performance. For example, Shepherd considered entrepreneurs' grief at the failure of a venture and how different levels of grief might affect how entrepreneurs learn from their experiences (Shepherd, 2003).

Research examining the influence that structures of experience have on entrepreneurs and entrepreneurship is widespread and diverse, though few have framed the research in terms of studying experience. However, studies on affect, cognition development, experiential learning, human and social capital, and even the value of previous entrepreneurship experience could all fall under the broad scope of experience, at least as it is conceived in the anthropology discipline. Even pedagogically, entrepreneurship programs have recognized the value of providing opportunities for students to accrue entrepreneurial experience, through business plan contests, facilitating consulting engagements at home or abroad, and fostering communication between experienced entrepreneurs and students. Within the anthropology lens, these experiences together create within students and schools structures of experience, which may lead to students identifying themselves as entrepreneurs and schools embracing entrepreneurship through collective expression. An example of entrepreneurship research regarding the structure of experience includes Corbett's study (2007) of the impact of experiential learning on opportunity identification. He draws on experiential learning theory, which echoes Schütz's notion that individuals acquire sets of experiences to which they retrospectively assign meanings (Corbett, 2007; Schütz, 1967). For Corbett, how individuals assign meaning to an experience (or information) can influence how they identify and evaluate opportunities.

Anthropologists' work on examining expression can influence how researchers study entrepreneurship. The ventures entrepreneurs create might be considered expressions of experience. In the purest form, "entrepreneurial acts . . . are readings of and contributions to different conversations, and successful entrepreneurs can join these conversational processes and move them in particular directions" (de Montoya, 2000, p. 343). These conversations, or expressions, might represent the venture itself or activities associated with the venture. A newly opened accounting firm will have meaning for the society in which it is embedded; it might have a different meaning for those who are associated with it as employees, suppliers or buyers; meanings can be attached to the marketing campaign it might launch; and meanings can be attached to the work the firm creates, which are expressions of experience in and of themselves. Downing (2005) has described how meanings might be attached to organizational narratives and how those narratives affect the organizational identity. Delmar and Shane (2004) and Karlsson and Honig (2009) use institutional theory to explain the role of business planning as a technique used to obtain legitimacy – the anthropologist's perspective might advance research by examining how these business plans represent expressions of the entrepreneur's experiences and how business plans might fit within society as broader social expressions. Similarly, how do ventures represent a product of an entrepreneur's enacted environment (Sarasvathy, 2003) – and in what ways can both the venture and the structure surrounding the venture be considered expressions of experience?

Finally, the anthropology perspective on experience and hermeneutics might provide a unique insight into the dialectical relationship between identifying opportunities and launching a venture to exploit those opportunities. For example, Doganova and Eyquem-Renault (2009) provide an interesting case example of the iterative process that exists between opportunity identification and creating a workable business model. In their study, Doganova and Eyquem-Renault illustrated the dialectic that exists between the entrepreneur and the market-based opportunity, and they described how the entrepreneur ultimately adopted a third path as a consequence of the dialectical process. This recursive process that exists between a venture and society represents an experienced-based dialectic: for the venture, as it and the people within it accrue experience in exploiting opportunity and serving customer needs, and for society, as it accrues experience of being served by the venture and of shaping and molding it through isomorphism or coercive forces.

CONCLUSIONS

This chapter outlines experience as it is understood within the anthropology literature. We open with a discussion on the elements of experience and describe the foundations of an experience-based perspective rooted in works by Durkheim, Levi-Strauss, and others. We next discuss one type of methodology used to study experience, which is strongly rooted in an interpretivist philosophy: hermeneutics. Hermeneutics, which focuses on incorporating the historical and cultural embeddedness of a subject into our understanding of that subject, has been argued as the only path to knowledge (Gadamer, 1976). Here, we describe a few guidelines for conducting hermeneutic research and focus on the iterative, reflexive interpretation of an expression of experience, whether a play, novel, poem, or even a business plan or a website. We conclude the chapter by describing certain influences anthropology has had on our understanding of entrepreneurship as well as how an anthropological view of experience might inform the research questions of entrepreneurship scholars. In the next chapter, we turn to psychology, where experience as a subject of study is concerned with how individuals perceive and attribute meaning to experiences.

NOTE

1. This originates from the notion that hermeneutics is dialectical – the most complete method for uncovering truth about subjective topics, where a researcher's openness is essential. Asking questions is a way to remain open and let the creation express its own meanings (Butler, 1998). Similarly, because absolute truth is impossible to discover, competing interpretations must not be seen in conflict with each other but rather as two participants in a larger dialectic process (Baronov, 2004).

REFERENCES

Abrahams, R.D. (1985), 'Our native notions of story', *New York Folklore*, **11**(1–4): 37–47.
Abrahams, R.D. (1986), 'Ordinary and extraordinary experience', in V. Turner and E. Bruner (eds), *The Anthropology of Experience*, Chicago, IL: University of Illinois Press, pp. 45–72.
Baker, T. and R.E. Nelson (2005), 'Creating something from nothing: resource

construction through entrepreneurial bricolage', *Administrative Science Quarterly*, **50**(3): 329–66.

Baron, R. (2008), 'Role of affect in the entrepreneurial process', *Academy of Management Review*, **33**(2): 328–40.

Baronov, D. (2004), *Conceptual Foundations of Social Research Methods*, Boulder, CO: Paradigm.

Brereton, D.P. (2009), 'Why sociocultural anthropology needs John Dewey's evolutionary model of experience', *Anthropological Theory*, **9**(1): 5–32.

Bruner, E.M. (1986), 'Experience and its expressions', in V. Turner and E. Bruner (eds), *The Anthropology of Experience*, Chicago, IL: University of Illinois Press, pp. 3–30.

Butler, T. (1998), 'Towards a hermeneutic method for interpretive research in information systems', *Journal of Information Technology*, **13**(4): 285–300.

Corbett, A.C. (2007), 'Learning asymmetries and the discovery of entrepreneurial opportunities', *Journal of Business Venturing*, **22**(1): 97–118.

Delmar, F. and S. Shane (2004), 'Legitimating first: organizing activities and the survival of new ventures', *Journal of Business Venturing*, **19**(3): 385–410.

de Montoya, L.M. (2000), 'Entrepreneurship and culture: the case of Freddy, the strawberry man', in R. Swedberg (ed.), *Entrepreneurship: The Social Science View*. Oxford: Oxford University Press, pp. 332–55.

Desjarlais, R. (1994), 'Struggling along: the possibilities of experience among the homeless mentally ill', *American Anthropologist*, **96**(4): 886–901.

Desjarlais, R. (1997), *Shelter Blues*, Philadelphia, PA: University of Pennsylvania Press.

Dew, N., S. Read, S. Sarasvathy and R. Wiltbank (2009), 'Effectual versus predictive logics in entrepreneurial decision making: differences between experts and novices', *Journal of Business Venturing*, **24**(4): 287–309.

Dewey, J. (1925), *Experience and Nature*, LaSalle, IL: Open Court.

Doganova, L. and E. Eyquem-Renault (2009), 'What do business models do? Innovation devices in technology entrepreneurship', *Research Policy*, **38**: 1559–70.

Downing, S. (2005), 'The social construction of entrepreneurship: narrative and dramatic process in the coproduction of organizations and identities', *Entrepreneurship Theory and Practice*, **29**(2): 185–204.

Durkheim, E. (1964), *The Division of Labor in Society*, New York: Free Press of Glencoe.

Durkheim, E. ([1912] 1995), *The Elementary Forms of Religious Life*, London: Allen.

Ermarth, M. (1978), *Wilhelm Dilthey: Critique of Historical Reason*, Chicago, IL: University of Chicago Press.

Gadamer, H.G. (1975), *Truth and Method*, New York: Seabury Press.

Gadamer, H.G. (1976), *Philosophical Hermeneutics*, Berkeley, CA: University of California Press.

Gadamer, H.G. (1988), *Truth and Method*, translated by J. Weinsheimer and D.G. Marshall, New York: Continuum, 2.

Garud, R. and P. Karnoe (2003), 'Bricolage versus breakthrough: distributed and embedded agency in technology entrepreneurship', *Research Policy*, **32**(2): 277–300.

Godlove, T.F. (1996), 'Is "space" a concept? Kant, Durkheim, and French neo-Kantianism', *Journal of the History of the Behavioral Sciences*, **32**(4): 441–55.

Husserl, E. (1997), *Experience and Judgment*, Evanston, IL: Northwestern University Press.

James, W. (1890), *The Principles of Psychology*, New York: Henry Holt & Co.

Karlsson, T. and B. Honig (2009), 'Judging a business by its cover: an institutional perspective on new ventures and the business plan', *Journal of Business Venturing*, **24**(1): 27–45.

Levi-Strauss, C. (1955), *Tristes tropiques*, Paris: Librarie Plon.

Levi-Strauss, C. (1967), *The Savage Mind*, Chicago, IL: University of Chicago Press.

Lindholm, C. and C. Lindholm (1982), 'Life behind the veil', in D.E.K. Hunter and P. Whitten (eds), *Anthropology: Contemporary Perspectives*, Boston, MA: Little, Brown & Company, pp. 231–4.

Madison, G.B. (1988), *The Hermeneutics of Postmodernity: Figures and Themes*, Bloomfield, IN: Indiana University Press.

Morris, M.H., D.F. Kuratko, M. Schindehutte and R. Spirack (2011), 'Framing the entrepreneurial experience', *Entrepreneurship Theory and Practice*, published online.

Morris, M.H., J.A. Allen, D.F. Kuratko and D. Brannon (2010), Experiencing family business creation: differences between founders, nonfamily managers, and founders of nonfamily firms, *Entrepreneurship Theory and Practice*, **34**(6): 1057–83.

Palmer, R.E. (1969), *Hermeneutics*, Evanston, IL: Northwestern University Press.

Parsons, T. (1937), *The Structure of Social Action*, New York: Free Press.

Rickman, H.P. (ed.) (1976), *Dilthey: Selected Writings*, Cambridge: Cambridge University Press.

Ricoeur, P. (1965), *De l'interpretation: Essai sur Freud*, Paris: Editions du Seuil.

Ricoeur, P. (1984), *Time and Narrative*, Chicago, IL: University of Chicago Press.

Sarasvathy, S. (2001), 'Causation and effectuation: toward a theoretical shift from economic inevitability to entrepreneurial contingency', *Academy of Management Review*, **26**(2): 243–63.

Sarasvathy, S. (2003), 'Entrepreneurship as a science of the artificial', *Journal of Economic Psychology*, **24**(2): 203–20.

Sarasvathy, S. (2008), *Effectuation: Elements of Entrepreneurial Expertise*, Cheltenham, UK and Northampton, MA, USA: Edward Elgar.

Scholte, B. (1973), 'The structural anthropology of Claude Levi-Strauss', in J. Honigmann (ed.), *Handbook of Social and Cultural Anthropology*, Chicago, IL: Rand McNally, pp. 637–716.

Schütz, A. (1967), *The Phenomenology of the Social World*, Evanston, IL: Northwestern University Press.

Scott, J. (1991), 'The evidence of experience', *Critical Inquiry*, **17**(4): 773–95.

Shepherd, D.A. (2003), 'Learning from business failure: propositions of grief recovery for the self-employed', *Academy of Management Review*, **28**(2): 318–28.

Throop, C.J. (2002), 'Experience, coherence, and culture: the significance of Dilthey's "Descriptive Psychology" for the anthropology of consciousness', *Anthropology of Consciousness*, **13**(1): 2–26.

Throop, C.J. (2003a), 'Articulating experience', *Anthropological Theory*, **3**(2): 219–41.

Throop, C.J. (2003b), 'Minding experience: an exploration of the concept of "experience" in the early French anthropology of Durkheim, Levy-Bruhl, and Levi-Strauss', *Journal of the History of Behavioral Sciences*, **39**(4): 365–82.

Turner, V. (1982), *From Ritual to Theater: The Seriousness of the Human Play*, New York: Performing Arts Journal Publication.

Turner, V. (1985), *On the Edge of the Bush: Anthropology as Experience*, L.B. Turner (ed.). Tucson, AZ: University of Arizona Press.

Turner, V. (1986), 'Dewey, Dilthey, and drama: an essay on the anthropology of experience', in V. Turner and E. Bruner (eds), *The Anthropology of Experience*, Chicago, IL: University of Illinois Press, pp. 33–44.

Turner, V. and E.M. Bruner, (eds) (1986), *The Anthropology of Experience*, Chicago, IL: University of Illinois Press.

3. Psychology and experience

Our natural way of thinking about these coarser emotions is that the mental perception of some fact excites the mental affection called the emotion, and that this latter state of mind gives rise to the bodily expression. My theory, on the contrary, is that the bodily changes follow directly the perception of the exciting fact, and that our feeling of the same changes as they occur IS the emotion.

(William James, 1890)

INTRODUCTION

The man with no memory is in-the-moment and of-the-world. He experiences, but these experiences flow past his consciousness and leave no trace and no meaning and no structure. He experiences the sight of an empty cup but doesn't remember the experience of drinking coffee. A mashed out cigarette but no experience of having smoked. A waking state without ever having experienced awakening. This man experiences, but the experiences do not congeal to form meaning, which he can later draw on, or structure, which helps him interpret subsequent experiences, or consciousness, with which he can say, "I am alive." This man experiences the moment, perhaps even more purely than the man with memory, yet he has no experience.

In 1985, Clive Wearing's structure of experience stopped developing. He had contracted encephalitis, a severe inflammation of the brain, which in earlier years would have killed him. He survived. His memory was destroyed, and he became the most severe case of amnesia ever recorded in medical history (Baddeley, 1990; Sacks, 2007). He doesn't retain memories of his present lived-through experiences, and he lost much of what he knew before his illness. For most people, experiences are absorbed, interpreted, and assigned meaning when they enter a person's structure of consciousness. Wearing's memory is shattered and he is, with a few intriguing exceptions, unable to add experiences to what he knew before he was struck with the disease. He was a music historian, musician, and conductor – he edited volumes on Renaissance composers – but cannot recall their names. He can recognize his children, but he is surprised about their even not-so-recent accomplishments (such as his son's graduation, which happened 20 years ago). His memory extends only a few seconds

– his wife, Deborah, says, it's as if his world resets with each blink (Sacks, 2007). Wearing keeps a journal, which he once filled with his experiences throughout a typical day. But:

> his journal entries consisted, essentially, of the statements "I am awake" or "I am conscious," entered again and again every few minutes. He would write: "2:10 P.M: This time properly awake . . . . 2:14 P.M: this time finally awake . . . . 2:35 P.M: this time completely awake," along with negations of these statements: "At 9:40 P.M. I awoke for the first time, despite my previous claims." This in turn was crossed out, followed by "I was fully conscious at 10:35 P.M., and awake for the first time in many, many weeks." This in turn was cancelled out by the next entry. (Ibid., p. 2)

Wearing is stuck in the present – he is in-the-moment and the experience-at-hand is his life. He is unaware of the experience of his own amnesia; the amnesiac never is (Sacks, 2007). Unable to draw on a lifetime of experiences, he constantly feels like he has just gained consciousness – the life he knows is only ever minutes or seconds old. And though he retains a remarkable ability to play the piano, conduct music, and exhibit striking devotion to his wife, without an accrued set of experiences, his life, for him, is like "Hell on earth – It's like being dead – all the bloody time" (Baddeley, 1990, p. 6).

Wearing illustrates the essential question of experience: what is the relationship between an experience and experience? As we have discussed, this question drives anthropologists, and it similarly drives psychologists – albeit with different foci and interests. Anthropologists study the *expressions* of experience. Coming upon unique cultures, either contemporary or of the past, they are able to construct an image of the community's collective experience through the community's expressions, such as rituals, dramas, literature or music. They are, in effect, studying the *artifacts* of experience. The objects of their interest are collective representations of experience. Psychologists studying experience take a *first-person view* of experience. How does someone embedded in a body – and thus separated from the world – experience the world? How does context influence experience? And what is the nature of the structure of experience – how does it change as a person accumulates new experiences or assigns meaning to old experiences? A psychology focused on experience finds its roots in philosophers such as Kierkegaard, Heidegger, Merleau-Ponty and Husserl, and psychologists such as James (Pollio et al., 1997). Its foundation is in existentialism and phenomenology, which is the study of the subjective nature of consciousness and the relation between a person and the world they experience.

This chapter will discuss experience as it is understood from a psychological perspective rooted in phenomenology. First, we will define and describe experience as a construct within psychology. Second, we will discuss phenomenological psychology and its use of experience in understanding consciousness. Third, we will turn to examine the methodology employed by psychologists to understand experience. Fourth, we will discuss the possible applications that phenomenological psychology may have in helping us understand entrepreneurship and the role of the entrepreneur.

EXPERIENCE IN PSYCHOLOGY

It is ironic that the drive for empiricism should be the reason psychologists have tended to neglect the role of experience (Bradley, 2005; Pollio et al., 1997) – an empiric is one who relies on experience (Merriam-Webster, 2011). William James, on whom so much of our understanding of experience is founded, eschewed the strictly abstract, objective approach to understanding psychology in order to lie "flat on his belly in the middle of experience" (James, 1909, p. 125). But because James embraced subjectivity, in the sense that an experience could only be viewed and interpreted through the perspective of the individual's perception, psychologists interested in testing causal theories of behavior were unlikely to adopt James's approach (Pollio et al., 1997). While the notion that subjective experience played a major role in the development of consciousness might have been accepted theoretically, it was seen as empirically impossible to parse out experience and its influence on the individual and behavior. A psychological perspective of experience and method appropriate for studying experience languished in the United States but ultimately emerged through a European gestalt tradition, and the work of existentialist and phenomenological philosophers.

The lived body lies at the root of a psychological perspective of experience (ibid.). According to Pollio and colleagues, "There seems to be no more significant problem than that of providing a coherent way of dealing with the fact that human beings both have a body and are a body" (ibid., p. 5) – they engage in both cognition and behavior. The boundary between the body and the environment is most clear in the third person. A surgeon about to dissect a body on an autopsy table is able to perfectly define what is within the body, and what is outside or without the body. Likewise, the psychologist analyzing a patient is easily able to delineate between that which is the patient and that which is not the patient. However, when one adopts a first-person perspective, this boundary is much more difficult to define – the notion of the body itself becomes more fluid and amorphous in this perspective as it moves through the environment, whether in a home

---

BOX 3.1 ELEMENTS OF EXPERIENCE IN PSYCHOLOGY

Intentionality: While two of us may be experiencing the same ontic occurrence, our points of view affect how we receive the experience. My point of view consists of my spatial or temporal relation to the experience and the context I bring with me to each experience, namely my life's worth of previous experiences.

Figure and ground: I can't experience without contrast. For example, the type on this page is only visible because of the white background of the page. When we focus on an object, we perceive only one aspect of the object, all the other potential aspects of that object fade away.

Continuity and change: The meaning of an experience is in constant flux. The moment I attach a meaning to an experience, that meaning already begins to change as I move through time and accumulate more experience.

---

or in a garden or in an office building. Or as it moves through the past, remembering, or moves through the future, desiring. When engaged in a familiar task that requires great skill, the body can almost fade away to nothingness – such as the athlete who feels she "is the ball" as she kicks it through the goal or the writer who is so in tune with the keyboard or pen that he does not notice as time slips away or that his body cries out for a drink of water.

Psychologists dissect experience into three components: intentionality, figure/ground, and continuity/change (Box 3.1). Let us briefly examine each of these.

Intentionality

During an experience, the body fades away to the lightest shades and the individual notices the immediately relevant environmental aspects most (Pollio et al., 1997). Pollio and colleagues point out that this notion constitutes intentionality, which is the first component of the psychological conceptualization of experience. Intentionality means that the person's experience and the person's perception of the world represent the same thing. That which is perceived is experienced (Horgan and Tienson, 2002); more specifically, individuals direct their attention toward some objects and not toward others. Husserl (1984) labeled the content of an experience, which includes the object being experienced as well as the affective content of the experience, "intentional matter." Intentionality can also be thought of as awareness: the fact that experiencing individuals can be aware of some objects in the environment and not aware of others (Strawson, 2004). Intentionality does not mean the common definition of intention, which is a person's purposeful action, but rather the person's point of view of the environmental context. A comedian may intend to be funny, but a member of the audience may be offended by the joke. While the comedian's experience of the night might be a successful gig, the audience member's experience is that of being offended. Both people underwent a similar ontic experience – that of being in a comedy club on a weekend evening – but they occupied slightly different situations in the overall event. This difference, which stems from how the individual is attached to the situation, is intentionality. It can require intentional effort or not – the intentionality as it pertains to a psychologist is based on each individual's point of view, which is the context from which they experienced the event or object (Pollio et al., 1997).

Harman (1990) describes the difference between the actual content of an experience and the perception or intentionality of an experience. For example, Harmon describes the man who feels pain in his leg caused by a slipped disk in his back. The content of the experience would place the location of the pain either at the point where the disk slipped in the back (or in the brain where the pain is processed), but the intentionality of the experience is that the pain is in the leg. Harmon also notes the possibility that one person may experience the redness of an apple as red, another may experience the color red as green. The content of the experience is the same thing – the redness of the apple is the foundation of both experiences, but the individual's perception of red can differ from another's. In that difference lies intentionality (ibid.).

An important corollary to intentionality within psychology is the notion that a person's experience of the environment precedes their experience of themselves. Pollio and colleagues (1997) note that individuals define themselves through their interactions with the outside world and objects, ideas, and people within that world. That boundary between the body and the outside, whether physical or cognitive, can only exist in the presence of contrast. People are able to identify and reinforce who they are through their contact with the external. The whiteness of the page is as essential to reading as the shape of the typeface, and the absence of darkness gives definition to light. Where a person's intentionality can highlight certain objects in the environment, conversely, these objects can be used to reveal what is important to the person (James, 1890; Pollio et al., 1997). Intentionality is thus linked to experience – individuals draw out and focus on objects with which they have familiarity (Strawson, 2004). Every experience has some conative attribute attached to it. As Zahavi (2005, p. 304) writes: "Every intentional experience is an experience of a specific type, be it an experience of judging, hoping, desiring, regretting, remembering, affirming, doubting, wondering, fearing, etc." This quality of experience represents intentionality. Experience, therefore, always precedes intentionality, and ultimately, consciousness (Husserl, 1984).

In instances of heightened intentionality, the body–environment barrier can fade entirely away in favor of the object in the environment on which the intentionality is focused. For example, Pollio (1982) describes the football player who is only aware of "me and the ball." This cliché of "keeping your eye on the ball" is yet another example of intentionality, and at the extreme end of this spectrum, individuals can become so involved in an experience with an object that they lose track of time and enter a state of high performance (Ghani and Deshpande, 1994). This experience of "optimal flow" has been most notably described by Csikszentmihalyi (1990) as a situation in which an individual voluntarily pursues an optimally challenging task for pure enjoyment's sake.

Figure and Ground

Intentionality implies that a human has focused on one object in the environment at the expense of focusing on other objects. Intentionality also carries with it the concept of contrast – that definition of the self and consciousness is only possible through experience. In other words, experience is attached to objects (figures) contrasted against a diffuse background (ground) (Thompson et al., 1989). Experiences are always part of more general events. In psychology, the broader events or context of the experiences give definition to the experience itself (Leibe and Schiele, 2006). Take, for example, the visual trick of reversible images (see Figure 3.1). In a black and white picture, an individual either notices the two black faces turned toward each other or the white vase. If the individual notices the two faces, the white space turns diffuse and fades away while the black spaces grow more intense. Conversely, if the vase is noticed first, the black spaces turn diffuse and the white space grows more intense.

Contrast, or figure/ground, is also linked to the concept of fringe, or the white space: those parts of experience that remain subconscious or unassigned with intentionality (Makkreel and Rodi, 1989). Our experiences with objects are always changing, and different focal points constantly come in and out of the fringe. As we increase focus on the image of the one white vase, the blackness of the two faces fade into the fringe. However, just as the person identifies the two faces, the whiteness is subsumed by

Figure 3.1   Sample field/ground image

the growing intensity of the experience of the two black faces, and the whiteness fades into the fringe. Take the experience of reading a newspaper in the morning. The initial experience might be of the paper as it sits in the driveway and the satisfaction of starting a morning routine. Take it out of the bag and scan the front page – you experience the sight and smell of the paper, but you are also experiencing the news and information that you see displayed across the page. Turn the page, and experience the feel – even the ink residue left on one's hand. Experience reading that morning's cartoons to your children and hearing them laugh. These are all different experiences brought about by your interaction with a single object. Your awareness of particular aspects of the experience necessarily requires that other aspects fade into the background (Wu, 2011). Husserl described this as the object's "inner horizon," which is to say that objects are not one-dimensional but instead possess ever-changing and interacting presences and fringes (in Pollio et al., 1997). For Pollio and colleagues there are two important broad categories of horizons or grounds. First, as we just discussed, the object itself carries with it any number of possible experiences, and the environment in which it is embedded also grounds the object. Second, the experiencing individual herself is grounded, not only in a particular social, cultural or geographic context, including language and religion, but also by a life's worth of accumulation of experience, or, as we discussed earlier, a structure of experience (Pollio et al., 1997; Schütz, 1967). This structure serves as a ground in so far as it affects the way people perceive and assign meaning to subsequent experiences.

Continuity and Change

William James (1899) describes a student's listening to a lecturer. At first the student is experiencing the content of the lecturer's talk. The student's focus, perhaps unintentionally, turns to the lecturer's voice or mannerisms. Or the student's attention jolts to another student in the classroom or perhaps even to remembering an event from the previous day. While researchers tend to discuss experiences as concrete, linear occurrences, with beginnings, middles, and ends, they are careful to note that experiences occur at the height of fluidity and are never static. James calls this the stream of consciousness, which he proposes has five characteristics: (1) events must be experienced by individuals; (2) consciousness is always changing; (3) consciousness is continuous; (4) consciousness always deals with objects; and (5) consciousness selects among its objects and events. Experiences must always be *experienced*, and a stream of consciousness is always *someone's* stream of consciousness (see Pollio et al., 1997). As we have discussed earlier, the experience is not in the concrete occurrence itself but lies in the perception and attachment of meaning by the experiencing person. This brings us to continuity and change. While some philosophers described experience as stopping points along a journey, James described experience as a continual flow – continuity lies in how preceding experiences affect subsequent experiences (James, 1899). While James's student listening to the lecture might suddenly jump from an experience of watching the lecturer's hands to experiencing thinking about that morning's breakfast, the experiences are nonetheless continuous: every subsequent experience is somehow influenced by the preceding experience (Natsoulas, 1988). James's last two points draw again on intentionality – that experiences are always a person's situated perspective on a particular object of attention.

EXPERIENCE IN PSYCHOLOGY RESEARCH

An experiential perspective within psychology has existed since the beginning of the twentieth century, but has only relatively recently begun to find traction as a field of research. Part of the problem, some scholars have argued, is that an experience-based psychology tends to ask qualitative questions – questions that begin with "why" not "how" (Giorgi, 1985). In psychology, a field that considers itself a natural science, asking the qualitative question is subordinate to asking the quantitative question. Psychologists have favored the laboratory setting and structuring test treatments to survey questions and analyzing descriptions. But for the psychologist interested in understanding experience, "descriptive psychology" as described by William Dilthey (1977) is the favored tradition. Giorgi (2006) points out that the natural science perspective of psychology is not exclusively useful in understanding non-physical forms, such as consciousness or experience. He argues that while empirical approaches have conceptualized experience so that it may be studied, they have done so with "severe distortion" (p. 46) of the phenomena. This section will outline the phenomenological approach to psychology, which is based on Husserl's work, as well as describe a few topics in psychology relevant to the discussion.

Psychology began as the science of consciousness or experience (Wundt, 1902), but the focus of research in the field turned toward studying behavior and the unconscious (Giorgi, 2006). Phenomenology is the study of how individuals perceive the objective world. While phenomenology owes its foundation to philosophical thinkers like Heidegger and Husserl, it has proven useful toward re-establishing an experienced-based perspective in psychology itself. Giorgi (ibid.), who considers himself a Husserlian, describes five key components of a phenomenological psychology.

First, Husserl erects a strict barrier between objects and the individual's perception of these objects (ibid.). Objects themselves cannot be part of consciousness, but the experiences of these objects are what make up consciousness. Additionally, since individuals cannot incorporate objects themselves into consciousness, they rely on their experiences, which are based on perception. This brings us back to the point Pollio and colleagues (1997) made about figure and ground – how objects can possess the potential for any number of experiences. Husserl makes a similar point – that is, because individuals rely on perception, which affords them only the vaguest outline of an object, perceptions can change as objects come in and out of focus during the experience.

Second, empiricism or naturalism is not sufficient for understanding consciousness (Giorgi, 2006). For Husserl, experience is not real in the way a tree or a building are real, which means it cannot be tested or measured. While a person may have an experience beholding a tree, which might conceivably be measured, a person may also have an experience with an idea, which cannot be exactly measured. Husserl proposed a phenomenological approach to psychology, and he suggested two approaches for arriving at pure consciousness or experience. He argued that researchers must attempt to separate present experiences from the influence of the body of accumulated experiences, and researchers must be willing to examine experiences as non-real entities (ibid.), or recognize that they are a person's perceptual creations and not necessarily related to the object on which an experience is based.

Third, whereas psychology has concerned itself with the real object's influence on consciousness, Husserl argues that psychology should instead be interested in the action of consciousness itself, which is intuition or the making of "the present" through experience and perception. There are many kinds of objects, irreal objects such as: ideas, memories, or fictional events; experiential objects such as dreams; and real objects such as trees, buildings, and newspapers (ibid.). Husserl argues that psychology should have focused on understanding the differing impacts that experiencing the various types of objects have on consciousness; instead, it focused on the real.

Fourth, while objects may be perceived in an infinite number of ways and are perpetually vague to consciousness, consciousness *itself* is understood absolutely (ibid.). The meanings and sensations attached to experiences are directly perceived – the barrier between body and environment doesn't exist between a person and consciousness. Lastly, Husserl notes the important role of intentionality in experience, which we have discussed above.

Phenomenology is a distinct school in psychology, and its scholarly adherents have advocated using it as a comprehensive approach to psychology research and education (Bradley, 2005; Giorgi, 2009; Husserl, 1965). There is not sufficient space in this chapter to present an exhaustive set of applied examples of phenomenological psychology. However, we will discuss two important areas of research where an experienced-based perspective of psychology is particularly relevant – visual perception and memory.

Visual Perception

Psychology presents vision as a dualistic process: first, the physiology of sight allows individuals to behold objects; and second, mental processes at the end of the process, including thinking and memory, translate the sensory data into meaningful information (Kruger, 1979). Individuals do not see an object as it is reflected in the retina nor do they see the object as it passes along the optical nerve to the brain (Kruger, 1979; McConville, 1978). Again, as Pollio and colleagues suggest (1997), a barrier presents itself between the body and the environment, this time creating separation between seeing and perceiving. In this two-stage process, individuals may first only receive the visual signals from objects – they are unable to control the physiological processes involved in sight – and for the psychologist, the mental processes involved in translating ontic visual signals to perception remain hidden.

This model of seeing presents a problem for the experienced-based perspective of psychology – individuals have intentionality toward the objects they experience. They must be involved with the objects they view. In the above model, individuals are merely passive recipients of visual sensory stimulation, which means intentionality is reduced and the figure/ ground distinction is eliminated as the object's and the perceiver's situatedness or context is rendered mute. However, research has indicated that visual perception may not be the one-sided affair depicted above. Kruger (1979) describes a case involving a reading instructor for the blind in the nineteenth century. At that time, at least two systems existed to enable blind individuals to read: the well-known Braille system and the Moon system. The Moon system consisted of reliefs of capital letters in English. Individuals who used this system were typically older and became blind later in life – they already knew how to read and found difficulty in picking up a new written language. One day, an instructor was teaching the Moon system to a patient who suddenly interrupted the lesson with the complaint that her eyes hurt. What was discovered is that readers using the Braille system would tend to focus their eyes on the horizon, and readers using the Moon system would look directly at the page, following along as their fingers felt the letters – they were trying to *see* the words they were reading. For the experienced-based perspective, which incorporates intentionality, this carries a significant implication: "To be able to see one looks" (p. 85). When the physiological process of sight does not function and visual sensory stimulation is impossible, intentionality can nevertheless influence physiology.

Perception is also rooted in meaning, and individuals perceive a meaning world while that which is meaningless fades in comparison. Consider the well-known video of four people, two dressed in white and two dressed in black, passing basketballs back and forth to each other (Simons and Chabris, 1999). Before presenting this video to a class, the instructor tells the students to count how many times the people in black pass the basketball to each other – the instructor has assigned meaning for the students watching the video. It is no surprise, then, that the students miss the person dressed in a gorilla costume as he walks through the middle of the scene. This example illustrates how meaning can affect how individuals experience a situation, regardless of what the actual visual sensory signals are. Unlike the model of sight described above, where meaning is attached at the very end of a physiological process, meaning and intentionality play a role throughout perception.

Memory

As mentioned at the beginning of this chapter, encephalitis destroyed Clive Wearing's ability to retain experiences as memories. While amnesia did not wipe out memories of his wife, children or his ability to play music, he is effectively locked into the moment, even though his memories reach up to a point in time in the 1960s and then stop (Sacks, 2007). Wearing has been rendered physically unable to experience or remember. However, researchers have noticed that he is somehow able, despite his physical detriment, to retain certain types of memories and even to learn. For example, Wearing is an experienced musician and can still expertly play the piano. Sacks writes that when Wearing's illness first set in, every time he would encounter a repeat sign in a piece of music, he would repeat and repeat the section, unaware that he had already done so. Over time, however, Wearing somehow developed a new awareness and began playing repeat signs only once (ibid.). In this instance, physiology is unable to fully explain Wearing's behavior.

Psychologists in the experienced-based perspective are critical of the physiological approach to memory, which they argue treats the brain only like some sort of computer, capable of separating long-term memory from short-term memory and recalling it, more or less, on demand (Kruger, 1979). These researchers question the mechanical and empirical understandings of knowledge and doubt that the pursuit of discovering some sort of physiologically real structure of memory is valuable. Just as in the experienced-based critique of visual perception, which added to the physiological understanding, the experienced-based perspective does not completely eschew a physiological component of memory, but it adds to our understanding of memory the role of intentionality (Schacter, 1987). For example, Kruger (1979) writes that while we may see every car driving down the road, we are unlikely to remember any of them because our focus was based on the destination or the road or some task we must perform later in the day – we remember the trip, but aspects we remember stand out only in so far as they were the objects of our attention (Kruger, 1979).

Memory is "the reactivating of the past as past, the past as it was then but as it appears now" (Kruger, 1979, p.99). The memory exists as it was experienced by the rememberer. Objects drop in and out of focus, in and out of intentionality, and in and out of memory (Wheeler et al., 1997). Kruger describes some acts of forgetting as a manifestation of

intentionality. For example, you may take a scarf off when you arrive at
your friend's house for dinner, and on leaving, forget about it and leave
it behind. Kruger further writes that this is not "forgetting" in the strict-
est sense of the term but rather an example of where the scarf fell out of
the experiencer's intentionality. Proper forgetting involves forgetting an
experience or a piece of an experience, such as forgetting the name with the
face. The rememberer is aware of the experience of forgetting the person's
name and the loss of the information becomes real to the rememberer, who
is unable to remember (Kruger, 1979).

METHODOLOGY FOR STUDYING EXPERIENCE IN PSYCHOLOGY

Wilhelm Wundt, who is considered the founder of modern experiential
psychology (Giorgi, 2006), confronted two general conceptualizations
about the mission of psychology. Wundt (1902) disagreed with the first
notion – that psychology sought to understand what he called metaphysi-
cal mind-substance, because it was too close to philosophy and ignored
physical reality. Wundt also dismissed the second notion – that psychology should strive to understand inner experience because it ignored the
role played by the experiential interface between the person and reality.
Instead, he called for a psychology that would investigate both inner
experience and outer experience, and he supported using empiricism in
order to pursue both goals. However, Wundt's contemporaries and other
early psychologists of the modern era embraced qualitative methods as
valid complements to quantitative methods (Giorgi, 2009). Giorgi draws
on work by James, Titchner, and others to show they used descriptions of
experience to draw conclusions about consciousness. Giorgi (1985, 2009),
who has published several books on the phenomenological approach to
psychology, likewise supports both empiricism and qualitative efforts
in understanding experience. He argues that a strictly understood and
followed descriptive method can be as empirical and scientific as other
research philosophies operative in natural science. Specifically, Giorgi
adapts Husserl's philosophical approach: (1) description; (2) phenomenological reduction; and (3) search for psychological meaning, to explicate a
phenomenological psychological methodology.

Description

The psychologist must first extract raw data from the experiencer. To do
this, she may either conduct an interview with the subject, which will later

be transcribed, or she may ask the subject to write down the experiences in as much detail as possible. According to Giorgi (2009), the researcher should not solicit specific experiences for the subject to describe; instead, let the subject choose the experiences and the semantics used in the description. Giorgi notes that two simultaneous phenomenological events are occurring in the collection of this raw data: first, the subject's description of lived-through events; and second, the psychologist's own experience of the data collection process, as well as the experience that is ultimately described. Some researchers have noted that this simultaneity causes methodological problems – how might a researcher's intentionality affect the way they describe someone else's experience? Giorgi admits that this phenomenon might be taking place, but he is also quick to note that the patient's description of an experience is written and public – which would mitigate, if not eliminate, the possible occurrences of bias in data collection. Giorgi also asserts that experiences are shareable with others because they take place in the world – that an ontic encounter with the environment is at the root of experience, which can be apprehended by others.

Phenomenological Reduction

Psychologists must adopt an approach that brings them as close to the subject's lived-through experience as possible. Husserl described a psychological phenomenological reduction (1977), wherein the researcher parses out the expressions of consciousness that are attached to a particular experience and those that are not (Giorgi, 2009). Again, the question is raised: since there are two people involved in analyzing any experience (i.e., the subject and the psychologist) and since the psychologist herself becomes an experiencer when encountered with the subject's experience, are there not methodological problems? Specifically related to phenomenological reduction, there is some question of whether both the subject and the psychologist should be familiar with reductionism. To what extent should a subject be trained to express a lived-through experience? Some qualitative studies trained the subjects about how best to describe their experiences (Giorgi, 2006, 2009). Giorgi raises arguments against the notion of training subjects themselves to adopt a phenomenological reductionist perspective. The first is practical: if psychologists can devote extensive study to reductionism themselves and still get it wrong, what chance do subjects off the street have in properly adopting the technique? The second is theoretical: the subject should remain naive regarding phenomenology and describe the experience as "complex and mixed precisely as it was lived, thick with its ambiguities and relationships" (Giorgi, 2009,

p. 99). According to Merleau-Ponty (1962) it is the role of the psychologist to interpret the experience and attempt to understand it better than the subject can. In fact, if the subject were to be given insight into phenomenology, they may attempt to relay conscious expressions directed at pleasing the researcher, thereby introducing bias (Giorgi, 2009).

Search for Psychological Meaning

Giorgi (ibid.) describes three steps to interpreting the subject's description of experience, which is bracketed by the researcher through phenomenological reduction: (1) obtaining a sense of the whole; (2) determination of meaning units; and (3) transformation of the subject's descriptions into generalizable phenomenological essences. During the initial phase, the researcher is attempting to obtain a holistic perceptive. Giorgi notes that any qualitative approach requires that the researcher first apprehends a general impression of the experience described in the transcript. However, from a phenomenological perspective, the goals of the qualitative pursuit change. For instance, the researcher must employ reductionism, as only the expressions related to the lived-through experience are sought. The next step in the process is to break down the transcription into individual pieces, or what Giorgi calls meaning units. The researcher begins rereading the text transcription of the experience description and notes when significant meaning changes occur – these shifts bracket individual meanings into units. In this step, the researcher should not attempt to analyze the content of the meaning but instead simply mark where they occur. Giorgi further notes that this step depends on the subjectivity of the researcher, which means the meaning units may not be consistent if the experience were to be analyzed by more than one person. In the last and most detailed step, the researcher must adopt a "psychological perspective" and begin the process of interpreting the meaning units of described experiences. The researcher attempts to examine the transcript a third time in order to more fully understand how the particular lived-though experiences manifest themselves in the expressed consciousness, and the researcher is also attempting to draw broader, more generalizable conclusions regarding the nature of consciousness – how "individual human subjects present the world to themselves and how they act on the basis of that presentation" (p. 135).

APPLICATION TO ENTREPRENEURSHIP

Applying the experienced-based perspective of psychology to the field of entrepreneurship has the potential to stimulate several interesting research questions. Whereas experience in anthropology focuses on the *collective* expressions of experience, a psychological perspective of experience is much more focused on the processes the *individual* uses to apprehend the external environment. The anthropologist's interests in entrepreneurship centers on understanding how entrepreneurs build structures of experience and how those structures manifest themselves in outward expressions – such as the organization (an artifact) that emerges during venture creation. In contrast, the psychologist would likely be more interested in understanding how the entrepreneur herself understands a particular entrepreneurship experience, either as it is lived-through or as she may later remember it.

Several of the research questions previously discussed in the preceding chapter on anthropology can be applied equally well through the psychological perspective. However, where the anthropologist's focus is on the external relics (or artifacts) of the expressions of experience, the psychologist turns the lens toward the experiencing individual. For example, we may ask, what is the nature of an entrepreneurial experience? For the psychologist, the question focuses on intentionality. Our engagement with objects within the external environment does not preclude the potential for infinite perspectives. An entrepreneur's specific experience during venture creation may hold a particular meaning while the event is being lived through, hold a similar meaning in the hours and days after the experience occurred, and hold an entirely different (perhaps opposite) meaning when the entrepreneur remembers it years afterward. Intentionality also raises certain questions about which objects enter into the entrepreneur's field of awareness. What problems prove to be most salient for an entrepreneur? Which problems are ignored? How might this change as the entrepreneur passes through the various phases of the entrepreneurship process? These questions might be informed by a phenomenological perspective of learning. Colaizzi (1971), for instance, found that an individual's experience of a set of learning materials changed as they became more familiar with them. Much research has been performed within the field of entrepreneurship on the effects of learning and expertise (Baron and Henry, 2010; Ericsson and Ward, 2007), that is, *how* questions. However, employing the phenomenological perspective has the potential to enhance our understanding of *why* learning might take place (Kruger, 1979).

Experienced-based psychology may also contribute unique insights on entrepreneurs and entrepreneurship. For example, meta-cognition – that is, thinking about thinking – has been researched and described in the phenomenological context (Pollio et al., 1997). Thinking about thinking is, itself, an experience – thought is intentional as it is always directed at an object. Thinking itself is what Descartes described as the quality that endows humanness or even existence (ibid.). This is particularly important for understanding the entrepreneurship process, which involves the encounter between an individual and an opportunity (Kirzner, 1979). Within entrepreneurship, meta-cognition has been described as a quantity that is accumulated through experience (e.g., Haynie et al., 2010; Mitchell et al., 2007) when viewed through a social cognition lens. If meta-cognition can develop over time, how might this affect the individual's perception of an opportunity? For the phenomenological psychologist, the question is not necessarily that the entrepreneur might miss the opportunity altogether, but rather that her perception of it may be different than another's perception of it. How individuals experience and perceive opportunities may also inform current entrepreneurship research on the differences between first-person and third-person opportunities (McMullen and Shepherd, 2006). The current conceptualization of opportunity exploitation tends to treat opportunities as objective phenomena, whereas phenomenology would focus on the subjectivity of opportunity – not simply how different individuals perceive opportunities, but also how the same person may perceive an opportunity differently from moment to moment. Better understanding of how entrepreneurs experience their own awareness (i.e., meta-cognition), could lead to a more thorough perspective on the processes that encourage an individual to exploit a perceived opportunity.

CONCLUSIONS

In this chapter, we explain the psychological perspective of how an individual experiences objects and events. We also explain how these individual experiences congeal to form an overall structure of experience, which is itself in a constant state of flux as new objects or events are experienced. We discuss the elements of understanding experience in psychology, which are intentionality, figure/ground, and continuity/change. Intentionality refers broadly to the individual's "point of view" during an experience. This point of view, which is affected by a broad array of contextual factors, influences the individual's experience, and it explains how individuals can each have different experiences of the same object or event. Figure/ground incorporates the element of contrast: the experience of an object or an event is dependent on the objects and events that are *not* experienced. To experience an event, it must stand apart from other events in a stream. Continuity/change explains the stream of experience and how subsequent and preceding experiences flow into each other and affect each other. We then describe several applications of an experience-based perspective within psychological research as well as outline a methodology used by phenomenological psychologists. We close the chapter with a discussion on the possibilities that an application of an experience-based perspective rooted in psychology may have for entrepreneurship research. In the next chapter, we outline experience as it is understood in sociological research. Sociology is concerned with understanding a very specific type of experience – the social interaction between individuals. Through social interaction, individuals interpret and share meaning, which ultimately affects how they understand, construct, and live reality.

REFERENCES

Baddeley, A. (1990), *Human Memory: Theory and Practice*, Boston, MA: Allyn & Bacon.

Baron, R.A. and R.A. Henry (2010), 'How entrepreneurs acquire the capacity to excel: insights from research on expert performance', *Strategic Entrepreneurship Journal*, **4**(1): 49–65.

Bradley, B. (2005), *Psychology and Experience*, Cambridge: Cambridge University Press.

Colaizzi, P.F. (1971), 'Analysis of the learner's perception of learning material at various phases of the learning process', in A. Giorgi, W. Fisher and R. Von Eckartsberg (eds), *Duquesne Studies in Phenomenological Psychology*, vol. 2, Pittsburgh, PA: Duquesne University Press, pp. 101–31.

Csikszentmihalyi, M. (1990), *Flow: The Psychology of Optimal Experience*, New York: Harper & Row.

Dilthey, W. (1977), 'Ideas concerning a descriptive and analytic psychology', in W. Dilthey (ed.), *Descriptive Psychology and Historical Understanding*, The Hague: Nijhoff.

Ericsson, K.A., and P. Ward (2007), 'Capturing the naturally occurring superior performance of experts in the laboratory: toward a science of expert and exceptional performance', *Current Directions in Psychological Science*, **16**(6): 346–50.

Ghani, J.A. and S.P. Deshpande (1994), 'Task characteristics and the experience of optimal flow in human–computer interaction', *The Journal of Psychology*, **128**(4): 381–91.

Giorgi, A. (1985), 'Introduction', in A. Giorgi (ed.), *Phenomenology and Psychological Research*, Pittsburgh, PA: Duquesne University Press, pp. 1–7.

Giorgi, A. (2006), 'The value of phenomenology for psychology', in P. Ashworth and M.C. Chung (eds), *Phenomenology and Psychological Science: Historical and Philosophical Perspectives*, New York: Springer, pp. 45–68.

Giorgi, A. (2009), *The Descriptive Phenomenological Method in Psychology: A Modified Husserlian Approach*, Pittsburgh, PA: Duquesne University Press.

Harmon, G. (1990), 'The intrinsic quality of experience', *Philosophical Perspectives*, **4**: 31–52.

Haynie, J.M., D. Shepherd, E. Mosakowski and P.C. Earley (2010), 'A situated metacognitive model of the entrepreneurial mindset', *Journal of Business Venturing*, **25**(2): 217–29.

Horgan, T. and J. Tienson (2002), 'The intentionality of phenomenology and the phenomenology of intentionality', in D.J. Chalmers (ed.), *Philosophy of Mind: Classical and Contemporary Readings*, New York: Oxford University Press, pp. 520–32.

Husserl, E. (1965), 'Philosophy as a rigorous science', in Q. Lauer (ed.), *Phenomenology and the Crisis of Philosophy*, New York: Harper Torchbooks, pp. 71–147.

Husserl, E. (1977), *Phenomenological Psychology*, The Hague: Martinus Nijhoff.

Husserl, E. (1984), *Logische Untersuchungen II*, The Hague: Martinus Nijhoff.

James, W. (1890), *The Principles of Psychology*, New York: Henry Holt & Co.

James, W. (1899), *Talks to Teachers on Psychology: And to Students on Some of Life's Ideals*, New York: Holt.

James, W. (1909), *A Pluralistic Universe*, Cambridge, MA: Harvard University Press.

Kirzner, I. (1979), *Perception, Opportunity and Profit: Studies in the Theory of Entrepreneurship*, Chicago, IL: University of Chicago Press.

Kruger, D. (1979), *An Introduction to Phenomenological Psychology*, Pittsburgh, PA: Duquesne University Press.

Leibe, B. and B. Schiele (2006), 'Interleaving object categorization and segmentation', in H.I. Christenson and H.H. Nagel (eds), *Cognitive Vision Systems*, Lecture Notes in Computer Science, **3948**: pp. 145–61.

Makkreel, R.A. and F. Rodi (1989), 'Introduction to volume 1', in R. Makkreel and F. Rodi (eds), *Wilhelm Dilthey Selected Works/Volume 1: Introduction to the Human Science*, Princeton, NJ: Princeton University Press, pp. 3–43.

McConville, M. (1978), 'The phenomenological approach to perception', in R.S. Valle and M. King (eds), *Existential Phenomenological Alternatives for Psychology*, New York: Oxford University Press, pp. 94–118.

McMullen, J.S. and D. Shepherd (2006), 'Entrepreneurial action and the role of uncertainty in the theory of the entrepreneur', *Academy of Management Review*, **31**(1): 132–52.

Merleau-Ponty, M. (1962), *The Phenomenology of Perception*, New York: Humanities Press.

Merriam Webster (2011), *Online Dictionary*, accessed 13 November 2011 at www.merriam-webster.com/dictionary.

Mitchell, R.K., L.W. Busenitz, B. Bird, C.M. Gaglio, J.S. McMullen, E.A. Morse and J.B. Smith (2007), 'The central question in entrepreneurial cognition research', *Entrepreneurship Theory and Practice*, **31**(1): 1–27.

Natsoulas, T. (1988), 'Gibson, James, and the temporal community of experience', *Imagination, Cognition, and Personality*, **7**(4): 351–76.

Pollio, H.R. (1982), *Behavior and Existence*, Monterey, CA: Brooks/Cole Publishing.

Pollio, H.R., T.B. Henley, and C.G. Thompson (1997), *The Phenomenology of Everyday Life*, Cambridge: Cambridge University Press.

Sacks, O. (2007), 'The abyss: a neurologist's notebook', *The New Yorker*, **83**(28): 100.

Schacter, D.L. (1987), 'Implicit memory: history and current status', *Journal of Experimental Psychology: Learning, Memory, and Cognition*, **13**(3): 501–18.

Schütz, A. (1967), *The Phenomenology of the Social World*, Evanston, IL: Northwestern University Press.

Simons, D.J. and C.F. Chabris (1999), 'Gorillas in our midst: sustained inattentional blindness for dynamic events', *Perception*, **28**(9): 1059–74.

Strawson, G. (2004), 'Real intentionality', *Phenomenology and the Cognitive Sciences*, **3**(3): 287–313.

Thompson, C.J., W.B. Locander and H.R. Pollio (1989), 'Putting consumer experience back into consumer research: the philosophy and method of existential-phenomenology', *Journal of Consumer Research*, **16**(2): 133–46.

Wheeler, M.A., D.T. Stuss and E. Tulving (1997), 'Toward a theory of episodic memory: the frontal lobes and autonoetic consciousness', *Psychological Bulletin*, **121**(3): 331–54.

Wu, W. (2011), 'What is conscious attention?', *Philosophy and Phenomenological Research*, **82**(1): 93–120.

Wundt, W. (1902), *Outlines of Psychology*, New York: G.E. Stechert.

Zahavi, D. (2005), 'Intentionality and experience', *Synthesis Philosophica*, **40**(2): 299–318.

4. Sociology and experience

> The body social is many things: the prime symbol of the self, but also of the
> society; it is something we have, yet also what we are; it is both subject and
> object at the same time; it is individual and personal, as unique as a fingerprint
> or odour plume, yet it is also common to all humanity . . . . The body is both
> an individual creation, physically and phenomenologically, and a cultural
> product; it is personal, and also state property.
> (Anthony Synnott, 1993)

INTRODUCTION

A man squeezes a lemon over a salad he's making for that evening's dinner,
and an errant drop lands in his daughter's eye. She flinches, engaging in a
behavior before she really knows the nature of what is in her eye, maybe
before she even recognizes that something hit her in the eye. She's simply,
suddenly, and perhaps only slightly aware that something, whatever it is,
has caused her discomfort. We find another man in another house similarly preparing a salad and likewise squeezing a lemon. This man's daughter, on witnessing him, makes a face and shudders. She doesn't like lemon
juice, and she wants her father to know it.

The difference between these brief sketches is the meaning behind each
girl's behavior. The first girl's behavior has no meaning. She's merely reacting, reflexively, to an impulse, perhaps conscious, perhaps not. The second
girl's behavior has meaning. She witnesses the lemon juice corrupting (in
her opinion) an otherwise fine salad, disapproves, and enacts her displeas-
ure. For sociologists, the question of what constitutes meaningful action
and how people interpret the meaning of others' actions lies at the heart of
what Max Weber described as interpretive sociology (Schütz, 1967). Weber
(1968) propounds the same systematic interpretive process to understanding social structure that others, including William Dilthey (1989), discussed
under the rubric of *Verstehen* and hermeneutics, which we discussed in
Chapter 2. The purpose of interpretive sociology is to examine and analyze
social action – a pursuit that has been critiqued by other sociologists since
its introduction – the most important of which, for our purposes, is Alfred
Schütz (1967) in *The Phenomenology of the Social World*. For Schütz,
experience lies at the heart of social action and its meaning.

In the preceding chapters, an experience-based perspective occupied a moderate-sized application within the anthropology and psychology fields. Within sociology, the experienced-based perspective has found a broader application and can be found under many names and traditions, including phenomenology, ethnomethodology, and symbolic interactionism (Adler et al., 1987; Maynard and Clayman, 1991; Tiryakian, 1965). This chapter will center around Schütz's discussion of experience and social action – a phenomenological perspective on sociology derived from Husserl – that has many elements in common with other perspectives. For example, symbolic interactionism, as described by Herbert Blumer (1969), is also closely tied to social action and its subjective meanings. The chapter will therefore examine one by one the several elements held in common by different schools of thought instead of attempting a comprehensive review of the various perspectives. Experience, behavior, action, meaning, subjectivity, and symbols are all incorporated within the different perspectives, and where they are used or understood differently we will note it in our discussion.

This chapter starts with a brief overview of the foundations and development of an experience-based perspective during the earlier years of sociology. Second, we discuss the elements that different schools of thought have in common. Next, we describe in more detail research streams within sociology that center on phenomenology, ethnomethodology, and symbolic interactionism. Lastly, we draw attention to the possible applications and implications of a sociological understanding of experience for entrepreneurship research.

EARLY DEVELOPMENT OF AN EXPERIENCED-BASED PERSPECTIVE

Two early schools of thought emerged in the late nineteenth century and early twentieth century, which today constitute the foundations of a sociology based in experience and meaning. First, a group of German philosophers, including Dilthey, Husserl, and Martin Heidegger, began work on developing phenomenology, which attempted to delineate consciousness as a collection of experiences, each subjectively apprehended by the first-person experiencer and fitted into a broader structure of experience (Tiryakian, 1965). This structure of experience ultimately constitutes consciousness. Foremost among these thinkers' concerns was the subjectivity of experienced reality – that individuals may perceive the same objective things, whether natural objects, other people or even non-physical entities like ideas, and experience them differently based on their intentionality and their previous body of accrued experience. The second school is grounded in the work of George Herbert Mead on pragmatism and behaviorism, and today lies in the body of work collected under the aegis of symbolic interactionism.

Phenomenology

Early phenomenology sought to explain *Weltanschauung*, or the "global perception of social reality" (Tiryakian, 1965, p. 675), the social expressions of which constituted the collective representations that interested sociologists, including Durkheim, and anthropologists up to today. As discussed in earlier chapters, these collective representations are expressions of meaning-laden experiences. Heap and Roth (1973) describe four strains of sociology that grew out of this movement. The first merely adopts phenomenology's concern with consciousness and subjectivity in interpreting social action. This strain – which influenced thinkers such as Max Weber and George Mead – is only loosely connected to phenomenology. It does not attempt to present a phenomenological-based theory of social structure but instead advocates the use of interpretive methods. The second strain is derived from Schütz's critique of Max Weber's ideas about ideal types and social action. Whereas the first strain did not attempt to create a framework for sociologists to use in understanding phenomena, Schütz lays the foundation for such a framework in sketching a theory explaining the subjectivity of meaning and the creation of a social world. According to Heap and Roth (1973), this second strain closely follows the methodology described by Husserl – that of bracketing individual experiences and interpreting their meanings through phenomenological reduction (also see Giorgi, 2009). The third strain of sociology that grew out of phenomenology adopts Schütz's perspective but also incorporates a greater degree of existentialism. For example, it abandons Weber's notion of ideal types as well as the methodology based on phenomenological reductionism. Instead, it recognizes that sociology itself is imbedded within the world and focuses on the role that both the experiencer and the observer/researcher plays in experiencing, describing, and interpreting an experience. The fourth strain of sociology falling under the umbrella of phenomenology is ethnomethodology, which is "the body of common-sense knowledge and the range of procedures and considerations by means of which the ordinary members of society make sense of, find their way about in, and act on the circumstances in which they find themselves" (Heritage, 1984, p. 4).

Ethnomethodology's founder, Harold Garfinkel, was critical of Durkheim's description of "social facts," which constitute the sociologist's object. For Durkheim, social facts are independent of, and outside, individuals. They are objective phenomena, and they influence individuals' behavior. According to Durkheim, individuals are constrained, encouraged, or stimulated to action by these social facts. In contrast, Garfinkel argues that social facts are not objective. Rather, their "objectivity" is an artifact of the methodology that sociologists employ to examine society. Ethnomethodology is phenomenological in that it focuses on the constantly ongoing and iterative interpretation, adaptation, and implementation of experience into social action, and its subject of study is the "immortal, ordinary society" of everyday life (Garfinkel, 1988, p. 104).

An often-cited example of ethnomethodology is Garfinkel's (1967) description of Agnes. In this study, Garfinkel refutes the common assertion that individuals are born man or woman and that they do not have to act in any particular way to be seen as such. He describes a process where gender, then an accepted biological if not social fact, is actually accomplished through learning behaviors. Agnes, on first glance and even close inspection, was a beautiful woman. She dressed and acted as such. She wore makeup, cared about her appearance, and might even be called "sexy." However, Agnes was a man seeking a sex-change operation. Garfinkel's sociological point was that gender, and other accepted objective facts, should not be taken for granted. It took more than wearing dresses and lipstick before Agnes could behave and fit into society as a woman – instead, she had to learn the appropriate gestures and behavior before others saw her as such (ibid.). Only after her experiences learning and implementing these behaviors could she ultimately come to define herself as a woman.

Symbolic Interactionism

The German thinkers that spearheaded the development of phenomenology – starting with Dilthey and Husserl, who influenced Weber, Schütz, and even economists including Ludwig von Mises – were bound by geographic and language barriers. It was not until Schütz's and Husserl's work was translated into English in the 1960s that American scholars began to pay attention (Adler et al., 1987). Meanwhile, a philosophy of pragmatism was taking form in the United States based on the work of John Dewey and William James (Ritzer, 2008). As we have discussed in previous chapters, Dewey and James in particular were just as interested in the nature of consciousness and experience as Dilthey and the other German scholars. This early philosophy of pragmatism also eschewed the notion of objective social facts that constrain and guide human behavior in favor of looking at humans as independent actors who are free to accept or reject social standards (Lewis and Smith, 1980).

George Herbert Mead's work, which occupies a major space in the foundation of symbolic interactionism, adopts a micro-sociological approach and rejects the pragmatism of Dewey and James. Mead's ideas are micro insofar as they examine and seek to understand the everyday interactions consequent of human action. However, Mead rejects the idea that individuals can transcend social forces. In his book, *Mind, Self and Society* (1934), Mead argues that social experience precedes and leads to human characteristics, including action, mind, and the notion of self. And similar to Schütz and the other phenomenologists, Mead (1982) saw action as the fundamental unit of study. For Mead (1938), action was constituted by four stages: (1) the *impulse*, which includes an external stimulation on the actor as well as the actor's immediate reaction to it, and which precipitates the determination that action needs to be taken; (2) *perception*, which influences how the actor may perceive a stimulus as well as assess mentally the potential responses before engaging in physical behavior; (3) *manipulation*, which Ritzer (2008) likens to an individual's evaluation of alternatives of which action might constitute the best response to the impulse; and (4) *consummation*, which is the actuation of a selected behavior to satisfy or respond to the impulse.

Mead's (1934) notion of action differed from that of Schütz's (which we will describe in more detail), but they shared some similarities. Both viewed action as social experience and the root from which individuals construct their understanding of the world. Both saw a difference between action directed at objects (which Schütz, with Weber, understood as mere behavior), and social action, which is action directed toward one or more people. Both believed that individuals used certain behaviors (Mead called them gestures; Schütz referred to expressive acts) to communicate meaning to others. Likewise, both developed their theories by drawing on symbols. Mead understood significant symbols as a gesture that would bring to mind the same meaning for anyone familiar with the symbol. Language is a commonly cited example of such symbols; anyone may clearly communicate their meanings to another person who is also familiar with the language.

Mead taught at the University of Chicago and influenced two sociologists who were both students at Chicago during and immediately after his tenure, and who would eventually expand on Mead's pragmatic philosophy and develop symbolic interactionism within sociology. The first of these is Herbert Blumer, who came to be regarded as the founder of symbolic interactionism, and the second is Erving Goffman, who focused on the mechanisms underlying social interactions, developed the dramaturgical perspective and set the stage for another viewpoint from which sociologists could study ritual. Blumer, Goffman, and symbolic interactionism are the focus of our discussion in the next section.

ELEMENTS OF AN EXPERIENCED-BASED SOCIOLOGY

In previous chapters, we have outlined how anthropologists and psychologists study and incorporate an understanding of experience in their work. Anthropologists study the relics of expression, which are found in the cultural expressions of collective experience: a culture's literature, theater, rituals, and myths. Psychologists seek to understand the relationship between experience and consciousness and how individuals process experience into meaningful units. Both perspectives do not limit the types of experiences individuals may have – for a phenomenological psychologist, an individual's experience with an orange may be as rich a field of study as that individual's experience with another person. The processes of perceiving, understanding, and attaching meaning to the experience are practically the same. However, the sociologist who is likewise interested in experience tends to limit her perspective to social experiences. Hence, the two primary perspectives within sociology (phenomenological sociology and symbolic interactionism) focus on the individual act, especially social acts. It is in the action, or interaction, with others that individuals accrue experiences necessary for understanding and operating in the social world.

The two important branches of experienced-based sociology – phenomenology and symbolic interactionism – share several similarities. A comprehensive description of both schools is not possible given space constraints, and thus we will attempt to parse out and describe the elements they have in common. These elements include meaning, behavior and action, symbols, and framing. Some elements are emphasized within phenomenology, such as Schütz's description of subjectivity and objectivity of meaning. Others are emphasized within symbolic interactionism, such as symbols and framing. Because Schütz builds on thinkers we have already discussed, such as Husserl, his thoughts will provide the framework on which we base the next discussion.

Meaning

An English translation of Alfred Schütz's work *Die sinnhafte Aufbrau der sozialen Welt* hit the United States in 1967 under the title *The Phenomenology of the Social World*. Literally put, it means "the meaningful construction of the social world," and in it Schütz lays the phenomeno-logical foundation of sociology. Schütz begins his discussion with a cri-tique of Max Weber's (1968) work *Economy and Society.* He agrees with Weber, who writes that sociology is an interpretive science and that its most important application is in understanding and interpreting social action. However, Schütz argues, Weber fails to adequately describe what he means by understanding or social action and his explanation of subjec-tive meaning falls short. For both scholars, meaning refers to a behavior that is always directed toward an object. Meaningful behavior is called action (Schütz, 1967). As Weber puts it, action is social if it is oriented toward another human being and possesses subjective meaning for the actor. Non-social action can be meaningful; for example, drinking water out of a glass or opening a door are both directed toward an object and are thus meaningful. Non-meaningful behavior is that which is reflexive (but even then, some degree of meaning must exist – such as in the stimulus that precipitated the reflex) (ibid.). Social action, in which two or more people interact with each other, requires that each interprets the meaning of the other's action. This infers a higher level of meaning. Weber (1968) uses the example of two cyclists who career into each other on a road, which he calls a "natural event." The situation where the cyclists first notice each other and swerve to avoid a collision constitutes social action. The cyclists interpreted the meaning of the other person's behavior and then took action as a consequence of the behavior they observed.

Schütz (1967) takes up the final piece of Weber's definition of social action – that it must possess "subjective meaning." Here, he critiques Weber's description of subjective and objective meaning. As Weber (1982, p. 192) himself writes, subjectivity "is this which distinguishes the empiri-cal sciences from action, such as sociology and history, from the dogmatic disciplines in that area, such as jurisprudence, logic, ethics, and esthetics, which seek to ascertain the 'true' and 'valid' meanings associated with the objects of their investigation." According to Schütz, this definition aligns with the common understanding of subjectivity, but it falls short of what even Weber meant. Every social action possesses subjective meaning, which simply refers to the actor's meaning for the action. An observer cannot discover this meaning through mere observation. Schütz offers the following example: a man witnesses another man cutting wood. The witness immediately beholds the objective meaning of the action: "wood cutting." However, the woodcutter's own meaning, his subjective meaning, remains hidden. He may be cutting wood to build a chair or to fuel a fire, to exercise the body or to work off some anger. The actor's subjective meaning includes first, the meaning the action has for the actor, but also the influence of his structure of experience, which we have described in previous chapters – the actor's accrued set of life experiences always influences the present experience, how he understands it, and how he assigns meaning to it. Therefore, the actor's subjective meaning for a behavior is almost impossible to decipher by the observer, who inevitably has not lived the actor's life and can only guess at how the actor's experiences may influence his current actions. Therefore, the observer can only understand the objective meaning of the action he beholds. Likewise, the observer is engaged in an action of his own: that of observing the woodcutter. And for him, this action will have subjective meaning.

A second type of objective meaning also involves the use of symbols (Schütz, 1967). For Schütz, objects have ontic qualities and meaningful qualities. For example, a stop sign is objectively red and octagonal, but these qualities are independent from its subjective quality, which is "Stop." Meaning defines objects within symbolic interactionism. Symbolic interactionists argue that objects, whether physical, social or abstract, are defined by their meanings – even further, that they are objects only in so far as they have a meaning – they "are the product of symbolic interaction" (Blumer, 1969, p. 10). Blumer describes meaning as preceding the object – the meaning of a rock or a tree affects how the individual observes it. Fundamentally, the object's meaning is defined through interaction with others and society. Because objects are social creations, they are constantly in a state of flux – they have no permanent meaning. For example, Blumer notes that stars meant something to ancient Egyptians and something else to current astronomers; marriage meant something to early Romans, something different to late Romans, just as it meant something to 1950s' Americans and something different today. In so far as symbolic interactionists discuss action and meanings of action, they discuss the vocalized rationalizations, or motives, that individuals give for their actions. As C. Wright Mills (1967, p. 441) writes: "Motives are words." Individuals have sets of vocabularies they use to explain their behavior because they want to maintain their social interactions with others (Brissett and Edgley, 1975). People might also solicit other's motives in an effort to categorize people into good and bad types, and this enables us to mete out justice against those who have unjustifiable motives or to reward others with pristine motives (Charon, 1995).

The Act

Schütz (1967, p. 57) writes: "In common usage we tend to distinguish action from behavior by simply saying that the former is 'conscious' or 'voluntary,' while the latter is 'reactive' in character and includes such things as reflexes." Phenomenology and symbolic interactionism generally share the viewpoint that the individual human act is the primary focus of sociology. The two perspectives also make a similar distinction between mere behavior and meaningful action, as Schütz described above. Behavior constitutes an action when it involves "protention," which is the notion that action must be directed toward bringing about some future state (Husserl, 1970). Symbolic interactionism states that action is always goal oriented, whether the goal is fulfilled or not (Charon, 1995). However, the underlying understanding of action within the two perspectives is each rooted in different philosophical foundations.

Phenomenology breaks action into two pieces: (1) *the act*, which is the projected future state; and (2) *the action*, which is the set of activities aimed at fulfilling the act. Acts cannot exist until they are achieved through action, and action is always directed toward a particular act. Schütz (1967) connects this idea with his earlier discussion of meaning: the meaning of any action is the act toward which it is directed. Action, and behavior in general, has an even more important role within phenomenology regarding experience. As we have discussed in previous chapters, not all lived experience is meaningful. It is not until the individual goes back retrospectively and assigns a meaning to an experience that the experience becomes differentiated from the individual's entire set of accrued experiences. Retrospection is what Husserl calls a meaning-endowing experience: the act of assigning meaning to an experience is an experience in and of itself, complete with intentionality and subjective meaning. Action, therefore, is very important to phenomenology because without it, experiences would remain dormant and meaningless within an undifferentiated structure of experience.

Action is always connected to the projected act, which also constitutes the action's meaning. Schütz offers a phenomenological explanation for why some acts may remain unfulfilled or even be altered during the course of an action. The meaning of an action may only be held retrospectively – once the act has been fulfilled. Until then, Schütz says it is inappropriate to say that a meaning has been "attached" to an action. First, acts may consist of a series of sub-acts, each of which expands the actor's set of experiences. Second, in order to keep on track toward fulfilling a projected act, an individual may occasionally look back over his completed actions – again, this constitutes yet another act, which expands the individual's set of experiences. These two phenomena serve to alter the individual's accrued set of experiences, which, in turn, inevitably alters the subjective meaning the individual has placed on the action. Third, the passage of time itself can alter the actor's intentionality – how he views the projected act. Altered intentionality can likewise change the subjective meaning an actor places on the act. As Schütz (1967) notes, this has a series of implications: (1) that meaning is always changing; and (2) that it is difficult for a researcher to grasp an actor's meaning without being aware of how the many actions within an act can alter the subjective meaning of the act itself.

Symbolic interactionism, which finds its roots in a philosophy of pragmatism, places far less emphasis on the role that an individual's consciousness plays with regard to action and meaning. In symbolic interactionism, the meaning of an action is more or less taken as a given – it is simply enough that human beings act; however, scholars in this tradition have nevertheless given attention to external objects that might impel an individual to action, such as goals, the environment, motives, and emotion. These objects are not a result of an individual's internal processes, such as Schütz and Husserl's subjective meaning. Instead, these objects are created through social interaction and lie outside the individual.

An individual action is the primary unit of measure in symbolic interactionism (Charon, 1995). However, an individual action takes place within a "stream of action"; for example, the act of opening a carton of eggs might fit within the broader act of making breakfast, which fits within the broader act of preparing for work, and continuing to an ever broader stream of action, which one might imagine ultimately terminating in the action of living. The perspective an individual takes when regarding her action is arbitrary, dependent on the purposes (such as researching an individual act or writing an autobiography) and conditions (e.g., five minutes might seem longer or shorter to a student waiting for school to end compared to an inmate awaiting execution).

This stream of action is guided by the decisions an individual makes. Individuals ascertain their situation and set goals toward which they direct their actions. Because individuals exist in a stream of action, wherein any number of long-term or short-term goals might be simultaneously overlapping and situations might change from moment to moment, these individuals are able to change their goals to adapt to the situation. Individuals make decisions about their action depending on their situation and the objects they notice (Blumer, 1981). For example, a family may have possessed a rug for generations, which has seen no end of abuse. The dogs sleep on it. The kids spill drinks on it. But one day, the father may get the notion to take the rug to an appraiser – perhaps he intends to sell the old thing so he can make way for a newer linoleum floor. On examining the rug, the appraiser informs the man that this rug is worth thousands of dollars. Suddenly, this old rug has become something different – the price placed on the rug has altered not only its value but its meaning as a social object. The man decides to no longer pursue his original goal, which was to sell the rug just to get rid of it, and instead decides to pursue a new goal, which is to protect the rug from further abuse.

Above, we noted Mead's (1938) four parts of action: impulse, perception,

Source: Charon (1995).

Figure 4.1   Action as embedded in situation

manipulation, and consummation. Neither Mead nor symbolic interactionists understand impulse as something that compels an individual to act. Impulse is merely a condition for action without any implications for what type of action might be possible. It is ultimately up to the individual to decide to act and what goal to act toward. Sociology in general proposes many different causes of action, such as society, cultural norms or personal traits. However, within symbolic interactionism, only the individual's *decision* to act is regarded as a cause. Decisions, in turn, are influenced by the individual's perception of the situation, which is itself influenced by the individual's background, history of social interactions, and past behavior – in other words, the individual's social construction of reality (Charon, 1995). Where phenomenology accords the individual's accrued set of life experiences a central role in the definition of action, symbolic interactionism regards it as an antecedent to how an individual defines the present situation (see Figure 4.1).

Past experience is important for three reasons. First, it helps individuals define the present situation. Mead (1934) conceptualizes intelligence as the ability to take past experience and apply it to present situations and determine potential outcomes. The "past" is not a static construct either – individuals may redefine their past, such as the new mother who comes to understand her own childhood in an entirely different light. Similarly, a country may redefine its past experience for political purposes. For example, France removed all of the trappings of monarchical religion during and after the Revolution. Second, past experience influences the present situation. The stream of action does not leap from point to point but flows continually: every current, ripple, and bend is a creation of upstream experiences, and will likewise influence downstream experiences. Decisions an individual made in childhood inevitably have some impact on where that individual finds herself today. Third, Charon (1995) notes that the beginning point – the headwaters of the stream of action – plays a major role in how an individual makes subsequent decisions. Whether born in poverty or riches, in this country or that, "our past enters in by starting us out. Nothing is inevitable after that, but it is foolish to ignore the starting line" (p. 135).

Symbols

Recall the individual observing the woodcutter. In order to determine the meaning of the woodcutter's action purely from the observable behavior, Schütz (1967) writes that the observer will attempt to place himself in the woodcutter's shoes and ask, "What would this action mean if I were performing it?" The observer draws on his own experiences to interpret the intended meaning of the beheld action if he should be the one doing the action. For Schütz, this is as close as anyone can approach the actor's subjective meaning based purely on observation and without engaging in some sort of social relationship with the actor. However, should the actor choose to express his subjective meaning, he would engage in expressive acts. According to Schütz, expressive acts are those gestures by which the actor chooses to project his subjective meaning so that it may be understood by others. Husserl describes a sign as an external object that signifies the existence of some other object. A sign has intrinsic, objective qualities itself, such as its shape, size, or color. A sign also has non-objective qualities, which are the qualities of the other object it signifies. Individuals do not behold signs based on their objective qualities (what Schütz would call an *adequate* interpretation); instead, individuals interpret a sign based on their experience with the object it signifies (a *non-adequate* interpretation). The non-adequate interpretation of a sign is embedded in the individual's familiarity and experience with the sign. For example, an adequate interpretation of the peace sign would be the upward and spread extension of the index and middle fingers, palm forward. A non-adequate interpretation of the same sign by an individual in 1960s' United States would be "peace." However, an individual in 1940s' London might more readily identify, and non-adequately interpret, the same sign as "victory." The non-adequate interpretation is based on the individual's own experiences as well as the meaning society has attached to the sign.

Schütz notes that signs are a consequence of experience for two reasons. First, signs are objects of expression, and for the observer or user of a sign to be familiar with the object as an expression, the observer must have had experience either using the sign or imagine using the sign. Second, signs are objects that fit within an interpretive context. For example, the word "nova" infamously means something different in the United States than it does in South America, which is based on the sign's interpretive scheme (in this case, language). Therefore, the individual must have had experience with the interpretive scheme in which the sign is embedded or have had experience in interpreting the sign. Schütz makes an additional point regarding the subjective and objective nature of a sign, for which he uses language as an example. The objective meaning of a word is the literal

definition found within a dictionary. The subjective meaning of a word
cannot be found in a dictionary but must instead be discovered within
the context of a sentence, a paragraph, an author's entire body of work
or even the political environment in which the word is written and read.
For example, the word "environment" means one thing to an organizational behaviorist and something else to a member of Green Peace. When
Winston Churchill displayed a "victory" sign in a bombed-out London,
it communicated much more than victory – perhaps resistance, British
pride, encouragement in the face of adversity, or even a recollection of
Churchill's own record of overcoming past failures.

Schütz's sign is comparable to symbolic interactionism's symbol.
Symbolic interactionism categorizes symbols as social objects. Objects
are social because they are defined for us by others and because we
understand them not through their intrinsic qualities but through their
usefulness to us (Blumer, 1969). Symbols are particular kinds of social
objects – Charon (1995) defines them as objects that enable individuals
to communicate and that are representations of meanings. He highlights
three qualities of symbols. First, they are social. Individuals are not born
knowing what symbols mean; instead, their understanding of symbols is a
consequence of social interaction and experience. Second, they are meaningful. Charon cites Shibutani's (1961) description of a flag – although it
is merely a colored piece of fabric, soldiers will risk their lives to prevent it
from falling onto the ground or be captured by the enemy. The risk they
take isn't for the flag itself, but for that which the flag represents. Third,
symbols hold significance for both the observer and the user. According
to Mead (1934), significance carries two implications: (1) the user is aware
of the symbol's meaning and intentionally uses it to communicate that
meaning; and (2) the observer is also aware of the symbol's meaning – the
actor deliberately chose the symbol in order to communicate a meaning
that he believed the observer would understand. Almost any act or object
can have symbolic meaning. Wearing a Rolex watch communicates power
or class. Reading a book alone in a café may be an actor's way of communicating intellectualism, or perhaps that he's looking for a date. A
doctoral candidate may feverishly work to meet a deadline to earn a grade
but also to communicate her dedication to a professor or to the program
in which she's enrolled. In fact, symbols are so ubiquitous that we're often
willing to perceive symbols where they don't exist. A friend doesn't return
a call – he must be angry with me. A student falls asleep in class – she must
be bored with my lecture. But these are not symbols if the actor does not
intend to communicate any meaning. Charon notes that this can lead to a
wide degree of ambiguity in human communication; nevertheless, symbols
and symbolic action remain an important component of social interaction.

Symbolic interactionists place a major emphasis on symbols. It is through symbols that individuals construct reality, and it is through symbols that society exists at all. Specifically, Charon (1995, p. 56) notes three critical reasons why symbols are vital to social existence. First, symbols are how the individual constructs and understands reality. Social interaction, or experience, is symbolic: "Whenever there is interaction between persons, there is meaning shared, and this meaning is symbolic in nature as is the reality toward which we act. Humans do not react to a physical reality but to a symbolic one." For example, language is one category of symbols. When we think to ourselves, we think in language – we are engaging in symbolic interaction with ourselves. When an individual calls out an experience and attaches a meaning to it, she is really symbolizing the experience. Therefore, the accrued set of experiences, which represents an individual's consciousness, cannot exist except as symbols.

Second, symbols enable society to exist. In our previous discussion on anthropology, we noted that cultural expressions, such as literature, drama or ritual, are merely a collective representation of experience. They are also symbols left behind by our social predecessors, they enable us to have an understanding of their lives and culture, and they allow us to fit our own culture into what came before. Libraries, archaeological sites, and theaters are among the various socially created symbol communicators – through these mechanisms and others, individuals are socialized and integrated into the group. Whether it's an orientation session during our first day at a new job, a ceremony that we might undergo to become a member of a church, or even our arrival at the airport terminal of a foreign country – these experiences facilitate our learning of the local symbols, as well as ease our integration into the group we have just entered.

Third, symbols, especially language, make humanness possible. We are able to categorize, label, and reflect on our experiences through language, which enables us to not only perceive our day-to-day lived-through experiences, but also to compare them to experiences we have already had as well as to project them against experiences we might have in the future (Hertzler, 1965). Language allows us to think – a task we often take for granted – and which Blumer (1969) describes as symbolic interaction with ourselves. Through thinking, we are also able to engage in more directed tasks, such as problem-solving or creativity. Creativity, especially, involves taking learned symbols and transforming, combining or redefining them (Charon, 1995). This often manifests itself as a one-off, or even parody, of a widely recognized symbol, such as the image of the bicycle seat and handle bars standing in for a bleached cattle skull (see Figure 4.2). Symbols enable us to transcend our own time and physical confinement. Written or oral histories allow us to live and understand

Figure 4.2   Picasso's Tête de Toro

lives and cultures past, and language allows us to escape our own perspectives and empathize with others. S. Morris Eames (1977) summarizes the importance the symbol possesses for the symbolic interactionist:

> Pragmatic naturalists conceive of humans as a part of nature. Although they share many organic processes with other animals in their life in nature, humans emerge above the animals in certain forms and functions. For instance, humans can construct symbols and languages, they can speak and write, and by these means they can preserve their past experiences, construct new meanings, and entertain goals and ideals. Humans can make plans and by proper selection of the means to the ends carry them through. They can write poetry and novels, compose music and painting, and otherwise engage in aesthetic experiences. They can construct explanatory hypotheses about the world and all that is in it, of electrons, protons, and neutrons, and solar systems far away. They can dream dreams, concoct fantasies, erect heavens above the earth which entice their activities to far-off destinies, and they can imagine hells which stimulate fears of everlasting torture. The emergent functions of symbolic behavior make it possible for humans to transcend parts of their immediate undergoing and experiencing and to know that death and all that it entails is a part of organic life. (Eames, 1977, pp. 40–41).

Frame

Symbolic interactionism rejects the notion that humans ever merely react to external stimuli. For them, action is always guided by the individual's decision to engage in a particular behavior. Schütz's (1967) phenomenological view of sociology allows for merely reflexive action, which he simply calls behavior – that is, physical gestures without meaning. Erving Goffman, who was a colleague of Herbert Blumer at Berkeley and later studied at the University of Chicago, is often afforded a chapter at the back of any book dedicated to symbolic interactionism. Although some of his ideas were outside the mainstream perspective of symbolic interactionism, he developed the greatest understanding of "self" within the symbolic interactionist paradigm. Goffman, who is known for his work on dramaturgy, impression management, and role identity, also developed the notion of frames, which is most salient with regard to experience and meaning. Goffman (1974) was interested in understanding the frameworks that underlie the vast majority of social interactions – while these frames do not compel individuals to action, they can serve to guide action and certainly enable individuals to attach meanings to their interactions. Goffman believed that social interactions conformed to socially created rules or guidelines and that only through understanding these schemes of interpretation can individuals understand the experiences in which they find themselves as well as be able to make themselves understood to others.

Frames are rules regarding how symbols are understood and interpreted, how actions are supposed to be experienced and how it all relates to the individual (Gonos, 1980). Frame is closely related to the phenomenological concept of intentionality – an individual's unique perspective within an experience means that she will define it differently than other individuals involved in the experience. However, frames transcend the personal interpretation and serve as a schema for all individuals involved to similarly define a particular experience. For example, the air traveler passing through a checkpoint and being frisked, as well as the security agent frisking the traveler, are both operating within the same schema of interpretation. However, it is also possible that the traveler may adopt a completely different frame – such as a frame of sexual assault – when passing through the checkpoint. Another example involves the idea that "one man's terrorist is another man's freedom fighter." Depending on the frame adopted, an armed gunman may be fighting for his country's freedom or terrorizing a civilian populace. Frame has come to be a crucial component of understanding social interactions – Snow (2007) argues that meaning might be altogether incommunicable without frames.

SOCIOLOGICAL RESEARCH CONDUCTED ON EXPERIENCE

In this section, we describe several studies sociologists have conducted regarding experiencing through social interaction. We outline studies in three particular sociological fields, phenomenology, ethnomethodology, and symbolic interactionism, because all three draw on foundational scholars on lived-through experience and employ methodologies that are particularly useful for examining experiencing as a phenomenon.

Phenomenology Research and Experiencing

Phenomenological sociology has been generally subsumed by ethnomethodology and by symbolic interactionism. Current sociological studies of phenomenology are few and generally focus on the perspective's role in influencing the early years of other sub-fields in sociology based on an understanding of experiences of "everyday life." However, some early research, influenced by Schütz, explicates the sorts of questions that a phenomenological sociology was interested in answering. Frank (1979) notes that empirical phenomenological studies are rare and that the perspective might best be used to enhance and inform other fields within sociology – a commentary that largely came to pass, as we'll see with ethnomethodology.

Two early studies on experience, rooted in an exclusively phenomenological perspective and based on field data, are Jehenson's (1973) study of typified roles in a psychiatric clinic and Berger and Kellner's (1970) study of marriage as a mechanism that allows individuals to construct reality. Jehenson (1973) opens his study with a discussion of the difference between consociates and contemporaries, which derives from intersubjectivity, or shared subjective meaning between two people. According to Schütz (1967) individuals can only approach subjective understanding of another's actions by adopting the point of view of that other person. This "thou orientation" allows the observer to place herself within the shoes of the actor, apply her own set of experiences to the action she beholds, and determine what the meaning of the action might be. When two individuals meet and interact through "thou orientations," reality itself begins to take shape – the two individuals simultaneously reinforce the other's experience through intersubjectivity. These two individuals might be called consociates (Jehenson, 1973). Schütz and Jehenson understood perfect intersubjectivity to be an ideal type: humans cannot ever completely understand another's subjective meaning, and intersubjectivity can only be accomplished when two individuals direct their intentionality toward the other and form a complete understanding (ibid.). In reality, most close relationships exist between contemporaries. Face-to-face meetings may be rare, and individuals act toward each other based on an objective understanding of action, as well as the expectation that others will behave typically. These "types" are derived from first-hand experiences with others (ibid.). For example, a young man on the first day of his first accounting job after graduation may still see himself as a college student. His new co-workers see him as an accountant. It is only after the man has gained experience within the organization that he, too, comes to see himself as an accountant and adopts the typical actions expected of him.

Jehenson applies Schütz's work to an organizational setting – a psychological research hospital – to better see how the organization itself and the typical roles people occupy within it affect social interactions. Through a series of interviews with all levels of staff – from the hospital director to nurses working on the floor – Jehenson is able to assemble and describe a picture of how interactions break down when individuals do not follow their typical roles, as established by the organization. He closely examines the staff's reaction to news that a low-importance but high-performing wing of the hospital is going to close down. A hospital administrator, who is himself a psychiatrist, engages in a bit of psychiatry to describe the actions of his subordinate psychiatrists and staff – he describes them as petulant children and himself as the father figure. Jehenson makes it clear that this administrator's behavior toward his subordinates is based largely on this assessment. However, when other psychiatrists in the hospital are told this about their supervisor, they are incensed. For them, the supervisor has stepped outside his typical role and adopted the role of a psychiatrist, and in that organizational setting, it was strictly taboo to engage in analyzing co-workers. As a consequence, their typification of the hospital director changed – they no longer understood him as one who serves a strictly bureaucratic function, but also as someone who was willing to break protocol and who was more than willing to perform a little psychoanalysis on his subordinates and colleagues. Jehenson's (ibid.) contribution was to show that typifications are far from static and do not represent "naive" ideal types. Instead, he argued that individuals' typifications are constructed through social experience and are far from the ideal-typical, which are reinforced by the organizational setting.

Separately, Berger and Kellner (1970) attempt to describe marriage as one of the processes that facilitates intersubjectivity and creates "for the individual the sort of order in which he can experience his life as making sense" (p. 50). Subjective meaning and an individual's private experiences are only real insofar as that individual perceives them to be real. Intersubjectivity, Berger and Kellner argue, takes the mirage out of subjective meaning and casts it as "massively objective" (p. 54). While marriage is able to solidify individual experiences by facilitating their sharing, it is also able to maintain the private sphere of one's life by erecting a barrier between self and society. In this way, marriage becomes one of the most important institutions for constituting reality.

Ethnomethodology Research and Experiencing

Ethnomethodology is essentially the study of how individuals conduct the day-to-day activities of their lives and how these actions constitute reality. Some scholars have argued that phenomenology and ethnomethodology are the same sociologies, travelling under a different name (Maynard and Clayman, 1991). Harold Garfinkel regarded Husserl and Schütz as a foundation for his work on ethnomethodology. Both sociologies are interested in understanding the construction of reality and meaning through experience, but where phenomenology places an emphasis on the individual's construction of reality by attaching meaning to experience, ethnomethodology takes a more behaviorist approach. Maynard and Clayman (ibid.) note that phenomenology has influenced ethnomethodologists, especially with regard to its methodology (i.e., the phenomenological reduction of expressions into self-contained, or bracketed, descriptions of experience), how rules relate to lived life (e.g., Wieder's, 1974 study of how individuals experience codes of rules and use them based on their own intentionality toward the code), and the nature of objective reality. These influences notwithstanding, ethnomethodology has emerged as a diverse and widely applied perspective in its own right, which focuses on the concrete activities, or ethnomethods, that individuals use to live their lives in a social world.

We've already discussed one study conducted under the ethnomethodology umbrella – Agnes's construction of a new gender identity (Garfinkel, 1967). This study falls under a broader category within ethnomethodology – the study of institutions. Ritzer (2008) notes that sociologists tend to examine the rules, structures, and traditions of institutions with an understanding that such examinations can explain the actions of individual members of the institution. However, ethnomethodologists refute this approach; the rules and procedures inherent in institutions do not simply compel individuals to fall into conformity – instead, these institutional expectations help individuals constitute reality. A famous category of such research includes the breaching studies conducted by Garfinkel (1967). In one, a test subject plays a game of tic-tac-toe with a researcher. During the course of the game, the researcher places his symbol on the line between two cells – the test subject's reaction is the material of an ethnomethodologist's study. Does the subject demand the tester place the symbol within a cell? Does the subject attempt to rationalize or otherwise explain why the symbol was placed on the line between two cells? Another simple example might involve turning around and facing the back of a moving elevator and recording the fellow passenger's reactions. Ethnomethodologists would then attempt to interpret the reactions with the understanding that the way individuals react to these institutional breaches is how they act in day-to-day life (see Handel, 1982). One study, conducted specifically in an institutional setting, is Button's (1987) examination of job interviews. Of particular importance to Button was how the workplace interview differed from other types of conversations, how the interviewer set guidelines for how the interview would work, how the interviewer might use tactics to prevent the interviewee from going back and revising answers, and how the conversation itself is acknowledged as an interview.

Symbolic Interaction Research and Experiencing

The field's influence is too broad and the volume of studies published so varied that a substantive overview of symbolic interactionism literature is beyond our current scope. However, several studies serve to illustrate our interests here – namely experience and meaning – as well as an interpretive methodology. One such study is Timothy Curry's (1993) interviews with a single person: Sam, a college wrestler. Curry wanted to know how Sam's definition of pain and injury was transformed during his wrestling career. Early in Sam's childhood, he was strongly influenced by his father, who believed that pain is worth suffering through. Sam came to identify pain with masculinity – something that everyone experiences and must simply be endured. His definition of pain began to shift through his interactions with coaches at the high school and college level. While pain endurance was still part of being a successful wrestler, Sam no longer understood it as something that accompanies manhood – instead, it was something to be avoided. The constant presence of team physicians and the actions of coaches reinforced this new meaning for Sam. His experience of interacting with others shaped how he came to understand the meaning of a social object – in this study, pain (ibid.).

Another, more recent study involves the connection between experience and identity. Stein (2011) conducted 20 interviews with Western vacationers in China in an effort to understand how their experience of vacation led to the creation of a "vacationer identity," complete with specific activities to bracket the experience off from their routinized, day-to-day activities. Through the experiences associated with beginning vacations, including buying tickets, packing bags, getting shots, and securing travel visas, the vacationers begin the process of constructing an identity of the "vacationer." This identity, in turn, affects how the vacationers behave while on vacation – including going beyond their normal boundaries and participating in karaoke, changing their dining behavior or otherwise taking advantage of a newfound freedom and anonymity. Once home, the vacationers transitioned back into their old identities through the performance of experience bracketing activities, such as restarting the mail or picking the pet up from the kennel. However, Stein noted that the transition *to* the vacation identity was asymmetric with the transition *from* vacation identity – people are reluctant to give up their vacation identity, so they engage in lingering tactics, such as keeping souvenirs or waiting a day or two from the return to unpack. Sometimes, souvenirs or other objects from the vacation are incorporated into the individual's day-to-day life. For example, one China vacationer redecorated a spare bedroom in her home in Chinese fashion, which objectifies her experience so that she can share it with others.

Lastly, a classic study (Becker, 1953) attributes marijuana use to emergent experiences as opposed to psychological traits or other motivations. After interviewing 50 marijuana users, Becker notes that habitual smokers share three things in common. First, the new user must learn how to smoke marijuana properly in order to experience its effects. Second, the smoker must recognize the effects of "being high" and attribute them to the marijuana. Third, the smoker must enjoy using marijuana. These steps – all based on experience with a social object (i.e., marijuana) and interactions with others (e.g., new users are taught how to smoke marijuana properly and new smokers sometimes have to be talked into enjoying the experience) – are necessary for a person to become a marijuana smoker. Becker argues that contemporary sociological and psychological theory (incorrectly) suggests that individuals are predisposed to behave in certain ways, either due to psychological traits or sociological pressures that lead to deviance. Instead, Becker (ibid., p. 242) writes that "if a stable form of new behavior toward the object is to emerge, a transformation of meanings must occur, in which the person develops a new conception of the nature of the object," and "this happens in a series of communicative acts in which others point out new aspects of his experience to him." Becker's study precedes Blumer's description of symbolic interaction and the translation of Schütz's phenomenological work from German – and yet it captures the essence of the sociology of experience.

SOCIOLOGY, EXPERIENCE, AND ENTREPRENEURSHIP

Entrepreneurship scholars begin from a premise shared by Mead, Schütz, Husserl, and Blumer: human beings, and especially entrepreneurs, do not merely react to environmental conditions. Instead, they act based on their appraisal of a situation through intentional decision-making (Baron, 2007; Shane et al., 2003). More importantly, the theory of action described by Mead and Schütz is very similar to Kirzner's (1985, p. 56) description of the "motivated propensity of man to formulate an image of the future." Schütz's and Mead's actor acts only insofar as she has a specific action or goal to achieve. The actions leading to the desired act or goal are meaningful only in relation to the desired end state the actor is trying to achieve. Likewise in entrepreneurship, action is undertaken by an actor striving to bring about a desired future state – the greater the difference between the current state and the entrepreneur's desired future, the greater the potential for entrepreneurial action (Kirzner, 1982).

Sociological perspectives on experience and meaning can have, and in some cases have had, influential effects on the study of entrepreneur-ship. While the field's influence is too broad to include a comprehensive summary here, a few examples stand out, especially with regard to sym-bolic interactionism. Interactionist perspectives have influenced every-thing from institutionalism (DiMaggio and Powell, 1991; Fine, 1993) and legitimacy (Starr and MacMillan, 1990; Stinchcombe, 1965), which are essentially the study of the experience of organizational settings and inter-actions; to signaling and screening theories (Sanders and Boivie, 2003); to the deployment of symbolic actions, such as Delmar and Shane's (2004) study of organizing activities that ventures undertake to obtain legitimacy. Strains of ethnomethodology can also be found within entrepreneurship research, particularly in research on bricolage (e.g., Garud and Karnoe, 2003), effectuation (e.g., Wiltbank et al., 2006) and structuration (e.g., Sarason et al., 2006). Not surprisingly, studies that are interested in the day-to-day constructions of reality (or opportunity or a venture) have a lot in common, including methodology, such as think-aloud protocols, which is the analysis of described, lived-through experience similar to the meth-odologies used in Garfinkel's breach experiments and institutional studies (Garfinkel, 1967). Think-aloud protocol studies in entrepreneurship fre-quently ask entrepreneurs to evaluate a fictional set of facts or product prototypes and verbalize their thoughts while identifying an opportunity or describing target markets based on those facts or products (e.g., Dew et al., 2011; Gregoire et al., 2010). Phenomenology, too, has begun to influ-ence entrepreneurship research. For example, Cope (2005) describes using phenomenological inquiry to better understand how lived experience affects entrepreneurial learning. Phenomenological inquiry is an approach used to understand experience where solicited individuals provide descrip-tions of meanings of what they've experienced. Cope describes his meth-odological process, and we explore this in more detail in Chapter 12.

The sociology of experience offers important insights as we consider the future of entrepreneurship. Work on the construction of reality and the construction of identity both can enrich our understanding of the emergent nature of ventures and entrepreneurs (see Chapter 8). Reality and identity are both based on experiences, the meanings of which constantly change, sometimes subtly and sometimes drastically, depending on any number of variables, including preceding or subsequent experiences or the inten-tionality with which the observer beholds her experiences. Thus, Downing describes the entrepreneurial firm and entrepreneurial identity as iterative, developing entities that emerge as an individual experiences interactions with stakeholders and the environment (2005). Other scholars have also noted the continuous flux that characterizes variables surrounding venture creation. Windows for opportunity open and close (Kirzner, 1979; Shane,

2003), opportunities change as the entrepreneur interacts with the environment (Bhave, 1994; Shah and Tripsas, 2007; Wood and McKinley, 2007), and the experience of entrepreneurs themselves can affect how they identify opportunities (Baron, 2006; Corbett, 2007; Shane, 2000). Identity theories in entrepreneurship are also indebted to sociological perspectives. For example, Cardon and colleagues' (2009) study of passion and entrepreneurial roles builds on identity theory (Stryker and Burke, 2000), which in turn is an extension of Erving Goffman's (1959) work on self and its social construction through interaction (see Chapter 10).

CONCLUSIONS

The experiences we have interacting with each other lie at the core of the sociological perspectives we have just discussed. Phenomenology explains how individuals experience social objects and understand the meanings of these experiences. It also seeks to explain how individuals come to understand the meanings of others' actions, thus creating intersubjective meaning, or shared meaning. Symbolic interactionism focuses on the tools of social communication. More specifically, symbolic interactionism explains how objects are socially defined and become symbols of subjective meaning. Individuals then use these symbols so that their meanings can be understood while interacting with others. The essence of ethnomethodology is in understanding the construction of reality. In other words, it focuses on how individuals erect meaningful realities for themselves and others through social interaction. In this chapter, we describe the historical development of these perspectives, the elements of experience in sociology, and several examples of research applications. We close with a discussion of the promise that sociological perspectives on experience can hold for future entrepreneurship research. In the succeeding chapters, we turn once again to the experiencing entrepreneur and portray the ways in which experiencing events shape an emerging venture and an emerging entrepreneur.

REFERENCES

Adler, P.A., P. Adler and A. Fontana (1987), 'Everyday life sociology', *Annual Review of Sociology*, **13**(1): 217–35.
Baron, R.A. (2006), 'Opportunity recognition as pattern recognition: how entrepreneurs "connect the dots" to identify new business opportunities', *Academy of Management Perspectives*, **20**(1): 104–19.

Baron, R.A. (2007), 'Behavioral and cognitive factors in entrepreneurship: entrepreneurs as the active element in new venture creation', *Strategic Entrepreneurship Journal*, **1**(1–2): 167–82.

Becker, H.S. (1953), 'Becoming a marihuana user', *American Journal of Sociology*, **59**(3): 235–43.

Berger, P. and H. Kellner (1970), 'Marriage and the construction of reality: an exercise in the microsociology of knowledge', in H.P. Dreitzel (ed.), *Recent Sociology No. 2*, New York: Macmillan, pp. 50–72.

Bhave, M.P. (1994), 'A process model of entrepreneurial venture creation', *Journal of Business Venturing*, **9**(3): 223–42.

Blumer, H. (1969), *Symbolic Interactionism: Perspective and Method*, Berkeley, CA: University of California Press.

Blumer, H. (1981), 'Conversation with Thomas J. Morrioni and Harvy A. Farberman', *Symbolic Interaction*, **4**(2): 9–22.

Brissett, D. and C. Edgley (eds) (1975), *Life as Theate*, Chicago, IL: Aldine.

Button, G. (1987), 'Answers to interactional products: two sequential practices used in interviews', *Social Psychology Quarterly*, **50**(2): 160–71.

Cardon, M.S., J. Wincent, J. Singh and M. Drnovsek (2009), 'The nature and experience of entrepreneurial passion', *Academy of Management Review*, **34**(3): 511–32.

Charon, J.M. (1995), *Symbolic Interactionism: An Introduction, and Interpretation, an Integration*, Englewood Cliffs, NJ: Prentice Hall.

Cope, J. (2005), 'Researching entrepreneurship through phenomenological inquiry: philosophical and methodological issues', *International Small Business Journal*, **23**(2): 163–89.

Corbett, A.C. (2007), 'Learning asymmetries and the discovery of entrepreneurial opportunities', *Journal of Business Venturing*, **22**(1): 97–118.

Curry, T.J. (1993), 'A little pain never hurt anyone: athletic career socialization and the normalization of sports injury', *Symbolic Interactionism*, **16**: 273–90.

Delmar, F. and S. Shane (2004), 'Legitimating first: organizing activities and the survival of new ventures', *Journal of Business Venturing*, **19**(3): 385–410.

Dew, N., S. Read, S. Sarasvathy and R. Wiltbank (2011), 'On the entrepreneurial genesis of new markets: effectual transformations versus causal search and selection', *Journal of Evolutionary Economics*, **21**(2): 231–53.

Dilthey, W. (1989), *Introduction to Human Sciences*, Princeton, NJ: Princeton University Press.

DiMaggio, P. and W. Powell (1991), 'Introduction', in W. Powell and P. DiMaggio (eds), *The New Institutionalism in Organizational Analysis*, Chicago, IL: Chicago University Press, pp. 1–38.

Downing, S. (2005), 'The social construction of entrepreneurship: narrative and dramatic processes in the coproduction of organizations and identities', *Entrepreneurship Theory and Practice*, **29**(2): 185–204.

Eames, S.M. (1977), *Pragmatic Naturalism*, Carbondale, IL: Southern Illinois University Press.

Fine, G.A. (1993), 'The sad demise, mysterious disappearance, and glorious triumph of symbolic interactionism', *Annual Review of Sociology*, **19**(1): 61–87.

Frank, G. (1979), 'Finding the common denominator: a phenomenological critique of life history method', *Ethos*, **7**(1): 68–94.

Garfinkel, H. (1967), *Studies in Ethnomethodology*, Englewood Cliffs, NJ: Prentice-Hall.

Garfinkel, H. (1988), 'Evidence for locally produced, naturally accountable phenomena of order, logic, reason, meaning, method, etc., in and as of the essential quiddity of immortal ordinary society (I of IV): an announcement of studies', *Sociological Theory*, **6**(1): 103–9.

Garud, R. and P. Karnoe (2003), 'Bricolage versus breakthrough: distributed and embedded agency in technology entrepreneurship', *Research Policy*, **32**(2): 277–300.

Giorgi, A. (2009), *The Descriptive Phenomenological Method in Psychology: A Modified Husserlian Approach*, Pittsburgh, PA: Duquesne University Press.

Goffman, E. (1959), *The Presentation of Self in Everyday Life*, Garden City, NY: Doubleday.

Goffman, E. (1974), *Frame Analysis: An Essay on the Organization of Experience*, New York: Harper Colophon.

Gonos, G. (1980), 'The class position of Goffman's sociology: social origins of an American structuralism', in J. Ditton (ed.), *The View from Goffman*, New York: St. Martin's Press, pp. 134–69.

Gregoire, D., P. Barr and D. Shepherd (2010), 'Cognitive process of opportunity recognition: the role of structural alignment', *Organization Science*, **21**(2): 413–31.

Handel, W. (1982), *Ethnomethodology: How People Make Sense*, Englewood Cliffs, NJ: Prentice Hall.

Heap, J.L. and P.A. Roth, (1973), 'On phenomenological sociology', *American Sociological Review*, **38**(3): 354–7.

Heritage, J. (1984), *Garfinkel and Ethnomethodology*, Cambridge: Polity Press.

Hertzler, J.O. (1965), *A Sociology of Language*, New York: McGraw Hill.

Husserl, E. (1970), *Logical Investigations*, New York: Humanities Press.

Jehenson, R. (1973), 'A phenomenological approach to the study of formal organizations', in G. Psathas (ed.), *Phenomenological Sociology*, New York: Wiley, pp. 219–47.

Kirzner, I. (1979), *Perception, Opportunity, and Profit: Studies in the Theory of Entrepreneurship*, Chicago, IL: University of Chicago Press.

Kirzner, I. (1982), 'Uncertainty, discovery, and human action: a study of the entrepreneurial profile in the Misesian system', in I. Kirzner (ed.), *Method, Process, and Austrian Economics*, Lexington, MA: Lexington Books, pp. 139–59.

Kirzner, I. (1985), *Discovery and the Capitalist Process*, Chicago, IL: University of Chicago Press.

Lewis, J.D. and R.L. Smith (1980), *American Sociology and Pragmatism: Mead, Chicago Sociology, and Symbolic Interactionism*, Chicago, IL: University of Chicago Press.

Maynard, D.W. and S.E. Clayman (1991), 'The diversity of ethnomethodology', *Annual Review of Sociology*, **17**(1): 385–418.

Mead, G.H. (1934), *Mind, Self, and Society: From the Standpoint of a Social Behaviorist*, Chicago, IL: University of Chicago Press.

Mead, G.H. (1938), *The Philosophy of the Act*, Chicago, IL: University of Chicago Press.

Mead. G.H. (1982), *The Individual and the Social Self: Unpublished Work of George Herbert Mead*, Chicago, IL: University of Chicago Press.

Mills, C.W. (1967), *Power, Politics and People: The Collected Essays*, Oxford: Oxford University Press.

Ritzer, G. (2008), *Sociological Theory*, Boston, MA: McGraw-Hill Higher Education.

Sanders, W.G. and Boivie, S. (2003), 'Sorting things out: valuation of new firms in uncertain markets', *Strategic Management Journal*, **25**(2): 167–86.

Sarason, Y., T. Dean and J.F. Dillard (2006), 'Entrepreneurship as the nexus of individual and opportunity: a structuration view', *Journal of Business Venturing*, **21**(3): 286–305.

Schütz, A. (1967), *The Phenomenology of the Social World*, Evanston, IL: Northwestern University Press.

Shah, S.K. and M. Tripsas (2007), 'The accidental entrepreneur: the emergent and collective process of user entrepreneurship', *Strategic Entrepreneurship Journal*, **1**(1–2): 123–40.

Shane, S. (2000), 'Prior knowledge and the discovery of entrepreneurial opportunities', *Organization Science*, **11**(4): 448–69.

Shane, S. (2003), *A General Theory of Entrepreneurship*, Cheltenham, UK and Northampton, MA, USA: Edward Elgar.

Shane, S., E. Locke and C. Collins (2003), 'Entrepreneurial motivation', *Human Resource Management Review*, **13**(2): 257–79.

Shibutani, T. (1961), *Society and Personality: An Interactionist Approach to Social Psychology*, Englewood Cliffs, NJ: Prentice Hall.

Snow, D.A. (2007), 'Frame', in George Ritzer (ed.), *The Blackwell Encyclopedia of Sociology*, Oxford: Blackwell, pp. 1778–80.

Starr, J.A. and I.C. MacMillan (1990), 'Resource cooptation via social contracting: resource acquisition strategies for new ventures', *Strategic Management Journal*, **11**(4): 79–92.

Stein, K. (2011), 'Getting away from it all: the construction and management of temporary identities on vacation', *Symbolic Interaction*, **34**(2): 290–308.

Stinchcombe, A.L. (1965), 'Social structure and organizations', in J. March (ed.), *Handbook of Organizations*, Chicago: Rand McNally, pp. 142–93.

Stryker, S. and P.J. Burke (2000), 'The past, present, and future of an identity theory', *Social Psychology Quarterly*, **63**(4): 284–97.

Synnott, A. (1993), *The Body Social: Symbolism, Self, and Society*. London: Routledge.

Tiryakian, E.A. (1965), 'Existential phenomenology and the sociological tradition', *American Sociological Review*, **30**(5): 674–88.

Weber, M. (1968), *Economy and Society*, New York: Bedminster Press.

Weber, M. (1982), 'Subjective meaning in the social situation I', in L.A. Coser and B. Rosenberg (eds), *Sociological Theory: A Book of Readings*, Prospect Heights, IL: Waveland Press, pp. 191–203.

Wieder, D.L. (1974), *Language as Social Reality*, The Hague: Mouton.

Wiltbank, R., N. Dew, S. Read and S.D. Sarasvathy (2006), 'What to do next? The case for non-predictive strategy', *Strategic Management Journal*, **27**(10): 981–98.

Wood, M.S. and W. McKinley (2010), 'The production of entrepreneurial opportunity: a constructivist perspective', *Strategic Entrepreneurship Journal*, **4**(1): 66–84.

5. Processing of the entrepreneurial experience

> It is the job of the sensemaker to convert a world of experience into an
> intelligible world.
> (Karl Weick, 2001)

INTRODUCTION

The core argument of this book is that entrepreneurship can best be understood by approaching it as an experience. The entrepreneur encounters a temporal sequence of salient events. The volume, velocity, and volatility of these events serve to define venture creation. At issue is what is actually happening when one is in the midst of a venture taking form. He or she is experiencing the problematic launch of a new product, the making of a financial commitment that could bankrupt the company, the achievement of a significant performance goal, a break-in resulting in significant theft, the hiring away of a key employee by a competitor, a lawsuit from an investor, and many hundreds of other developments. Such events have to be interpreted, given meaning, and made sense of.

Central to experiencing, then, is how the individual actually processes these events. How do they enter into one's consciousness, and in what ways might they elicit unconscious reactions? Each individual has their own unique way of perceiving, interpreting, and responding to the events surrounding creation of a venture. This processing, in turn, results in changes to the individual, who then perceives, interprets, and responds to future stimuli, in a cumulative, path-dependent process.

In this chapter, we explore how entrepreneurs process events and event streams. A general framework to capture relationships between events, experiential processing, and behavioral outcomes is introduced. We approach processing as a complex and multi-level set of bi-directional interactions among cognition, affect, and physiology. We then examine the application of key elements of the proposed framework to the entrepreneurial context.

AN EXPERIENTIAL PROCESSING FRAMEWORK

Experiences are idiosyncratic. The way in which one individual interprets and responds to the environment may be very different from the way in which another individual interprets and responds to the exact same stimuli. These idiosyncrasies can be traced to approaches to processing the stimuli that are individual-specific. Moreover, mounting empirical evidence confirms that consciousness plays a limited role in producing behavior (Wilson, 2002). A primary function of consciousness is the development of novel adaptive responses by bringing together new combinations of knowledge, skills, and other resources. This is of critical importance in novel or unfamiliar situations such as new venture creation.

Within the cognitive science literature, the theory of connectionism has emerged as one way to tease apart these "black box" phenomena of computational models that rely on logical rules, where cognition is viewed as symbolic, rational, structured, and algorithmic (McClelland et al., 1986; Phaf and Wolters, 1997). In connectionist systems, the neural network instantiations are intrinsically embodied and rely on parallel processing of non-symbolic distributed activation patterns based on statistical properties (O'Brien and Opie, 1999). Different processing and memory units (nodes) are linked together in concurrently operating networks of mutually cooperating and competing units. A key feature of connectionism is that "the system's connectivity becomes inseparable from its history of transformations and related to the kind of task defined for the system" (Varela, 1991, p. 242). Each of these processing and memory modules has limited processing capacity, exhibits interdependence with other modules in the network, and has a range of activation levels. It is this pattern of linkages between these memory and processing units that, once established, enable faster processing of similar stimuli (Rosch, 1978). The connectionist model allows for multiple aspects of an experience to be coded by the modules or units (McClelland et al., 1986). According to a connectionist view, perception is concerned with the acquisition of sensory data to enable effective action and complements cognitive processes that unfold in real time in a synchronous manner with events in the environment.

Accordingly, we use this theory to develop an integrative model (see Figure 5.1) that reflects a cross-sectional view of our conceptualization of the overall fluid and emergent process of experience. The integrative model consists of multi-dimensional components and multi-level processes with recursive loops that are embedded, interconnected, networked, and interdependent. The six key components are numbered and each consists of (a) a set of *parts* and (b) the set of their *relations*. The six numbered components depict the following: (1) the environment consisting of events

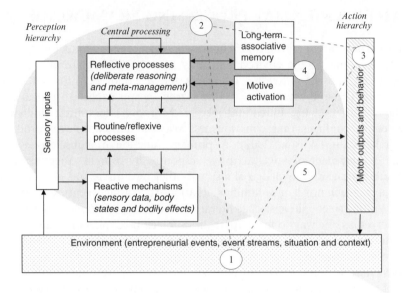

Note: 1 = environment; 2 = mind–body; 3 = behavior; 1+2+3 triangle = system;
4 = meaning making (space-of-action); 5 = sense-making (thought–action routines);
4+5 = knowledge construction and learning.

Figure 5.1   A framework to capture experience processing

and situations within an entrepreneurial context; (2) the entrepreneur
who experiences perceptual and cognitive processes in an embodied mind;
(3) an action hierarchy of motor processes and behavior; (4) the components involved in making meaning; (5) the sense-making components
and process; and (6) the combined effect of the experience and learning.
Although each of the main processes and their individual components will
be explained independently, it is our contention that, following connectionist theory, these dimensions are interdependent and that interaction
occurs simultaneously and influences the resultant outcomes in a recursive
and path-dependent manner.

Overarching Framework Components

Bandura (1997) argues there are three major classes of determinants of
human experience: internal personal factors in the form of cognitive, affective, and biological developments; the external environment; and behavior. These three determinants interact in "triadic reciprocal causation."

Experience is the emergent result of this network of interacting components, both external and internal to the body. Accordingly, the framework is situated within contextually sensitive multiple-level feedback loops between the environment (with event- and individual-specific influences), the individual (as an embodied cognizer), and an action system.

The experience starts when environmental cues (events) activate the implicit/automatic behavior-generation system that shapes mental representations and behavioral tendencies continuous with evolutionary ancestors through a learning process (Gollwitzer, 1999). The experience in turn could cause new events and a single event can trigger one or many experiences that could have several meanings depending on who, where, why, and when.

Embodied, Situated, and Social Cognition

Our processing framework centers on a constructivist and interactionist perspective that treats cognition as more than what takes place in the individual mind (Clark, 1999). Accordingly, cognition is viewed as a continuous process of perception–action loops that is social, embodied, and situated. The relevant situation in which entrepreneurial cognition takes place is almost always a social situation, whether it entails social interactions between individuals or within a wider social context. Social cognition is concerned with individual cognitive processes involving social information, such as attention, perception, memory, and internal mental representations. A key theme in situated cognition is a focus on action through an action–perception matching system. Furthermore, thoughts originate in the tactile-kinesthetic body, and therefore experiences matter for cognition and our way of knowing the world, in addition to their role in creating perceptual-motor pathways (Sheets-Johnstone, 1994). Lakoff (1987) and Johnson (1987) created a program called "Experiential Cognition," and argue that meaning is rooted in mind–body unity such that it is primarily tied to what is experientially available to an embodied mind. Cognition is therefore embodied such that there is interaction between levels of activity on a continuum of bodily, endocrinal, involuntary neural, emotional, and rational systems (Damasio, 2003).

Processing Levels and Modes

In their work on affect, motivation, cognition, and behavior, Ortony et al. (2005) argue that processing associated with individual events occurs at three interconnected levels: reactive (visceral), routine (behavioral/deliberate), and reflective (meta-management). Each level requires increasing degrees of consciousness and sophisticated reasoning. At the most elementary or reactive level, processing is concerned with the individual's approach and avoidance behavior and results in rapid judgments (e.g., good/bad and safe/dangerous) that interrupt and send signals to the motor system as well as the rest of the brain (i.e., signaling the higher levels).

The routine level encompasses all non-reactive-level processing that is executed automatically, without conscious control (such control exists at the reflective level). At the routine level, elementary units from the reactive level are organized into more complex patterns embodied in skills or procedural knowledge. The routine level is concerned with the execution of well-learned behaviors, and affect begins to show features of emotions but in a limited manner. Behavior and cognition at the routine level can be initiated by activity generated at the reactive level, the reflective level, by other routine-level activity, or by the output of sensory systems.

Actions generated at the routine level are in turn inhibited or enhanced by the reflective level, which is the highest level of cognitive functioning and consciousness. Here, individual differences in motivational structures, such as promotion and prevention focus, and cognitive representations, such as attribution of success and failure, come into play. The complex interplay between motivation and cognition leads to complex affective and behavioral responses. At the reflective level, alternative behaviors and their impact on the environment can be modeled consciously. Importantly, the reflective level of processing does not have direct access to sensory input or the control of behavior but instead "watches over, reflects upon and tries to bias the routine or behavioral level" (Norman et al., 2003, p. 40). The nature of the goal of the perceiver determines whether the processing mode is internally focused (e.g., thoughts and feelings) or externally focused (e.g., physical characteristics of object in the world through sensory-mediated channels) (Lieberman, 2007), not the intrinsic property of the stimulus. Additionally, the individual adaptively switches processing modes flexibly and without conscious awareness based on situational demands.

Processing Systems and Feedback Loops

According to Epstein's (1994) cognitive-experiential self-theory (CEST), individuals use two systems, one rational and the other experiential, for processing information. The rational system operates at the reflective level in the framework. The process is verbal, affect-free, context-independent, effortful, analytical, abstract, and requires logical justification with empirical verification for decision-making. By contrast, the experiential system operates at the routine level and is non-verbal, affect-laden, context-specific, automatic, outcome-oriented, intuitive, concrete, associative, and relies on self-evident "truths."

With CEST, the two information processing systems operate both sequentially and simultaneously as they interact to co-create behavior. Although the two systems are qualitatively different, neither is regarded to be superior, and the two systems are not engaged to the same extent in all situations (Epstein et al., 1996). For instance, individuals are more likely to engage the experiential system when confronted with a problem, in emotionally charged situations, and when under time pressure. Other factors influencing the likelihood that information will be processed one way or the other include individual psychological characteristics and whether the decision relates to a general trend, specific event or information within an area of expertise (Sherman et al., 1999). While experiential processing is prone to a variety of judgment errors because of biases, it may produce better results than can be achieved by rational processing in some situations. Most importantly, although verbal/symbolic thought deals with abstract properties of objects, it is the demands of situations and embodiment that determine the relevance for action of the abstract properties, making the action subservient to motivational constraints (Semin and Smith, 2002).

Brain and Body

Vernon et al. (2007) suggest that "cognition is intrinsically linked with the ability of an agent to act prospectively; to operate in the future and deal with what might be, not just what is" (p. 156). Consequently, the primary model for cognitive learning is anticipative skill construction, which contrasts with cognitivist approaches that focus on knowledge acquisition. In our processing framework, affect and cognition are intimately connected within a single integrated, bi-directional representation system. The two-way link between affect and cognition means there are consequences of emotions and feelings for cognitive processes as well as cognitive antecedents of affect.

Affect influences behaviors via cognitive processes that impact how individuals prefer to act (Foo et al., 2009). According to the Affect Infusion Model (AIM), this happens through two different mechanisms (Forgas, 1999). With the first of these, affect as information, a person makes a judgment based on how he or she feels about an event or development. The emotion becomes the information being used to judge or decide, and this affective information is used as a heuristic to speed up the judgment-making process. The second mechanism is called affect priming, where affect indirectly influences judgments through its impact on information processing. Specifically, information is selected or ignored based on its congruence with the current affect. Also, as a set of new information inputs are encoded, more weight is put on those inputs that are congruent with the current affect. Further, past information held in memory is retrieved by the individual based on its congruency with the current affect. Where individuals rely on more open, as opposed to closed, searches for information, as is typically the case with entrepreneurial situations, there is a greater likelihood that emotion-laden information will influence and become incorporated into judgment processes (Podoynitsyna et al., 2011).

Processing of affect associated with individual events occurs at the reactive, routine, and reflective levels discussed earlier. Affect at the reactive level is simple and unelaborated. With the routine level, affect begins to show features of emotions but in a limited manner. The reflective level, as the locus of higher-level cognitive functions and consciousness, is where emotions are full-fledged and cognitively elaborated. At the reflective level, alternative behaviors and their impact on the environment can be modeled consciously. Affective processing is biologically determined and starts at the reactive level, but can be inhibited or enhanced by control signals from the reflexive level (Ortony et al., 2005). The internal processing includes initial recognition of positive or negative affect as an "innately structured, non-cognitive evaluative sensation that may or may not register in consciousness" (Zajonc, 1998), which then becomes evaluated in sync with the physical and cognitive elements to identify a "feeling" (Masters, 2000). Affect can prime the kind of associations used in the interpretation and evaluation of stimuli. Appraisals made about the significance and worth of an event, rather than the event itself, determine whether and which emotion will be experienced (Stein and Levine, 1999). Where events are pivotal, significant emotional responses may be elicited that lead to goal modification.

The outcome of these internal processing stages creates emotion, defined as a psychosocially constructed, dramatized feeling (Masters, 2000). At the reactive level, the physiological response category includes a variety of body-level responses driven by neuron-based signal transport mechanisms, leading to the release of hormones, such as adrenaline, heart rate fluctuations, sweating, nausea, shaking, and other aspects that influence the individual's degree of arousal (Krauss and Putnam, 1985). Based upon the consequences of how the individual responds to this stimulus, and the outcome of that response, the linkages between the physical, emotional, and cognitive elements will be created, modified, or strengthened (Hummel and Holyoak, 2003). The physiological response interacts with both cognitive and affective processing via mutual influence. Over time, an accumulation of certain physiological responses may have an effect on the individual's health.

From Perception to Action and Memory

Drawing from Hoch and Deighton's (1989) stage model of consumer learning, internal processing occurs as a result of four stages: (1) exposure to and encoding of evidence; (2) depending on whether the stimulus is novel or not, either an elaboration ("bottom-up") or activation ("top-down") process will occur; (3) outcomes of this process include the integration of this new information with prior beliefs and/or belief revision, or learning; and finally (4) the individual enters the stage of hypothesis generation, which involves the creation of new expectations for what will happen next. These expectations will then interact with future stimuli in the individual's future perception and processing. Prior processing feeds into future processing in a recursive manner and embeds experience in a multi-layered feedback loop.

The work of Phaf and Wolters (1997) is especially instructive here. They explain that, via learning mechanisms, memory traces are laid down in a distributed fashion over the network as a result of activation and elaboration processes such that routes are specific to a given stimulus. Links between processing units will be *created* when the individual is presented with a novel stimulus, *modified* when past processing was incorrect based on outcomes to prior responses, or *strengthened* when reinforced by outcomes, just as indicated by classical conditioning. In the situation where an individual is exposed to a novel stimulus, elaboration processes occur that involve responses to novel stimuli requiring active attention. In this case, new links are established, and a "bottom-up" type of processing occurs, where perception is data driven, guided by the objective characteristics of the stimulus (Hoch and Deighton, 1989). The automatic consequence of the novelty of the stimulus information is called *elaboration learning*. In the scenario where an individual is exposed to a stimulus resembling stimuli previously exposed to, an *activation process* occurs. This is a subconscious process by which existing associations in memory are automatically activated and strengthened when a stimulus is presented (Phaf and Wolters, 1997). It has also been referred to as top-down processing or concept-driven perception guided by prior knowledge (Hoch and Deighton, 1989). A result of activation processing is a reduction in future processing time and strengthening of linkages, referred to as *activation learning* in the connectionist literature (Phaf and Wolters, 1997).

The conscious or subconscious retrieval of learned lessons from memory is dependent upon the reactivation of these links (ibid.). These links are reactivated through *associative recall*, a process where the present perceptual process makes contact with the trace of a similar process of the past, and content associated with this trace (Wallach, 1949). The reactivation of links or associative recall is supported by the literature demonstrating that environmental cues, such as a familiar scent or internal states such as mood, affect memory recall (ibid.). At any point in time, an individual might be induced by some trigger or stimulus to reflect upon past experience, upon which the individual will process a collection of instances from the past selected by associative recall or the reactivation of the linkages formed during processing activities. This new reflective processing is recursive in that each of these recalled instances and streams become the stimuli feeding into the processing framework shown in Figure 5.1. The processing of these memories often elicits emotional, physiological, and cognitive responses. In essence, this type of reflection forms another layer of internal processing by processing past instances and can be considered "meta-processing." The long-term memory sector includes all retained prior experiences, knowledge, beliefs, attitudes, predispositions, intentions, values, cognitive networks, schema, scripts, motives, the individual's personality, feelings, impressions, images, expectations, and so forth (Forgas, 1999).

Although perceptual and motor processes are similar in nature at the reactive (neural) and routine (behavioral) levels, at the reflective level internally reactivated sensorimotor structure plays a crucial role in social cognition (especially emotive states) through simulation mechanisms (Nielsen, 2002). According to Barsalou and colleagues (2003) four types of phenomena in social cognition are explained by simulation of bodily states: (1) social stimuli produce bodily responses (e.g., facial expressions) automatically and unconsciously in tandem with cognitive responses; (2) perceiving bodily states produces bodily mimicry (e.g., watching someone yawn often causes one to yawn); (3) bodily states (e.g., facial expressions or postures) can induce emotion states and influence evaluative and non-evaluative judgments; and (4) performance is enhanced by compatibility between bodily states and affective states.

REVISITING THE ENTREPRENEURIAL EXPERIENCE

We now return to the question "What is the entrepreneurial experience?". As noted in earlier chapters, the extant literature provides few clues regarding the nature of this experience apart from considering it as prior knowledge or learning. In our conceptualization, experiences are the result of the contextualization of events resulting from the interaction between the entrepreneur and the entrepreneurial context. This has important implications for the practicing entrepreneur as it suggests that the entrepreneurial act is essentially an opportunity to learn about oneself. Our interest is in the reciprocal interaction between entrepreneur and the venture (or world), particularly the self-knowledge derived from this interaction. With this in mind, it is useful to distinguish between evidence-based self-knowledge derived from conscious processing at the reflective level in *low-experience* domains and intuition-based self-knowledge that is a non-reflective, automatic way of knowing in *high-experience* domains that occurs at the routine level of our framework. For the purpose of our discussion below, meaning-making happens in high-experience domains whereas sense-making occurs in low-experience domains.

The relevance of our integrative processing framework with its key components as a representation of the entrepreneurial experience is discussed below. For our analysis of the component parts of this experience, specific attention is devoted to the following: (1) the environment including antecedents, individual factors and contextual factors; (2) interactive effects of the three core dimensions (cognitive, affective, and physiological) and the resultant effect on the entrepreneur; (3) the perceptual process involved in meaning-making; (4) the process of sense-making; and (5) outcomes such as entrepreneurial action, learning, and memory.

Impact of Contextual Factors on Entrepreneurial Experiencing

The entrepreneur's processing mechanism is dependent upon the context in which they find themselves. According to Semin and Smith (2002), situatedness is derived from the interaction of situation and context. They argue that the context influences and determines the specific situation in which actions take place such that in a given situation there are several different, possibly overlapping contexts. At least five general characteristics of the venture creation context can be proposed: ambiguity, lack of control, uncertainty, autonomy, and stress (see Chapter 6 for a more detailed discussion). Although these are but a few of the ways in which entrepreneurship might be characterized, they represent a beginning point in efforts to decipher the implications of an experiential view of the venture creation process. If successful entrepreneurs are found to have a high tolerance for ambiguity then it logically follows that the experience possesses ambiguous qualities, penalizing those who cannot tolerate such conditions. Similarly, the entrepreneur's need for control is reflective of a context that is relatively uncontrolled, subject to unpredictable environmental forces, where the venture eventually creates its own momentum and evolves in unique ways. The presence of a multiplicity of obstacles and demands, unclear job responsibilities, limited information for decision-making, and high levels of uncertainty regarding outcomes and the future all serve to reinforce the entrepreneur developing an ability to cope with uncertainty and to penalize uncertainty avoidance. That entrepreneurs prefer a degree of independence and autonomy suggests they are drawn to contexts demonstrating meaningful room for individual action. The relative autonomy found within the entrepreneurial venture may also create a sense of loneliness tied to personal assumption of responsibility. And the characteristics described herein coupled with the extreme velocity and volatility of the context not only heighten stress but reward the development within the entrepreneur of a greater ability to perform at high levels under stressful circumstances.

Other individual characteristics that shape the experience include self-efficacy (Zhao et al., 2005), prior knowledge and experience (Madsen et al., 2003), practical intelligence (Baum, 2005) or cognitive ability (Baron and Ensley, 2006), and intentions (Zhao et al., 2005). At the reflective level of processing, the entrepreneur's motivation (prevention and promotion focus) and cognitive representations (e.g., attribution of success and failure) become especially relevant (see Baron, 2004).

Components of the Entrepreneurial Experience

Many cognitive tasks require entrepreneurs to go beyond the available information and use associations, inferences, and interpretations to construct a judgment or make a decision, particularly when confronting complex and ambiguous social information (Heider, 1958). Factors influencing processing choices and thus mediating mood effects include task familiarity, complexity, and typicality of task, personal relevance, personal motivation, processing capacity, and mood effects on processing (Lord and Maher, 1990). As we have noted, affect can prime the kind of associations used in the interpretation and evaluation of stimulus. Appraisals made about the significance and worth of an event (either external or internal to the person), rather than the event itself, determine whether and which emotion will be experienced. Without occurrence of a pivotal significant event, goals will not change and no emotional response will be elicited.

According to Stein and Levine (1999) a number of questions related to the components of experience reflect the temporal and causal constraints of mental schemas used to interpret and respond to emotion-laden events:

- What happened?
- How did the event affect my goals?

- How do I feel about it?
- What do I want to do about it?
- What did I do?
- What were the results of my actions?

Further, there is a process of understanding that accompanies emotional experience. The presence of emotion signals perception that a personally significant goal has been attained, blocked or threatened. The experience of emotion depends upon prior knowledge, beliefs, and appraisals about the causes and consequences of an event (not the event itself). Emotions occur involuntarily and unexpectedly in response to novel aspects of an event or situation. Causal thinking and goal appraisal unfold continuously during the experience of an emotion. The unfolding of an emotion episode is described by the dimensions of content, process (causal sequencing), and function.

Under conditions endemic to entrepreneurship such as uncertainty, time constraints, ambiguity, and emotional load, experiential processing is often the preferred problem-solving approach because it is fast, efficient, holistic, and encodes reality in images, metaphors, and narratives (Epstein and Pacini, 1999). An example of this holistic representation is the instantaneous gut-level response when faced with unexpected critical events under time constraints or in stressful contexts. To date, this intuitive capacity could not be adequately explained by using a cognitive lens that distinguishes between intuitive cognition and analytical cognition (Busenitz and Barney, 1997), nor can intuitive capacity be ascribed to a stock of prior concrete experiences in Kolb's experiential learning cycle (Cappon, 1994; Kolb, 1984). Moreover, Tversky and Kahneman (1971) contend that intuition should be regarded with proper suspicion, and the decision-maker should replace impression formation by computation whenever possible. By contrast, Cappon (1994) considers intuitive feelings to be underrated aspects of the experience, especially when the entrepreneur doesn't act like a "cognitive miser" during information processing and decision-making. For example, Loewenstein and colleagues (2001) recently developed a "risk as feelings" hypothesis to explain entrepreneurs' risk-taking propensity. They found that individuals react at a gut level to risky situations based on the severity of outcomes and likelihood of occurrence. The gut-level reaction is influenced by anticipated and experienced emotions, not by a rational or cognitive assessment of various factors. This type of processing differs from "fast and frugal reasoning" in a limitedly rational paradigm that relies on recognition and the favoring of familiar objects over unfamiliar ones (Gigerenzer and Todd, 1999).

The Meaning-making Process of the Experience

The intuitive-experiential processing system operating in high-experience domains shares many operating characteristics with connectionist models, such as parallel processing and sub-symbolic pattern matching (McClelland et al., 1986). The routine level in our processing framework is the source of a more sensorily influenced context in which sensory feedback from emotion-related body changes make important contributions to emotion-related schemata. This high-experience domain is conducive to a holistic, implicit level of meaning that Gendlin (2003) describes as a "felt sense." According to Teasdale and Barnard (1993, p.91), "the implicational code provides a 'common currency' in which 'sensory' and 'cognitive' contributions can be expressed, integrated and can modulate the production of emotion." In addition, Lakoff (1987) proposes that meaningful conceptual structures arise from two sources: (1) the structured nature of bodily and social experience and (2) one's innate capacity to imaginatively project from certain well-structured aspects of bodily and interactional experience to abstract conceptual structure.

Building on Kolb's experiential learning model, Politis (2005) distinguishes between two stages in the learning process that he refers to as the "grasping of knowledge" and "transformation of knowledge." Most existing studies focus on the second aspect, transformation of knowledge, which is an experiential process where the personal experience of an entrepreneur is transformed into knowledge, which in turn can be used to guide the choice of new experiences. We conceptualize the meaning-making process of the entrepreneurial experience as a form of inquiry in experiential learning of a different, but complementary, nature that corresponds with the first part of the learning process, grasping of knowledge. Sensory, cognitive, and affective inputs are precursors of, as well as an evolutionary part of, the experiential processing of information from the entrepreneurial environment in a recursive feedback loop. As a result of this "grasping of knowledge," decisions can be made about appropriate action to take in response to stimuli from the entrepreneurial context.

Our integrative processing framework therefore has potential implications for the central learning process by which routines develop through an alternative route as a result of "experience accumulation" (Zollo and Winter, 2002). The contemporary notion is that routines reflect experiential wisdom in that they are the outcome of trial and error learning and the selection and retention of past behaviors (Gavetti and Levinthal, 2000). According to our framework, experiential wisdom refers to a certain "internal knowing" that is acquired personally in repeated multi-modal choices, which in turn provides the input for future behavior instead of being the outcome of past behaviors. This view is consistent with the activity theory of knowledge (Blackler, 1995) in which mental models or schemas of knowledge are developed from experience when interacting with the physical and social world. Scripts and mental schemas constitute the foundation for representing and understanding common, recurrent experiences and these internally structured concepts are embedded within broader prototypical knowledge structures.

From Meaning-making to Sense-making

In recent years, entrepreneurship seems to have an especially strong prefer- ence for processing by boundedly rational agents using causation or effec- tuation, decisional algorithms, non-linear differential equation models, and real options logic. Recent investigations into the role of affect relate only to sense-making and treats affect as an interfering mechanism rather than an integral part of cognition (Baron, 2008). However, in a connec- tionist view affect and cognition are integrally linked within an associative network of cognitive representations, where "affect is not incidental but an inseparable part of how we see and represent the world around us, the way we select, store and retrieve information, and the way we use stored knowledge structures in the performance of cognitive tasks" (Forgas, 1999, p. 593). The proposed integrative processing framework, founded upon connectionism and sharing some qualities with Epstein's (1994) cognitive-experiential self-theory (CEST), expands upon these rational perspectives by adding experiential processing. This multi-dimensional experiential processing facilitates short-term decision-making, learning, and behavior, based not only upon cognition but also emotions and physi- ological responses. The entrepreneur uses both conscious and unconscious processes to understand, evaluate, and respond to external events that evoke emotion. Appraisal, thinking, and planning can occur in real time during the experience of an emotion or retrospectively when recalling events that are emotionally meaningful. Sense-making occurs at the reflec- tive level of our processing framework – it is concerned with concepts and specific meanings, and although it has no direct influence on emotion, it mediates "cool" thinking about emotion-related topics (Teasdale, 1999). Sense-making is related to interactions with the environment and relates to deliberate "what if" reasoning related to action taken to make events happen.

In situations involving uncertainty, motivational conflict, or mul- tiple difficult-to-discriminate alternatives for action, they typically draw on symbolic thought in which they devote conscious and effortful consideration to their plans and action. People use dual processing in a range of situations, including problem-solving, analyzing persuasive messages, perceiving persons, and generating behavior from attitudes, among others (e.g., Chaiken and Trope, 1999; Fazio, 1986; Sloman, 1996). In fact, Epstein et al. (1999) found that decisions made quickly from the gut are sometimes better than when rationally analyzed. A sudden exposure to highly emotional stimuli may create strong and new associations equivalent to what would result from extensive practice, such as the experiences of serial entrepreneurs. However, emotional and physiological processes are assumed by some to be undesirable and interfere in rational decision-making. Consequently, the tendency is to encourage separation of emotion from facts in the decision process. Researchers have found attenuation of an emotional response during increasing levels of cognitive load (e.g., Pessoa et al., 2002). Studies using Positron Emission Tomography (PET) show that higher levels of dispositional negative affect are associated with a greater metabolic rate (Abercrombie et al., 1998). Such findings highlight the importance of understanding interactions between the three processes. Consequently, dual processing in CEST might shed new light on the risk perceptions of entrepreneurs who rely more heavily on experiential/affective processing such that "risk is a feeling" that serves as an "early warning system."

Making New Connections: The Role of Memory and Reflection

Recursive loops between the reactive, routine, and reflective levels in the framework result in thinking and tacit knowledge and produce several outcomes including learning, changes in beliefs, attitudes, intentions, impressions, judgments (e.g., of risk), and so forth. The knowledge that underpins adaptive behaviors are either procedural (implicit, tacit, embodied in skills) or declarative (explicit, associated with thought, deliberation, and theorizing) (Schneider and Chein, 2003). Procedural knowledge is cognitively impenetrable and although very effective in similar circumstances, procedural skills and behaviors cannot be transferred or adapted without costly trial and error. By contrast, declarative knowledge in the form of events, actions, and relations can be readily adapted or recombined to model changed circumstances and the impact of alternative behaviors. Declarative knowledge answers questions such as what, where, why, and is described as "knowledge that." Entrepreneurship scholars have largely ignored the role of automated, unconscious procedural knowledge in favor of declarative knowledge that is in awareness. At the same time, tacit knowledge is revered as a source of competitive advantage in the strategy literature without much attention given to its source or function. Our focus on the entrepreneur's experience viewed through the lens of connectionism provides some interesting insight.

The prediction of future impacts of behavior enables actions to anticipate future events through declarative modeling, which reduces the need for costly trial and errors in the face of novel situations or events. Implicit information eventually becomes explicit in a process that Karmiloff-Smith (1992) labels "representational redescription." After being revised and improved using the slow serial processing of consciousness (declarative knowledge) the particular skills and behavior again become automatic and unconscious through a process of proceduralization, freeing up the limited resources of conscious processing. Only the outputs of the "post-declarative" proceduralized skills and behaviors enter consciousness, enabling performance of specialist functions intuitively (Dreyfus and Dreyfus, 1990). This explains how complex situations or solutions to difficult problems can be understood at a glance.

In essence, the notions of "knowledge that," "knowledge why," "knowledge who," and "knowledge how" can be represented as sets of relationships that are imposed on entrepreneurial events. This view is consistent with existing conceptualizations of habitual entrepreneurship that rely upon the development of expert skills and behaviors. However, in our processing framework of the entrepreneurial experience, instead of requiring successive start-up experiences, the entrepreneur is a learning laboratory that garners and integrates knowledge. Cognitive understanding emerges from co-determined exploratory learning. Through cognition the entrepreneur breaks free of the present – by anticipating and predicting the future, as well as assimilating and adapting to actual events, the entrepreneur learns in a virtuous cycle that is acquired through declarative transitions that unfold at different times and rates, progressively building a range of new resources and cognitive skills as part of the emergent entrepreneurial mindset. It is this process of emergence over time that we turn our attention to in Chapter 8.

CONCLUSIONS

The current chapter has explored an integrative, multi-dimensional, and multi-level framework for capturing how events and event streams are processed by the entrepreneur. It emphasizes interactions between elements of the mind and body and their combined influences upon the perceptions, beliefs, and behaviors of the entrepreneur.

In our framework, the entrepreneur is situated within a specific new venture context and experiences events, which are then processed and responded to. The framework centers on internal personal factors in the form of cognitive, affective, and physiological developments, the environment as a source of novel events, and behavior. Cognition is viewed as a continuous process of perception–action loops that is social, embodied, and situated. Affect includes both state (shifts in current moods) and dispositional (more stable emotional tendencies) forms, and plays a role both as a source of information and as a vehicle for priming the encoding, retrieval, and selective use of information when making judgments. Physiological responses include a range of involuntary reaction to events such as increased heart rate fluctuations, release of adrenaline, loss of appetite, and sleeplessness.

Processing of events occurs at the reactive, routine, and reflective levels, with each level requiring increasing degrees of consciousness and sophisticated reasoning. The nature of affect and its impact evolve across these three levels. Two systems are used in processing information, one rational and the other experiential, and operate at different levels in the framework. Four stages are involved in internal (bottom-up or top-down) processing, and corresponding roles for perceptions, memory, association, learning mechanisms, motives, and action come into play over these stages. Following connectionist theory, the components and processes within the framework are interdependent and interaction occurs simultaneously and influences the resultant outcomes in a recursive manner.

The outcomes of this processing are more than just decisions and behaviors. Ultimately, the kind of venture that emerges is defined by these processes. Further, the entrepreneur himself or herself is being formed. These outcomes will be examined in greater detail in Chapter 8. Before that, however, let us further explore the critical role of affect in experiential processing in Chapter 6.

REFERENCES

Abercrombie et al. (1998), 'Metabolic rate in the right amygdala predicts negative affect in depressed patients', *Neuroreport*, **9**(14): 3301–7.
Bandura, A. (1997), *Self-efficacy: The Exercise of Control*, New York: Freeman.
Baron, R.A. (2004), 'The cognitive perspective: a valuable tool for answering entrepreneurship's basic why questions', *Journal of Business Venturing*, **19**(2): 221.
Baron, R.A. (2008), 'The role of affect in the entrepreneurial process', *Academy of Management Review*, **33**(2): 328–40.
Baron, R.A. and M.D. Ensley (2006), 'Opportunity recognition as the detection

of meaningful patterns: evidence from comparisons of novice and experienced entrepreneurs', *Management Science*, **52**(9): 1331.

Barsalou, L.W., W.K. Simmons and A. Barbey (2003), 'Grounding conceptual knowledge in modality-specific systems', *Trends in Cognitive Sciences*, **7**(2): 84–91.

Baum, J. Robert (2005), 'The practical intelligence of high potential entrepreneurs', University of Maryland, Smith School of Business working paper, College Park, MD.

Blackler, F. (1995), 'Knowledge, knowledge work and organizations: an overview and interpretation', *Organization Studies*, **16**(6): 1021–46.

Busenitz, L. and J. Barney (1997), 'Differences between entrepreneurs and managers in large organizations: biases and heuristics in decision making', *Journal of Business Venturing*, **12**(1): 9–30.

Cappon, D. (1994), *Intuition and Management: Research and Applications*, Westport, CT: Quorum Books.

Chaiken, S. and Y. Trope (eds) (1999), *Dual-process Theories in Social Psychology*, New York: Guilford Press.

Clark, L.S. (1999), 'Learning from the field: the journey from post-positivist to constructivist methods', paper presented to the International Communication Association, San Francisco.

Damasio, A. (2003), *Descartes' Error: Emotion, Reason, and the Human Brain*. New York: Putnam.

Dreyfus, H. and S. Dreyfus (1990), 'Making a mind versus modeling the brain: artificial intelligence back at a branch-point', in M.A. Boden (ed.), *The Philosophy of Artificial Intelligence*, Oxford: Oxford University Press, pp. 308–33.

Epstein, S. (1994), 'Integration of the cognitive and the psychodynamic unconscious', *American Psychologist*, **49**(8): 709–24.

Epstein, S. and R. Pacini (1999), 'Some basic issues regarding dual-process theories from the perspective of cognitive-experiential self-theory', in Shelly Chaiken and Yaacov Trope (eds), *Dual-process Theories in Social Psychology*. New York: Guilford Press.

Epstein, S., S. Donovan and V. Denes-Raj (1999), 'The missing link in the paradox of the Linda conjunction problem: beyond knowing and thinking of the conjunction rule, the intrinsic appeal of heuristic processing', *Personality and Social Psychology Bulletin*, **25**(2): 204–14.

Epstein, S., R. Pacini, V. Denes-Raj and H. Heier (1996), 'Individual differences in intuitive-experiential and analytical-rational thinking styles', *Journal of Personality and Social Psychology*, **71**(2): 390–405.

Fazio, R. (1986), 'How do attitudes guide behavior?', in R.H. Sorrentino and E.T. Higgins (eds), *The Handbook of Motivation and Cognition: Foundations of Social Behavior*, New York: Guilford Press, pp. 204–43.

Foo, M., M.A. Uy and R.A. Baron (2009), 'How do feelings influence effort? An empirical study of entrepreneurs' affect and venture effort', *Journal of Applied Psychology*, **94**(4): 1086–94.

Forgas, J.P (1999), 'On feeling good and being rude: affective influences on language use and request formulations', *Journal of Personality and Social Psychology*, **76**(6): 928–39.

Gavetti, G. and D. Levinthal (2000), 'Looking forward and looking backward: cognitive and experiential search', *Administrative Science Quarterly*, **45**(1): 113–37.

Gendlin, E. (2003), 'Beyond postmodernism: concepts through experiencing', in R. Frie (ed.), *Understanding Experience: Psychotherapy and Postmodernism*, London: Routledge, pp. 100–115.

Gigerenzer, G. and P. Todd (1999), *Simple Heuristics That Make us Smart*, New York: Oxford University Press.

Gollwitzer, P. (1999), 'Implementation intentions: strong effects of simple plans', *American Psychologist*, **54**(7): 493–503.

Heider, F. (1958), *The Psychology of Interpersonal Relations*, New York: Wiley.

Hoch, S.J. and J. Deighton (1989), 'Managing what consumers learn from experience', *Journal of Marketing*, **53**(2): 1–20.

Hummel, J.E. and K.J. Holyoak (2003), 'A symbolic-connectionist theory of relational inference and generalization', *Psychological Review*, **110**(2): 220–64.

Johnson, M. (1987), *The Body in the Mind: The Bodily Basis of Meaning, Imagination, and Reason*, Chicago, IL: Chicago University Press.

Karmiloff-Smith, A. (1992), *Beyond Modularity*, Cambridge, MA: MIT Press.

Kolb, D.A. (1984), *Experiential Learning: Experience as the Source of Learning and Development*, Upper Saddle River, NJ: Prentice-Hall.

Krauss, R.M. and L.E. Putnam (1985), 'Dimensions of emotion in facial and autonomic responses', paper presented at the annual meeting of the American Association for the Advancement of Science, Los Angeles, CA.

Lakoff, G. (1987), *Women, Fire and Dangerous Things: What Categories Reveal About the Mind*, Chicago, IL and London: University of Chicago Press.

Lieberman, M.D. (2007), 'Social cognitive neuroscience: a review of core processes', *Annual Review of Psychology*, **58**(1): 259–89.

Loewenstein, G., E. Weber, C. Hsee and N. Welch (2001), 'Risk as feelings', *Psychological Bulletin*, **127**(2): 267–86.

Lord, R. and K. Maher (1990), 'Alternative information-processing models and their implications for theory, research and practice', *Academy of Management Review*, **15**(1): 9–28.

Madsen, H., H. Neergaard and J. Ulhøi (2003), 'Knowledge-intensive entrepreneurship and human capital', *Journal of Small Business and Enterprise Development*, **10**(4): 426.

Masters, R. (2000), 'Compassionate wrath: transpersonal approaches to anger', *The Journal of Transpersonal Psychology*, **32**(1): 31–51.

McClelland, J.L., D. Rumelhart and G.E. Hinton (1986), 'The appeal of parallel distributed processing', in D. Rumelhart, J. McClelland and the PDP Research Group (eds), *Parallel Distributed Processing: Explorations in the Microstructure of Cognition: Vol. 1. Foundations*, Cambridge, MA: MIT Press, pp. 3–44.

Nielsen, L. (2002), 'The simulation of emotion experience', *Phenomenology and the Cognitive Sciences*, **1**(3): 255–86.

Norman, D.A., A. Ortony and D.M. Russell (2003), 'Affect and machine design: lessons for the development of autonomous machines', *IBM Systems Journal*, **42**(1): 38–44.

O'Brien, G.U. and J. Opie (1999), 'A connectionist theory of phenomenal experience', *Behavioral and Brain Sciences*, **22**(1): 127–96.

Ortony, A., D. Norman and W. Revelle (2005), 'Add-affect and proto-affect in effective functioning', in M. Arbib (ed.), *Who Needs Emotions?*, New York: Oxford University Press, pp. 173–202.

Pessoa, L., M. McKenna, E. Gutierrez and L. Ungerleider (2002), 'Neural processing of emotional faces requires attention', *Proceedings*, National Academy of Science, pp. 11458–63.

Phaf, R.H. and G. Wolters (1997), 'A constructivist and connectionist view on conscious and nonconscious processes', *Philosophical Psychology*, **10**(3): 287–307.

Podoynitsyna, K., H. Van der Bij and M. Song (2011), 'The role of mixed emotions in the risk perception of novice and serial entrepreneurs', *Entrepreneurship Theory and Practice*, accessed 16 November at http://onlinelibrary.wiley.com/journal/10.1111/%28ISSN%291540-6520/earlyview.

Politis, D. (2005), 'The process of entrepreneurial learning: a conceptual framework', *Entrepreneurship Theory and Practice*, **29**(4): 399.

Rosch, E. (1978), 'Principles of categorization', in E. Rosch and B.B. Lloyd (eds), *Cognition and Categorization*, Hillsdale, NJ: Erlbaum.

Schneider, W. and J.M. Chein (2003), 'Controlled and automatic processing: behavior, theory, and biological mechanisms', *Cognitive Science*, **27**(3): 525–59.

Semin, G.R. and E.R. Smith (2002), 'Interfaces of social psychology with situated and embodied cognition', *Cognitive Systems Research*, **3**(3): 385–96.

Sheets-Johnstone, M. (1994), *The Roots of Power: Animate Form and Gendered Bodies*, Chicago, IL: Open Court Publishing.

Sherman, S., D. Beike and K.R. Ryalls (1999), 'Dual-processing accounts of inconsistencies in responses to general versus specific cases', in S. Chaiken and Y. Trope (eds), *Dual-process Theories in Social Psychology*, New York: Guilford Press.

Sloman, S.A. (1996), 'The empirical case for two systems of reasoning', *Psychological Bulletin*, **119**(1): 3–22.

Stein, N. and L.J. Levine (1999), 'Early emergence of emotional understanding and appraisal', in T. Dalgleish and M. Power (ed.), *Handbook of Cognition and Emotion*, New York: John Wiley, pp. 383–408.

Teasdale, J.D. (1999), 'Emotional processing: three modes of mind and the prevention of relapse in depression', *Behaviour Research and Therapy*, **37**(Supplement 1): S53–S77.

Teasdale, J.D. and P. Barnard (1993), *Affect, Cognition and Change: Remodeling Depressive Thought*, Hove: Lawrence Erlbaum.

Tversky, A. and D. Kahneman (1971), 'Belief in the law of small numbers', *Psychological Bulletin*, **76**(2): 105–10.

Varela, F.J. (1991), *The Embodied Mind: Cognitive Science and Human Experience*, Cambridge, MA: MIT Press.

Vernon, D., G. Metta and G. Sandini (2007), 'A survey of artificial cognitive systems: implications for the autonomous development of mental capabilities in computational agents', *Evolutionary Computation, IEEE Transactions*, **11**(2): 151–80.

Wallach, Hans (1949), 'Some considerations concerning the relation between perception and cognition', in J.S. Bruner and D. Krech (eds), *Perception and Personality: A Symposium*, New York: Greenwood, pp. 6–13.

Weick, Karl E. (2001), *Making Sense of the Organization*, Oxford and Malden, MA: Blackwell Business.

Wilson, M. (2002), 'Six views of embodied cognition', *Psychonomic Bulletin and Review*, **9**(4): 625–36.

Zajonc, R.B. (1998), 'Emotions', in D.T. Gilbert, S.T. Fiske and G. Lindzey (eds), *Handbook of Social Psychology, Vol. 1*, 4th edn, New York: Oxford University Press, pp. 591–632.

Zhao, H., S.E. Seibert and G. Hills (2005), 'The mediating role of self-efficacy in the development of entrepreneurial intentions', *Journal of Applied Psychology*, **90**(6): 1265–72.

Zollo, M. and S. Winter (2002), 'Deliberate learning and the evolution of dynamic capabilities', *Organization Science*, **13**(3): 339–51.

6. Experiencing and the entrepreneur: the role of affect

> Experiences occur as a result of encountering, undergoing or living through
> things . . . they provide sensory, emotional, cognitive, behavioral, and
> relational values that replace functional values.
> (Bernd Schmitt, 2010)

INTRODUCTION

Emotions and feelings, or affect, play a large role in entrepreneurship. Fear, joy, anger, shame, and other strong emotions not only drive the entrepreneur, but impact how he or she processes information, responds to various stimuli, and makes decisions. If an entrepreneur experiences a prolonged period of depression, feelings of being under assault, or an enduring sense of joy and excitement, it is quite likely that his or her tendency to take risks, persevere, act creatively, or challenge convention will be meaningfully impacted.

Our experiential framework provides a lens for better understanding the role of emotions and feelings in venture creation. As we shall see, affect lies at the very heart of experiencing. This conclusion is reinforced by Slovic et al. (2002), who characterize the experiential mode as intuitive, automatic, natural, and based on images to which positive and negative affective feelings are attached. They note (p. 130):

> One of the main characteristics of the experiential system is its affective basis. Although analysis is certainly important in some decision-making circumstances, reliance on affect and emotion is a quicker, easier and more efficient way to navigate in a complex, uncertain and sometimes dangerous world. Many theorists have given affect a direct and primary role in motivating behavior.

Affect plays a complex role in experiencing. As various events occur over time, emotions will influence the saliency given to each of them, how they are interpreted, the nature of any response, and what learning takes place. Moreover, emotions do not operate in isolation. They influence and are influenced by cognitive and physiological processes.

In this chapter, we further explore the affective nature of the entrepreneurial experience. We begin by reviewing the growing body of work
on emotions and feelings in entrepreneurship. We then examine how
the findings of this work might be reinterpreted using the experiential
perspective. Attention is next devoted to identifying key emotions that
entrepreneurs and researchers tend to associate with the venture creation
experience. Building on this foundation, the underlying dimensionality of
the affective experience is examined. Finally, the concept of an affect space
is introduced to capture the changing affective state of the entrepreneur
as a venture is launched, takes shape, and becomes (or fails to become)
sustainable.

RESEARCH ON AFFECT AND THE ENTREPRENEUR

Feelings and emotions are prominent in any business. Researchers have
examined how emotions undermine rational decision-making in companies, how they can facilitate rationality, and how they are inextricably
connected to and influence cognitions (Ashforth and Humphrey, 1995;
Fineman, 1999; Jayasinghe et al., 2008). The bottom line is that affective
processes have a significant influence on judgment and behavior (Hayton
and Cholakova, 2011).

Yet, only recently has much attention been given to the influence of
emotions in an entrepreneurial context. This seems surprising, as the
early-stage venture would seem especially susceptible to the moods and
feelings of the founder. The entrepreneur invests heavily in their venture,
and this includes an emotional investment. As a result, the intertwinement
of venture with self finds the individual attributing business accomplishments and deficiencies to their own capabilities and inadequacies (Cardon
et al., 2005).

Despite this recent attention, affect was actually quite prominent in the
early, classical work of Joseph Schumpeter (Goss, 2005). At a base level,
Schumpeter emphasized the will to win, to fight and conquer, and the joy
of creation and problem-solving as keys to succeeding at the unknown
and at breaking with convention. Yet, his work implies that the absence
of routine is upsetting for many, while the continual advocacy of innovation or departures from the norm can cause emotional distress that the
entrepreneur must surmount.

The seminal work to date on affect and entrepreneurship can be found
in the contributions of Robert Baron (2008). He argues that the venture
creation context, due to its uncertainty, rapid rates of change, and need for
quick decisions, is one where affect is especially likely to influence behavior

and decision-making. Entrepreneurs are forced to make it up as they go along, and their emotions and feelings are prominent factors in how things are interpreted. Further, many of the activities in which the entrepreneur is engaged (e.g., creativity, persuasion, decision-making, formation of working relationships), are ones where the evidence suggests a stronger susceptibility to the influence of affect.

Baron distinguishes what he terms "state affect" from "dispositional affect." State affect is event generated, and refers to shifts in current moods that result from external events. Dispositional affect concerns stable tendencies to experience particular affective reactions across different situations over time. While they derive from different sources, Baron argues that both forms of affect produce parallel and similar effects across situations.

Separately, Goss (2005) refers to an emotional tone among entrepreneurs that is durable from situation to situation. The entrepreneur is broadly characterized as "feeling up" or "feeling down," and this emotional energy influences the maintenance of social order. Moreover, it accumulates over time. Entrepreneurs move through the chain of encounters that make up the venture creation experience on an up-and-down flow of emotional energy. Goss (ibid.) further discusses how emotional energy can center broadly on either a pride mode or a shame mode. The former finds the entrepreneur acting within the venture on the basis of pride, and this tends to be reinforced by family and the type of social network to which he or she strives to be connected. Pride is also felt when others defer to the entrepreneur's new way. The latter finds the entrepreneur driven by self-righteous anger, aggression, and shame, where externally-directed hostility or aggressiveness is prominent in the actions of the entrepreneur and his or her venture. Such aggressive behavior represents a reaction to a perceived lack of acceptance, loss of status, or sense of ridicule. Both general forms of high emotional energy can be sources of attraction for employees and other stakeholders.

Emotional energy that produces general states of being up or down would seem somewhat analogous to the notions of positive and negative affect. Positive affect is reflective of emotions that are more favorable, promising, constructive or good. Joy or excitement would be examples. Negative affect describes emotions that can be distressing, unpleasant, disagreeable, and even destructive. Feelings of fear, humiliation, and anger are examples. Baron (2008) proposes that experiencing positive affect enhances one's ability to recognize opportunities and to creatively solve problems. It can also improve the ability to acquire resources by enhancing the entrepreneur's persuasiveness. Further, entrepreneurs experiencing positive affect are more likely to expand their skill sets and build their social networks. They will be better at dealing with high levels of stress. Finally, positive affect is associated with responding more effectively to highly dynamic environments and with quicker decision-making. Negative affect will tend to produce the opposite results. In a separate study, Foo et al. (2009) found that negative affect was positively associated with effort devoted to venture tasks requiring immediate attention, while positive affect was positively related to venture effort beyond what is immediately required. The latter relationship was mediated by the entrepreneur's future temporal focus. Positive affect is thought to make one feel that the present environment is safer, allowing one to focus on the future, while also widening one's scope of attention.

Positive and negative affect have also been linked to the early stages of the entrepreneurial process, namely idea generation and the intention to develop the idea. Hayton and Cholakova (2011) present a model in which positive affect increases the probability of perceiving idea-stimulating information, of storing and readily retrieving more of such information from memory, and of combining such information in novel and creative ways. Moreover, experiencing positive affect will lead to a stronger belief that one's effort devoted to seeking uncertainty-reducing information will be successful, that continued pursuit of the idea will enable the generation of more secondary outcomes associated with uncertainty reduction, and that the valence for continued pursuit of the idea will be stronger. At the same time, affect is believed to play less of a role in entrepreneurial idea development when individuals have more familiarity and knowledge related to the idea, where ideas are less complex and conventional, and when the idea is more closely associated with the core self-identity of the individual.

The notion that a venture has affective qualities, or that it is a generator of emotional reactions in entrepreneurs, is made clear by Cardon et al. (2005). They propose a framework wherein the entrepreneur at any given time experiences a core affective state. Developments within the venture evoke a varied set of positive and negative emotions, some of which may be quite intense. These venture-generated emotions serve to cause some degree of change in the entrepreneur's core affective state. This change is referred to as "attributed affect," and it is processed subconsciously. However, the individual also consciously appraises the emotional changes they are experiencing, and this attempt at understanding and labeling is termed "an emotional meta-experience." Cardon et al. (ibid.) conclude that this process of experiencing changes one's core affective state and that attributing these changes to aspects of the venture makes the resulting affective state a consciously accessible experience.

A given emotion does not typically operate in isolation. By this we mean that people frequently experience multiple emotions at a time, and these can include both positive and negative emotions. The likelihood of experiencing multiple emotions grows as situations become more ambiguous (Larsen et al., 2004). Entrepreneurial ventures are a case in point, especially the more they center on innovation, creation of new markets, development of novel technologies, and achievement of aggressive growth. To understand the potential implications of mixed emotions, consider a scenario where the entrepreneur experiences anger, fear, and nervousness, but also hopefulness and pride. As there are three negative and two positive emotions, the positive emotions are considered *conflicting*, while the negative ones are considered *dominating* (Podoynitsyna et al., 2011). Conflicting emotions are especially significant, as they lead to ambivalence, which impacts judgments and actions. Podoynitsyna et al. (ibid.) have found that mixed emotions lead entrepreneurs to perceive higher risk and to engage in more cautious, conservative behaviors.

Two different approaches have been applied to assessing emotional responses. The first of these, the valence-based approach, has received the greatest emphasis. Here, as with the work of Baron or Cardon and colleagues above, emotions are perceived as being relatively more positive or negative. The second approach is the cognitive appraisal tendency approach, and it finds the individual assessing differences between emotions of the same valence, and judging them on such factors as their relative certainty and controllability (Podoynitsyna et al., 2011). Two emotions may be negative, but one may be judged as more certain and controllable. Possible implications are found in the work of Lerner and Keltner (2001), who demonstrate that fearful people (negative affect) made risk-aversive choices and angry people (negative affect) made risk-seeking choices, and that the angry people more closely resembled happy people (positive affect) in their judgments than they resembled those experiencing other types of negative affect. It may be that anger is more certain and controllable than fear.

Some attempt has been made to apply the concept of emotional intelligence (EQ) to entrepreneurs (e.g., Rhee and White, 2007). EQ, or the ability to appraise, regulate, and use emotions in the self and with others, has been associated with leadership and workplace success (Dulewicz and Higgs, 2000; Goleman, 1998). Cross and Travaglione (2003) have extended these findings to entrepreneurs. They found high levels of overall emotional intelligence among a set of high-profile entrepreneurs. They also note high scores on each of the sub-scales of the leading EQ models, with scores on the regulation of emotions sub-scale being the highest. In a related vein, Akgün and co-authors (2008) provide evidence that the abilities of early-stage ventures to perceive, understand, track, and utilize their members' emotions in its operations was positively associated with various measures of venture performance, with this impact moderated by levels of environmental dynamism.

HOW DOES VENTURE CREATION "FEEL"?

What is it like when one is in the midst of starting a venture? General descriptions of venture creation in the literature represent a beginning point for deciphering the fabric of the entrepreneurial experience. For instance, it has been observed that the experience possesses ambiguous qualities, penalizing those who cannot tolerate such conditions (McClelland, 1986). Such ambiguity refers to conditions where many phenomena (e.g., opportunities, markets, competitor behavior) are vague or indistinct and often subject to different interpretations. Ambiguity extends to the roles fulfilled by the entrepreneur, how those roles should be approached, and the relative priority to be given to a given role. It is a context where the entrepreneur may have little sense of what is working, what is not, and why. Moreover, the emergent nature of the venture creation context suggests that what is working today may not work tomorrow.

Coupled with this ambiguity, the act of creation takes place in circumstances where the individual has relatively little control over conditions and outcomes (Bird, 1989). Moltz (2003) uses the metaphor of trying to control a rollercoaster while riding it. The entrepreneur is dependent on the decisions and behaviors of a wide range of stakeholders over which he or she often has relatively little influence. Further, one is operating in a chronic state of uncertainty, as the entrepreneur does not know exactly what price to charge, which market segments to prioritize, which products to feature, which employees to hire, what location is best, which assets to acquire, the correct hours to operate, which operating processes to rely upon, the kind of technology in which to invest, how much debt to incur, and so forth. Schindehutte et al. (2006) describe the venture context in terms of a multiplicity of obstacles and demands, unclear responsibilities, and information that is limited both in quantity and quality.

The relative autonomy found within a venture may also produce a sense of loneliness or isolation (Boyd and Gumpert, 1983). The entrepreneur can feel a heavy burden in terms of continually making right or wrong decisions that affect employees' lives and the survival of the business. As one errant move can spell the demise of the venture, fear is another aspect of the experience. Such fear can also be tied to events somewhat beyond the entrepreneur's control. One might fear the bank calling a loan, the landlord cancelling the lease, the supplier refusing to provide critical raw materials, or key customers switching to competitors. And faced with impending failure, Shepherd and colleagues (2009) describe an experience they label "anticipatory grief."

Entrepreneurship is a temporal experience, one with a fairly clear beginning but an unclear middle or ending (Cope and Watts, 2000). Many of the developments that occur over time are unplanned and unexpected. Especially in the early days of a venture, cause-and-effect relationships are not well-defined and are often elusive, while there is ongoing exposure to newness and novelty (Sarasvathy, 2004). Each day can represent an entirely new set of problems and challenges. Exposure to novel phenomena can lead one to question assumptions and lessons learned as the entrepreneur struggles to make sense of things. Shane (2008) adds the observation that the early stages of venture formation can entail extreme velocity and volatility as the pace and diversity of stimuli continually tax the ability of the individual to cope.

Various observers have noted the importance of passion in entrepreneurial success (e.g., Smilor, 1997). Cardon et al. (2005) argue that such passion is borne out of enduring bonds of identification and attachment between entrepreneur and venture. It is a discrete emotion of high intensity and arousal that is nurtured and reinforced by the affective nature of the venture creation experience.

Given this set of conditions, it is not surprising that the experience takes a toll on the entrepreneur. Buttner (1992) demonstrates that entrepreneurs experience more stress, more health problems, and less ability to relieve work-related tension than managers. Certain levels of stress can lead to greater focus, clarity of purpose, and an orientation towards action. However, excessive stress impacts the ability to properly interpret developments and heightens the potential for emotions to drive decision-making. It can also produce various dysfunctional behaviors such as alcoholism, poor eating and sleeping habits, abuse of co-workers and family members, divorce, and engagement in unethical or illegal activities.

IDENTIFYING DESCRIPTORS OF THE AFFECTIVE EXPERIENCE

To get a richer sense of the affective nature of the new venture context, a study was undertaken by the authors for this volume. Specifically, a content analysis was conducted to identify words used to describe the entrepreneurial experience. The review was conducted using the following sources: (1) academic articles on venture creation appearing in the *Journal of Business Venturing*, *Entrepreneurship Theory and Practice*, and *Small*

BOX 6.1   DESCRIPTORS ASSOCIATED WITH ENTREPRENEURSHIP AS AN EXPERIENCE

Invigorating	Humiliating	Sense of having to
Disappointing	No rules to follow	outwork others
Powerful	Lonely	Fun
Exhausting	Adventurous	Empowering
Panic	Motivating	Burdensome
Sense of	Tedious	Chaotic
inadequacy	Passionate	Ambiguous
Energizing	Overwhelming	Intimidating
Joy	All-consuming	Difficult
Complex	Feeling of	Strange
Humbling	insignificance	Creative
Challenging	Frightening	Unstable
Demanding	Exciting	Dynamic
Uncertain	Empty	Threatening
Hopeful	Stressful	Feeling free
Alienating	Exhilarating	Terrifying
Self-fulfilling	Novel	Sense of being lost

Business Economics over a five-year period; (2) six leading entrepreneurship textbooks; and (3) 650 interviews of entrepreneurs conducted by trained MBA students over five years. These interviews focused on ventures between two and five years old, with at least ten employees, where no employee in the company was related to the interviewee. They employed a structured format to examine the entrepreneur's personal journey as he or she started and grew the business, and lasted an average of 90 minutes. To be retained for use in the second stage, a given descriptor had to appear at least three times. Where terms were clearly overlapping (e.g., motivating and motivational) a single adjective was used. Following this methodology, a total of 48 descriptors were produced. The final set of descriptors is itemized in Box 6.1.

The terms that emerged, such as stressful, fulfilling, uncontrollable, ambiguous, and all-consuming, suggest a multi-faceted experience that is both rich and intense. An examination of these descriptors suggests 14 of them would appear to reflect positive affect (e.g., joyful, hopeful, feeling free), another 24 are suggestive of negative affect (e.g., disappointing, intimidating, sense of being lost), and ten are more neutral terms (e.g., complex, humbling, novel). The stronger presence of negative terms is not necessarily suggestive that the overall venture creation experience is a negative one, only that it can be a difficult journey where some of the low points resonate at least in terms of how the experience is recalled or described.

TOWARDS UNDERLYING DIMENSIONALITY

While terms such as those in Box 6.1 reinforce the affective nature of entrepreneurial experiences, they also suggest a varied and diverse experience. Taken a step further, it may be possible to identify an underlying dimensionality to the venture creation experience. Work on consumer experiences by Mano and Oliver (1993) provides valuable insights. These authors provide extensive evidence that affective experiences can be described in terms of two primary dimensions: pleasantness and arousal. While other dimensions may exist, they tend to be unstable across studies. Pleasantness describes a stimulus or context that is agreeable, enjoyable, comfortable or pleasing. It is more positive than negative. Arousal is a reflection of a person's relative emotional intensity, fervor, stimulation or excitement. It regulates consciousness, attention, and information processing. Figure 6.1 illustrates these two dimensions as what we might call an "experience space."

In earlier work, Watson and Tellegen (1985) approach the configuration in Figure 6.1 as a circumplex. A 45-degree rotation of the pleasantness–arousal space produces two independent dimensions, labeled positive and negative affectivity, and engagement is positively correlated with these two axes, positioned at 45 degrees between them. Others (Cantor et al., 1991) have also found that affective valence and engagement level emerge as dominant factors in the structuring of experiences. In addition, particular emotions tend to load on the affective valence (e.g., optimistic–pessimistic, stressful–relaxed) and others on the level of engagement (e.g., active–passive, distant–intimate, exciting–boring).

Based on Mano and Oliver (1993), there could be an experience of moderately engaged negative affectivity (e.g., feelings of slight distress), such as person A in Figure 6.1; strongly engaged positive affectivity (e.g., feelings of elation) such as person C; neutral or nondescript affectivity (e.g., boredom) as with person B, or low arousal–low negative affect (e.g., calmness) such as person D. It would also seem plausible that there are stages to the venture experience, where an individual effectively moves around in the space, reflecting the highs and lows, stressful and less demanding points in time, and slower and faster periods of activity.

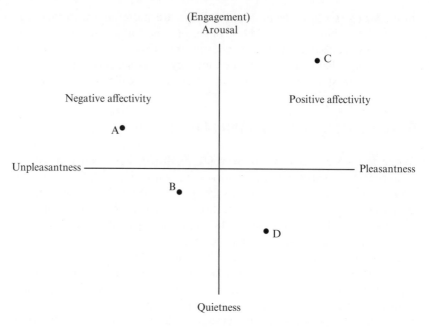

Source: Adapted from Mano and Oliver (1993).

Figure 6.1   The experience space

Consistent with this conceptualization, Morris et al. (2010) have system-atically assessed the applicability of the comprehensive set of descriptors in Table 6.1 to the entrepreneurial experience (see also Chapter 11). They demonstrate underlying dimensionality to the experience that reflects high levels of positive and negative affectivity. Factors such as exciting and pas-sionate reflected a strongly positive experience, while exhausting, threaten-ing, ambiguous, and tedious were indicative of a negative experience.

The volatility of the entrepreneurial experience and the likelihood of strong positive affect are supported in work on peak experience, peak performance, and flow. Schindehutte et al. (2006) found evidence that entrepreneurs experience episodes of superior functioning, periods that surpass normal levels of intensity, meaningfulness, and richness, and tran-scendent states of well-being characterized by total focus and absorption. Such episodes are reflective of an entrepreneurial experience filled with highs and lows.

Figure 6.2 takes us a step further and introduces the temporal nature of the entrepreneurial experience. The plotted points are suggestive of an entrepreneur effectively moving around in the space as he or she processes

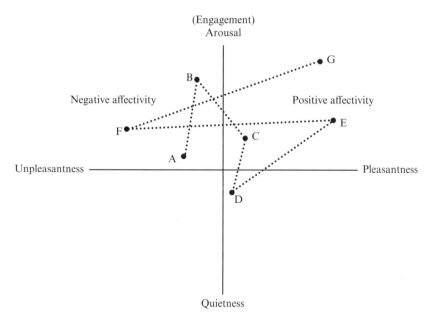

Source: Adapted from Mano and Oliver (1993).

Figure 6.2 *Temporal dynamics and the experience space*

events and streams in the venture creation experience. Here, we see an entrepreneur moving from an initial point (A) where he or she is trying to get the business launched, unable to generate enough resources, having difficulty making sales happen, and working out quality problems with products. The experience may be exciting, but is highly stressful, some-what unpleasant, and affect is generally negative. At a subsequent point in time (B), the entrepreneur is still struggling and unable to meet payroll. Stress levels remain high, arousal levels are extremely high, and affect is negative as the entrepreneur works intensely over long hours. Events continue to unfold to a point in time (C) where the entrepreneur is experiencing more consistent sales, a stable cash flow, and a much-needed loan has come through. Overall affect is positive, and arousal remains high but not as intense. And so the experience continues (points D through G), reflecting the highs and lows, stressful and less demanding times, slower and faster periods of activity. If we again think of the entrepreneurial experience in terms of peaks and valleys, then the relative volatility would seem especially pertinent in explaining movement around the experience space. Similarly, movement might be influenced by exposure to demands outside the entrepreneur's current knowledge, skills, and background, and the variance over time in the size of the knowledge gap as new experiential events are encountered.

ADDITIONAL CONSIDERATIONS

While this discussion has emphasized the occurrence of positive or negative affect in reacting to a stream of events, it is possible that both occur simultaneously. Earlier in the chapter, we noted the co-existence of mixed emotions, with the likelihood of a dominant affective orientation emerging (positive or negative). Larsen et al. (2001) note a general tendency for people to be either happy or sad, but observe instances where a given event elicited both happiness and sadness. Larsen et al. (2004) found simultaneous evidence of negative and positive affect when experiencing good outcomes that one anticipated could have been better, or bad ones that could have been worse. This bivariate experience could complicate the entrepreneur's processing of events, resulting in more moderate impacts on decisions entailing risk and change or outcome variables such as satisfaction.

Again returning to our earlier discussion, it should also be noted that the strength of the entrepreneur's affective reaction to an event is also influenced by his or her more permanent or enduring affective traits (e.g., a person who is more neurotic). These predispositions impact both which events generate a reaction, and the potential for that reaction to be magnified (Weiss and Beal, 2005). Hence a person high in neuroticism will react more strongly to negative events when they occur.

And finally, affect has implications for overall satisfaction with the entrepreneurial experience. Satisfaction ultimately results from an integrative assessment of the diversity, vitality, and richness of the events and streams that unfold as a venture emerges. There is strong evidence that affect is an antecedent to, and necessary for, satisfaction (Mano, 1997). Mano and Oliver (1993) further illustrate that satisfaction with an experience is predicated on assessments of both its instrumental or utilitarian performance (e.g., financial goals), and its aesthetic or hedonic performance (e.g., its intrinsically pleasing properties). The importance of aesthetic performance is especially important in high-arousal and high-engagement experiences, such as venture creation. As a result, personal assessments of the entrepreneurial life may be impacted by financial returns, but are more a function of how that life is aesthetically experienced. To the extent that venture creation provides a rich affective experience, it might be argued that the destination may indeed be the journey.

CONCLUSIONS

Central to experiencing is affect, or the feelings and emotions of the entrepreneur. Affect plays a dual role in impacting what people think and how they think. Forgas (1999, p. 593) explains, "affect is not incidental but an inseparable part of how we see and represent the world around us, the way we select, store and retrieve information, and the way we use stored knowledge structures in performing cognitive tasks." For their part, emotions occur involuntarily in response to novel aspects of an event. Emotional experiencing is linked to prior knowledge, beliefs, and appraisals about causes and consequences of an event. Causal thinking and goal appraisal occur continuously during the unfolding of an emotion or retrospectively when recalling emotionally meaningful events. Further, emotional (and cognitive) states are influenced by knowledge of approaching events and corresponding expectations.

In this chapter, we have explored the central role that affect plays in defining the experience of new venture creation. The entrepreneurial context is one where emotions and feelings are especially likely to play a meaningful part not only in defining the experience, but in explaining decisions, behaviors, and organizational outcomes. Environments with high levels of uncertainty, ambiguity, chaos, and complexity, and those compressed in time tend to elicit stronger affect, with a greater tendency for it to influence cognitive processes. Similarly, emotions and feelings are more likely to come into play in environments where one has significant amounts of time, energy, effort, money, reputation, and self-esteem at stake.

Despite its significance, affect only began to receive attention from entrepreneurship scholars in the past few years. Most of the work to date has been theoretical or conceptual, with frameworks, models, and research propositions being introduced, but relatively little empirical work. Yet, there is emerging evidence to suggest that a number of critical variables surrounding venture creation are impacted by affect. Among these are information search, opportunity recognition, persistence in pursuing an idea, risk proclivity, resource acquisition, ability to deal with stress, speed of decision-making, relative effort devoted to tasks requiring immediate attention versus those beyond immediate requirements, learning and skill enhancement, and creative problem-solving. Especially noteworthy in this regard is the favorable impact of positive affect on variables such as these.

We have also examined what it is actually like to create a new venture. When the entrepreneur is in the moment, experiencing the day-to-day developments as a venture is implemented, takes form, and hopefully becomes sustainable, he or she is experiencing novelty, volatility, uncertainty, ambiguity, emergence, lack of control, autonomy, pressure and stress. Of course, there are many different kinds of ventures and they vary in terms of the relative presence of these characteristics. Importantly, characteristics such as these give rise to a range of emotions and feelings. Based on a synthesis of perspectives from the literature and interviews with hundreds of entrepreneurs, 48 terms were identified to capture the affective nature of venture creation. Examples include "frightening," "joyful," "exhausting," "humiliating," and "empowering."

Building on work in psychology, we introduce the notion of an "experience space" to capture the structure of the entrepreneurial experience. In essence, a circumplex is built around two dimensions, affectivity valence and engagement level. Particular emotions will be associated with these two dimensions. The entrepreneur in effect moves around this space, experiencing highs and lows as he or she processes hundreds if not thousands of salient events as a venture unfolds. It is the processing of these events to which we turn in the next chapter.

REFERENCES

Akgün, A.E., H. Keskin and J. Byrne (2008), 'The moderating role of environmental dynamism between firm emotional capability and performance', *Journal of Organizational Change Management*, **21**(2): 230–52.

Ashforth, B.E. and R.H. Humphrey (1995), 'Emotion in the workplace: a reappraisal', *Human Relations*, **48**(2): 97–121.

Baron, R.A. (2008), 'The role of affect in the entrepreneurial process', *Academy of Management Review*, **33**(2): 328–40.

Bird, B. (1989), *Entrepreneurial Behavior*, London: Scott Foresman.

Boyd, D. and D. Gumpert (1983), 'Coping with entrepreneurial stress', *Harvard Business Review*, **61**(2): 44–64.

Buttner, H.E. (1992), 'Entrepreneurial stress: is it hazardous to your health?', *Journal of Managerial Issues*, **4**(2): 223–40.

Cantor, N., J. Norem, C. Langston, S. Zirkel, W. Fleeson and C. Cook-Flanagan (1991), 'Life tasks and daily life experience', *Journal of Personality*, **59**(3): 425–51.

Cardon, M.S., J. Wincent, J. Singh and M. Drnovsek (2005), 'Entrepreneurial passion: the nature of emotions in entrepreneurship', *Best conference papers*, Academy of Management Annual Conference, pp. 1–6.

Cope, J. and G. Watts (2000), 'Learning by doing: an exploration of experience, critical incidents and reflection in entrepreneurial learning', *International Journal of Entrepreneurial Behaviour & Research*, **6**(3): 104–24.

Cross, B. and A. Travaglione (2003), 'The untold story: is the entrepreneur of the 21st century defined by emotional intelligence?', *International Journal of Organizational Analysis*, **11**(3): 221–8.

Dulewicz, V. and M. Higgs (2000), 'Emotional intelligence: a review and evaluation study', *Journal of Managerial Psychology*, **15**(4): 341–72.

Fineman, S. (1999), 'Emotion and organising', in S. Clegg, C. Hardy and W. Nord (eds), *Studying Organisation: Theory and Method*, London: Sage.

Foo, M., M.A. Uy and R.A. Baron (2009), 'How do feelings influence effort? An empirical study of entrepreneurs' affect and venture effort', *Journal of Applied Psychology*, **94**(4): 1086–94.

Forgas, J.P. (1999), 'On feeling good and being rude: affective influences on language use and request formulations', *Journal of Personality and Social Psychology*, **76**(6): 928–39.

Goleman, D. (1998), *Working with Emotional Intelligence*, London: Bloomsbury Publishing.

Goss, D. (2005), 'Schumpeter's legacy? Interaction and emotions in the sociology of entrepreneurship', *Entrepreneurship Theory and Practice*, **29**(2): 205–18.

Hayton, J.C. and M. Cholakova (2011), 'The role of affect in the creation and intentional pursuit of entrepreneurial ideas', *Entrepreneurship Theory and Practice*, accessed 17 November at http://onlinelibrary.wiley.com/journal/10.1111/%28ISSN%291540-6520/earlyview.

Jayasinghe, K., D. Thomas and D. Wickramasinghe (2008), 'Bounded emotionality in entrepreneurship: an alternative framework', *International Journal of Entrepreneurial Behaviour & Research*, **14**(4): 242–58.

Larsen, J.T., A.P. McGraw and J. Cacioppo (2001), 'Can people feel happy and sad at the same time?', *Journal of Personality and Social Psychology*, **81**(4): 684–96.

Larsen, J.T., A.P. McGraw, B.A. Mellers and J.T. Cacioppo (2004), 'The agony of victory and thrill of defeat: mixed emotional reactions to disappointing wins and relieving losses', *Psychological Science*, **15**(5): 325–30.

Lerner, J.S. and D. Keltner (2001), 'Fear, anger, and risk', *Journal of Personality and Social Psychology*, **81**(1): 146–59.

Mano, H. (1997), 'Affect and persuasion', *Psychology and Marketing*, **14**(4): 315–36.

Mano, H. and R.L. Oliver (1993), 'Assessing the dimensionality and structure of the consumption experience', *Journal of Consumer Research*, **20**(3): 451–66.

McClelland, D.C. (1986), 'Characteristics of successful entrepreneurs', *Journal of Creative Behavior*, **21**(3): 219–33.

Moltz, B. (2003), *You Need to be a Little Crazy*, Chicago, IL: Dearborn Publishing.

Morris, M.H., J. Allen, D. Kuratko and D. Brannon (2010), 'Experiencing family business creation: differences between founders, non-family managers and founders of non-family firms', *Entrepreneurship Theory and Practice*, **34**(6): 1057–84.

Podoynitsyna, K., H. Van der Bij and M. Song (2011), 'The role of mixed emotions in the risk perception of novice and serial entrepreneurs', *Entrepreneurship Theory and Practice*, accessed 17 November at http://onlinelibrary.wiley.com/journal/10.1111/%28ISSN%291540-6520/earlyview.

Rhee, K.S. and R.J. White (2007), 'The emotional intelligence of entrepreneurs', *Journal of Small Business and Entrepreneurship*, **20**(4): 409–26.

Sarasvathy, S.D. (2004), 'The questions we ask and the questions we care about: reformulating some problems in entrepreneurship research', *Journal of Business Venturing*, **19**(5): 707–17.

Schindehutte, M., M.H. Morris and J. Allen (2006), 'Beyond achievement: entrepreneurship as extreme experience', *Small Business Economics*, **27**(4): 49–68.

Schmitt, B. (2010), 'Experiential marketing', *Journal of Marketing Management*, **15**(1–3): 53–67.

Shane, S. (2008), *The Illusions of Entrepreneurship*, New Haven, CT: Yale University Press.

Shepherd, D.A., J. Wiklund and J.M. Haynie (2009), 'Moving forward: balancing the financial and emotional costs of business failure', *Journal of Business Venturing*, **24**(2): 134–48.

Slovic, P., M. Finucane, E. Peters and D.G. MacGregor (2002), 'Rational actors or rational fools: implications of the affect heuristic for behavioral economics', *Journal of Socio-Economics*, **31**(4): 329–42.

Smilor, R.W. (1997), 'Entrepreneurship: reflections on a subversive activity', *Journal of Business Venturing*, **12**(3): 341–6.

Watson, D. and A. Tellegen (1985), 'A consensual structure of mood', *Psychological Bulletin*, **98**(2): 219–35.

Weiss, H.M. and D. Beal (2005), 'Reflections on affective events theory', in N.M. Askanasy, W. Zerbe and C.E.J. Hartel (eds), *Research on Emotion in Organizations: The Effect of Affect in Organizational Settings, Vol. 1*, Oxford: Elsevier Ltd, pp. 1–21.

7. A conceptual model of entrepreneurial experiencing*

> To "learn from experience" is to make a backward and forward connection
> between what we do to things and what we enjoy or suffer from things in
> consequence. Under such conditions, doing becomes a trying; an experiment
> with the world to find out what it is like; the undergoing becomes instruction –
> discovery of the connection of things.
> (John Dewey, 1916)

INTRODUCTION

Experiencing represents the essence of entrepreneurship. It is difficult, if not impossible, to grasp the reality of venture creation, particularly at a micro-level, without considering how the disjointed series of novel events encountered along the entrepreneurial path are received by and reacted to by the founder of a venture. Stated differently, it is not enough to simply describe venture creation as stressful or ambiguous or uncertain. The real question concerns how the entrepreneur encounters and processes the various events that give rise to ambiguity or stress or uncertainty. Yet, relatively little is known regarding what it is like to be in the moment as a venture unfolds.

The founder of a venture, particularly if it is his or her first venture, is attempting to learn how to be an entrepreneur. Engaged in creating something where there was nothing, he or she is acting out a multiplicity of roles for which there are no scripts. All the while, the entrepreneur is affecting change (e.g., in markets, value chains, the competitive environment, technology, a local economy) while operating within a context where one has relatively little control. Things are neither well-defined nor deterministic, but instead they are emergent.

If we accept that entrepreneurship is an emergent phenomenon (Gartner, 1993), then neither the entrepreneur who is in the middle of creating the venture, nor the scholar who is observing the venture as it takes form, has an accurate idea of what will ultimately emerge. In fact, what takes form is heavily influenced by the ongoing behaviors and actions of the emerging entrepreneur, and these behaviors and actions are not carefully planned in advance, or merely the result of rational analysis. They are heavily influenced by events as they occur and the extent to which these events are experienced as threatening, exhausting, ambiguous, exciting, tedious, humiliating or complicated, among other possibilities. Venture creation can be experienced as slow or fast, easy or hard, intense or passive, positive or negative.

To develop richer insights into the nature of entrepreneurship as it is experienced, we need a framework for capturing how experiencing fits within the context of venture creation. Toward this end, in this chapter we introduce a conceptual model that identifies key inputs that define what gets experienced and then link these inputs to experiential processing, which in turn is linked to entrepreneurial outcomes. A number of propositions are made concerning key relationships among variables in the model. A model such as the one presented in this chapter represents a beginning point for efforts to demonstrate how approaching entrepreneurship as it is experienced can shed light upon many of the other phenomena that contemporary entrepreneurship researchers are focused upon. The model also serves as a foundation for a number of the chapters to follow, as we elaborate upon these variables and relationships.

A CONCEPTUAL MODEL

Capturing the entrepreneurial experience is an elusive undertaking, both conceptually and from a measurement standpoint. While we will turn to the measurement issues in subsequent chapters, we begin by addressing conceptual issues and attempt to bring some structure to the way we think about the venture creation experience. Figure 7.1 represents a model that will serve to guide our efforts.

The model, in essence, first suggests that the entrepreneur comes to the venture with a cumulative stock of life experiences. As the venture unfolds, it produces any number of salient events and event streams, and these can vary in terms of volume, velocity, and volatility (see Chapter 1). The velocity and volatility of the entrepreneurial experience, and the likelihood of a strong impact on the entrepreneur, is supported in work by Schindehutte and colleagues (2006) on peak experience, peak performance, and flow. These events are subject to experiential processing, resulting in affective reactions and social learning, both of which influence the decision-making behaviors of the entrepreneur. Affective outcomes and ongoing behaviors, in turn, impact the development of the entrepreneur and the kind of venture that emerges. Let us further examine each of the elements in the model.

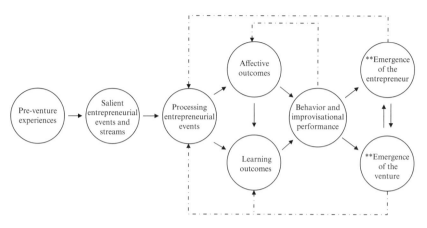

Notes:
** The solid arrows between the emergence of the entrepreneur and the emergence of the venture demonstrate the connection between the two. Please note that emergence does not follow the preceding boxes, but is continuous and ongoing, happening in tandem with the other boxes (variables).
Solid lines = direct relationships.
Dotted lines = feedback loops.

Figure 7.1   *Conceptual model of entrepreneurial experiencing*

Prior Experience

The term "experience" has been used by entrepreneurship scholars in five ways: (1) the outcome of involvement in previous entrepreneurial activities (Baron and Ensley, 2006); (2) experientially acquired knowledge and skills that result in entrepreneurial know-how and practical wisdom (Corbett, 2007); (3) the sum total of things that have happened to a founder over their career (Shane and Khurana, 2003); (4) the collective set of events that constitute the entrepreneurial process (Bhave, 1994); and (5) direct observation of, or participation in, activities associated with an entrepreneurial context (Cope and Watts, 2000). Of these, the most common usage is to describe prior knowledge and skills gained either in business or when creating ventures. As an antecedent condition, researchers have emphasized the role of prior experience as a factor in explaining self-efficacy (Baron and Ensley, 2006), entrepreneurial intentions (Krueger, 2007), information processing (Cooper and Folta, 1995), business practices (Cliff et al., 2006); learning from failure (Shepherd, 2003), habitual entrepreneurs (Westhead et al., 2005), and meta-cognition in decision-making (Haynie et al., 2010).

The greatest amount of attention has been devoted to prior experiences in corporate management and in venture creation within particular industries, both of which have been associated with venture performance (Gimeno et al., 1997). Especially noteworthy in this regard is work on serial entrepreneurs. Prior entrepreneurial experience enhances both the ability to recognize viable opportunities and to overcome liability of newness challenges as a venture is created (Politis, 2005). As with the study of meta-cognition, prior experience can be expected to play a role both in determining which events are processed and the manner in which they are processed.

The significance attached to a given experience, no matter how novel, is influenced by one's stock of previous experiences (Reuber and Fischer, 1999). Weiss and Cropanzano (1996), in their work on affective events theory, suggest that this significance is tied to the degree to which an event is perceived to be beneficial or harmful to the entrepreneur's well-being. Thus, the relatively higher success rates that habitual entrepreneurs demonstrate may be tied to their ability to better interpret and place saliency on particular events, suggesting novice entrepreneurs are less able to put a particular event in proper context. A possible implication is that the "volume" of salient events that constitute the venture creation experience will be lower for those having more prior entrepreneurial experience. The entrepreneur is more likely to properly interpret the typicality, meaning, and impact, and hence the significance of a given event. Further, prior experience can be expected to influence the affective response to an event, where the tendency to get frustrated, feel stress, or otherwise respond will be tempered by one's experiential background (Baron, 2008). The ability to focus on or emotionally respond to fewer salient events suggests the entrepreneur is experiencing less velocity in terms of the pace at which novel events must be processed. Also, when interpreting the event, greater expertise can lead to more reliance on exploratory modes of cognitive processing and employment of effectual reasoning (Politis, 2005). The result might be that more prior experience results in less "volatility" in the entrepreneurial experience, where volatility refers to the relative intensity due to the peaks and valleys in the series of events given salience by the entrepreneur. Based on this discussion, we offer the following proposition:

Proposition 1   The stock of prior experiences an entrepreneur brings to a new venture affects the saliency attached to unfolding events as they occur, serving to define the volume, velocity, and volatility of events that constitute the venture creation experience. All other things being equal, the greater this stock, the less will be the volume, velocity, and volatility of events.

Salient Entrepreneurial Events and Streams

Experiences occur at points in time and over time. Individual moments of experience, which we have called "events" (see Chapter 1), represent parts of an emerging structure. Many thousands of events occur in a given week or month of the venture creation experience. Our interest, however, is events that are salient, meaning they diverge from the norm and are given serious attention. The question becomes one of determining what makes an event salient.

A salient event is one that implies changes for what one is currently experiencing (Weiss and Cropanzano, 1996). Hence, significance is a function of a number of criteria, including the event's novelty, expectedness, complexity, consistency with the individual's assumptions and knowledge base, and perceived implications. Of these, novelty is likely the most critical factor. Something novel must be interpreted to give it meaning and sense must be made of it. However, any of these criteria could contribute to the saliency attached to an event, and not all need be present. Thus, the need to sell some personal asset to keep the business going could be expected or unexpected, but dealing with it, especially the first time it occurs, is a novel experience, and so the event is likely to be salient. Similarly, an event could have been anticipated and may have occurred before, such as the loss of a key account, but it remains salient because of its serious implications for company survival.

Weiss and Beal (2005) argue that there are two stages involved in appraising a given event. The first of these finds the event being assessed for relevance to well-being in simple positive and negative terms. This initial assessment includes an importance evaluation that fuels the intensity of emotional reaction. The secondary appraisal focuses on context and associated consequences, attributions, and coping potential, and triggers discrete emotions.

As events occur during the launch and early years of a venture, some will be strongly related in terms of their underlying themes or focus, and so we have referred to a cumulative set of related events as a stream of experience. A stream is a series of episodes that have a coherent thematic organization (Beal et al., 2005). There is a path-dependent quality to the stream, such that each instance interacts with the next in the creation of the stream. A stream will vary in duration depending on the boundaries arbitrarily assigned to an experience. It will also vary with regard to the volume, velocity, and volatility of the events that are embedded in the stream. An example of a stream might include building a team, which could include taking on a partner, a number of key hires, the need to fire an employee who does not fit, having a vital employee hired away, and critical mistakes made as the entrepreneur learns how to delegate and empower others. In effect, streams are defined by the entrepreneur in terms of sets of events that he or she conceptually links to one another, particularly as new and novel events occur and he or she looks for a reference point in trying to interpret and make sense of these new events.

One might expect, in a new venture context, that streams would tend to relate to the different roles the entrepreneur plays (e.g., a selling role, a financing role, a supervising role). However, streams will not necessarily follow this sort of functional delineation or categorization. It could be that the entrepreneur associates a set of events with one another for reasons unrelated to the task involved or the skills required in addressing those events. For instance, a stream of events might have the shared characteristic of bringing the entrepreneur joy and making him or her take pride in the venture.

The total set of events and streams associated with the creation of a given venture form the experience stock. Overall assessments can be made by the entrepreneur (e.g., positive–negative, intense–passive) of this stock. This evaluation is dependent upon the memories (events and streams) recalled and included in the experience stock. It is idiosyncratic in nature, such that two people are not likely to delineate the parameters of the same type of experience in similar ways. Each memory may be weighted differently depending on the relative importance assigned to it and by factors influencing which memories are recalled (Bandura, 1986). Other relevant issues might include the relative concentration or dispersion of key events across time, and the tendency for seminal events to come earlier or later as the venture unfolds. At a given moment of recall, then, there is a stock of experience used to define overall feelings about the venture creation experience. Based on this discussion, the following proposition is put forward:

Proposition 2   Venture creation represents an uncertain temporal experience, the parameters of which are delineated by the entrepreneur as he or she uniquely constructs and processes a stock of salient events and event streams.

Processing Entrepreneurial Events

The entrepreneur attempts to impose structure on events as they are received into consciousness, making them intelligible. Experiencing, then, centers on the processing of events. This processing involves the interaction of cognition, emotions, feelings, and bodily reactions within the individual. Further, this interaction occurs at multiple levels as the information generated from experiencing is processed (Epstein et al., 1996).

Additionally, processing of experiences results in efforts at meaning-making and sense-making, which can produce learning and new organizational routines.

Consider particular salient events, such as having the firm's product fail when being used by a major customer, achieving the first month of profitability, the spoiling of a large volume of inventory, or embezzlement of a significant amount of money by an employee. Each of these will elicit cognitive reactions, such as an analysis of why the event happened or greater mental focus. They will likely generate emotional responses, such as fear, joy, or anger, which can vary in intensity. And there may be various physiological reactions such as sleeplessness, headaches, or adrenaline-induced energy.

Based on the interaction between cognitive, affective, and physiological elements as events and streams of experience play out, entrepreneurs give meaning and make sense of their context. The meaning of a particular experience is a cognitive construal of a coordinated set of actions (Barsalou et al., 2003). The recursive process of meaning-making involves situated activity that depends on the part/whole relationship between the entrepreneur and characteristics of the situation. In this sense, entrepreneurship is a sequence of performative and transformative events that are interpreted and cohere through time as the individual attempts to impose meaning. The entrepreneur derives meaning by translating experiences into how he or she feels and thinks, while meaning also acts as a guide and explanation for his or her experience. Knowing and doing are interlocked, inseparable, and embedded in the context. The temporal nature of experiencing has important implications here, as the meaning of an action differs based on the point in time from which it is observed.

Sense-making is the process of creating situational awareness and understanding amid complex, uncertain situations so decisions can be made. It is a "motivated, continuous effort to understand connections (among people, places, events) in order to anticipate their trajectories and act effectively" (Klein et al., 2006, p. 71). Sense-making relates to deliberate "what if" reasoning related to action taken to make events happen. As Weick and colleagues (2005) note, sense-making in organizations often occurs amid intense emotional experience. Unexpected or disruptive events force individuals to make sense of ambiguous stimuli in ways consistent with their own identity needs. The entrepreneur predicts alternative courses of action using objective information obtained by deliberative reasoning or recall of prior knowledge and experiences (Haynie et al., 2010). Based on this discussion, we propose the following:

Proposition 3 Experiential processing involves interactive effects between physiological, affective, and cognitive reactions to salient events.

Sense-making on the part of the entrepreneur is derived from these interactions as events are processed over time.

Learning Outcomes

Entrepreneurs learn from events as they unfold. A distinction exists, then, between the events experienced by an entrepreneur and the knowledge acquired from those events through learning. Learning is more than simply grasping and interpreting objective knowledge. The entrepreneur is immersed in events, generating knowledge as a function of his or her interactions with the venture context and larger environment. Politis (2005) explains entrepreneurial learning as a transformation process applied to experiences that is continually created and recreated. Minniti and Bygrave (2001, p. 8) refer to "the process of updating the probabilities of choosing any particular action as new information on its consequences is received."

Learning is also tied to the nature of the events being experienced. There is evidence, for instance, that learning is greater the more diversity there is in the portfolio of events to which the individual is exposed over time (McCall et al., 1988). Reuber and Fischer (1999) posit that the more novel events are relative to the entrepreneur's stock of experience at any point in time, the greater the learning. In addition, learning is greater with the first or second encounter with a particular type of event, such that diminishing returns ultimately set in.

In a venture creation context, Politis (2005) examines the manner in which entrepreneurs transform experiences into knowledge, arguing they follow either an exploitative or explorative path. Exploitation centers on learning what has worked in the past and finding ways to replicate it. Exploration involves learning by exploring new possibilities. Exploration involves a broader and wider scope, while exploitation entails a narrower, more local scope. Extant research on affect and cognitive processes contends that positive affect increases one's scope of attention by encouraging people to play and experiment (Carver, 2003). Fredrickson (1998) asserts that positive affect increases a person's thought–action repertoire by signaling that the environment is a safe place to experiment. In contrast, negative affect signals that something is wrong and encourages an individual to focus more narrowly on one's current domain. Gasper and Clore (2002) found that individuals who experience positive affect apply a global approach toward their immediate environment while negative affect results in the use of a more local approach. Basso and colleagues (1996) found that personality traits related to negative affect such as anxiety and depression were associated with a local bias (narrowed attentional focus) while traits linked with positive affect such as optimism related to a global bias (broadened focus). Based on this discussion of learning outcomes, the following propositions are offered:

Proposition 4   Learning outcomes are the result of experiential processing, where the diversity and novelty of the stock of events give rise to enhanced learning.

Proposition 5   Positive and negative affect will influence the global or local direction of the entrepreneur's processing of events. Events strong in positive affect will drive the global or explorative learning direction while events strong in negative affect will drive the local or more exploitative learning.

Affective Outcomes

While a key outcome of experiencing is learning, it is not the only outcome. For its part, learning is ongoing and subject to change and modification. New experiences produce data that challenge earlier lessons. Cumulative knowledge at any point in time can be markedly inadequate for dealing with emerging developments or encounters with novelty. More fundamentally, any number of reactions and behaviors occur separate from, or in spite of, whatever learning is taking place.

Emotions and feelings are especially important in this regard. Observers in different disciplines have demonstrated that experiential processing results in outcomes that are predominantly affective (e.g., Feldman, 1995; Mano and Oliver, 1993). Experiences are felt and produce emotional responses. Affect levels fluctuate over time, with patterns of affect traceable to endogenous (e.g., known cycles in mood or affective disposition) and exogenous (e.g., salient events) components. Affective responses are especially strong when events occur that fundamentally undermine or contrast with the individual's beliefs, understandings, and sense of self (Weiss and Cropanzano, 1996).

Further insights can be gained by considering the work on affect by Mano and Oliver (1993). These authors build on extensive evidence from psychology that affective experiences can be described in terms of two primary dimensions: pleasantness and arousal. Other dimensions may exist but tend to be unstable across studies. Pleasantness describes a stimulus or context that is agreeable, enjoyable, comfortable, or pleasing. It can be more positive or negative. Arousal is a reflection of a person's relative emotional intensity, fervor, stimulation or excitement. It regulates consciousness, attention, and information processing. Further, Watson and Tellegen (1985) approach this configuration as a circumplex. They suggest that a 45-degree rotation of the pleasantness–arousal space produces two primary independent dimensions, labeled positive and negative affectivity, and that engagement is positively correlated with these two axes, positioned at 45 degrees between them. Others (Cantor et al., 1991) have also found that affective valence and level of engagement emerge as dominant factors in the structuring of emotional experiences. In addition, particular emotions tend to load on the affective valence (e.g., optimistic–pessimistic, stressful–relaxed) and others on the level of engagement (e.g., active–passive, distant–intimate, exciting–boring).

Overall, evaluations of the entrepreneurial experience ultimately reflect an integrative assessment of the diversity, vitality, and richness of the events and streams that unfold as a venture emerges. There is strong evidence that positive affect is an antecedent to, and necessary for, satisfaction (Mano, 1997; Weiss and Cropanzano, 1996). Mano and Oliver (1993) further illustrate that satisfaction with an experience is predicated on assessments of both its instrumental or utilitarian performance (e.g., financial goals), and its aesthetic or hedonic performance (e.g., its intrinsically pleasing properties). The importance of aesthetic performance is especially important in high-arousal and high-engagement experiences. Applied to venture creation, personal assessments of entrepreneurial events and streams are a function of how those events and streams are aesthetically experienced. Based on this discussion of affective outcomes, the following proposition is offered:

Proposition 6 The ongoing processing of experiential events impacts the entrepreneur's affective state, characterized in terms of positivity/ negativity and levels of engagement. Where this processing results in more positive and intense affect, satisfaction with the entrepreneurial experience will be higher.

Behavior and Improvisational Performance

Our model posits that learning and affective outcomes directly influence entrepreneurial behaviors. These behaviors tend to be improvisational in nature (Hmieleski and Corbett, 2008). Politis (2005) concludes that knowledge derived from experiencing first and foremost has an influence on the strategic choices made by entrepreneurs. One possibility is that learning leads to employment of trusted heuristics and routinized behaviors once the entrepreneur figures out what works, and can eventually produce inertia within the venture. Salient events serve to disrupt this flow, however, and this volatility can foster discovery through experimentation and improvisation. Sarasvathy (2001) demonstrates that encountering a stream of unexpected events results in a greater reliance on effectual reasoning, experimentation, creativity in decision-making and value creation.

Intuition plays a role here. Johannisson (1998), in examining entrepreneurship as action learning, argues that the stock of concrete experiences contributes to the formation of an intuitive capacity, which can be used to produce analogies when addressing unexpected developments or events as they arise. This sort of repertoire becomes the basis for interpreting and making decisions about unexpected situations deemed to be categorically similar to past events, and hence for the formation of schema that serve as maps to guide behaviors.

Learning is not limited to the venture. As the entrepreneur learns things about himself or herself, such as his or her comfort level with ambiguity, risk tolerance, ability to handle stress, and need for control, decision-making is likely to be impacted (Bandura, 1986). Willingness to innovate, expand operations, invest in new technologies, or move into unfamiliar markets will vary depending on what one has come to understand about their own capabilities, values, and personal needs.

All experiences share the common feature of a central actor who is "in the moment." But a distinction can be drawn based on whether the individual is an active participant in the event and how their participation affects what is being experienced. The entrepreneurial experience centers on the critical roles of performance and transformation in an environment with relatively little control. The venture context becomes a medium for performance. The individual, as active participant in streams of experience, is performing in fund-raising events, marketing events, human resource management events, and so forth. This performance is more complex than simple acting, as the entrepreneur does not know in advance what he or she is going to do – especially given that what he or she does is influenced by emotional inputs that arise in the midst of the event. Existing within the work, he or she is constructing reality. To paraphrase Bruner (1986, p. 25), entrepreneurs not only construct their worlds, but watch themselves doing the construction and then enter and believe in their constructed worlds. So, each event is an improvisational performance that is lived through and felt, with uncertain outcomes. But the performance of an entrepreneur must ultimately result in new combinations – in the transformation of resources, business models (mental frameworks), and ongoing transformation of a venture. Emerging in a non-deterministic manner, the venture is continually forming. The same is happening to the entrepreneur.

Affective outcomes also influence the course a venture takes. Baron (2008) argues that the impact of affect on behavior is especially likely in

Entrepreneurship as experience

uncertain, less predictable environments and when pursuing entrepreneurial tasks. The emergent nature of a new venture is such that formulaic approaches and established scripts are not effective, and, hence, owners and managers must "make it up as they go along" (p. 329). He concludes that affective states can influence the individual's perceptions of the external world, levels of creativity, use of heuristics in decision-making, memory, motives, and cognitive strategies. Further, there is an impact on speed of decision-making and choices regarding resource acquisition, development of skills and social networks, and how to respond to environmental dynamics.

In assessing the impact on behavior of affective reactions to events, a distinction can be drawn between affect-driven and judgment-driven behaviors (Weiss and Beal, 2005). The former includes behaviors, decisions, and judgments that are proximal consequences of being in a particular affective state. The latter introduces evaluative judgments, or attitudes (which themselves are influenced by affective reactions), and is the consequence of decision processes where the context is part of the decision matrix. Accordingly, seminal events can occur that generate strong affective responses that influence how subsequent events are interpreted and the ongoing actions of the entrepreneur. Earlier experiences can create biases, preoccupations, and priorities that determine the subsequent willingness to incur debt, work with partners, interact with certain suppliers, or engage in any number of other behaviors.

While both positive and negative affect influence behavior, evidence suggests that negative emotional reactions have disproportionately stronger effects (Taylor, 1994) and thus may have a greater influence on favorable and unfavorable outcomes of the experience. Negative events produce stronger mobilization responses in terms of physiological, affective, cognitive, and behavioral activity than positive ones, taxing individual resources more than positive and neutral events (Weiss and Beal, 2005). We can posit behavioral outcomes from quadrants representing combinations of valence and engagement. Consistent with Baron (2008), the entrepreneur experiencing positive affect/high arousal may be more likely to take risks, innovate, and approach the future optimistically. Learning can also be enhanced. A positive affect/low arousal state might produce less risk-taking, innovation, and experimentation, and a lower willingness to persevere. Negative affect/high arousal should lead to more adaptive experimentation as the entrepreneur attempts to address adversity, and a heightened need for control. In a negative affect/low arousal state, there may be a tendency to withdraw effort. Low arousal could increase the probability of creating lifestyle over growth ventures. This discussion can be captured in the following propositions:

Proposition 7a　Event streams that are more disruptive (i.e., higher velocity and volatility) will produce (i) more intense and stronger affective responses, and (ii) greater reliance on improvisational behavior.

Proposition 7b　Affective reactions to event streams that are more positive and intense will result in a greater tendency to engage in improvisational behaviors that reflect greater innovation and risk-taking as the venture unfolds.

Emergence of the Entrepreneur

Valliere and O'Reilly (2007) draw an analogy between entrepreneurs and mountaineers, pointing to commonalities such as goal-setting, risk, and resource constraints. Yet, what is missed in comparing how entrepreneurship is *like* mountain climbing is that both are individualistic experiences, and the structure of these experiences forms the person, just as the person forms the experience. The entrepreneur is an active player in the experience – not simply a passenger on a journey across time. He or she is a participant in the formation of reality. It is through the lens of his or her experience that the entrepreneur interprets life events and constructs a sense of self.

Those creating their first venture often have little in their backgrounds to prepare them to be an entrepreneur. Moreover, considerable variability exists in individual motives for venture creation. If we consider work on traits and skills of entrepreneurs, we find an emphasis on tolerance of ambiguity, calculated risk-taking, independence, ability to learn, social skills, and adaptability, among others (e.g., Bird, 1989). Yet, the individual does not necessarily start with such characteristics. As the context itself is filled with events that are ambiguous, uncertain, and require adaptability, it is possible that exposure to such conditions results in self-development as the entrepreneur learns to cope, especially when these events give rise to strong negative and positive affect. The individual does not start as an entrepreneur but becomes one.

The characteristics of the entrepreneurial context pose unique challenges for finding meaning. As we have seen, meaning-making is a sensory process that includes cognitive, emotional, and physiological reactions to experiences as the entrepreneur constructs knowledge. Constructs are formed regarding oneself and the venture, which subsequently drive actions. As an individual assigns meaning to experiences, he or she is putting them in context with the rest of his or her life and exemplar experiences (Weick et al., 2005). The entrepreneur is placing them in an existing mental classification schema, relying on experience in securing and shaping a personal identity in the face of disruptive and often highly emotional events that influence knowledge construction (Murnieks, 2007). The entrepreneur is being continually reconstructed in real time through mutual entrepreneur–venture interaction. Thus, Polkinhorne (1991) suggests that identity is constructed by the iterative best-fitting together of remembered events into plots, while Downing (2005) concludes that identity is produced simultaneously with organization.

The nature of the affective experience may require the individual to build a new mental framework, one that enables development of an entrepreneurial mindset. Heuristics and cognitive mechanisms previously learned must be abandoned, which does not happen easily. The new framework finds the individual revisiting deceptively simple questions about what he or she believes to be true about himself or herself, the venture, the market, and other aspects of the emerging context. New meanings are arrived at in a manner that finds emotion interacting with cognition and physiology. Hence, Cardon and colleagues (2009) emphasize the significant role of entrepreneurial passion in catalyzing identity. The individual is becoming something; an identity is being created. The entrepreneur is constructing new knowledge, which produces an enlightened understanding of self and venture by seeing new meaning in terms of value that can be created, what the product can represent, company vision and values, and more.

Proposition 8   The development of key personal characteristics associated with entrepreneurs (e.g., tolerance of ambiguity, calculated risk-taking, achievement motivation) is facilitated by the ongoing processing of salient events as a venture unfolds.

Proposition 9   The likelihood of the individual developing an entrepreneurial mindset is greater where experiential processing results in more intense and positive affective states.

Emergence of the Venture

The uncontrollable nature of the venture creation process suggests that what is successfully created is likely to differ meaningfully from what was initially planned. Changes that occur in organizations are often more emergent than predictable (Plowman et al., 2007). Many actions are unplanned and reflect situational conditions and encounters with novelty. The path to a sustainable venture involves considerable trial and error. The ability to recognize and address errors, when in the midst of experiencing them, is tied to how the individual is processing immediate events, connecting them to past events, and anticipating the future. This processing includes the interplay of rational analysis, positive and negative affect, biases and perceptual distortions, bodily responses, and more. It can be difficult to assign meaning to cues, especially where experienced events are novel. The resultant stream of actions (or inactions) can profoundly impact the venture. A richer understanding of entrepreneurship requires that we focus on the creation of structure out of experiential events, not the creation of events out of structure. Thus, affective events define the structure of entrepreneurship, rather than being a by-product of that structure.

The entrepreneur's risk orientation is an example of a factor affecting the sort of venture that emerges. One's risk orientation is not static, and can be influenced by ongoing experiencing. A useful perspective is the "risk as feelings" hypothesis developed by Loewenstein and colleagues (2001), which posits that individuals react at a gut level to risky situations, and the reaction is influenced by anticipated and experienced emotions. Thus, where entrepreneurs find venture creation filled with peak experiences and flow, their actions might be expected to reflect more risk, while an experience characterized by low arousal affect might lead the entrepreneur to be more risk averse.

Also relevant are the entrepreneur's goals for the type of venture they create. The way in which a person experiences events is influenced by what they are trying to accomplish (Magnusson, 1981). Events that are important for goal accomplishment will be experienced as more emotionally involving. Yet, as experiences are processed, goals are subject to modification (Harlow and Cantor, 1994). The adaptive nature of goals establishes parameters around the kind of venture that satisfies the entrepreneur. Streams of experiences resulting in higher engagement and more positive affect can lead to more ambitious goals for the activity or behavior in question (ibid.). Thus, experience-informed goals have much to do with whether what was intended as a lifestyle venture becomes a high-growth firm, or vice versa. Such temporally-based changes in growth orientation are common, though not well understood.

In the final analysis, the relationship between the emergent entrepreneur and emergent venture is interactive and dynamic. The entrepreneur is creating while being created. Each significant instance that defines the venture experience is processed at multiple levels involving the interplay of cognition, affect, and physiology. Engagement level and affectivity valence vary with peaks and valleys of ongoing experiencing. Meaning-making and sense-making result in decisions and behaviors that determine what is being created. Ongoing actions and outcomes in turn represent new events and experience streams that influence thinking, feeling, and acting.

Meanwhile, identity is being formed and modified, and an entrepreneurial mindset emerges, further affecting behavioral choices. The emergence of the venture is captured in the following proposition:

Proposition 10   Experiential processing influences the type of venture that emerges. Individuals whose experiential processing results in more positive and intense affective states are more likely to create innovative, growth-oriented ventures.

CONCLUSIONS

Entrepreneurship represents a cumulative series of salient events, each of which is processed, contributes to sense-making, facilitates learning, influences affective states, and can produce behavioral responses. The overall venture creation experience will vary in the volume, velocity, and volatility of events processed by the entrepreneur, leading to an array of emotions and feelings characterized in terms of positive and negative affect. By focusing on the experienced event as the basic building block, we move away from an instrumental view (e.g., entrepreneurs create ventures and ventures produce outcomes), and allow for the possibility that the venture emerges, in the process developing the entrepreneur. This is consistent with the structuration view of Sarason et al. (2006), who portray the entrepreneur and opportunity as a duality where the entrepreneur is enabled/constrained by the opportunity identified and the structured processes of the venturing process, while the opportunity and the structuring processes are constructed and reconstructed in the entrepreneur's actions.

This discussion suggests an alternative way for conceptualizing the entrepreneur. Experience is the continuous present. It is pragmatic and it is personal. As an actor in an unscripted temporal performance and embedded within the venture context, the entrepreneur is continually encountering novelty. He or she constructs units of experience without controlling them. These experiences take on properties rooted in affect and emotion. Relying on experience-based concepts to create meaning, the entrepreneur filters inputs from the world to produce his or her own unique reality. In the constructivist sense, it could be argued that we can only know ourselves in terms of what we have previously created and experienced. The entrepreneur constructs and reconstructs both an identity and a venture by applying motivation, intention, and affective reactions to past and present experiences and the anticipated future.

Approached in this manner, we begin to focus on the entrepreneurial journey itself as an exploratory activity that leads to development of the venture and the entrepreneur. The perceptions, beliefs, time horizons, goals, and actions of entrepreneurs are rooted in the unique way they experience. Many entrepreneurial decisions are outgrowths of the highs and lows, negative and positive affect, and engagement levels that are woven into the fabric of temporal sequences of events. While choices are certainly influenced by analysis and rational thinking, they are also a product of one's sense that the emerging venture context represents an experience of panic, flow, difference-making, overwhelming burden, self-actualization, and so forth.

NOTE

* This chapter is adapted from Morris, M.H., D.F. Kuratko, M. Schindehutte and A. Murdock, 'Framing the entrepreneurial experience'. *Entrepreneurship Theory and Practice* (forthcoming), early view available at: http://onlinelibrary.wiley.com/journal/10.1111/(ISSN)1540-6520/earlyview; accessed 17 November 2011.

REFERENCES

Bandura, A. (1986), *Social Foundations of Thought and Action*, Englewood Cliffs, NJ: Prentice-Hall.

Baron, R.A. (2008), 'The role of affect in the entrepreneurial process', *Academy of Management Review*, **33**(2): 328–40.

Baron, R.A. and M. Ensley (2006), 'Opportunity recognition as the detection of meaningful patterns: novice and experienced entrepreneurs', *Management Science*, **52**(9): 1331–52.

Barsalou, L.W., W.K. Simmons and A. Barbey (2003), 'Grounding conceptual knowledge in modality-specific systems', *Trends in Cognitive Sciences*, **7**(2): 84–91.

Basso, M.R., B.K. Schefft, M.D. Ris and W.N. Dember (1996), 'Mood and global-local visual processing', *Journal of the International Neuropsychological Society*, **2**(3): 249–55.

Beal, D.J., H.M. Weiss, E. Barros and S. MacDermid (2005), 'An episodic process model of affective influences on performance', *Journal of Applied Psychology*, **90**(6): 1054–68.

Bhave, M.P. (1994), 'A process model of entrepreneurial venture creation', *Journal of Business Venturing*, **9**(3): 223–43.

Bird, B. (1989), *Entrepreneurial Behavior*, London: Scott Foresman.

Bruner, E. (1986), 'Experience and its expressions', in V. Turner and E. Bruner (eds), *The Anthropology of Experience*, Urbana, IL: University of Illinois Press, pp. 3–32.

Cantor, N., J. Norem, C. Langston, S. Zirkel, W. Fleeson and C. Cook-Flanagan (1991), 'Life tasks and daily life experience', *Journal of Personality*, **59**(3): 425–51.

Cardon, M.S., J. Wincent, J. Singh and M. Drnovsek (2009), 'The nature and experience of entrepreneurial passion', *Academy of Management Review*, **34**(3): 511–32.

Carver, C.S. (2003), 'Pleasure as a sign you can attend to something else: placing positive feelings within a general model of affect', *Cognition and Emotion*, **17**(2): 241–61.

Cliff, J., P. Jennings and R. Greenwood (2006), 'New to the game and questioning the rules: experiences and beliefs of founders of imitative vs. innovative firms', *Journal of Business Venturing*, **21**(5): 633–50.

Cooper, A.C. and T. Folta (1995), 'Entrepreneurial information search', *Journal of Business Venturing*, **10**(2): 107–22.

Cope, J. and G. Watts (2000), 'Learning by doing – an exploration of experience, critical incidents and reflection in entrepreneurial learning', *International Journal of Entrepreneurial Behaviour & Research*, **6**(3): 104–19.

Corbett, A.C. (2007), 'Learning asymmetries and discovery of entrepreneurial opportunities', *Journal of Business Venturing*, **22**(1): 97–114.

Dewey, J. (1916), *Democracy and Education*, New York: Macmillan, p. 140.

Downing, S. (2005), 'The social construction of entrepreneurship: narrative and dramatic processes in the coproduction of organizations and identities', *Entrepreneurship Theory and Practice*, **29**(2): 185–204.

Epstein, S., R. Pacini, V. Denes-Raj and H. Heier (1996), 'Individual differences in intuitive-experiential and analytical-rational thinking styles', *Journal of Personality and Social Psychology*, **71**(3): 390–415.

Feldman, L.A. (1995), 'Valence focus and arousal focus: individual differences in the structure of affective experiences', *Journal of Personality and Social Psychology*, **69**(2): 153–66.

Fredrickson, B.L. (1998), 'What good are positive emotions?', *Review of General Psychology*, **2**(3): 300–19.

Gartner, W.B. (1993), 'Words lead to deeds: toward an organizational emergence vocabulary', *Journal of Business Venturing*, **8**(3): 231–40.

Gasper, K. and G.L. Clore (2002), 'Attending to the big picture: mood and global versus local processing of visual information', *Psychological Science*, **13**(1): 34–40.

Gimeno, J., T. Folta, A. Cooper and C. Woo (1997), 'Survival of the fittest? Entrepreneurial human capital and the persistence of underperforming firms', *Administrative Science Quarterly*, **42**(4): 750–83.

Harlow, R. and N. Cantor (1994), 'Social pursuit of academics: side effects and spillover of strategic reassurance seeking', *Journal of Personality and Social Psychology*, **66**(2): 386–97.

Haynie, J.M., D.A. Shepherd, E. Mosakowski and P.C. Earley (2010), 'A situated metacognitive model of the entrepreneurial mindset', *Journal of Business Venturing*, **25**(2): 173–244.

Hmielski, K.M. and A. Corbett (2008), 'The contrasting interaction effects of improvisational behavior with entrepreneurial self-efficacy on new venture performance and entrepreneur work satisfaction', *Journal of Business Venturing*, **23**(4): 482–96.

Johannisson, B. (1998), 'Personal networks in emerging knowledge-based firms: spatial and functional patterns', *Entrepreneurship and Regional Development*, **10**(4): 297–312.

Klein, G., B. Moon and R. Hoffman (2006), 'Making sense of sensemaking 1: alternative perspectives', *IEEE Intelligent Systems*, **21**(4): 70–73.

Krueger, N.F. (2007), 'What lies beneath: the experiential essence of entrepreneurial thinking', *Entrepreneurship Theory and Practice*, **31**(1): 123–42.

Loewenstein, G.F., E.U. Weber, C.K. Hsee and N. Welch (2001), 'Risk as feelings', *Psychological Bulletin*, **127**(2): 267–86.

Magnusson, D. (1981), *Toward a Psychology of Situations*, Hillsdale, NJ: Lawrence Erlbaum.

Mano, H. (1997), 'Affect and persuasion', *Psychology & Marketing*, **14**(4): 315–36.

Mano, H. and R.L. Oliver (1993), 'Assessing the dimensionality and structure of the consumption experience', *Journal of Consumer Research*, **20**(3): 451–66.

McCall, M., M. Lombardo and A. Morrison (1988), *The Lessons of Experience*, New York: Lexington.

Minniti, M. and W. Bygrave (2001), 'A dynamic model of entrepreneurial learning', *Entrepreneurship Theory and Practice*, **25**(2): 5–16.

Murnieks, C.Y. (2007), 'Who am I? The quest for an entrepreneurial identity and its relationship to entrepreneurial passion and goal-setting', doctoral dissertation at University of Colorado, Boulder.

Plowman, D., L. Baker, T. Beck, M. Kulkarni and D. Villarreal (2007), 'Radical change accidentally: the emergence and amplification of small change', *Academy of Management Journal*, **50**(3): 515–43.

Politis, D. (2005), 'The process of entrepreneurial learning: a conceptual framework', *Entrepreneurship Theory and Practice*, **29**(4): 399–424.

Polkinhorne, J.C. (1991), *Reason and Reality: The Relationship Between Science and Theology*, Philadelphia, PA: Trinity Press.

Reuber, A. and E. Fischer (1999), 'Entrepreneurs' experience, expertise, and performance of technology-based firms', *IEEE Transactions on Engineering Management*, **41**(4): 365–84.

Sarason, Y., T. Dean and J.F. Dillard (2006), 'Entrepreneurship as the nexus of individual and opportunity: a structuration view', *Journal of Business Venturing*, **21**(3): 286–305.

Sarasvathy, S. (2001), 'Causation and effectuation: toward a theoretical shift from economic inevitability to entrepreneurial contingency', *Academy of Management Review*, **26**(2): 243–88.

Schindehutte, M., M.H. Morris and J. Allen (2006), 'Beyond achievement: entrepreneurship as extreme experience', *Small Business Economics*, **27**(4): 49–68.

Shane, S. and R. Khurana (2003), 'Bringing individuals back in: the effects of career experience on new firm founding', *Industrial and Corporate Change*, **12**(3): 519–43.

Shepherd, D.A. (2003), 'Learning from business failure: propositions of grief recovery for the self-employed', *Academy of Management Review*, **28**(2): 318–37.

Taylor, S. (1994), 'Waiting for service: the relationship between delays and evaluations of service', *Journal of Marketing*, **58**(2): 56–69.

Valliere, D. and N. O'Reilly (2007), 'Seeking the summit: exploring the entrepreneur–mountaineer analogy', *International Journal of Entrepreneurship and Innovation*, **8**(4): 293–304.

Watson, D. and A. Tellegen (1985), 'A consensual structure of mood', *Psychological Bulletin*, **98**(2): 219–35.

Weick, K.E., K. Sutcliffe and D. Obstfeld (2005), 'Organizing and the process of sensemaking', *Organization Science*, **16**(4): 409–21.

Weiss, H.M. and D. Beal (2005), 'Reflections on affective events theory', in N.M. Askanasy, W. Zerbe and C.E.J. Hartel (eds), *Research on Emotion in*

Organizations: The Effect of Affect in Organizational Settings, vol. 1, Oxford: Elsevier Ltd, pp. 1–21.

Weiss, H.M. and R. Cropanzano (1996), 'Affective events theory: a theoretical discussion of the structure, causes and consequences of affective experiences at work', in B. Shaw and L.L. Cummings (eds), *Research in Organizational Behavior*, Greenwich, CT: JAI Press, pp. 1–74.

Westhead, P., D. Ucbasaran and M. Wright (2005), 'Decisions, actions, and performance: do novice, serial, and portfolio entrepreneurs differ?', *Journal of Small Business Management*, **43**(4): 393–418.

8. Emergent outcomes of the entrepreneurial experience

> When you are in the middle of a story, it isn't a story at all, but only a confusion, a dark roaring, a wreckage of shattered glass and splintered wood, like a house in a whirlwind, crushed by the icebergs or swept over the rapids, and all aboard powerless to stop it. It's only afterwards that it becomes anything like a story at all, when you are telling it to yourself, or to somebody else.
>
> (Margaret Atwood, 1997)

INTRODUCTION

The real-time experiencing of events as they unfold can be jarring, rewarding, disrupting, reinforcing, disappointing, and much more. The signals these events send are often confusing, and their underlying meaning and implications are frequently unclear and subject to ongoing reinterpretation. Events define the fundamental nature of venture creation and are the source of core venture characteristics such as ambiguity, uncertainty, lack of control, and stress. They continually force the entrepreneur to re-examine a host of variables that surround the venture, including assumptions, perceptions, beliefs, behaviors, and decision alternatives. They give rise to strong emotions that influence how these variables are re-examined, and can lead to courses of action that differ significantly from those one might have followed based purely on rational analysis.

Ultimately, however, the processing of events over the months and years during which a new venture is conceptualized, launched, and developed has a much more fundamental set of outcomes. In a sense, the venture context represents a crucible, a place in which concentrated forces cause development or change in some object. The entrepreneur is the raw material that is being formed and shaped in this crucible. At the same time, the venture is being formed and shaped, frequently into something unplanned or unintended. The interplay between events, the individual, and the venture drives this forming and shaping. Moreover, this forming and shaping is continuous, with no clear endpoint.

In this chapter, we focus on the emergence of both the individual as an entrepreneur and the venture as an economic and social entity. We first examine the concept of emergence and how it is approached by contemporary scholars. Building on this foundation, we look at what is known about entrepreneurs, and then attempt to re-examine this knowledge base through an experience and emergence lens. Following this, we extend insights on the entrepreneur to the emergence of the venture. The chapter concludes with implications of the dynamic interplay between emergent entrepreneur and venture.

BEING IN THE MIDST: VENTURE CREATION AS CONTINUOUS FLUX

We return to the question of what it is like when one is in the midst of venture creation, processing events as they come. Venture creation is idiosyncratic, experienced differently by every entrepreneur. So, the nature of any one person's experience depends on interactions among that individual, streams of events, and the venture context. These interactions produce experiential states that can be strong in affect (see Chapter 6), but about which we know relatively little. Further consideration of these states can shed light on outcomes of venture creation.

In earlier chapters, we conceptualized the venture creation experience in terms of volume (how many events), velocity (the pace at which these events occur), and volatility (the relative highs and lows that these events represent). As illustrated in Figure 8.1, a large number of combinations of these three variables are possible. Each of them speaks to a different type of experience. Hence, a venture where little occurs in terms of salient events, the pace is relatively slow and there are no wide up and down swings could be perceived by some as less engaging, somewhat monotonous, and/or less fulfilling. Alternatively, having to process large numbers of salient events that come at one continuously and that fluctuate widely from severely threatening or disruptive to extremely rewarding or reinforcing might produce high levels of anxiety, stress or mental and physical exhaustion.

Another way to conceptualize ongoing experiencing is to consider the gap or incongruity between the individual's skills and the nature of the event-based challenges he or she faces (i.e., context complexity) at any point in time. New events produce incongruities that are either positive, where challenges exceed skills, or negative, where skills exceed challenges. Relative congruency between challenges and skills produces "flow," a concept we first encountered in Chapter 6 (Nakatsu et al., 2005) and we will explore in depth in Chapter 9. Flow is immersion based on high engagement and an energized focus, where emotions are positive and

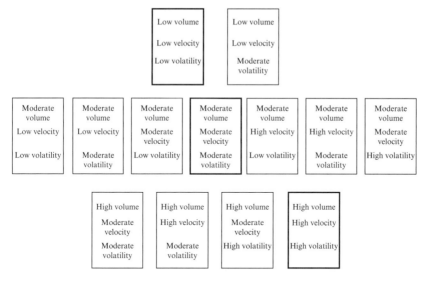

Figure 8.1   The entrepreneurial experience as combinations of volume, velocity, and volatility

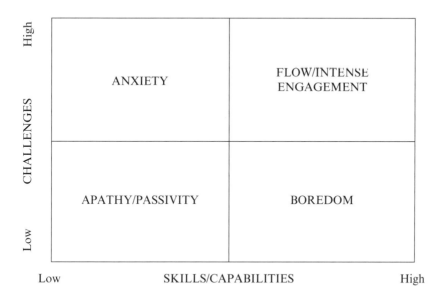

Source: Adapted from Nakatsu et al. (2005).

Figure 8.2   Skills, challenges, and flow experiences

aligned with the task at hand. Consistent with the cells in Figure 8.2, high amounts of negative incongruity can produce experiences of boredom where the individual is not especially engaged, ultimately unsatisfied, and may withdraw. Of course, boredom could find the entrepreneur looking for ways to increase the context complexity by trying new things, assuming the context lends itself to such experimentation. Alternatively, overly high positive incongruity can result in high levels of agitation and anxiety, which might also result in greater engagement, but also work against flow.

In a new venture context, the individual's ability to learn (changing their skills and capabilities, typically through trial and error), is a key factor determining whether the incongruity remains at acceptable levels. Negative affect is the likely outcome of positive and negative incongruities that exceed a tolerable range. Over time, the entrepreneur's learning system must keep pace with the complexity of the context, where complexity is driven by the volume, velocity, and volatility of salient events being encountered.

A related conceptualization of the experience explicitly links affect and engagement levels (see Chapter 6). Venture creation is an active and performative experience that requires physical, emotional, and mental presence. Yet, presence is not engagement. Central to experiencing is how immersed into or captivated by the venture the entrepreneur is. There is also likely to be an interactive effect between engagement and event generation, where highly engaged entrepreneurs are trying more new things, which in turn produces more unexpected or novel events, which may then require even more engagement (and could eventually produce burnout). In Figure 8.3, we capture engagement levels as they might relate to negative and positive affect, each of which varies from low to high. Thus, an experience high in positive affect produces the highest engagement levels, while high negative affect also forces the entrepreneur to be fairly engaged. On balance, positive affect might be expected to be more highly associated with engagement levels than is negative affect, especially over time.

We can conclude from these perspectives that venture creation involves an unceasing dynamic as the individual copes with the volume, velocity, and volatility of events; as these events produce ongoing incongruities and changing realities, and as they result in different levels of engagement and negative or positive affect. At their essence, then, the events that make up the entrepreneurial experience produce continual flux. Approaching things through an experiential lens, change becomes the essential aspect of venture creation. Encounters with novelty are the norm in the early days of a business. Events represent disruptions that punctuate the everyday, colliding with whatever sense of order has been achieved. Tsoukas and Chia (2002) argue that change means entrepreneurs, while trying to bring order

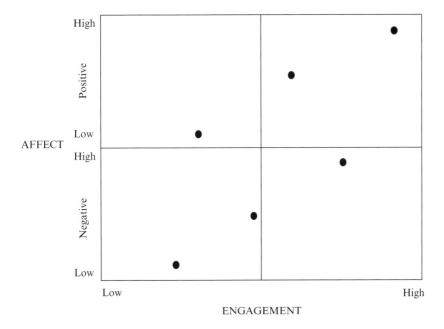

Figure 8.3   Examples of combinations of affect and engagement levels

to their circumstances, must continually reweave their webs of beliefs and habits of action to accommodate new experiences. They explain (p. 575) that change is experienced as "an unfolding process, a flow of possibilities, and a conjunction of events and open-ended interactions in time."

While the entrepreneur may seek the establishment of routines and stability, he or she is forced to improvise and adapt as events create new realities. In effect, events introduce variety to the venture context and this variety feeds individual learning and exploratory behavior. Learning, in turn, is instrumental in the individual's ability to adapt. Improvisational and adaptive behaviors serve to generate new events and realities. In this way, the temporal experience becomes a crucible where change, improvisation, learning, adaptation, and the ongoing challenges to one's assumptions, perceptions, and beliefs find that a business is being molded, and an entrepreneur is being formed. Both are emergent phenomena.

EXPERIENCING AND EMERGENCE

While change is the norm in venture creation, change is not the same as emergence. Change is about modifications to what exists, or alterations to the initial state of the system (Lichtenstein et al., 2006). Emergence is the creation of a new context where elements of the previous state continue to exist together with new elements. It is not simply pursuing a new path or direction, but instead is a new type of order. The entity is in the process of becoming something it was not before.

With roots in philosophy, emergence has received considerable attention in recent years from scholars in the area of complex systems. From a systems theory standpoint, emergence finds some new phenomenon arising in a system that wasn't in the system's specification to start with (Standish, 2001). It is "the arising of novel and coherent structures, patterns and properties during the process of self-organization in complex systems" (Goldstein, 1999, p. 54). Emergence is neither simple growth nor is it the simple result of the process of interactions (i.e., a new state or entity). Rather, it takes place during the process of interacting (McKelvey, 2004). Emergent properties arise when components combine in unpredictable ways and component parts form something unlike the parts themselves. These properties are novel when they are unpredictable, unexplainable, and irreducible to component parts (Humphreys, 1997).

Emergence has been investigated in a wide variety of contexts over the years. Consider three examples. In a classic study, Becker (1953) characterizes how one becomes a marijuana user. He concludes that the behavior emerges as a result of a sequence of social experiences during which the activity is given meaning and judgments of objects and situations are modified. Fundamental changes take place in the person and their perceptions of the activity and the experience it represents. Notably, Becker argues that it is not fruitful to focus on determining traits that might cause the behavior, but rather one must concentrate on the process of emergence that produces the behavior.

In a very different context, Barnard and Solchany (2002) examine the emergent nature of motherhood. They discuss fundamental physical, emotional, and psychological transformations of women as they become mothers. This becoming includes reciprocal interactions between mother and child, which results in structural changes within each party. The authors describe a dynamic process with unceasing change that can be overwhelming, where the woman must flexibly adapt to transformations and concomitant losses together with an ongoing range of feelings that can include conflict, ambivalence, contentment, hostility, joy, aggression, and regression. What emerges can include some level of mothering capacity, maternal role attainment, and changes in both personality and identity. Beyond the mother herself, how these elements emerge has significant implications for multiple outcomes related to the child.

As a third example, Morris et al. (2011) provide an example of emergence applied to an inner city entrepreneurial development project initiated by a university. They describe an emergent social process that unfolds in a non-linear manner, a system poised between order and disorder, adaptive tensions that create new connections, amplification of initial changes into far more dramatic developments, and modifications that overlapped, occurred in parallel, and interacted with one another. The end product is an outcome state that is fundamentally different from initial intentions and inputs.

Based on these examples and many others, we can conclude that emergence of order in structures, processes, and routines is a messy process. As such, the emergence of any given phenomenon can be difficult to explain. This difficulty is traceable to some of the underlying properties of emergence, properties that are context dependent. Within an entrepreneurial context, some relevant properties might include:

- time irreversibility;
- dynamic instability and tensions;
- presence of non-linear change and feedback, where small inputs can produce large outcomes;
- components combining in unpredictable ways, and component parts forming something unlike the parts themselves;
- surprise, where non-obvious or unexpected behaviors come from the object in question;
- reciprocal interactions between micro-level events and behaviors and emergent macro-structures;
- co-evolution among components of the system and increasing complexity;
- ongoing creation of new knowledge;
- enhanced improvisational capabilities and related competencies.

Venture creation actually finds three major emergent phenomena: the opportunity being exploited, the individual driving the venture, and the venture itself. For our current purposes, we are especially concerned with emergence of the entrepreneur and the venture.

EMERGENCE OF THE ENTREPRENEUR

Who is the entrepreneur? This question has received considerable attention from scholars over the years. A variety of sometimes conflicting findings exist regarding the sociology and psychology of the entrepreneurial prototype. Lack of cross-situational consistency is traceable, at least in part, to significant methodological problems. Samples are often small or unrepresentative. The validity and reliability of the measures employed are frequently not apparent, measures are applied long after the individual has done anything entrepreneurial, and it is often not clear if the researchers are focusing only on successful entrepreneurs, on people who have started small businesses, on people who identify themselves as entrepreneurs, or on some other delimiter. Given these issues, it is not surprising that the findings of empirical studies have been mixed and controversial. With this in mind, it is possible to make some general observations.

What Do We Know About Entrepreneurs?

On the sociological side, researchers have noted the high rates of entrepreneurship among immigrant populations, found mixed evidence regarding the importance of birth order within families, and suggested a role for education, previous experiences, age and milestone years in prompting start-ups (e.g., Bird, 1989; Ronstadt, 1984; Sexton and Van Auken, 1982). Bird (1989) synthesizes a wide array of findings from the literature to demonstrate how the prototypical entrepreneur is the product of specific developments in his or her social, economic, and family environments. Hence, the individual's social, cultural, historic and economic context explains much of what happens in launching and building a venture. She highlights such variables as a society that supports the development of an authoritarian personality, the existence of family poverty, childhood family dynamics, the father's absence or remoteness and mother's dominance, and personal identity conflicts as conditions that give rise to developing personality characteristics (e.g., rebelliousness, suspiciousness, need for control) that are (at least stereotypically) associated with entrepreneurs.

Separately, a range of perspectives has been generated regarding traits of entrepreneurs (see Box 8.1 for a list of traits associated with the entrepreneurial personality). Six of the more common findings include the following:

- Based on the classic studies of McClelland (1986), entrepreneurs are thought to be achievement motivated. They are driven by the task, the challenge, the chance to make a difference, or the opportunity to accomplish what others said could or should not be done.
- Entrepreneurial individuals demonstrate a strong internal locus of control. They see themselves as able to change their environments.
- Entrepreneurs are calculated risk-takers. They are willing to pursue a course of action that has a reasonable chance of costly failure. It is

---

BOX 8.1 TRAITS AND CHARACTERISTICS ASSOCIATED WITH THE ENTREPRENEUR

Achievement motivation
Internal locus of control
Calculated risk-taking
Tolerance of ambiguity
Perseverance/tenacity
Independence
Self-confidence
Dedication/strong work ethic
Organizing skills
Opportunistic
Adaptability/versatility
Initiative/energetic
Resourcefulness
Creativity
Perceptiveness
Assertiveness
Persuasiveness

Source: Adapted from Morris (1998).

---

calculated in the sense that the individual recognizes key risk factors and attempts to mitigate these risk factors.
- Entrepreneurs demonstrate a high "tolerance of ambiguity." Things do not have to be precise, fit a precast mold, or follow an exact process.
- Entrepreneurs tend to be independent. They are self-motivated, self-reliant, and prefer a degree of autonomy when accomplishing a task. The perception that they have room to maneuver in affecting their own destiny is highly valued.
- It is generally thought that entrepreneurs are tenacious and demonstrate significant perseverance.

Other common findings, about which there is less consensus, suggest that entrepreneurs are versatile, persuasive, creative, well-organized, extremely hard-working, and competitive (i.e., have a need to win).

According to some observers, there is also a "dark side" to entrepreneurs.

Kets de Vries (1985) argues that many entrepreneurs have an excessive need for control, which may produce a tendency to micro-manage or do other people's jobs for them. They can also demonstrate a tendency toward suspicious thinking that goes beyond thinking someone will steal their concept. Other characteristics include impatience, a need for applause, seeing the world in terms of black and white, defensiveness, and the externalizing of internal problems.

Yet a different angle has involved exploring skills and capabilities of entrepreneurs (e.g., Baron and Markman, 2000). We believe that entrepreneurs develop not only managerial competencies (e.g., cash flow management, organizing work, selecting and supervising employees, performance assessment), but also entrepreneurial competencies. We recently completed a Delphi study in which 12 core entrepreneurial competencies were identified by panels of successful entrepreneurs and leading entrepreneurship academics. These competencies included:

- recognizing opportunity;
- assessing opportunity;
- conveying a compelling vision;
- creative problem-solving;
- leveraging resources;
- guerrilla skills;
- mitigating and managing risk;
- planning when nothing exists;
- innovation – developing concepts that work;
- building and managing social networks;
- ability to maintain focus yet adapt;
- implementation of something novel or new.

Still others have examined the entrepreneur through a cognitive lens, attempting to look at how they process information, think, and approach decision-making. Considerable attention has been devoted to entrepreneurial cognition over the past decade. An excellent synthesis is provided by Robert Baron (2004). Examples of some of the tendencies associated with entrepreneurs include cognitive biases, such as an overly optimistic bias or a tendency to draw major conclusions from very limited data, alertness to new opportunities, engaging in less counterfactual thinking, risk adversity with respect to gains and risk-seeking with respect to losses, a greater concern with recognizing stimuli that are present than properly concluding stimuli are not present, and a greater likelihood that behavior will be regulated from a promotion versus a prevention focus. Box 8.2 summarizes some of Baron's key conclusions.

BOX 8.2   INSIDE THE MIND OF THE
          ENTREPRENEUR: COGNITIVE
          PROCESSES

While the research is limited, below are some of the phenomena that reflect beliefs regarding how entrepreneurs may tend to think, process information, and approach decision-making:

Cognitive biases: Optimism bias (inflated tendency to expect things to turn out successfully), sense of infallibility, the illusion of control (belief that one's abilities and efforts can influence outcomes even where chance clearly plays a larger role), and the law of small numbers (the tendency to use a small sample of information as a basis for firm conclusions).

Entrepreneurial alertness: A motivated propensity to formulate an image of the future. Alertness is reflected in how information is processed, assumptions are challenged, and opportunities are identified. While entrepreneurs can be expected to vary in terms of their alertness, it may well be that successful entrepreneurs are more alert to stimuli that represent untapped opportunities.

Counterfactual thinking: Tendency to imagine different outcomes in a given situation than what actually occurred – what might have been. Entrepreneurs tend to engage in less counterfactual thinking, accepting what happens and thinking that focusing on what might have been is a waste of time.

Prospect theory: Does the entrepreneur focus more on potential losses or potential gains; does he or she overstate one or understate the other? In general, a loss of $10 000 is felt more strongly than a gain of $10 000 – so that entrepreneurs are risk-averse with respect to gains and risk-seeking with respect to losses. They prefer to avoid risk when they focus on gains, but seek risk when they focus on losses. So, if they had a choice of a 50 percent chance of losing $1000 or a certain loss of $500, they would choose the former, even though both have the same expected value – they are risk-seeking because they framed this choice in terms of losses. If asked whether they prefer a certain gain of $500 or a 50 percent chance of gaining $1000, they will prefer the former, since they are focusing on gains – they are risk averse and prefer the sure thing. So, entrepreneurs tend to frame many situations in terms of losses – they focus more on the opportunities for economic gain they will forfeit if they ignore or overlook an opportunity. To the extent they focus on losses, they are risk-seeking.

Signal detection: In situations where individuals attempt to determine whether a stimulus is present or absent, four possibilities exist: (1) the stimulus does exist and the perceiver correctly concludes this; (2) the stimulus exists but the perceiver fails to recognize it; (3) the stimulus does not exist and the perceiver concludes it is present; and (4) the stimulus does not exist and the perceiver correctly concludes it does not exist. The entrepreneur might be expected to be more concerned with recognizing stimuli that are present than with correctly concluding stimuli are not present.

Regulatory focus: The tendency to approach the regulation of one's own behavior from a promotion (an emphasis on accomplishment, on exploring multiple possible means to achieve goals) versus a prevention focus (an emphasis on avoiding negative outcomes, considering fewer options, and not making mistakes). Those adopting a promotion focus will recognize more opportunities compared to those having a prevention focus. If we assume that both the promotion and prevention focus are operating in most entrepreneurs, it may be that an individual will rely more on one or the other depending upon the demands and circumstances he or she faces within the venture. It may be that those who successfully build high-growth ventures demonstrate more of a promotion focus.

Acceptance of sunk costs: Willingness to stick with decisions that generate initial negative results.

Source: Adapted from Baron (2004).

Prototyping the Entrepreneur

The work on traits, skills, and cognitive styles is useful, but perhaps not for the obvious reasons. To talk about common characteristics of an entrepreneur is to suggest there might be some sort of prototype or general model that represents a standard against which we compare individuals. This is an erroneous notion, however, as decades of research have failed to produce such a prototype and it remains impossible to predict who will be an entrepreneur, much less who will be an entrepreneurial success.

A more fruitful path might be to identify general types or categories of entrepreneurs. Unfortunately, no general typology has received widespread acceptance among scholars. Early work in this area distinguished the "craftsperson" and "opportunistic" entrepreneurs (Smith and Miner, 1983). The former is characterized by narrowness in education and training, low social awareness and involvement, a feeling of incompetence in dealing with the social environment, and a limited time orientation. The latter has more breadth in education and training, high social awareness and involvement, confidence in their ability to deal with the social environment, and an awareness of, and orientation to, the future. Opportunists are thought to produce more growth-oriented, adaptable ventures. Vesper (1980) organizes entrepreneurs based on the essence of the type of venture they create, such as solo self-employed individuals, team-builders, independent innovators, and pattern multipliers. Others categorize individuals based on how many ventures they start and how many they operate at once. Hence, Westhead et al. (2005) identify underlying characteristics of novice, serial, and portfolio entrepreneurs.

A promising attempt at classification can be found in the work of Miner (1996). Tracking a large sample of company founders for a number of years, he distinguished four major categories of entrepreneurs:

- *The personal achiever*: High need for achievement, need for performance feedback, desire to plan and set goals, strong individual initiative, strong personal commitment and identification with the venture, internal locus of control, belief that work should be guided by personal goals, not those of others.
- *The super-salesperson*: Capacity to understand and feel another and to empathize, desire to help others, belief that social processes are important; social interaction and relationships are important, need to have strong positive relationships with others.
- *The real manager*: Desire to be a corporate leader, desire to compete, decisiveness, desire for power, positive attitudes to authority, desire to stand out from the crowd.
- *The expert idea generator*: Desire to innovate, love of ideas, curious, open-minded, belief that new product development is a crucial component of company strategy; intelligence as a source of competitive advantage, desire to avoid taking risks.

Miner notes some possibility that one could fall into more than one category. While insights are provided on how each of these types of entrepreneurs succeed or fail, and the need for fit between type of entrepreneur and type of venture, there is less insight in how these different types are developed or formed. The implication is that individuals come to the venture with a given orientation or skill set. However, as we discuss below, the venture itself may have some impact on the development of a given type.

This extended discussion is not meant to suggest any definitive description of the entrepreneur, but instead to introduce the reader to the range of perspectives and findings regarding the entrepreneurial individual. However, the experiential view presented in this book suggests that it is extremely difficult to generalize about entrepreneurs. Of the millions of people in the world who start ventures, or start successful ventures, or start successful ventures that achieve meaningful growth, there is far more diversity than commonality. Perhaps it is enough to say that entrepreneurs as a group are more achievement motivated or tolerant of ambiguity than is society at large, or when compared to managers, while acknowledging that entrepreneurs differ meaningfully in terms of any particular characteristic.

Yet the real implication of the extant research on entrepreneurs, at least from our vantage point, is that individuals do not start out as entrepreneurs or entrepreneurial types, they become these things. While some may have some of these core characteristics before they start, or at least rudiments of these characteristics, many others do not. In fact, it is possible that they start out with none of the characteristics and descriptors presented above. The venture experience becomes the medium where many of these traits, skills, competencies, and cognitive styles are developing within the entrepreneur as the business unfolds.

What is Emerging in the Entrepreneur?

As a business idea is conceptualized and implemented, the individual is engaged in an ongoing process of assigning meaning to events, streams, and stocks of experiences. This process of enactment leads to the emergence of an entrepreneur. According to Deleuze's (1994) philosophy of becoming, the entrepreneur is always in the middle, there is no beginning or end. The body operates in the present moment – it reacts to what is. By contrast, the mind processes the responses from the body and tracks understanding of past experiences, goals, and aspirations. The mind also analyzes the gap between what is, what was, and what could be. In this process of becoming, the focus is on "what could be" (Chia, 1995). Instead of reproducing worlds, the entrepreneur is in a continuous process of creating them.

This experiential perspective is consistent with a situated view of entrepreneurial action, which emphasizes the interface between inner and outer environments (Berglund, 2007). Meaning is derived from the structure of experiences, not from measures and numbers. Further, meaning is not stable or predetermined by one's background or acquired skills. Instead, everyday actions and feelings are important, especially during early phases of entrepreneurial enactment because "the everyday is the scene where social change and individual creativity take place as a slow result of constant activity" (Steyaert, 2004, p. 10).

Each individual's venture creation experience is unique, and every individual is affected differently by their experiences. The individual is being formed and transformed into something he or she was not before. In effect, events introduce variety to the venture context and this variety feeds individual learning and exploratory behavior. Learning, in turn, is instrumental in the individual's development as an entrepreneur. The degree of formation or transformation is specific to the individual. So, any two individuals can emerge from a similar context in very different ways. The question thus becomes one identifying the variables around which the entrepreneur is being formed. While there certainly may be others, our focus is on four core variables: business skills, entrepreneurial competencies, an entrepreneurial mindset, and an entrepreneurial identity (see Box 8.3).

We begin with business skills. The entrepreneur is becoming a manager, ultimately responsible for all facets of a self-created organization and its performance outcomes. While these skills can include technical capabilities such as selling, budgeting, or production, they also include development of a leadership style, the ability to delegate, the individual's need for control, and an ability to create and maintain an ethical climate, among other capabilities. Events are instrumental in the formation of these skills, as they introduce variety, disruption, feedback, and reinforcement. A person that knows nothing about and is even uncomfortable with selling learns to become adept at the sales process through the dynamic interactions, tensions, unexpected behaviors, generation of new knowledge, and related properties of emergence. Or, consider the earlier discussion of the so-called dark side of the entrepreneur. Although elements in a person's background might create a tendency to be obsessed with control, even absent such elements a series of events that generate strong negative affect, or that reflect wide, high, and low swings in terms of velocity, might be critical factors that transform someone into a micro-manager.

With regard to entrepreneurial competencies, it is our position that venture creation requires a number of capabilities that the typical entrepreneur has neither received formal training in nor has been engaged in prior to the venture (at least to any significant extent). Competencies referred to in the earlier discussion, such as leveraging capabilities, guerrilla skills, the ability to assess opportunities, or adeptness at managing and mitigating

---

BOX 8.3   WHAT IS EMERGING WITHIN THE ENTREPRENEUR?

Managerial skills	*Entrepreneurial competencies*	*Entrepreneurial mindset*	*Entrepreneurial identities*
Planning	Opportunity recognition	Self-efficacy	As an organization builder
Organizing		Optimism	
Staffing	Opportunity assessment	Opportunity alertness	As a job creator
Budgeting			As a risk-taker
Reviewing	Conveying a vision	Tolerance of ambiguity	As an innovator or achiever
Directing			
Operating	Mitigating risks	Independence	As a change agent
Coordinating	Leveraging resources	Attitudes toward:	
		risk-taking	As a community builder/ contributor
	Creative problem-solving	control	
		change	As a woman, minority, veteran immigrant, disabled, gay or other affinity group member who has created a venture
		growth	
	Innovation	time	
	Guerrilla skills	Proactiveness	
	Building and managing networks		
	Focus while adapting		
	Implementing something new		

---

risk, are acquired from everyday experiencing in the venture. The individual does not set out to learn or develop these capabilities. Circumstances (unfolding events) produce conflicts and crises that force the entrepreneur to experiment with activities that are indicative of such competencies. Such experiments grow out of observation of other entrepreneurs, advice received from various parties, as well as the resourcefulness, inventiveness, and cleverness of the individual entrepreneur. As with becoming a great piano player, competencies such as these develop as a function of practice. Hence, the more one leverages or comes up with effective guerrilla tactics, and adjusts based on results, the better one becomes at such behaviors. Further, the competencies can interact with one another, such as where attempts to mitigate risk are accomplished by resource leveraging or reliance on guerrilla tactics. The entrepreneur's capabilities emerge as a function of these interactions and their outcomes. Moreover, as we saw in Chapter 6, the exploratory activity, creativity, and learning that underlie these competencies are fostered to the extent that experiencing by the entrepreneur results in positive affect and higher engagement levels.

One of the most intriguing emergent outcomes is some sort of "entrepreneurial mindset." This is a construct widely referred to both in academic circles and in practice, but one about which there is little consensus regarding its definition or make up. Hence, Ireland et al. (2003) define this mindset as the ability to sense, adapt, and react under conditions of uncertainty. McGrath and Macmillan (2000) claim it includes alertness to new opportunities, approaching opportunities with enormous discipline, selection, and focus on certain opportunities, adaptive execution, and leveraging capabilities. Carsrud and Brannback (2009) indicate that individuals with this mindset continue to be motivated to create products, processes, markets, and ventures. A mindset is reflected in a person's overall attitudes, assumptions, inclinations, disposition, and outlook. It is a kind of personal philosophy and is formed over time by one's previous experiences. It produces a strong incentive to behave in certain ways. Thus, the entrepreneurial mindset represents an ongoing way of thinking and acting that is an outcome of experiencing.

Some of the perspectives on the entrepreneurial mindset seem to confuse development of competencies or skills, such as adaptation, leveraging capabilities, or execution skills, with an emerging mindset. In Box 8.3, we identify key elements that might constitute a philosophy or outlook that might be labeled "entrepreneurial." Here we include entrepreneurial self-efficacy, or the belief that one is capable of undertaking entrepreneurial initiatives, an optimistic outlook, alertness to emerging opportunities, tolerance of ambiguity, a desire for independence, and a proactive attitude (Bird, 1989; Chen et al. 1998; Hmieleski and Baron, 2009; Tang et al., in press). We also suggest that an emerging entrepreneurial mindset finds the individual developing a more enlightened or calculated attitude toward risk, a lessened need for control, greater openness to change, more desire for growth, and a longer time horizon.

This kind of mindset emerges from experiencing. Let us take, for instance, the entrepreneur's tolerance of ambiguity as a component of this mindset. Although there is research to suggest that successful entrepreneurs are tolerant of ambiguity, there is no evidence that entrepreneurs are more tolerant of ambiguity if the measure is taken before or at the time of start-up. Events produce ambiguity, and as these events are given meaning and made sense of, the individual learns to survive and progress in the midst of such ambiguity. Unconsciously, and over time, he or she reinterprets the relative need for clarity or exactitude that is required to comfortably perform. Of course, this happens to differing degrees with any given entrepreneur. The critical role played by experiencing in producing the entrepreneurial mindset is further reinforced by the work on serial entrepreneurs, as these individuals often demonstrate such a mindset borne out of earlier ventures in which they were involved (McGrath and MacMillan, 2000).

Lastly, let us turn to the formation of identity. Anthropologists argue that performance of the self in experiential events becomes a means of forming an identity (Bruner, 1986). Psychologists note that ongoing states of activity (engagement, evaluation) are instrumental in forming self-identity (Barab et al., 2001). An identity emerges through a process of negotiation as social realities are shaping the individual and the individual is shaping social realities (Turner, 1982). Hoang and Gimeno (2005) conceptualize identity as a structure of meanings relating to the self that changes over time and over successive roles, and so as a dynamic construct intimately linked to emergence processes. People can have multiple identities. Consistent with these perspectives, they develop an entrepreneurial identity as a function of the venture creation experience.

Entrepreneurial identity is not one thing. It is defined by at least four dimensions: identity attributes (i.e., personal traits associated with the role, such as being an individualist or risk-taker), identity content (i.e., the task of the entrepreneur, such as opportunity identification or organization building), role regard (i.e., positive or negative assessments the individual has of the entrepreneurial role as well as how he or she thinks others view this role), and identity centrality (i.e., the subjective importance of the entrepreneurial identity vis-à-vis other identities that make up the individual's self-concept) (Hoang and Gimeno, 2005). These dimensions are interacting as individuals experience the venture and engage in social interactions, resulting in updates to and refinements of the entrepreneurial identity.

Building on the work of a number of researchers (e.g., Down and Reveley, 2004; Hoang and Gimeno, 2005; Morris et al., 2006; Murnieks and Mosakowski, 2007; Shepherd and Haynie, 2009), we believe that entrepreneurial identity can be built around a number of different elements. This is illustrated in Box 8.3, where the emergent identity could center on that of organization builder, job creator, taker of risks, change agent, contributor to society, or innovator. Further, role identities interact. As a result, the gay individual who creates a venture may well see himself as a gay entrepreneur, or as an entrepreneur that happens to be gay (Schindehutte et al., 2005). The same can be said for the female, immigrant, handicapped individual, member of an ethnic group, or other affinity group member.

Entrepreneurial identity is further defined by the type of venture one creates and the roles one plays in creating that venture. This is because the events and experiences being processed, and how they are processed, will vary significantly depending on venture context. Hence, the identity one develops in building a lifestyle venture can differ from the person creating a high-growth venture, just as it is likely to differ if one is creating something alone or with partners or family members.

It is also important to note that venture outcomes all along the way will impact entrepreneurial identity formation. For instance, positive and negative outcomes (and affect) can lead to changes in role regard and/or to the centrality placed on the entrepreneurial identity relative to other self-identities (e.g., mother, person of faith, environmentalist) the individual holds. A further dynamic finds that, as identity emerges, it will tend to affect information processing, learning, and behavioral choices. As a result, the processing of ongoing events is being affected. Hence, experiencing leads to identity formation, which in turn influences how things are experienced. The interplay or experiencing and identity formation impacts many variables, among them the individual's decision to persevere or leave the venture.

EMERGENCE OF THE VENTURE

Ventures also emerge, both in terms of their commercial focus and how substantial they become. Thus, what often starts as an incomplete or ill-conceived business model can morph into something quite different. Peter Drucker (1985, p. 189) explains:

> When a new venture does succeed, more often than not it is in a market other than the one it was intended to serve, with products and services not quite those with which it has set out, bought in large part by customers it did not even think of when starting, and used for a host of purposes besides the ones for which the products were designed.

Drucker's insight is borne out by findings of many other researchers (e.g., Ardichvili et al., 2003; Lichtenstein et al., 2006; Nicholls-Nixon et al., 2000; Sarasvathy, 2001) and highlights the unplanned and unpredictable nature of venture emergence.

Similarly, the scale and scope of the venture that actually develops may not be what was intended at the outset. Box 8.4 summarizes five general types of businesses that entrepreneurs create. In some cases, the

---

BOX 8.4   GENERAL TYPES OF VENTURES CREATED BY ENTREPRENEURS

What sort of organization does the entrepreneur create? While other variations exist, below is a typology consisting of five categories within which virtually any entrepreneurial venture can be categorized:

Survival venture: Usually a solo, self-employed individual who generates enough revenue to pay current bills; the business tends to produce a hand-to-mouth type of financial existence.

Lifestyle venture: Once a workable business model is arrived at, the business produces a decent living for the individual and his or her family; it is a stable business that typically employs people and requires maintenance management, but generates limited wealth.

Managed-growth venture: The business seeks ongoing, relatively steady growth, often by regularly adding new products, services, locations or markets.

Aggressive-growth venture: The business expands rapidly, seeking to become an industry leader, or to create an entirely new industry; competitive dynamics are significantly affected by the business.

Speculative venture: The business is created just long enough to demonstrate that the business model can or does work, and is then sold.

---

entrepreneur may give little thought to whether he or she is trying to create a managed-growth business or a high-growth venture. However, even where the entrepreneur has a very clear outcome in mind, the dream one begins with is likely to become something very different. As the venture unfolds, goals and motives change, decisions are taken that open or close doors, and the organization adapts or fails to adapt to developments. Acting in multiple roles without a script, the entrepreneur's actions reflect trial and error, where things work or do not work, and lessons are learned or not learned. As a result, while the entrepreneur sought to build an aggressive-growth venture, what turns out is a lifestyle venture, or what started out to be a small, family business becomes a publically traded company.

Whether it is the business model or the scope and scale of the business, events and the experiences they produce drive the emergence process in new ventures. They introduce uncertainty, complexity, diversity, and surprise, which force improvisation and adaptation, and this, in turn, produces new events that must be processed and responded to. They help demonstrate why one's initial conception of an opportunity was errant in whole or in part, and they open doors to new aspects of opportunity. They contradict or reinforce assumptions, routines, and behaviors. They are experienced at multiple levels through the interactions of cognition, affect, and physiological reactions. As a result, the manner in which events are experienced ultimately determines what kind of venture is created.

In a sense, individuals do not start ventures but initiate a process of organizational becoming. It is true that there is a point in time that we can call "start-up" where one creates some sort of legal entity that holds certain assets and begins operations on a certain day. But start-up is not venture creation. A venture is something that unfolds as structure is created and modified, goals are set and changed, new resources are acquired, a culture takes root, processes and routines are implemented and updated or replaced, and the core elements of a business model are played with until something emerges that works, and often further experimented with until something emerges that works even better. Tsoukas and Chia (2002, p. 570) explain:

> Organization is an attempt to order the intrinsic flux of human action, to channel it towards certain ends, to give it a particular shape, through generalizing and institutionalizing particular meanings and rules. At the same time, organization is a pattern that is constituted, shaped, *emerging* from change. [Original emphasis]

In effect, then, while attempting to stem change, the organization represents an outcome of change.

Organizational emergence refers to how organizations become manifest, or how they come into being. Gartner (1993) concludes that the ability to understand the process of organizational emergence requires an appreciation for the particular space–time context of a given venture, and a recognition that the order of events is critical to the process. The question becomes one of determining the point at which there is an "organization." For our purposes, what is emerging under the guise of an organization is an operational business model that is economically sustainable. Sustainability means the entrepreneur is creating variation in organizational forms and business models that will enable the organization to adapt and survive. Of course, some ventures never become sustainable. Others go beyond mere sustainability to achieve meaningful growth. For still others, the sustainable business model becomes a platform for continuous innovation, and they emerge as sizeable entities.

An important attempt to longitudinally capture how a venture comes to be can be found in the work of Lichtenstein and colleagues (2006). They provide evidence of underlying change over time in the basic modes of organizing employed by the entrepreneur. These authors note what they call punctuating shifts in the organization of the vision, strategy, and tactics or behaviors that guide the venture. These punctuating shifts occur roughly in conjunction with one another. Further, they posit that shifts in tactical organizing come just before shifts in strategic organizing, which then produce shifts in vision. They conclude that what emerges from this core set of shifts is fundamentally different from what preceded. In seeking the triggers of these shifts, Lichtenstein and colleagues point to conflict, frustration, fear, and other aspects of negative affect over time, together with the entrepreneur's own self-awareness and agency. This interpretation is consistent with the temporal experiential processing perspective advocated in this book.

Examining the entrepreneurial experience from the vantage point of different combinations of positive/negative affect and high/low engagement may be fruitful for explaining ongoing decision-making and organizational outcomes. Strong affect and high engagement fuel emergence of the entrepreneur, which in turn strongly impacts emergence of the venture. As business skills, entrepreneurial competencies, an entrepreneurial mindset, and identity take root, the entrepreneur begins to see the venture differently, affecting what he or she does and how it is done. Baron (2008) concludes that the impact of affect on managerial behavior is most likely in uncertain environments and when pursuing entrepreneurial tasks. It may be that particular combinations of arousal and valence are more likely to result in risk-taking or experimentation, while the tendency to create a lifestyle versus growth venture is more associated with other combinations. Ongoing processing can influence how founders think and act, and hence how mental models are interpreted and approached.

Relying on experience-based concepts to create meaning, individuals filter inputs from the world to produce their own unique reality. The perceptions, beliefs, time horizons, goals, and actions of entrepreneurs become rooted in the unique way they experience. Business decisions are outgrowths of the highs and lows, negative and positive affect, and engagement levels woven into the fabric of temporal experiences. Choices transcend rational thinking and become a product of one's sense that the evolving venture context represents an experience of excitement, passion, threat, ambiguity, emptiness, and similar dimensions.

Yet, in the early stages of a venture, these business decisions often must reflect improvisation and adaptation, which lie at the heart of organizational emergence. Improvisation involves deliberately chosen activities that are spontaneous, novel, and involve the creation of something while it is being performed (Moorman and Miner, 1998). Solutions are created "on the fly" and one creatively addresses problems with novel combinations of tools and materials at hand. Weick (1998) makes the point that improvising is close to the root process in organizing. He talks about a continuum that ranges from interpretation through embellishment and variation and ending with improvisation. The entrepreneur is likely to be engaged in all four as events unfold, with true improvisation resulting in the greatest organizational change. However, unlike the well-practiced jazz musician, the first-time entrepreneur may have relatively little background to draw upon when improvising in the very early stages of a venture.

In building an organization, the entrepreneur attempts to establish routines and order, but this effort is continually disrupted by events and experiences. Improvisation represents an attempt to accommodate and make sense of new experiences. It leads to new products, services, processes, as well as changes to routines, norms, and mores. As the volume, velocity, and volatility of events producing these experiences increase, the need for improvisation likely increases. The ability to meet this challenge is enhanced by experiences producing positive affect and high engagement levels. Moreover, ongoing improvisation improves one's abilities at creating in the moment and increases the repertoire he or she has to draw upon when doing so (although there may be some level of velocity where improvisation becomes more difficult to accomplish). Improvisation, in turn, produces new events, any number of which are unanticipated or represent surprises. The organization is continually being transformed.

We also want to emphasize that organizational emergence is affected by behaviors that are less novel or improvisational. A characteristic of emergence is the potential for small inputs to have unpredictably large or unintended impacts. In an organizational context, Weick (1979) argues that small occurrences often become major influences on behaviors and outcomes. He discusses (p. 43) "small wins," or concrete, complete, implemented outcomes of moderate importance that become the basis for a pattern of achievement. Hence, reactions to less unfolding events may find the entrepreneur putting in extra (or fewer) hours in a given period, making more (or less) than the usual number of phone calls, meeting with more (or fewer) external stakeholders, taking more (or fewer) business trips, and so forth (Gartner, 1993). These immediate behaviors may ultimately lead to some significant outcome in terms of the development of the business.

In the end, at least for those who succeed, a business comes to be. It is molded around an interacting set of employees, facilities, products, markets, structures, rules, processes, systems, technologies, values, and more. A unique organizational personality takes form. The company occupies a definable niche in the marketplace. It has a cogent business model. And while it continues to evolve through life cycle stages, the core DNA of the organization is established.

CONCLUSIONS

In this chapter, we extend the earlier model in Chapter 7 to more fully explore the outcomes of entrepreneurial experiencing. While there are many outcomes of the venture creation experience, our focus has been on the emergence of the individual as an entrepreneur and the emergence of the venture as a sustainable entity.

Our theme has been one of emergence. Emergence is more than change or modification to what exists. It is about an entity becoming something it was not before. The process of becoming involves a number of properties, including dynamic instability, non-linear change and feedback, amplification of initial changes into far more dramatic developments, reciprocal interactions, and co-evolution among components of a system, among others. The uncontrollable and unpredictable nature of entrepreneurship is tied to such properties.

The generative mechanisms of emergence are events and the experiences they produce. Occasions of experience are the fundamental elements that define venture creation, with every occasion influenced by prior experiences and influencing subsequent experiences. Engagement with these events becomes the key to finding meaning, learning, improving, adapting, and ultimately surviving. The processing of these events impacts what the entrepreneur creates and who the entrepreneur becomes.

Researchers have lamented how little we know about the social formation of the entrepreneurial self (e.g., Down and Reveley, 2004). Our position is that one is formed into an entrepreneur as a function of the processing of streams and stocks of salient events, and that the event volume, velocity, and volatility are instrumental in shaping what kind of entrepreneur one becomes. The venture context represents a crucible within which business skills, entrepreneurial competencies, an entrepreneurial mindset, and an entrepreneurial identity are being developed.

The kind of individual who emerges from a venture creation experience fits no single prototype and, in fact, resists categorization. Hence, we have the person who becomes a "mom and pop" proprietor and sees the venture as a formulaic job and source of income substitution. An entrepreneurial mindset and identity are hard to discern in this individual. At another extreme is the high-growth entrepreneur who develops adroit business and entrepreneurial capabilities and emerges with a strong entrepreneurial mindset and a core entrepreneurial identity centered on innovation and affecting change. Yet, these are but two examples of the many thousands of different types of entrepreneurs molded by the venture creation experience.

A venture is also being formed. Organizational emergence involves the construction of reality based on efforts to create order and make sense of developments (Weick, 1995). Yet, even as the organization represents an attempt to bring order and stem change, it is being shaped by and emerges from change. The building of a company is a trial-and-error journey. The journey is complicated by ongoing events and event streams that introduce conflict, crises, and complexity, as well as new opportunities and possibilities. Entrepreneurs act, figure out what happens, adjust, and adapt. They make lots of mistakes. They continually improvise. And just as the venture context is forming them into entrepreneurs, they are building something that takes a form, shape, and purpose that can differ significantly from what they started out to create.

REFERENCES

Ardichvili, A., R. Cardozo and S. Ray (2003), 'A theory of opportunity identification and development', *Journal of Business Venturing*, **18**(1): 105–23.

Atwood, M. (1997), *Alias Grace*, New York: Anchor Books, pp. 162.

Barab, S., K. Hay and L. Yamagata-Lynch (2001), 'Constructing networks of action-relevant episodes: an in situ research methodology', *Journal of Learning Sciences*, **10**(1 and 2): 63–112.

Barnard, K. and J. Solchany (2002), 'Mothering', in M. Bornstein (ed.), *Handbook of Parenting: Being and Becoming a Parent, Vol. 3*, Mahwah, NJ: Lawrence Erlbaum, pp. 3–26.

Baron, R.A. (2004), 'The cognitive perspective: a valuable tool for answering entrepreneurship's basic "why" questions', *Journal of Business Venturing*, **19**(2): 221–39.

Baron, R.A. (2008), 'The role of affect in the entrepreneurial process', *Academy of Management Review*, **33**(2): 328–40.

Baron, R.A. and G. Markman (2000), 'Beyond social capital: how social skills can enhance entrepreneurs' success', *Academy of Management Executive*, **14**(1): 106–16.

Becker, H.S. (1953), 'Becoming a marihuana user', *American Journal of Sociology*, **59**(3): 235–42.

Berglund, H. (2007), 'Entrepreneurship and phenomenology: researching entrepreneurship as lived experience', in H. Neergaard and J. Ulhøi (eds), *Handbook of Qualitative Research Methods in Entrepreneurship*, Cheltenham, UK and Northampton, MA, USA: Edward Elgar, pp. 75–96.

Bird, B. (1989), *Entrepreneurial Behavior*, London: Scott Foresman.

Bruner, E. (1986), 'Experience and its expressions', in V. Turner and E. Bruner (eds), *The Anthropology of Experience*, Urbana, IL: University of Illinois Press, pp. 3–32.

Carsrud, A. and M. Brannback (2009), *Understanding the Entrepreneurial Mind*, Heidelberg, Germany: Springer.

Chen, C., P. Greene and A. Crick (1998), 'Does entrepreneurial self-efficacy distinguish entrepreneurs from managers?', *Journal of Business Venturing*, 13(4): 295–316.

Chia, R. (1995), 'Modern to postmodern organizational analysis', *Organization Studies*, 16(4): 579–604.

Deleuze, G. (1994), *Difference and Repetition*, New York: Columbia University Press.

Down, S. and J. Reveley (2004), 'Generational encounters and the social formation of entrepreneurial identity', *Organization*, 11(3): 233–50.

Drucker, P. (1985), *Innovation and Entrepreneurship*, New York: Harper & Row, pp. 189.

Gartner, W.B. (1993), 'Words lead to deeds: towards an organizational emergence vocabulary', *Journal of Business Venturing*, 8(3): 231–9.

Goldstein, J. (1999), 'Emergence as a construct: history and issues', *Emergence: Complexity and Organization*, 1(1): 49–72.

Hmieleski, K. and R.A. Baron (2009), 'Entrepreneurs' optimism and new venture performance: a social cognitive perspective', *Academy of Management Journal*, 52(3): 473–88.

Hoang, H. and J. Gimeno (2005), 'Becoming an entrepreneur: a theory of entrepreneurial identity', INSEAD working paper, Fountainbleu, France, pp. 1–38.

Humphreys, P.W. (1997), 'Emergence, not supervenience', *Philosophy of Science Supplement*, 64(4): 337–45.

Ireland, R.D., M. Hitt and D.G. Sirmon (2003), 'A model of strategic entrepreneurship: the construct and its dimensions', *Journal of Management*, 29(6): 963–82.

Kets de Vries, M. (1985), 'The dark side of entrepreneurship', *Harvard Business Review*, 85(6): 160–67.

Lichtenstein, B., K. Dooley and T. Lumpkin (2006), 'Measuring emergence in the dynamics of new venture creation', *Journal of Business Venturing*, 21(2): 153–75.

Lichtenstein, B., N. Carter, K. Dooley and W. Gartner (2007), 'Complexity dynamics of nascent entrepreneurship', *Journal of Business Venturing*, 22(2): 236–53.

McClelland, D.C. (1986), 'Characteristics of successful entrepreneurs', *Journal of Creative Behavior*, 21(3): 219–33.

McGrath, R. and I. MacMillan (2000), *The Entrepreneurial Mindset*, Boston, MA: Harvard Business Press.

McKelvey, B. (2004), 'Toward a complexity science of entrepreneurship', *Journal of Business Venturing*, 19(3): 313–41.

Miner, J. (1996), *The Four Routes to Entrepreneurial Success*, San Francisco, CA: Berrett-Koehler.

Moorman, C. and A.S. Miner (1998), 'Organizational improvisation and organizational memory', *Academy of Management Review*, 23(4): 698–723.

Morris, M.H. (1998), *Entrepreneurial Intensity*, Westport, CT: Quorum Books.

Morris, M.H., N. Miyasaki, C. Watters and S. Coombes (2006), 'The dilemma of growth: understanding venture size choices of women entrepreneurs', *Journal of Small Business Management*, 44(3): 221–44.

Morris, M.H., C. Watters, M. Schindehutte and V. Edmonds (2011), 'Inner city engagement and the university: mutuality, emergence and transformation', *Entrepreneurship & Regional Development*, **23**(5–6): 287–316.

Murnieks, C. and E. Mosakowski (2007), 'Who am I? Looking inside the "entrepreneurial identity"', in *Frontiers of Entrepreneurship Research*, Wellesley, MA: Babson College Entrepreneurship Research Conference.

Nakatsu, R., M. Rauterberg and P. Vorderer (2005), 'A new framework for entertainment computing: from passive to active experience', in F. Kishino, Y. Kitamura, H. Kato and N. Nagata (eds), *Entertainment Computing*, Heidelberg: Springer, pp. 1–12.

Nicholls-Nixon, C.L., A.C. Cooper and C.Y. Woo (2000), 'Strategic experimentation: understanding change and performance in new ventures', *Journal of Business Venturing*, **15**(4): 493–521.

Ronstadt, R. (1984), *Entrepreneurship*, Dover, MA: Lord Publishing.

Sarasvathy, S.D. (2001), 'Causation and effectuation: toward a theoretical shift from economic inevitability to entrepreneurial contingency', *Academy of Management Review*, **26**(2): 243–88.

Schindehutte, M., M. Morris and J. Allen (2005), 'Homosexuality and entrepreneurship: implications of gay identity for the venture-creation experience', *International Journal of Entrepreneurship and Innovation*, **6**(1): 27–40.

Sexton, D. and P. Van Auken (1982), *Experiences in Entrepreneurship and Small Business Management*, Englewood Cliffs, NJ: Prentice-Hall.

Shepherd, D. and M. Haynie (2007), 'Birds of a feather don't always flock together: identity management in entrepreneurship', *Journal of Business Venturing*, **24**(3): 316–37.

Smith, N.R. and J.B. Miner (1983), 'Type of entrepreneur, type of firm, and managerial motivation: implications for organizational life cycle theory', *Strategic Management Journal*, **4**(3): 325–40.

Standish, R.K. (2001), 'On complexity and emergence', *Complexity International*, **9**, accessed 18 November 2011 at http://arxiv.org/abs/nlin.AO/0101006.

Steyaert, C. (2004), 'The prosaics of entrepreneurship', in D. Hjorth and C. Steyaert (eds), *Narrative and Discursive Approaches in Entrepreneurship*, Cheltenham, UK and Northhampton, MA, USA: Edward Elgar.

Tang, J., K. Kacmar and L. Busenitz (in press), 'Entrepreneurial alertness in the pursuit of new opportunities', *Journal of Business Venturing*.

Tsoukas, H. and R. Chia (2002), 'On organizational becoming: rethinking organizational change', *Organization Science*, **13**(5): 567–82.

Turner, V. (1982), *From Ritual to Theatre*, New York: Performing Arts Journal Press.

Vesper, K. (1980), *New Venture Strategies*, Englewood Cliffs, NJ: Prentice-Hall, Inc.

Weick, K.E. (1979), *The Social Psychology of Organizing*, Reading, MA: Addison-Wesley.

Weick, K.E. (1998), 'Introductory essay: improvisation as a mindset for organizational analysis', *Organizational Science*, **9**(5): 543–55.

Westhead, P., D. Ucbasaran and M. Wright (2005), 'Decisions, actions, and performance: do novice, serial, and portfolio entrepreneurs differ?', *Journal of Small Business Management*, **43**(4): 393–417.

9. Entrepreneurship as peak experience*

> There were probably about five games in my career where everything was
> moving in slow motion and you could be out there all day, totally in the zone,
> and you don't even know where you are on the field, everything is just totally
> blocked out.
> (Lawrence Taylor, American football player)

INTRODUCTION

As an experience, entrepreneurship represents a complex and evolutionary phenomenon, and its more salient aspects remain unclear. In this
chapter, we explore the manner in which the higher-intensity aspects
of an entrepreneurial venture are experienced. Three interrelated constructs from psychology would seem to offer promising insights into
these high-intensity periods: peak experience, peak performance, and
flow. Maslow's (1971) notion of peak experience, if applied to entrepreneurship, approaches venture creation and growth as an aspect of
self-actualization and optimal emotional functioning. Peak performance
concerns situations where individuals are motivated by circumstances to
perform at unusually high levels (Privette, 1981). Flow is a positive experiential state where the individual is totally connected to the task and
personal skills are equal to the required challenges (Csikszentmihalyi,
1997).

These three constructs are relevant in explaining how entrepreneurs
experience the venture creation process and, importantly, whether their
personal performance is affected by the nature of the experience. A conceptual model linking these three constructs to one another and to the
entrepreneurial process is presented. To assess the model, results are
reported of a series of in-depth interviews with a cross-sectional sample
of entrepreneurs. The relevance of these three constructs is assessed
using both qualitative and quantitative analyses, with specific reference to a series of entrepreneurial events at representative stages of the
entrepreneurial process.

THE ENTREPRENEURIAL EXPERIENCE AS PEAKS AND VALLEYS

Various researchers have noted that entrepreneurial ventures involve peaks and valleys in terms of the intensity and complexity of the pressures and demands placed on the founder (Boyd and Gumpert, 1983; Hornaday and Aboud, 1971; Rabin, 1996). This might imply that there are periods of high pressure and stress, higher relative uncertainty about outcomes, more ambiguity, and less sense of control, and periods that are slower, more stable, and more predictable. Moltz (2003), in describing the entrepreneurial process, uses the metaphor of trying to control a rollercoaster while riding it. We can refer to the relative peaks and valleys that an entrepreneur goes through as the *volatility* of the experience, while the speed or pace at which these peaks and valleys transpire can be thought of as the *velocity* of the experience.

The relative frequency of high-intensity periods would seem a function not only of circumstances surrounding the venture itself, but also of the choices made by the entrepreneur (Shane et al., 2003). That is, the entrepreneur is a key player in determining pathways for the venture that result in a higher or lower frequency of high-intensity periods, and the degree of intensity. To the extent that such periods are positive experiences or are a source of utility or benefit to the entrepreneur, they become desirable. In this manner, high-intensity experiences may become a source of motivation to the entrepreneur.

A key question concerns what happens during higher-intensity periods, such as when the ability to obtain a key order will make or break the firm, or the likelihood of completing a major contract on time and under budget appears problematic, or a bank loan is about to be called and the firm's payroll cannot be met.

HIGH-INTENSITY ACTIVITIES: THREE PSYCHOLOGICAL CONSTRUCTS

What is it like for the entrepreneur during high-intensity periods? Are there particular psychic, sensory, or emotional aspects that define the manner in which individuals experience the pressures and uncertainties that characterize these periods? The field of psychology offers three key phenomena that may be useful in furthering our understanding of the more intense periods that occur when creating and growing a venture. These phenomena are termed peak experience, peak performance, and flow. Privette (2001) suggests that each of these represents a type of integrative human experience, as opposed to a type of human behavior, and that each is a unique aspect of a particular individual and context.

Peak performance can be defined as an episode of superior functioning or reaching the upper limits of human potential as manifested in excellence, productivity, or creativity. It is performance that transcends what normally could be expected in a given situation. Manifestations of efforts that exceed one's predictable level of functioning (Privette, 1981) might include physical strength in a crisis, prowess in sporting events, creative expression in art, intellectual mastery of a problem, or a rich human relationship (Privette, 1982). It is associated with exceptional energy, extraordinary strength, speed, and endurance where athletes rise to a level of performance that seems impossible, almost superhuman (Murphy and White, 1995). The performance is intentional, as the person has a will to behave in a superior way, but the action seems to just flow out of the person. Experiential discriminators of peak performance include spontaneity, a click of functional autonomy, strong sense of self, fascination, prior interest, involvement, intentionality, and peak experience (Privette, 1981). Examples of peak performance outcomes, each of which is an extrinsic motivator, include financial gain, glory, pursuit of personal best, and setting a world record, among others.

Peak performance may affect and be affected by *peak experience*. Peak experience is a prototype of feeling. It is defined as an intense and highly-valued moment or period that surpasses the usual level of intensity, meaningfulness, and richness both perceptually and cognitively (Privette and Bundrick, 1991). Although peak experience is often the result of a peak performance (Maslow, 1971), the interrelationship of the two is reciprocal and statistically significant. Peak experiences are emotional, highly memorable, and personally significant (McAlexander and Schouten, 1998) and are associated with intense feelings of joy, fun, peace, serenity, exhilaration, and happiness (Csikszentmihalyi, 1997). They are characterized by personal absorption and immediate involvement, strong focus, singleness of purpose, self-validation, and can result in self-transformation or self-renewal and a deeper sense of meaning in life (Arnould and Price, 1993). Hence they have emotional as well as intellectual components. They can vary in duration, and can be a single event, occur periodically, or be a progression towards an ultimate experience based on numerous optimal experiences that build upon one other.

Flow refers to the psychological state underlying peak performance. It is a state of focused energy, a transcendent state of well-being, involving a spiritual dimension and a euphoric sensation and ecstatic moments, and is characterized by total focus and absorption of transcendent awareness (Jackson and Csikszentmihalyi, 1999; Waitley, 1991). Flow is an autotelic experience, one that is intrinsically rewarding that we choose to do for its own sake (Csikszentmihalyi, 1990). It is a positive experiential state where the performer is totally connected to the performance in a situation where personal skills equal required challenges. Others have described flow as a mystical experience with exceptional feats of strength and endurance (Murphy and White, 1995), an uplifting event, with a sense of mastery and control or a sense of invincibility. Flow-like states are considered to be similar to hypnotic states in which there is a dissociation or detachment from one's surroundings, with total absorption in the present moment, and perceptual distortions such as altered perceptions of time (Grove and Lewis, 1996).

In some instances, flow enhances performance and contributes to optimal performance (i.e., maximum or greater than maximum perform-ance levels) by allowing one to continue against the odds and overcome fatigue and pain to finish a task or meet a challenge. With flow, nothing extraneous is allowed to interfere, and the person often senses a loss of time and space and self, boundless energy, and a perception of mastery and control. He or she finds purpose and intrinsic reward in the activ-ity itself, especially when the challenge matches the individual's skill. Although being "in the zone" is often associated with a rush (Lewis, 2002), flow does not always involve an emotional high. Qualities of the "zone" include profound joy, acute intuition (almost precognition), a feeling of effortlessness in the midst of intense exertion, feelings of awe and perfection, increased mastery and self-transcendence (Csikszentmihalyi, 1997). Conditions necessary for the zone include craftsmanship, devotion, and total immersion (Cooper, 1998). These are intrinsically rewarding moments associated with a sense of self-mastery and a spiritual experi-ence. Csikszentmihalyi and Csikszentmihalyi (1988) characterized flow on nine dimensions: (1) challenge–skill balance (e.g., "was challenging but also seemed automatic"); (2) action–awareness merging (e.g., "being in the groove"); (3) clear goals (e.g., "really knowing what you were going to do"); (4) unambiguous feedback (e.g., "receiving feedback from my movements that I was at the right pace"); (5) concentration on the task at hand (e.g., "feel really focused"); (6) sense of control (e.g., "feel like I can do anything in that state" or "you can't imagine anything going wrong"); (7) loss of self-consciousness (e.g., "doing things instinctively and con-fidently"); (8) transformation of time; and (9) autotelic experience (e.g., "really enjoyable, may leave you on a high").

There can be a strong reciprocal relationship between peak performance and peak experience (Privette, 1981) that in extreme situations is associ-ated with flow, which in turn enhances performance (see Figure 9.1). Flow occurs in situations where there is a balance between the challenge of the

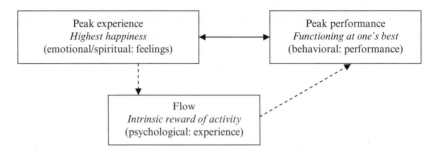

Figure 9.1   Three interrelated constructs

task and the skills of the person, while peak experience occurs where both challenges and skills lie above the average level. Flow happens during episodes that involve both positive performance and positive feeling, but is not associated with optimal joy or performance (Privette, 1983). Privette (1986) notes that the antitheses of peak performance and peak experience are failure and misery, respectively. Although each experience is a distinct, positive, and subjective experience, the three experiences share many qualities such as absorption, joy, spontaneity, a sense of power, personal identity, and involvement (Privette and Sherry, 1986). The three phenomenological experiences may occur in isolation, such as when a crisis results in peak performance that is not accompanied by peak experience or flow. However, when a single event involves more than one of these experiences, each offers a different perspective of the event. The most salient features of the three constructs are contrasted and compared in Table 9.1. These features are helpful in determining when an experience is exclusively peak performance, peak experience, or flow, and when it involves more than one of these constructs.

Linkages to Entrepreneurship

Researchers have examined these three constructs in a variety of contexts, including competitive sports, whitewater rafting, acting, motorcycling, prayer, encounters in nature, product consumption, and near-death episodes (e.g., Allen, 2002; Arnould and Price, 1993; Dodson, 1996; McAlexander and Schouten, 1998; Pates et al., 2001). For instance, Privette (1981) reports on athletes from a range of sports who describe similar peak experiences characterized by clarity and sharpness of focus, total absorption, a sense of confidence in performance, boundless energy, spontaneous behavior that allows forceful action that is effortless, and a strong desire to perform well. Prior interest and fascination with the

Table 9.1   Contrasting and comparing peak experience, peak performance, and flow

	Peak Experience	Peak Performance	Flow
Prototype construct	Feeling: extreme level of positive feeling	Performance: extreme level of performance	Does not imply, but may include peak experience or performance
Definition	Intense and highly valued moment	Episode of superior (almost superhuman) functioning	Capacity for full engagement in an activity
Distinguishing characteristics	Fulfillment, significance, and spirituality	Full focus and self in clear process	Play, outer structure, and the importance of other people
Descriptors	Joyful, transitory, rare, unexpected, extraordinary, cosmic, ecstasy, highly memorable	Spontaneity, functional autonomy, strong sense of self, involvement, intentionality	Challenge–skill balance; action–awareness merging, clear goals, unambiguous feedback, sense of control, concentration
Triggers	Art, nature, sexual love, religion, creative work, exercise/ movement, childbirth, music, scientific knowledge, recollection/ introspection	Physical strength in a crisis, prowess in sporting events, creative expression or acts, intellectual mastery of a problem	Transcendental/ peak/religious experiences, collective ritual, zen, yoga, meditation
Passive mode	Perceptual/ receptive	Transactive/ responsive	Active/interactive
Unique quality	Intense feelings of joy, fun, peace, serenity, exhilaration, happiness	Exceptional energy Extraordinary strength Endurance	Intrinsically enjoyable or autotelic experience Transpersonal/ mystical associated with fusion and loss of self

Table 9.1   (continued)

	Peak Experience	Peak Performance	Flow
Antitheses	Misery	Failure	Not in sync, disjointed
Other people	Companionable and contributing	Not important/relevant; focus is on personal performance	Interactive and often important contributors

activity were also commonly found. Dodson (1996) provides evidence of a relationship between having a peak experience when mountain biking and incorporating the bike into the individual's extended self. Allen (2002) demonstrates relationships between peak experiences of motorcyclists and both their personal values and a number of attitudinal measures.

Privette and Bundrick (1987) allow for the occurrence of peak performance and peak experience in a work context, and note significant commonalities in the underlying characteristics of both constructs in work and non-work contexts. Csikszentmihalyi (1990) cites examples of flow in people's work lives, especially where work is meaningfully related to people's identities and their ultimate goals. He also associates work-related flow events in terms of increasing levels of complexity of challenges and the transformation of opportunities in one's environment into action. Separately, Privette (1983) suggests flow is especially likely when pursuing endeavors at the frontier of a field. Accordingly, entrepreneurship would seem an especially rich area within which to examine these constructs.

Research on these three constructs suggests that they are more typically experienced under conditions of absorbed concentration, higher demands, adversity, unanticipated stress, visualized goals, as well as situations where control is possible, when pursuing endeavors at the frontier of a field, and when undertaking activities involving required learning of skills, feedback, high levels of motivation, commitment and self-confidence (Gould et al., 1992; Privette, 2001; Williams and Krane, 1998). The role of stress is particularly noteworthy, in that it must be accompanied by perceived limits that one believes can be transcended. Further, it is important to periodically engage in a process of disciplined recovery from stress (Loehr and Schwartz, 2001). Otherwise, stress is a disruptive factor that can lead to negative, regressive experiences.

These conditions would seem to aptly describe the entrepreneurial context, that is, the activities and events that occur over the stages of the entrepreneurial process, or as a new venture is conceptualized, implemented, grown, and harvested. Ventures are said to vary in terms of how entrepreneurial they are based on their relative levels of innovativeness, risk, and proactiveness (Morris, 1998) and their relative growth orientation (Zahra and Dess, 2001).

Accordingly, we should expect that entrepreneurs will meaningfully identify with the concepts of peak experience, peak performance, and flow, and that those in a high-growth context will tend to do so to a stronger degree than entrepreneurs in a low-growth context. More specifically, it is proposed that high-growth situations produce more high-intensity situations, such that entrepreneurs have more peak experiences and these enhance personal performance. Peak experiences are accompanied by feelings of joy and ecstasy, and can provide turning points in life. The entrepreneur has an epiphany that changes his or her perceptions of life. Also, in high-growth situations, entrepreneurs are more likely to experience flow, and this contributes to higher personal performance. Latent abilities are released for transcendent functioning. Optimal experiences give direction to capabilities. The entrepreneur's own performance is characterized by functioning that is more efficient, more productive, and in some ways better than his or her normal behavior. Peak crisis responses have a long-term positive impact on the entrepreneur. The entrepreneur emerges with renewed self-awareness.

A CONCEPTUAL MODEL

To ascertain the extent to which these three psychological constructs apply to the entrepreneurial experience, cross-sectional descriptive survey research was undertaken. To guide the research, a conceptual model was developed. As illustrated in Figure 9.2, the entrepreneur's performance at various stages of the entrepreneurial process sets the context. The entrepreneur has certain expectations about his or her own performance relative to his or her normal performance levels and that of others, based on a number of subjective criteria. The entrepreneur's ongoing response to events that occur during venture start-up and growth impacts the entrepreneur's performance levels. Specifically, a single event (challenging situation) could involve only one construct (e.g., either peak performance or peak experience or flow), a combination of any two of these constructs (e.g., peak performance and flow), or all three constructs simultaneously. The constructs individually or collectively offer different perspectives on the event. Mediating effects or triggers that lead to peak experience and peak performance might include mental preparation, goal-setting and motivation, experience, anxiety, a sense of self, and the extent to which

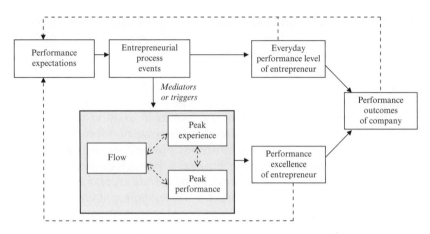

Figure 9.2   Conceptual model

the challenging situation threatens the entrepreneur's ego or the survival of the company, among others (Privette, 2001). The level of performance effort subsequently results in superior performance outcomes and potentially self-actualization if individual performance exceeds expectations. In the absence of any of the three constructs or in the event that the entrepreneur's performance merely meets expectations, the result is average performance and satisfaction.

Testing the Model

A series of structured personal interviews were conducted with two samples of entrepreneurs. The typical interview lasted approximately one hour and was conducted at the entrepreneur's business location. The survey instrument included qualitative and quantitative elements. A set of open-ended questions were used to determine normal or typical levels of performance in performing the work of an entrepreneur, assess whether respondents could recall incidents or experiences where they performed at unusual or superlative levels, and, if so, to characterize the nature of those experiences. Other questions explored the relevance of being "in the zone," experiencing moments of harmony, getting "a rush," and experiencing "highly-valued moments" when performing entrepreneurial tasks.

In addition, the instrument included 34 scaled items from psychometrically validated scales to measure flow (Jackson and Marsh, 1996; Privette and Bundrick, 1991), peak experiences (Dodson, 1996; Privette and Bundrick, 1991), and peak performance (Privette, 1982). These items were accompanied by a five-point strongly agree–strongly disagree response scale. Privette and Bundrick (1991) have conducted psychometric studies to support construct validity. Reported reliabilities (Cronbach's alpha) for these three sub-scales have ranged from 0.75 to 0.95. Finally, respondents were asked to provide information on personal and business characteristics.

Delmar et al. (2003), among others, have drawn a distinction between small businesses and entrepreneurial ventures, where the latter are characterized by goals of profitability and growth, and employ innovative strategic practices. Because of its emphasis on growth and innovation, and the accompanying peaks and valleys in terms of activity levels, pressures, and uncertainties, the entrepreneurial venture would seem an especially conducive environment for producing peak experiences, encouraging peak performance, and enabling flow. Accordingly, and for comparative purposes, a total of 140 in-depth interviews were conducted with founding entrepreneurs from 70 high-growth and 70 low-growth enterprises.

The high-growth sample was selected from a list of rapid-growth companies prepared by the chambers of commerce in three geographically distinct metropolitan areas, while the low-growth sample was drawn from the general chamber memberships. In each instance, the founder was contacted by telephone prior to the field interview to solicit participation and verify the firm's growth orientation. The distinction between high- and low-growth firms was based on measures of growth aspirations and reported growth rates, together with observable indicators of growth (e.g., market definition, scope of operations, financing structure). High-growth businesses demonstrated strong growth aspirations, served regional, national or international markets, and were often equity financed. They reported a peak in annual growth rates beyond the first two years ranging from 51 to 500 percent. While a number were high-tech firms, this group also included restaurant chains, specialized manufacturers, and logistics management companies, among others. Alternatively, low-growth businesses operated in local markets with one or a few locations, most often as retail and service firms, relied on self, family, and friends for start-up capital, and reported annual growth rates beyond the first two years (revenues) below 25 percent.

Qualitative Results

The entrepreneurs generally viewed themselves as high performers relative to other business professionals. The most frequently mentioned criteria used by respondents in defining high performance included work "commitment level" (e.g., more than 100 percent, seven days a week), "making sacrifices," "passion," the "ability to anticipate/react quickly/

seize opportunities," "knowledge of the business," and "making right choices."

More noteworthy was a strong tendency to identify with the concepts of peak performance, peak experience, and flow. The large majority (82 percent) of entrepreneurs were clearly able to cite extraordinary experiences where they performed at truly superlative levels in their ventures. When asked about words that best describe how the entrepreneur felt when functioning at his or her personal best in their venture, the most frequently cited terms were excitement/enthusiasm, adrenaline/energy, joy/elation/triumph, pride, confidence, focus, awareness, and fear. In describing flow events, respondents regularly used such terms as natural, perform on instinct, clarity of purpose, being "on" in an unexpected way, in control, magical, everything just starts going right, you forget time and space, everything clicks, and total focus.

Representative examples of respondents' descriptions of peak performance incidents, as well as peak experiences and flow are shown in Table 9.2. As illustrated in the table, respondents recalled incidents that can be explicitly linked to various stages of the entrepreneurial process. In some instances, only one of the three constructs was in evidence, while in others two or all three were experienced simultaneously. The range of examples provided by respondents suggests that incidents of high emotional intensity and intense physical or mental performance were associated with all phases of the venture process.

A different selection of examples from the interviews illustrating each of the components in the conceptual model (see Figure 9.2) is provided in Table 9.3. Incidents during which respondents could recall experiencing peak performance, peak experience or flow usually involved intense activity, tight deadlines, extreme pressure, and lots of change. Some of the more frequently recalled events included sales presentations, negotiating a deal, and IPO road shows. The presence of the three constructs and the resultant impact on performance effort are confirmed in the examples cited. Peak performance was often described in terms of a rollercoaster experience in which extreme highs were followed by extreme lows. Three words most often mentioned as being part of peak performance events were confidence, determination, and exhilaration. A number of respondents expressed the feelings they experienced during an event in a cognitive manner with words such as vision, clarity of action, keen awareness, and focus. By contrast, others explained that "awareness is almost tangible . . . everything you touch is magical."

Factors that triggered higher performance included setting goals, passion, optimism, competitive spirit, and strong desire to win. Several respondents mentioned challenges on the scale of David against Goliath

Table 9.2 Examples of peak experience, peak performance, and flow at particular stages in the entrepreneurial process

Step in process	Associated with	Representative example from respondent interviews
Opportunity	Peak performance, peak experience and flow	"We had proposed to do an equipment management program for one of the largest EPA contractors. And this program concept had been my idea originally many, many years before. I had been talking about it and talking about it and in fact I made a presentation to this company probably four years before they came back to me and said we remember the conversation and would like you to come in and talk to us about it. And we made the presentation and were awarded the proposal. No one was doing this in the business. We had never done it either but I knew what we could do and how we should do it. The excitement started with me writing the proposal. And it was a government contract so they had to go out for bids, but I knew there was no one else who was going to respond. I was probably going 20 hours a day for probably ten days. And it was just wild. I was coming into the office at 3:30 in the morning and just typing away creating stuff. I had the jazz music playing and I'm getting choked up, it was so cool. Ah, it was great! What I was doing was I was creating and I had jazz music going and was just a maniac and the people could see."
Concept	Peak experience	"Let me think . . . maybe there are two of them that are slightly different. One was more for the enterprise, one was more personal. At XXXX apart from developing a $100m business in three years we made it a pledge when we started the company that we will be very connected to our community in Washington DC and we had our own charitable foundation – that we set up – our employees contributed a parallel payroll deduction to this and made our vendors do matching gifts and we supported a number of charities very early on. And . . . the *Washington Post* presented me with a community service award . . . you know some big black tie thing in Washington . . . and I guess that felt very good because not only were we successful in promoting our business and pushing the industry, and creating a great environment from a polluter standpoint but we also were recognized for all this effort and got a community service award from the *Washington Post* at a big black tie dinner of 3000 business leaders in Washington. Yes that was quite a moving experience . . . unexpected too."

Table 9.2 (*continued*)

Step in process	Associated with	Representative example from respondent interviews
Resources	Peak experience	"[B]ut it probably goes back to the day when I met with my banker and she said we're not sure where this is going and the way I read that is that she not only didn't believe in me but she didn't believe in the business. At that time I probably had 30 employees. It meant that I would have been a failure to these 30 people that had invested their lives with me. And that bothered me overwhelmingly. Instead of saying ok, ok, though, I took it to the next level. The negative situation triggered a response from my end that encouraged me to find alternative sources of financing, which I did. And I found it in two people who believed in me. And I think they said 'you know, we're not only betting on your company's assets but we're betting on you as a human being, as a positive credit risk and that's how we're making our decision.' Nobody had ever said that to me in my career. One of the greatest levels of satisfaction I ever had was when I found the note, which was a two-page document believe it or not for a multimillion dollar loan, and I said 'is this all I sign?.' And they said 'that's it, we believe in you.' . . . When I signed my name, it was absolute euphoria to me because I was ridding myself of an organization who I felt didn't believe in me as a person, that didn't believe in my dream, my goals, my skills, and I was aligning myself with a partner, a team that did believe in me as a human being, as a person, as an organization. It was absolutely fantastic. On the payments thereafter I felt a high satisfaction of making each one. That was a significant emotional experience."
Management	Peak performance	"I think it's the competitive spirit. It's the – figuring out a way to win. It's a belief that there's a solution for every problem, the adrenaline that kicks in when you have something going that can be tremendously successful. Whether it's negotiating a deal, getting a contract, we have an automotive supply business where we get into bidding and negotiations with major auto manufacturers for machine parts they have. We got a couple of major contracts that we've won because . . . it's hard to explain. There are certain situations where the game is on the line. You have to take your thinking process and gamesmanship to another level."

Growth	Flow, peak performance and peak experience	"It very much applies. You could be having a presentation to a customer or a prospect that you hope to make into a customer and everything starts going right and you just forget time and space and everything and it just may be going well. I'd say that is in the zone and you're just going on instinct and it's not rehearsed or anything like that and you're just doing the right thing, saying the right thing at the right time. I think another aspect of that is also in the technology area . . . we are developing very sophisticated software and there are times where we just make huge strides in advancing the technology in a very short period of time and other times we are just banging our heads against the wall for months. That again, you feel like you're in the zone and everything is going right and what you're doing . . . customers see it and they go crazy over us because you just advanced the state of the art. So there are periods where I think everything is just clicking and it feels wonderful and just natural and you don't even need to think about it."
Harvest	Peak performance	"We were trying to get an IPO done and at the beginning of 1996 the climate was fairly good for getting an IPO done and so we put together a blue chip team of underwriters Solomon Bros and Montgomery Securities and our lawyers and accountants worked getting the IPO prospectus finished. And the day before we had to start the road show marketing of the offering the markets just collapsed. And so the underwriters said no, we are not just going to go out and market the offering . . . we've got to wait . . . the decision we made at the time was to get another underwriter and set Sept 1st as the date we were going to try to scale it and it was part of that decision we did not fold the growth back, so it was a very risky decision . . . and we found a new underwriter, Freeman and Ramsey in Washington and sure enough the economy did come back after Labor Day and we were the first ones to get the IPO on a road show and we got our $60 million financing done at the end of September. So our company stayed on the same path and enjoyed this stable operating investment when we got the $60 million in operating capital we were really ahead. So during that time period it was holding everything together and keeping the current investors in line, keeping the company optimistic that the future was going to provide some capital and figuring out a way to get the financing done and like I said, conventional wisdom was that it couldn't be done. So we got it done."

199

Table 9.3 Examples of experiences that support elements in the conceptual model

Component in model	Representative example from respondent interviews
Performance expectations	"I think it's the desire. I just hate to lose. I absolutely hate to lose whether it's an order. Whether it's hiring somebody that you really want to hire. Whether it's getting excited about providing opportunities for people who want to work for you. And I guess it's just the passion of success is so significant and maybe driven by the fear of failure. I mean I think both of those push you in the same direction but two at the other end of the spectrum of feelings. But both drive, I believe, in a high-energy entrepreneur."
Entrepreneur process events	"[A]nd some issue we faced and the conventional wisdom would have said: how did we ever make it out of that? How did we ever make that decision? How did we get that customer to sign on at that period in time . . . again there is this unexplainable mustering of resources to be able to lead through and make decisions during these very troubling and turbulent times. And . . . yeah I do . . . you look back and you think . . . how did we get into that, how did we get that customer to be a reference, how did we ever solve what looked like an insurmountable technical problem?"
Peak experience, flow, and peak performance	"Senses are heightened . . . you are prepared and know your stuff . . . you feel like nothing can disrupt you and you can overcome everything . . . I would do road show presentations and I had them feeding out of my hand . . . energy level is almost unnatural . . . you are fully engaged mentally and typically emotionally . . . you feel ethereal, untouchable, impervious."
Performance excellence (not normal performance)	*Superior performance in terms of the company* "The criteria in my mind would be the company's results . . . a reflection on the entrepreneur that is leading the company. In this particular marketplace, we are a high-tech company. In the high-tech market there are an awful lot of companies that have gone out of business or who are in really deep trouble financially. So, I look at that and now there are others who are growing and doing well but they are in a small minority. So, I think the fact that we have survived this period, we're growing, we're getting good results, we have low attrition rates, people like it here. All the criteria I would use on stability, growth, and results of the company's efforts would say you have to have someone who is making the right decisions and doing the right thing."

200

Superior performance of the entrepreneur

"Performance is measured only by results. I'm in top 10–20 percent, minute and detail elements in which performance is measured. The ability to make quick decisions and quality decisions. My company is one of the best . . . I call it analysis with speed. It is easy to have the speed and not the quality analysis and it is easy to have analysis but no sense of urgency. That generally delivers higher throughput . . . ability to do more in less time. Common sense, analysis with speed, and the last thing is the ability to work on 80/20. More than 20 percent of the things on the agenda deliver 80 percent of the results. That's how you hire, drive hire . . . there are 24 hours in a day, no one can work more than 24 hours, no one can work productively more than 16 hours I believe on a consistent basis. That's where these plateaus are. I work around 12–14 hours a day effectively. That comes to about 70 hours a week, after which my effectiveness goes away. So the challenge is how to do what other people do in 140 hours in 70 hours."

Meet performance expectations versus exceed performance expectations

"In a negotiation with capital providers I took a capital structure that would have had me own 51 percent of the company along with a couple of partners, and the venture firm would have had warrants for 49 percent of the company. We would have had to invest 1 million dollars based on projected rate of return 30 percent annually. What I did was negotiated the warrants away so we had 100 percent ownership sub-debt to the venture firm at a maximum annual return of 25 percent to the venture firm. We purchased a business that had a value of 4 million with 500k in cash. The rest was with various forms of debt. We then turned that business around to a point that one year after we purchased it the 4 million business was worth 15 million. We had paid off all the debt and taken out the entire capital structure. That provided us with free cash flow that financed the acquisition over the next four years of an additional 15 radio stations. And ultimately was the basis for creating a business that was later sold six years out for 200 million on a 500k investment. It was above average. It was a very intense negotiation with experienced bankers and venture capitalists that led to a dramatic change in the terms that they were proposing, still getting the deal done. Literally quadrupled what became an almost infinite rate of return."

Table 9.3 (*continued*)

Component in model	Representative example from respondent interviews
Feedback from self and others	"[B]eing able to stand up in front of a group and verbally walk them through slowly and precisely answer questions they field, and be able to respond quickly and adeptly on your feet to criticism and being able to modify that plan in your head and on your feet and explain to them how you would do that to accomplish their desired goals. Modifying layouts of streets or access points or landscaping plans so that they all of a sudden have comfort with it and being able to achieve that goal of approval on the development plan very quickly, and in a sense effortlessly. Because you do it over and over again you develop a level of comfort with talking about things like this at a high level, not just say, well here's the plan and how I'm going to do this, but here's the plan, now let me walk you through it and explain what you're going to see when we drive in and how it plays out and how it's going to benefit the overall community, how it's going to serve the residents, and enhance what you have around and expand on that and have them start to get excited about it."

and fear of failure as key factors resulting in enhanced performance effort. Moreover, respondents could clearly identify when their own personal performance was superior to normal, everyday levels. In periods of more typical performance, they were not aware of intensely emotional moments or the presence of an adrenaline rush. They noticed substantial increases in work commitment level, energy levels, willingness to make sacrifices, as well as an ability to anticipate potential outcomes and react quickly. Interestingly, respondents also mentioned performance excellence in terms of outcomes related *to the company* when there were whole periods of intense activity rather than more isolated intense events. Specific company performance measures that signaled exceptional performance were growth spurts, higher sales levels, and improved financial results. Additionally, the effects of peak performance, flow or peak experience on performance levels were reinforced by the positive emotions generated during the event as well as immediate feedback from others. One respondent expressed this as follows: "you get the right information, present the right features and benefits at the right time with the right chemistry . . . I can just feel it . . . you get instantaneous feedback."

One respondent specifically mentioned the role of peak experience in terms of self-actualization through his venture:

> I was selected to be on the cover of *Forbes* magazine with eight other people – Meg from eBay, Bill Hambrecht, the guy that started Idealab, Bill Gross, and that was emotional because it was recognition for me that reflected back . . . my family was proud, my kids were proud about that . . . a tremendous sense of accomplishment and pride . . . . And for me personally it was more a sense of after 15 years when you get some kind of self-actualization – you work yourself up and get on the cover of *Forbes* magazine and your eldest daughter goes and buys 10 copies and keeps them around the house.

Quantitative Results

The scaled measures of the three constructs were then evaluated. To assess the internal consistency of the items used to measure peak experience (12 items), flow (12), and peak performance (10), corrected item-total correlations were examined for each scale. Items with correlations < 0.35 were eliminated from further analysis. This procedure resulted in deleting two items from the peak experience scale, "I was totally absorbed in the task at hand and lost a sense of time" and "My business seemed like it was a part of me." Four items were deleted from the flow scale: "I did things instinctively and confidently without having to think about it," "It was no effort to keep my mind on what I was doing," "My goals were very clear to me and I knew what needed to be done," and "I was not concerned with what others may have been thinking of me." Three items were also deleted from the peak performance scale: "I felt compelled to continue until finished," "My performance was enhanced because it was an emergency/crisis situation," and "I was aware that others were paying attention."

Next, responses on the remaining scale items were summed for each of the constructs and individual item correlations with constructs they purport to measure were compared to their correlations with other constructs. Items not significantly ($p < 0.05$) correlated higher with intended constructs were candidates for deletion. This procedure resulted in deleting only one flow item, "I felt I understood something new and important as a result of the experience," that was highly correlated with the peak experience scale.

Cronbach's alpha (α) was used to assess overall scale reliability. Applying the criterion of 0.70 for satisfactory reliability (Nunnally, 1978), computed α of 0.73 for flow, 0.85 for peak experience, and 0.70 for peak performance demonstrated reliability adequate for the analysis to proceed. Items surviving the procedures outlined above were summed to form composite measures of their respective constructs. Descriptive statistics for included items along with a summary of scale reliability is provided by constructs in Table 9.4.

Mean scores on each of the constructs were relatively high for the overall sample (see Table 9.5). These means compare favorably to those reported in studies of the three constructs in non-business contexts (competitive sports, mountain biking) (e.g., Dodson, 1996; Privette, 1981). An attempt was then made to determine whether the high-growth context, ostensibly with its greater frequency of high-intensity or peak periods, resulted in higher mean scores on the three constructs than the low-growth context. A multivariate procedure that retains all available information regarding the constructs was employed. Using a series of individual t-tests would preclude the possibility that correlation among the constructs as a set provides evidence of overall group differences (Hair et al., 1998). Theoretical descriptions of the three constructs suggest much commonality (see Privette, 1983 for a review) and Bartlett's test of sphericity ($p < 0.00$) confirmed the existence of significant inter-correlation. Consequently, a one-way multivariate analysis of variance (MANOVA) was performed to test for significant ($p \leq 0.05$) overall differences and any univariate effects on individual constructs. For the analysis, group differences were considered as two levels of one independent factor and the three constructs as a set of related dependent measures.

Results of the MANOVA are presented in Table 9.5. Because the test is directional, that is, respondents classified as high-growth entrepreneurs ($n = 68$) are expected to outscore those who are low growth ($n = 70$),

Table 9.4 Descriptive statistics and reliability for the composite scales

Item/scale	Mean	Standard deviation	Item-total correlation	Alpha (α)
Peak experience:	36.67	6.61		0.85
The experience was a highly valued moment	4.39	0.73	0.41	
The experience made me reflect on who I really am	3.50	1.01	0.60	
I felt all-powerful joy	3.85	0.96	0.57	
I felt a sense of completeness after the incident	4.03	0.87	0.65	
Words are not enough to describe the experience	3.53	1.03	0.62	
I had confidence in myself that I didn't have before	3.46	1.14	0.45	
The experience was emotionally unlike normal work or life experiences	3.70	0.98	0.62	
The experience stands out in my mind because it was so emotionally intense	3.80	1.02	0.51	
Experience caused me to feel differently about myself	3.12	1.14	0.59	
I discovered new things about myself	3.28	1.11	0.58	
Flow:	26.48	4.12		0.73
The challenge and my skills were at an equally high level	4.11	0.81	0.46	
I was very aware of how well I was performing	3.98	0.92	0.41	
My total focus and attention were on the task at hand	4.25	0.80	0.42	
It felt like time stopped while busy with my activities	3.75	0.95	0.45	
I find experiences like this one are their own reward	4.19	0.91	0.48	
I felt transformed by the experience	3.30	1.13	0.46	
I felt I could do anything and nothing could go wrong	2.90	1.13	0.42	
Peak performance:	24.02	4.33		0.70
The ordinary sense of things faded	3.37	0.93	0.41	

Entrepreneurship as experience

Table 9.4 (*continued*)

Item/scale	Mean	Standard deviation	Item-total correlation	Alpha (α)
It seemed things went right without any special effort	3.23	1.23	0.45	
I found myself determined to do better than usual	3.86	1.02	0.41	
Reality was more real than usual during the incident	3.28	0.95	0.57	
My strength came from an unfamiliar source	2.77	1.14	0.35	
I thought of nothing but what was happening at that moment	3.60	1.05	0.35	
My performance was more spontaneous and effortless	3.90	0.86	0.37	

Table 9.5 *MANOVA results for high-growth vs. low-growth sub-groups*

Dependent variable	Mean	Standard deviation	F	p-value*
Peak experience:			8.05	< 0.01
High-growth	38.54	5.56		
Low-growth	35.23	7.01		
Flow experience:			5.17	0.01
High-growth	27.43	4.25		
Low-growth	25.76	3.90		
Peak performance:			3.85	0.03
High-growth	24.89	4.33		
Low-growth	23.36	4.25		

Notes:
Wilks' lambda λ (3,119) = 0.93, p = 0.02.
Bartlett's test ~ $\chi^2(3)$ = 128.16, p < 0.00.
* One-tailed test of significance reported.

p-values for a one-tailed test are reported. The multivariate Wilks' lambda [λ = 0.93] used to assess the overall effect of the independent variable on the set of dependent measures was significant (p = 0.02). Univariate F-tests were used to determine which of the constructs contributed to the overall difference. Observed differences for the group comparisons are significant

($p \le 0.03$) for all three of the constructs. An inspection of the group means clearly shows a pattern of response that is higher for entrepreneurs of high-growth compared to low-growth businesses.

A number of other MANOVAs were performed to test for group differences on such organizational characteristics as type and location of the company, growth rates and revenue achieved, size of the company in employees, number of years in operation, and the percentage of equity respondents had personally invested in the company. Differences in response were also examined with regard to respondents' personal characteristics of gender, age, education, ethnicity, and whether they perceived themselves as a high performer or not.

An overall significant effect ($\lambda = 0.93$, $p = 0.04$) was found for ethnicity. Significant univariate comparisons indicated mean differences in response that were higher for Caucasians vs. others on two of the constructs, peak performance and flow ($p \le 0.05$ for a two-tailed test), but not on *peak experience* ($p = 0.46$). For the rest of the group comparisons, none of the mean differences were large enough to be statistically significant, suggesting that respondents' identification with the constructs is similar along these characteristics.

CONCLUSIONS

The results suggest that sensory and emotional elements can play a prominent role in entrepreneurship. Specifically, the findings demonstrate that peak experience, peak performance, and flow are salient aspects of the entrepreneurial context. The process of achieving success in an environment characterized by stress, a multiplicity of obstacles and demands, and uncertainty regarding outcomes can produce a type of peak performance. Further, the entrepreneur can find such performance to be rewarding or self-actualizing, resulting in a peak experience. He or she periodically experiences a state of flow when applying personal skills and efforts to the myriad demands of a venture.

These findings have implications for entrepreneurial motives. Motives associated with entrepreneurship, such as achievement, drive, and egoistic passion, may be especially relevant during peak experiences, in that high levels of energy and stamina, a desire to meet challenging goals, and a love of the work enable the entrepreneur to function at peak levels (e.g., Morris, 1998; Shane et al., 2003). Further, entrepreneurs are more driven by achievement than extrinsic rewards such as money, while entrepreneurship offers a variety of intrinsic rewards (Bird, 1989; McClelland, 1961). The findings here shed light on the nature of these intrinsic rewards

and manner in which they are experienced. In essence, both researchers and practitioners may find it relevant to approach entrepreneurship
as a vehicle for self-actualization. Dodson (1996) notes that a defining
characteristic of a peak experience is the renewal of self and a deeper
sense of meaning and purpose in life. This perspective is consistent with
Csikszentmihalyi's (1990) suggestion that work undertaken as a flow
activity is the best way to fulfill human potentialities. Such an approach
would represent a departure from the traditional emphasis on entrepreneurship as a vehicle for wealth generation, job creation, economic development, and innovation.

The pursuit of an entrepreneurial venture is an evolutionary process
involving a multiplicity of decisions before, during, and following the
actual start-up of a firm. Multiple motives likely drive the entrepreneur
during this process, and these motives might be expected to evolve and
change as a venture unfolds. The entrepreneurial process itself, when a
positive experience, can become a source of these motives. Specifically,
where the entrepreneur achieves peak performance, has a peak experience,
or encounters flow, the corresponding sense of meaningfulness, fulfillment, self-validation, richness, or joy may become an end in itself. To
the extent that this is the case, the entrepreneur becomes further engaged
in the venture, producing further growth, or is keen to start additional
ventures. To some degree, then, entrepreneurship becomes an end in itself.

While the successful pursuit of entrepreneurship inherently involves
rational decision-making processes, emotional and sensory elements are
important interwoven elements in explaining the way an entrepreneur
thinks and acts. Hence, the occurrence of peak performance, peak experience, and flow might be expected to influence the entrepreneur's cognitive processes (Baron, 2004). For example, Brockner et al. (2004) discuss
the entrepreneur's "regulatory focus," or the tendency to approach the
regulation of one's own behavior from a promotion versus a prevention
orientation. The three phenomena examined in this chapter would seem
to encourage the regulation of one's behavior more from the vantage
point of opportunity achievement (promotion) rather than loss avoidance
(prevention), such that more opportunities are pursued. They might also
correlate with levels of entrepreneurial alertness, defined as a motivated
propensity to formulate an image of the future (Gaglio and Katz, 2001).
Baron (2004) posits a positive relationship between alertness to previously
unrecognized opportunities and a person's relative emphasis on attain-
ing positive outcomes over avoiding negative outcomes. To the extent
that the individual finds peak experience, peak performance, and flow
episodes to be enjoyable or fulfilling, these phenomena would also seem
consistent with a greater emphasis on achieving the positive rather than

avoiding the negative. Positive achievements are typical outcomes of these psychological phenomena.

Another linkage to cognitive processes can be found in signal detection theory (Swets, 1992). Entrepreneurs are thought to be more concerned with recognizing stimuli that are present than with correctly concluding stimuli are not present. Peak performance could also contribute to the entrepreneur's proficiency in recognizing the presence of stimuli, and especially in assessing risks, in that the individual is experiencing more spontaneity, a stronger sense of self, greater fascination, and higher involvement. Further, the presence of such cognitive biases as overconfidence and the willingness to endure sunk costs would seem consistent with the high level of absorption and immediate involvement, strong focus, singleness of purpose, and sense of infallibility associated with flow.

It appears that peak performance, peak experience, and flow are highly interrelated constructs in an entrepreneurial context. Each construct has contrasting as well as common aspects, all of which may not be found in any one event. A diverse mix of examples were provided by the entrepreneurs in our sample, sometimes with the same event used to describe all three constructs, while in other cases completely unique events were used to describe each of the constructs.

It is also noteworthy that the three constructs apply both to low- and high-growth ventures, but more so to the latter. While high-growth entrepreneurs strongly identified with the notions of peak experience, peak performance, and flow, so too did a large number of the lower-growth entrepreneurs. Although the demands of growth appear to heighten the tendency to achieve peak experiences, peak performance, and flow, the very nature of creating something from nothing, owning one's venture, and personal responsibility for results may contribute as much or more to the ability to experience the three constructs as do the demands and stress of rapid growth.

Given the extensive emphasis placed on the traits, values, and skills of entrepreneurs in the extant literature, it would seem especially relevant to explore whether individual differences affect the ability to experience peak performance, peak experiences, and flow, on the one hand, and whether interactions between personal characteristics and these three constructs affect organization performance. The degree of fit between entrepreneur and venture may affect and be affected by the ability to realize peak experience, peak performance, and flow. It may also be valuable to revisit the nature versus nurture issue as it applies to the achievement of peak performance levels in entrepreneurship.

A key question concerns the extent to which entrepreneurs can better prepare themselves to experience peak moments and peak performance, and whether such events can be created, engineered, or managed. For example, is it possible to re-engineer the subconscious/unconscious to eliminate inhibiting influences during periods of intense pressure? By relying on mechanisms such as letting go and learning to trust complex subconscious mechanisms, can the entrepreneur open the way for instinct and intuition? Can entrepreneurs make their own peak performance a frequent event? The joys of being in the zone can serve as a motivational tool that encourages entrepreneurs to push their performance to higher levels and achieve subsequent contentment and success. It would seem that entrepreneurs are able to enhance their cognitive capacities, most notably their focus, time management, positive thinking, and critical-thinking skills (Loehr and Schwartz, 2001). They must attempt to break the linearity of goal-oriented activity. Peak performance training programs can include relaxation, imagery, goal-setting, concentration, and cognitive self-management. Meditation and other non-cognitive activities can slow brainwave activity and stimulate a shift in mental activity from the left hemisphere of the brain to the right. The beneficial effects of self-management behavioral strategies (e.g., mental imagery, self-dialog on performance as a result of enhanced cognitions, behaviors, and affect) have been supported in a variety of sporting and business contexts. Manz and colleagues (1988) found that thought patterns of higher-performing managers differed significantly from those of lower-performing managers. It would seem that the exhilaration of peak performance can be attained by learning from athletes how to combine physical abilities, skills, and training with mental preparation that include relaxation techniques, focus, concentration, and emotional/ psychological as well as spiritual dimensions. An integrated model of high performance considers the body, the emotions, the mind, and the spirit (Loehr and Schwartz, 2001).

A number of other questions warrant attention if we are to understand the functioning of these three constructs in an entrepreneurial context. From a managerial standpoint, it is important to determine if it is possible to identify degrees of peak experience, and the implications of different degrees both for the individual and the venture. Do entrepreneurs conceptualize feeling and performance components of the venture experience and organize these experiential states in identifiable gradients? In addition, further insights are needed regarding the triggering events that result in peak experiences and peak performance. Can entrepreneurial success or failure be empirically linked to peak performance and flow? Being in the zone may allow the entrepreneur to continue against great odds and overcome obstacles in order to succeed. Research should also focus on the role of other people, both within and outside the venture, in achieving extraordinary experiences. As the entrepreneur does not operate in a vacuum, it would seem likely that a multiplicity of roles (initiator, facilitator, inhibitor, participant, etc.) might be played by others. Finally, it would seem possible to identify particular environmental conditions that encourage or inhibit peak performance.

NOTE

* This chapter draws extensively on previous research by two of the authors. Please see Schindehutte, M., M.H. Morris and J. Allen (2006), 'Beyond achievement: entrepreneurship as extreme experience', *Small Business Economics*, **27**(4), 349–68.

REFERENCES

Allen, J. (2002), 'Bikers' extraordinary experiences, sub-cultural values, and attitudes', University of Central Florida College of Business Administration working paper, Orlando, FL.

Arnould, E.J. and L.L. Price (1993), 'River magic: extraordinary experience and the extended service encounter', *Journal of Consumer Research*, **20**(1): 24–45.

Baron, R.A. (2004), 'The cognitive perspective: a valuable tool for answering entrepreneurship's basic "why" questions', *Journal of Business Venturing*, **19**(2): 221–39.

Bird, B. (1989), *Entrepreneurial Behavior*, London and Glenville, IL: Scott, Foresman and Co.

Boyd, D.P. and D.E. Gumpert (1983), 'Coping with entrepreneurial stress', *Harvard Business Review*, **61**(2): 46–56.

Brockner, J., E.T. Higgins and M.B. Low (2004), 'Regulatory focus theory and the entrepreneurial process', *Journal of Business Venturing*, **19**(2): 203–20.

Cooper, A. (1998), *Playing in the Zone: Exploring the Spiritual Dimensions of Sports*, Boston, MA: Shambala Publications, Inc.

Csikszentmihalyi, M. (1990), *Flow: The Psychology of Optimal Experience*, New York: Harper Perennial.

Csikszentmihalyi, M. (1997), *Finding Flow: The Psychology of Engagement with Everyday Life*, New York: Basic Books.

Csikszentmihalyi, M. and I.S. Csikszentmihalyi (1988), *Optimal Experience: Psychological Studies of Flow in Consciousness*, Cambridge and New York: Cambridge University Press.

Delmar, F., P. Davidsson and W.B. Gartner (2003), 'Arriving at the high-growth firm', *Journal of Business Venturing*, **18**(2): 189–216.

Dodson, K.J. (1996), 'Peak experiences and mountain biking: incorporating the bike into the extended self', *Advances in Consumer Research*, **23**(1): 317–22.

Gaglio, C.M. and J. Katz (2001), 'The psychological basis of opportunity identification: opportunity alertness', *Journal of Small Business Economics*, **16**(2): 95–111.

Gould, D., R.C. Ecklund and S.A. Jackson (1992), '1988 U.S. Olympic wrestling excellence: I. Mental preparation, pre-competitive cognition and affect', *The Sport Psychologist*, **6**(4): 358–82.

Grove, J.R. and M.A.E. Lewis (1996), 'Hypnotic susceptibility and the attainment of flow-like states during exercise', *Journal of Sport & Exercise Psychology*, **18**(4): 380–91.

Hair, J.F., R.E. Anderson, R. Tatham and W.C. Black (1998), *Multivariate Data Analysis*, Upper Saddle River, NJ: Prentice Hall.

Hornaday, J.A. and J. Aboud (1971), 'Characteristics of successful entrepreneurs', *Personnel Psychology*, **21**(2): 141–53.

Jackson, S.A. and M. Csikszentmihalyi (1999), *Flow in Sports: The Keys to Optimal Experiences and Performances*, Champaign, IL: Human Kinetics Publishing.

Jackson, S.A. and H. Marsh (1996), 'Development and validation of a scale to measure optimal experience: the flow state scale', *Journal of Sport and Exercise Psychology*, **18**(1): 17–35.

Lewis, S.M. (2002), 'Cycling in the zone', accessed 19 November 2011 at http:/// www.athleticinsight.com/Vol1Iss3/Bicycle_Zone.htm.

Loehr, J. and T. Schwartz (2001), 'The making of a corporate athlete', *Harvard Business Review*, **79**(1): 120–28.

Manz, C.C., D. Adsit, S. Campbell and M. Mathison-Hance (1988), 'Managerial thought patterns and performance: a study of perceptual patterns of performance hindrances for higher and lower performing managers', *Human Relations*, **41**(6): 447–65.

Maslow, A. (1971), *The Farther Reaches of Human Nature*, New York: Viking Press.

McAlexander, J.H. and J.W. Schouten (1998), 'Brandfests: servicescapes for the cultivation of brand equity', in J.F. Sherry Jr. (ed.), *Servicescapes: The Concept of Place in Contemporary Markets*, Chicago, IL: NTC Business Books.

McClelland, D. (1961), *The Achieving Society*, New York: Von Nostrand.

Moltz, B.J. (2003), *You Need to be a Little Crazy*, Chicago, IL: Dearborn Press.

Morris, M.H. (1998), *Entrepreneurial Intensity: Sustainable Advantages for Individuals, Organizations and Societies*, Westport, CT: Quorum Books.

Murphy, M. and R. White (1995), *In The Zone: Transcendent Experience in Sports*, New York: Penguin Books USA, Inc.

Nunnally, J.C. (1978), *Psychometric Theory*, New York: McGraw Hill.

Pates, J., I. Maynard and T. Westbury (2001), 'An investigation into the effects of hypnosis on basketball performance', *Journal of Applied Sport Psychology*, **13**(1): 84–102.

Privette, G. (1981), 'Dynamics of peak performance', *Journal of Humanistic Psychology*, **21**(1): 56–67.

Privette, G. (1982), 'Peak performance in sports: a factorial topology', *International Journal of Sport Psychology*, **13**(4): 242–9.

Privette, G. (1983), 'Peak experience, peak performance and flow: a comparative analysis of positive human experiences', *Journal of Personality and Social Psychology*, **45**(6): 1361–8.

Privette, G. (1986), 'Experience as a component of personality theory: phenomenological support', *Psychological Reports*, **57**(2): 558.

Privette, G. (2001), 'Defining moments of self-actualization: peak performance and peak experience', in K.J. Schneider, J. Bugenthal and J.F. Pierson (eds), *The Handbook of Humanistic Psychology*, Thousand Oaks, CA: Sage.

Privette, G. and C.M. Bundrick (1987), 'Measurement of experience: construct and content validity of the experience questionnaire', *Perceptual and Motor Skills*, **65**(1): 315–32.

Privette, G. and C.M. Bundrick (1991), 'Peak experience, peak performance and flow: correspondence of personal descriptions and theoretical constructs', *Journal of Social Behavior and Personality*, **6**(5): 169–88.

Privette, G. and D. Sherry (1986), 'Reliability and readability of questionnaire: peak performance and peak experience', *Psychological Reports*, **58**(2): 491–4.

Rabin, M.A. (1996), 'Stress, strain, and their moderators: an empirical comparison of entrepreneurs and managers', *Journal of Small Business Management*, **34**(1): 46–58.

Shane, S., E.A. Locke and C.J. Collins (2003), 'Entrepreneurial motivation', *Human Resource Management Review*, **13**(2): 257–79.

Swets, J.A. (1992), 'The science of choosing the right decision threshold in high-stakes diagnostics', *American Psychologist*, **47**(4): 522–32.

Vesper, K. (1998), *New Venture Experience*, Seattle, WA: Vector Books.

Waitley, D. (1991), *The New Dynamics of Winning*, Palatine, IL: Quill Publishing.

Williams, J.M. and V. Krane (1998), 'Psychological characteristics of peak performance', in J.M. Williams (ed.), *Applied Sports Psychology: Personal Growth to Peak Performance*, Mountain View, CA: Mayfield Press, pp. 158–70.

Zahra, S. and G. Dess (2001), 'Entrepreneurship as a field of research: encouraging dialog and debate', *Academy of Management Review*, **26**(1): 8–11.

10. Applications of the experiential lens: intuition, effectuation, and passion

> [S]ince [intuition] comes from some stratum of awareness just below the conscious level, it is slippery and elusive, to say the least. . . . New ideas spring from a mind that organizes experiences, facts, and relationships to discern a path that has not been taken before. Somewhere along this uncharted path, intuition compresses years of learning and experience into an instantaneous flash.
>
> (Roy Rowan, 1986)

> Sustaining, persevering, striving, paying with effort as we go, hanging on, and finally achieving our intention – this is action, this is pure effectuation in the only shape in which, by a pure experience-philosophy, the whereabouts of it anywhere can be discussed.
>
> (William James, 1912)

INTRODUCTION

How can the experiencing perspective inform some of the big issues being examined by entrepreneurship scholars? Throughout this volume, the entrepreneur has been approached as someone who encounters diverse streams of events while engaged in venture creation. Some of these events go unnoticed by the individual while others represent important, salient moments that can challenge the entrepreneur's expectations and drive their behavior. Over time, these accumulated events assist the entrepreneur in interpreting new events as they are encountered. In this chapter, we select three significant topics from the contemporary entrepreneurship literature – intuition, effectuation, and passion – and re-examine them from an experience-based perspective. Sense-making and identity theories are also incorporated into the discussion, as they play a role in the linkages between experiencing and these other constructs.

While we touch on how these variables interact with each other, our primary intent is to offer a unique perspective on each independently. To assist with the flow of the discussion, Figure 10.1 provides a simple model

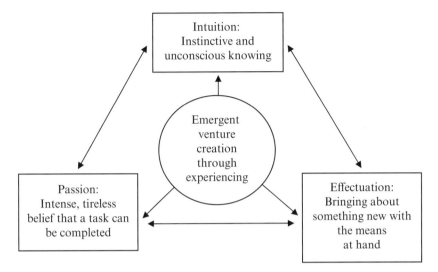

Figure 10.1   Three core variables associated with entrepreneurial experiencing

of meaning construction in entrepreneurship built around the constructs being explored in this chapter. Entrepreneurs begin to make sense of events and their surroundings, using *intuitive* decision-making to surmount the uncertainty represented by a salient event. As the venture emerges through a process of *effectuation*, the meanings the entrepreneur constructed are externalized from the consciousness of the entrepreneur to the firm itself through sense-making. The effectuated firm also serves as a framework for making sense of new events. As the venture takes on importance and saliency in the entrepreneur's life, the venture comes to influence the entrepreneur's identity, which is reflected in the entrepreneur's *passion* for the venture. Passion helps the entrepreneur overcome negative events and leads to creative problem-solving. We draw on two perspectives – sense-making and identity theory to build the connections. Intuition represents individual-level sense-making; effectuation represents organizational-level sense-making; and passion is strongly rooted in identity theory.

This chapter will proceed by considering each of the three constructs individually, recasting them from an experience-based perspective. Applications and implications of the recasted constructs and their interactions will be explored. While we have selected three constructs here to examine, an experienced-based perspective can be applied to virtually any aspect of current entrepreneurship research as well as spawn research topics of its own.

INTUITION: MAKING SENSE OUT OF NONSENSE

Intuition is a cognitive conclusion based on applying previous experience to a unique event (Burke and Miller, 1999). It is the meaning an individual makes to overcome uncertainty. The uncertainty caused by an event that challenges an entrepreneur's expectations triggers intuition – the more uncertainty in a given event stream, the more likely you are to encounter an entrepreneur using intuition to make sense of the situation (Burke and Miller, 1999; Crossan et al., 1999; Weick, 1995). Uncertainty can manifest as either a novel event, a variance between what the actor expects and what the actor perceives, or a problem-solving situation (Griffith, 1999). Intuition entails instinctive knowing and is preconscious and preverbal (Behling and Eckel, 1991). The gut feeling is hard to explain in words, can be triggered by the smallest cues, and relies on highly personal sets of experience that are not accessible to others. As an individual accumulates experiences, her reaction to new events can be based less on deliberative cognitive processes and instead occur almost unconsciously (Crossan et al., 1999). When entrepreneurs are able to put their intuition into words, it is often in the form of metaphors and analogies, which are selected based on previous experience and tailored for a specific audience (Cornelissen and Clarke, 2010).

Note that intuition is also strongly linked to expertise or past experience (Polanyi, 1967; Prietula and Simon, 1989; Weick, 1998). The jazz clarinetist is only able to improvise his way through a musical set because he is intimately aware of everything from how his instrument works, the key he's playing in, or even how his band tends to interact with an improvisationist. This sort of intimacy, or at least familiarity, with the experience is necessary before an actor may intuit his situation. As we describe in Chapter 7, an entrepreneur's intuitive capacity is dependent on the set of accrued experiences (Johannisson, 1998). For example, a payroll clerk driving to work in the morning takes his usual route: the trip itself occurs almost at a subconscious level as it is so ingrained in routine, until he notices brake lights suddenly appear directly ahead. Now, this variance from what he expected is enough to grab his attention, pull him back into the here-and-now, and force him to determine whether a traffic jam lies ahead that he should avoid or whether the driver ahead of him just accidentally tapped the brakes. Whatever he intuits, it is inevitably based on his experience: brake lights and traffic jams have social definitions, which he's learned through his experience with them and interactions with others.

From an experience-based perspective, salient events can trigger intuition as a step in a broader sense-making process. When preconceived, legitimized schemas, behavioral scripts and meanings break down, actors must instantiate new situations or meanings of reality (Weick, 1993). Thus, sense-making is a creative process through which individuals place unique, unexpected or novel environmental stimuli within a new framework, assign meaning, and act according to these new meanings through interactions with others (Weick et al., 2005). Sense-making is the process through which individuals interpret new events and determine a course of action. For example, the entrepreneur's experience of hiring a first employee can be a highly uncertain event. Especially absent previous hiring experiences, she is unlikely to be aware of cues that indicate whether the applicant in front of her would make a good employee. She may instead draw on her experiences with her son's friends or former co-workers, which help her pick up on cues such as whether the applicant has black fingernail polish or has misspelled words on a résumé. These cues stimulate the entrepreneur to apply intuition to extrapolate a sense of the applicant during the event.

Sense-making can be broken down into several sequential activities. First, as Schütz (1967) reminds us, experience or pure duration exists in an undifferentiated flow. Events run into each other and have no clear endings and beginnings – experience is a "coming-to-be and passing-away that has no contours, no boundaries, and no differentiation" (p. 47). Potential triggers for sense-making (i.e., opportunities to deploy intuition) exist in this tumultuous mix and flow of events, and it all goes unnoticed as the actor is living through the moment. Suddenly, the actor encounters something in the environment that doesn't fit his expectations. Recall our payroll clerk driving into work who's snapped out of his routine by the perception of brake lights. He may be thinking about any number of things – his breakfast that morning, his date that night, a terse encounter with a boss the previous day – and perhaps least on his mind is the actual drive to work. But the brake lights – signaling a potential threat – cause the driver to bracket his attention around the current situation, and he's suddenly focused on the here-and-now of the drive. His intuition kicks in as he searches for patterns and retrospectively considers previous experience in order to create sense out of the current situation (Weick et al., 2005). Perhaps the driver remembers a previous traffic jam on the same highway, which causes him to remember the consequences he incurred for being late to work. Maybe the driver's experience allows him to analyze and diagnose the current traffic slowdown as a minor accident – perhaps only one lane of traffic appears to be moving slowly while the others are flowing along fine – or alternatively as a major shutdown – ahead, he notices the traffic stops altogether, which means he might get stuck on the highway for hours. Of course, the driver is merely able to presume what lies ahead; his intuition is based on the cues he observes. The sense he makes is either confirmed or disconfirmed, but in either case, true sense is iterative. If he were to pull off the highway and attempt to take a quicker route to work, he won't know whether his intuition was mistaken until he sees that the pace of traffic quickened just ahead. "The *now* of mistakes collides with the *then* of acting with uncertain knowledge. *Now* represents the more exact science of hindsight, *then* the unknown future coming into being" (Paget, 1988, p. 48; original emphasis).

Intuition is an internal cognitive decision an entrepreneur makes regarding a salient event. Intuition occurs while in the midst of operating a venture, such as one's intuition regarding which logo to go with for the firm, or concerning the decision to follow up with a potential customer even after having been soundly rejected in an earlier attempt to get an order. It can also occur pre-venture – for example, intuition enables the entrepreneur to pick up on cues and patterns in event streams and thus discover opportunity (Baron and Ensley, 2006). Intuition is more than meaning-making because it represents a behavioral component: it inevitably leads to the question, "What do I do next?" (Weick et al., 2005, p. 412). When entrepreneurs intuit an event, they are *deciding* what an event means and how they should proceed.

Using our experiential framework, implications can be drawn for entrepreneurial intuition, especially within a sense-making framework. As we have seen in previous chapters, experiencing has strong affective consequences, in addition to cognitive and physiological attributes. For its part, intuition takes place in-the-moment, and because it is embedded in the tumult of the event itself, it can have strongly emotional characteristics. Bolte et al. (2003) explain intuition as a mix of both cognitive capacity and affective state. Positive affect opens cognitive access to fields of information in the memory that are only weakly associated with the current situation, providing the individual greater opportunity to recombine unique pieces of information. Negative affect has the opposite effect: it closes down remote fields of information, and the individual must rely on closely associated fields of information. Bolte et al. (ibid.) empirically demonstrated that individuals with positive affect were more likely to intuit a situation correctly as well as intuit more quickly than individuals with negative affect.

Consider the case of an entrepreneur who is faced with a decision about signing a lease on a warehouse at an attractive price but with a minimum three-year commitment. Only six months after start-up, the entrepreneur has achieved some major sales and discovers she is almost out of space in the garage at her home where she maintains her inventory and so must consider renting space. This event is not the only pressing matter she must address. The entrepreneur only has two months of cash reserves left in the bank. She has just found out that a potential partnership with a distributor was rejected. A machine critical to her manufacturing processes was supposed to have arrived from Germany days ago, and she fears that it has been lost along the way, which could have painful ramifications for the business. Handed a three-year lease for a warehouse she might not be able to afford, the question concerns whether her intuition kicks in, or she delays a decision until more information can be gathered and analysis performed.

The scenario above is filled with events having both positive and negative affect. If the net result is an entrepreneur whose affective state is positive given the marketplace successes the business has achieved, and this is reinforced by her strong passion for the venture, then she may be more apt to rely on her intuition about the lease. Positive affect is also related to self-confidence, suggesting the entrepreneur may believe no more time, information or other inputs are required to make a decision. Further, positive affect may also contribute to her intuitive decision being a good one.

For the entrepreneur with less passion and/or who is experiencing negative affect, we might expect a different result. Perhaps one of the simultaneous events we mentioned represents a "last straw" – for instance, the distributor who rejected her proposal was not the first to do so. Or perhaps she has come to believe that her family life is suffering because of her devotion to the business. In any event, negative affect means the entrepreneur is more likely to engage in analytical thinking (Bolte et al., 2003). It has the effect of narrowing an individual's cognitive processes, limiting her focus to the specific details of the here-and-now. And because she has limited access to her own internal sources of information, the entrepreneur is more likely to delay a decision and engage in a more rational decision-making process. Also, negative affect is associated with low self-confidence, which would tend to reinforce her need for supplementary information.

Event characteristics can have an influence on whether intuition is used as well as its accuracy. Velocity, or the speed at which events are experienced by the entrepreneur, is positively related to the use of intuition, especially where the entrepreneur is experiencing positive affect. As opposed to analytical or rational decision-making processes, intuition is made on the fly, while in the midst of an experience. If the entrepreneur is experiencing positive affect, then high event velocity could lead to the entrepreneur's absorption in the task, and her intuition would tend to be more accurate than an individual experiencing negative affect. At the high end of event velocity, intuition plays a critical role as the entrepreneur enters peak performance, which we describe in the previous chapter.

Intuition can help the entrepreneur process highly volatile and salient events as well, though the wide emotional swings inherent in volatile events may mitigate the use and effectiveness of intuition insofar as they introduce negative affect. As we mentioned above, positive affective states mean individuals have access to cognitive areas that are loosely associated with the current situation, which makes intuition a probable decision-making tool. Where events are novel, unexpected or disconfirming, entrepreneurs with positive affect are more likely to use intuition and come up with creative or unique solutions to the situation. Conversely, entrepreneurs with negative affect are likely to avoid intuition altogether in the face of these events and engage in analytical-style decision-making. As levels of event velocity and volatility increase, so do levels of negative emotions such as anxiety or stress. At the extreme end of this continuum, where velocity and volatility are highest, we would expect to see entrepreneurs' intuition become less effective and less commonly used.

EFFECTUATION: THE EMERGENT VENTURE AS INTERPRETIVE FRAMEWORK

Effectual reasoning holds that entrepreneurs draw less on formal plans or recipes and more on creative combinations of the resources at hand to create a venture and that ventures themselves are iterative. We suggest that an experiencing lens validates the logic of effectuation because it accounts for the iterative nature of entrepreneurship as a consequence of experiencing and processing events. The experiencing lens also helps us better understand core components of effectuation theory.

In addressing the question "What makes entrepreneurs entrepreneurial?" Sarasvathy (2001b) concludes it is their proclivity for effectuation. Effectual reasoning is the opposite of causal or predictive rationality, where a given set of means is employed to achieve a predetermined goal. The optimal path (best resource, best strategy, best process) is sought and pursued. Effectual reasoning does not try to predict the future. Instead, it enacts the future through creative use of the means at hand. Our experiential perspective reinforces the conclusion that entrepreneurship is inherently effectual in nature. As explained in Chapter 8, routines, processes, goals, identity, entrepreneurial mindset, business models, and venture itself are all emergent – they are in an ongoing state of becoming. Exploratory behavior, improvisation, experimentation, and trial and error are mainstays of entrepreneurship when approached as both experience and as effectuation.

In practice, entrepreneurs employ both effectual and causal reasoning, but the early years of a venture find greater reliance on effectuation. This reality is dictated by events that are novel, unexpected, and/or conflict with the entrepreneur's beliefs and assumptions. While the causal thinker seeks to avoid or minimize surprises, the effectual thinker understands that events are the raw material of venture creation. Beyond simply responding to events, Sarasvathy (ibid.) suggests that entrepreneurs open themselves to novel and unexpected developments, with their actions putting themselves into the path of such events. They are able to turn the unexpected into opportunity and profit. The unpredictability of the venture creation experience is consistent with outcomes of effectuation.

Effectual thinking is inherently creative, imaginative, and can entail greater risk-taking compared to causal thinking (although effectuation also involves more creative approaches to mitigating risk and the downside exposure). It is characterized by leveraging resources, risk management efforts, guerrilla actions, and bootstrapping. It highlights adaptability and flexibility. And ultimately, it centers on action. Through actions and interactions with events and with others, errors are made, new pathways are discovered, new combinations are attempted, and new opportunities or aspects of opportunities are uncovered. The entrepreneur's set of means and the set of possible effects change and get reconfigured.

The experience-based lens has important implications for elements of effectuation theory. Using the means at hand is a critical component of effectuation theory. Sarasvathy includes "who I am," "what I know," and "whom I know" as the three means available to an entrepreneur (2001a, p. 253). The experience-based lens has much to say about "who I am" and "what I know." As we describe in Chapter 8, the entrepreneur emerges through experiencing entrepreneurial events. The skills, entrepreneurial competencies, mindset, and identity she develops influence the venture as she interacts with new, salient events. As the entrepreneur develops through experiencing, the entrepreneur's means change and grow. "What she knows" is enhanced with the competencies and skills she learns as an outcome of experiencing, and "who she is" is fundamentally altered as she develops an entrepreneurial mindset and identity, which influence her aspirations or how she identifies opportunity patterns or tolerates risk. "Who she is" also includes her intuitive capacity and affective state, which influence how she processes and endures events.

Sarasvathy (2001a) also links effectuation to Weick's work on sense-making and the idea that the venture can be a framework for interpreting new events. Sense-making, which is the construction of explicit, verbal descriptions of meaning, is the processual link between meaning and action. Cornelissen and Clarke (2010, p. 543) write that "inner thoughts and imaginations of entrepreneurs matter, [but] they are not spoken or even necessarily speakable." For meaning to become actionable, sense-making is critical: it turns entrepreneurs' tacit meaning constructions "into a situation that is comprehended explicitly in words and that serves as a springboard to action" (Taylor and Van Every, 2000, p. 40).

Effectuation and sense-making get at two sides of the same coin. Sense-making, especially at the organizational level, is the process through which individuals and groups create meaningful representations of reality that enable them to understand new events. Though action is an important component of the sense-making process (Weick, 1995), it is secondary. Effectuation picks up where sense-making leaves off and focuses on the actions entrepreneurs undertake to enact their representations of reality – how do individuals create organizations that reflect these representations of reality? How do they control the environment instead of merely reacting to it?

Sense-making and the creation of external meaning produce an organization that both represents reality for the entrepreneur and provides a framework for the entrepreneur to interpret new events. Effectuation's focus on controlling an unpredictable future rather than predicting an uncertain one echoes this sentiment (Sarasvathy, 2001a, p. 252). Specifically, through adopting this non-predictive strategy, the entrepreneur abandons the use of predictive models of the future and instead capitalizes on what she and her organization can control (Wiltbank et al., 2006). Predictive strategies assume the entrepreneur has no control over the environment and what may happen in the future – the environment moves inexorably forward, and the best the entrepreneur can do is make an educated guess about where it might be heading. Non-predictive strategy flips this on its head. Here, the assumption is that the environment of the future doesn't exist at all but is actually created by the entrepreneur's actions (Lazonick, 1991; Wiltbank et al., 2006). For example, Apple created a new market space by developing a converged media world and strong brand identity. While competitors may attempt to take on certain technological aspects of the iPhone or iPad, the competitive market wouldn't have existed at all if it weren't for the meaningful environment Apple constructed.

We see the emergence of external meanings in the entrepreneurial venture. New ventures collect meanings held by individuals and transform them to external meanings, and new ventures collect roles held by individuals and create generalized positions. External meanings are crucial for enabling entrepreneurs and their ventures to interpret new events, but in the early stages of an entrepreneurial venture, it can be hard to externalize meaning. For example, an entrepreneurial team is working hard during the first year of a start-up, and everyone is putting in 80-hour weeks just to stay ahead of an upcoming major product launch. During this year, one member of an entrepreneurial team, the controller, may notice that the last month's books do not balance and are off by \$100, so he spends hours trying to track down the error. After a whole day of searching and coming up with nothing, the controller tells the team's lead entrepreneur, who isn't happy. The controller is surprised when the lead entrepreneur criticizes him for wasting a whole day and hundreds of dollars of pay just to track down a small error, especially with the impending launch. Had the controller been in tune with the overall meaning of the firm and understood the more salient mission, he might have ignored the small error and simply added an adjustment entry. Instead, he misattributed saliency to the event because of a breakdown in external meaning.

Our experiential perspective provides a framework within which effectual reasoning takes place. Streams of salient events are processed and produce affective outcomes and levels of engagement. Strong affect and high engagement lead to the improvisation that is the *sine qua* of effectuation. Exploratory behaviors and creativity are fostered where positive affect is experienced.

Events are the raw material of venture creation. The key is how these events are processed. At low levels of event velocity and volatility, causal logic may prove effective. As the velocity and volatility of events increase, causal logic becomes more elusive because the dots become harder to causally connect. Under such conditions, the entrepreneur may either be lost and finds herself grasping at straws, or she comes to understand that it is all about effectuation. But as event streams increase in velocity and volatility, effectual behavior becomes especially impactful in capitalizing upon unfolding developments. In fact, studies have suggested that proactive and innovative entrepreneurs and firms perform better in unstable environments (e.g., Covin and Slevin, 1989; Simsek et al., 2010). Further, as more events are experienced, processed, and responded to, effectual skills can be enhanced. Stated differently, many entrepreneurs are not natural-born effectuators, nor have they ever been taught effectuation. It's through real-time experiencing that they learn to escape the bounds of causal reasoning. The entrepreneurial experience finds them forced to experiment, and with ongoing experiencing, they come to appreciate the logic of effectuation.

PASSION: "I *AM* AN ENTREPRENEUR"

Another key variable in the entrepreneurship literature is passion. Passion is a strong, positively affective state that enables entrepreneurs to process events as well as handle negative emotional states such as anxiety and stress. Passionate entrepreneurs set more challenging goals and exhibit greater absorbance in the task at hand. Passion is associated with performing roles that are strongly associated with the entrepreneur's identity. In this section, we discuss passion and how it can be viewed through an experiencing lens.

Passion is defined as a "strong inclination toward an activity people like, that they find important" (Vallerand et al., 2003, p.757). From this definition, two things are clear. First, that passion is associated with enacting behavioral roles, and second, that the actor considers these roles to be salient in their lives. That is, passion is associated with performing behaviors that are central to one's identity. Cardon and colleagues (2009) argue that entrepreneurial passion is the "consciously accessible, intense positive feelings experienced by engagement in entrepreneurial activities associated with the roles that are meaningful and salient to the self-identity of the entrepreneur" (p.517).

While the emergent venture may embody roles that an entrepreneur eventually internalizes, this can work the other way around, too. The entrepreneur may have a particular passion for a certain activity, and when the entrepreneur builds a venture, that activity occupies a central place in the venture. For example, one entrepreneur with a passion for jogging finds that conventional baby strollers are not built to withstand his favorite activity, so he builds and markets a new stroller that is (Shah and Tripsas, 2007). Another well-known example is Phil Knight, a high-school and college athlete, who built a business around making better equipment for athletes (Frisch, 2009). In both instances, the entrepreneur's passion preceded the venture and became a major part of the entrepreneurial experience.

Passion has also been linked to improvisation, or bricolage, and it has been empirically shown to be positively related to creative problem-solving (Bierly et al., 2000). Bricolage, like effectuation, requires improvisation and the ability to shape strategy in the face of a barrage of ever-changing events. Because passion enhances decision-making and creativity (e.g., Amabile et al., 2005), passionate entrepreneurs are better able to uniquely recombine resources as well as make better decisions regarding the acquisition of future resources. Moreover, passion is linked to the ability to recognize opportunities (Shane et al., 2000). Passion is intrinsically associated with behavioral roles, and these roles, serving as schema or frameworks of meaning, enable the entrepreneur to make sense of new events by comparing them to previous experiences to determine their significance and meaning. Passion, therefore, enables entrepreneurs to process event streams and identify patterns in the environment, which leads to opportunity discovery and exploitation, as well as to innovative interpretations regarding the day-to-day occurrence of entrepreneurial events.

Entrepreneurial passion manifests when an entrepreneur performs an activity that is connected to a behavioral role central to her identity. The more broadly an individual applies a role across contexts, the more central that role is to the individual's identity. Identity theory is rooted in social psychology and the work of George Herbert Mead and contains several components. First, organizations establish behavioral roles. Individuals are free to enact these behavioral scripts as is, or they may alter them (Giddens, 1986). Through script enactment or alteration, individuals shape the organization. However, in an entrepreneurial venture, these roles have not necessarily been established. As the entrepreneur or other team members act in response to events, they are creating patterns that might ultimately become routinized as the venture develops. Second, these roles are associated with specific social relationships, such as the role of "teacher," "tennis player," "nurse," "salesperson," "inventor," etc. Third, the individual may choose one identity script over another based on whichever social situation she finds herself in (Stryker and Burke, 2000). When at home, an entrepreneur may adopt a "father" role, while at work adopting a "developer" or "inventor" role. Alternatively, an entrepreneur may constantly perform an "inventor" role, even in varied contexts such as at church or at home. Lastly, identity saliency refers to the likelihood that an individual will enact a particular role across life contexts. The more broadly an individual enacts a role, the more salient that role is to an entrepreneur's identity.

Early entrepreneurship research was concerned with developing an ideal-typical entrepreneur – someone who embodied an "entrepreneurial" identity (Down and Warren, 2008). There is little question that society contains such roles (Blumer, 1967; Somers, 1994). For example, Nicholson and Anderson (2005) describe a common social conception of an entrepreneur as depicted in the media as a heroic agent working for the broader good. While this general role can also come to comprise an entrepreneur's identity, we are discussing here specifically those roles that are embodied in the entrepreneurial venture. As the entrepreneur works to establish a venture, certain behaviors will, over time, become routinized and become a framework through which to interpret new events, reducing the entrepreneur's uncertainty (Giddens, 1986). These routinized behaviors become roles in the firm. Scholars have also suggested that entrepreneurial passion is associated with three generalized roles in new ventures: the inventor, the founder, and the developer (Cardon et al., 2009). The inventor's passion is for developing products and services that exploit new opportunities. The founder's passion is for creating an organization that facilitates opportunity exploitation. The developer's passion is for finding ways to grow a new venture. These roles are generalized and can each include a range of activities. Cardon and her colleagues (ibid.) write that an entrepreneur may exhibit passion for one or more of these roles and that the saliency a role holds for an entrepreneur may change throughout the life of the venture.

Our experience-based perspective suggests that entrepreneurial passion can occur through the emergence of its antecedent, which is a salient identity. We have written that identity is an emergent phenomenon, tied directly to the experiences of venture creation (see Chapter 8). As the venture emerges, so do behavioral roles within the venture. The entrepreneur becomes engaged in the venture and adopts these roles. She finds greater identity saliency in them, and these roles ultimately become an intrinsic part of her identity. She begins to define social relationships in terms of her entrepreneurial identity, and she applies the identity across life contexts. As the venture assumes an intrinsic place in the entrepreneur's identity, her passion for the venture also emerges.

Passion is associated with the strong desire toward some sort of identity-related pursuit – it is directed toward objects, whether it be a goal, a task, a person, a cause or some other phenomenon (e.g., Cardon et al., 2005; Frijda, 2005). It is a positive emotion that stirs individuals to action. Researchers have also argued that passion is related to entrepreneurial performance: it compels entrepreneurs to work hard and stick to tasks, even in the face of daunting uncertainty (Baum et al., 2001; Jelinek and Litterer, 1995). Passion is linked to positive affect (e.g., Rockwell, 2002), which contributes to entrepreneurial performance (Baron, 2008). Cardon and her colleagues (2009) write that passion in the pursuit of a founder, inventor, or developer identity will mean the entrepreneur will exhibit greater self-regulation toward pursuing opportunity exploitation. More specifically, they argue that these entrepreneurs will display creative problem-solving, perseverance, and absorption in their work.

Passion is a strong positive emotion associated with physiological and cognitive effects (Cardon et al., 2009). As explored in earlier parts of this book (see Chapters 5 and 6), strong positive affect helps entrepreneurs process new events. Positive affect can stimulate cognitive processes, which enable the entrepreneur to creatively draw on new and old sources of information and recombine them in creative ways such as in bricolage. Moreover, passion as positive affect can help entrepreneurs perform even in the face of highly dynamic and rapid events as well as cope with negative emotions associated with processing event streams, such as anxiety and stress. All of these factors mean that the passionate entrepreneur is more highly engaged in their venture, which enables them to persevere during events that might cause other, less passionate entrepreneurs to abandon a project. For example, the entrepreneur who is less committed to their venture, identifies with their venture less, and exhibits less passion for the venture is also less likely to bounce back and learn from experiences such as being rejected by ten different banks for a loan.

However, Cardon et al. (ibid.), also write that excessive passion can actually hinder entrepreneurial performance. Sometimes, excessive passion can lead to blind, emotional responses regardless of rational, cognitive processes. Entrepreneurs with too much passion might filter out and ignore information that they deem irrelevant to the task at hand, which blinds them to other opportunities that may exist. Also, passionate entrepreneurs can become obsessed with their role, so much so that their passion for the venture begins to harm other areas of their life.

Passionate entrepreneurs are quick, efficient decision-makers, even in dynamic environments, which suggests that they are better able to process events of high velocity and volatility. Cardon et al. (ibid.) argue that passionate entrepreneurs are also more likely to set challenging goals, which means that passion not only helps entrepreneurs process highly volatile events but may actually lead to the entrepreneur seeking highly volatile events. In turn, challenging goals cause the entrepreneur to devote even more time and resources to the venture. Passionate entrepreneurs ignore non-goal-related information and tightly focus on goal pursuit, and they are likely to be more absorbed with their task and more motivated to pursue the goal. This pursuit causes an intense, positive emotional feedback for the entrepreneur. However, the uncertainty and difficulty of processing increasingly volatile events associated with challenging goals may ultimately lead to the entrepreneur finally abandoning the goals, especially since failure in a task could harm the entrepreneur's self-identity (Cardon et al., 2005).

CONCLUSIONS

In employing an experience-based lens on the venture creation process, we have attempted to portray the emergence of the entrepreneurial venture as different manifestations of meaning construction that enable the entrepreneur to make sense of and act on new events. We touch on three different topics in entrepreneurship literature: intuition, effectuation, and passion, in order to illustrate the different elements of meaning construction within the context of venture creation. Through this discussion, we hope to illustrate the possible application of an experience-based perspective in describing some of the cognitive and behavioral influences underlying opportunity identification and exploitation.

We believe this chapter includes three important insights. First, it recasts three important concepts within entrepreneurship in an experience-based perspective. The purpose of this chapter is to demonstrate how an experience-based lens can inform subjects that are already commonly researched in entrepreneurship. Second, it presents an experience-based lens of the entrepreneurship process in which actors operating in an uncertain environment create their own versions of reality, which ultimately manifest as an emerging venture. In some ways, this brings entrepreneurship theory full circle. The field, which began in part as a description from Austrian economists, such as Mises, Hayek, and Kirzner, about how individuals make decisions based on unique information (Hayek, 1945) and are highly creative and innovative, ends with the description of experience, meaning, and emergence based on work by Edward Husserl and Alfred Schutz wherein individuals make sense of and enact their own meaningful environments. Early phenomenologists were influential in the development of Austrian economics. Schütz was particularly influenced by Austrian economists, especially Mises (Chiles et al., 2007). Third, the chapter reconceptualizes uncertainty, which comes in the form of salient events, as a trigger to the entrepreneurship process instead of as a barrier, as it is commonly portrayed (e.g., McMullen and Shepherd, 2006). In fact, the greater the degree of uncertainty represented by an event, the greater the potential for entrepreneurship. This notion, which draws on Kirzner (1982), means that entrepreneurial action exists in the difference between the future as it would have unfolded without action compared to the future enacted by a sense-making entrepreneur. In this model, uncertainty does not stymie the entrepreneur – instead, it gives the entrepreneur reason to act. For the entrepreneur, uncertainty may resemble less a shackle than it does a pair of wings.

REFERENCES

Amabile, T., S. Barsade, J. Mueller and B. Staw (2005), 'Affect and creativity at work', *Administrative Science Quarterly*, **50**(3): 367–403.

Baron, R.A. (2008), 'The role of affect in the entrepreneurial process', *Academy of Management Review*, **33**(2): 328–40.

Baron, R.A. and M.D. Ensley (2006), 'Opportunity recognition as the detection of meaningful patterns: evidence from comparisons of novice and experienced entrepreneurs', *Management Science*, **52**(9): 1331–44.

Baum, J.R., E.A. Locke and K.G. Smith (2001), 'A multidimensional model of venture growth', *Academy of Management Journal*, **44**(2): 292–303.

Behling, O. and H. Eckel (1991), 'Making sense out of intuition', *Academy of Management Executive*, **5**(1): 46–54.

Bierly, P., E. Kessler and E. Christensen (2000), 'Organizational learning, knowledge and wisdom', *Journal of Organizational Change Mangement*, **13**(6): 595–618.

Blumer, H. (1967), 'Society as symbolic interaction', in J. Mannis and B. Meltzer (eds), *Symbolic Interaction: Reader in Social Psychology*, Boston, MA: Allyn and Bacon, pp. 139–48.

Bolte, A., T. Goschke and J. Kuhl (2003), 'Emotion and intuition: effects of positive and negative mood on implicit judgments of semantic coherence', *Psychological Science*, **14**(5): 416–21.

Burke, L.A. and M.K. Miller (1999), 'Taking the mystery out of intuitive decision making', *Academy of Management Executive*, **13**(4): 91–9.

Cardon, M.S., J. Wincent, J. Singh and M. Drnovsek (2009), 'The nature and experience of entrepreneurial passion', *Academy of Management Review*, **34**(3): 511–32.

Cardon, M.S., C. Zietsma, P. Saparito, B.P. Matherne and C. Davis (2005), 'A tale of passion: new insights into entrepreneurship from a parenthood metaphor', *Journal of Business Venturing*, **20**(1): 23–45.

Chiles, T., A. Bluedorn and V. Gupta (2007), 'Beyond creative destruction and entrepreneurial discovery: a radical Austrian approach to entrepreneurship', *Organization Studies*, **28**(4): 467–93.

Cornelissen, J.P. and J.S. Clarke (2010), 'Imagining and rationalizing opportunities: inductive reasoning and the creation and justification of new ventures', *Academy of Management Review*, **35**(4): 539–57.

Covin, J. and D. Slevin (1989), 'Strategic management of small firms in hostile and benign environments', *Strategic Management Journal*, **10**(1): 75–87.

Crossan, M.M., H.W. Lane and R.E. White (1999), 'An organizational learning framework: from intuition to institution', *Academy of Management Review*, **24**(3): 522–37.

Down, S. and L. Warren (2008), 'Constructing narratives of enterprise: clichés and entrepreneurial self-identity', *International Journal of Entrepreneurial Behaviour and Research*, **14**(1): 4–23.

Frijda, N. (2005), 'Emotion experience', *Cognition and Emotion*, **19**(4): 473–97.

Frisch, A. (2009), *Built for Success: The Story of Nike*, Mankato, MN: Creative Editions.

Giddens, A. (1986), *The Constitution of Society*, Berkeley, CA: University of California Press.

Griffith, T.L. (1999), 'Technology features as triggers for sensemaking', *Academy of Management Review*, **24**(3): 472–88.

Hayek, F.A. (1945), 'The use of knowledge in society', *American Economic Review*, **35**(4): 519–30.

James, W. (1912), 'The experience of activity', in *Essays in Radical Empiricism*, Lincoln, NE: University of Nebraska Press, p. 181.

Jelinek, M. and J. Litterer (1995), 'Toward entrepreneurial organizations: meeting ambiguity with engagement', *Entrepreneurship Theory and Practice*, **19**(3): 137–68.

Johannisson, B. (1998), 'Personal networks in emerging knowledge-based firms: spatial and functional patterns', *Entrepreneurship and Regional Development*, **10**(4): 297–312.

Kirzner, I. (1982), 'Uncertainty, discovery, and human action: a study of the entrepreneurial profile in the Misesian system', in I. Kirzner (ed.), *Method, Process, and Austrian Economics*, Lexington, MA: D.C. Heath & Co, pp. 139–59.

Lazonick, W. (1991), *Business Organization and the Myth of the Market Economy*, Cambridge: Cambridge University Press.

McMullen, J.S. and D.A. Shepherd (2006), 'Entrepreneurial action and the role of uncertainty in the theory of the entrepreneur', *Academy of Management Review*, **31**(1): 132–52.

Nicholson, L. and A.R. Anderson (2005), 'News and nuances of the entrepreneurial myth and metaphor: linguistic games in entrepreneurial sense-making and sense-giving', *Entrepreneurship Theory and Practice*, **29**(2): 153–73.

Paget, M.A. (1988), *The Unity of Mistakes*, Philadelphia, PA: Temple University Press.

Polanyi, M. (1967), *The Tacit Dimension*, London: Routledge.

Prietula, M.J. and H.A. Simon (1989), 'The experts in your midst', *Harvard Business Review*, **61**: 120–24.

Rockwell, I. (2002), *The Five Wisdom Energies: A Buddhist Way of Understanding Personalities, Emotions, and Relationships*, Boston, MA: Shambhala.

Rowen, R. (1986), *The Intuitive Manager*, New York: Little, Brown & Co, p. 3.

Sarasvathy, S.D. (2001a), 'Causation and effectuation: toward a theoretical shift from economic inevitability to entrepreneurial contingency', *Academy of Management Review*, **26**(2): 243–63.

Sarasvathy, S.D. (2001b), 'What makes entrepreneurs entrepreneurial?', working paper, accessed 20 November 2011 at: http://ssrn.com/abstract=909038.

Schütz, A. (1967), *The Phenomenology of the Social World*, Evanston, IL: Northwestern University Press.

Shah, S.K. and M. Tripsas (2007), 'The accidental entrepreneur: the emergent and collective process of user entrepreneurship', *Strategic Entrepreneurship Journal*, **1**(1–2): 123–40.

Shane, S., E. Locke and C. Collins (2000), 'Entrepreneurial motivation', *Human Resource Management Review*, **13**(2): 257–79.

Simsek, Z., C. Heavey and J. Veiga (2010), 'The impact of CEO core self-evaluation on the firm's entrepreneurial orientation', *Strategic Management Journal*, **31**(1): 110–19.

Somers, M.R. (1994), 'The narrative constitution of identity: a relational and network approach', *Theory and Society*, **23**(5): 605–49.

Stryker, S. and P.J. Burke (2000), 'The past, present, and future of an identity theory', *Social Psychology Quarterly*, **63**(4): 284–97.

Taylor, J.R. and E. Van Every (2000), *The Emergent Organization: Communication as its Site and Surface*, Mahwah, NJ: Lawrence Erlbaum Associates.

Vallerand, R.J., G.A. Mageau, C. Ratelle, M. Leonard, C. Blanchard, R. Koestner and M. Gagne (2003), 'Les passions de l'ame: on obsessive and harmonious passion', *Journal of Personality and Social Psychology*, **85**(4): 756–67.

Weick, K.E. (1993), 'The collapse of sensemaking in organizations: the Mann Gulch disaster', *Administrative Science Quarterly*, **38**(4): 628–52.

Weick, K.E. (1995), *Sensemaking in Organizations*, Thousand Oaks, CA: Sage.

Weick, K.E. (1998), 'Introductory essay: improvisation as a mindset for organizational analysis', *Organization Science*, **9**(5): 543–55.

Weick, K.E., K.M. Sutcliffe and D. Obstfeld (2005), 'Organizing and the process of sensemaking', *Organization Science*, **16**(4): 409–21.

Wiltbank, R., N. Dew, S. Read, S.D. Sarasvathy (2006), 'What to do next? The case for non-predictive strategy', *Strategic Management Journal*, **27**(10): 981–98.

11. Comparing experiences of different types of entrepreneurs*

> A thing may be present to a man a hundred times, but if he persistently fails
> to notice it, it cannot be said to enter into his experience. . . . On the other
> hand, a thing met only once in a lifetime may leave an indelible experience
> in the memory.
> (William James, 1890)

INTRODUCTION

In this chapter, we explore how venture creation might be experienced in
unique ways by different individuals. Specifically, we compare differences
in the affective experiences between founders of family and non-family
ventures, and between family business founders and non-family managers
in the same venture. A methodology is introduced for measuring the affective experiences of each of these three groups and drawing comparisons
among them.

We focus on family versus non-family businesses because of fundamental differences in the two contexts. Beyond the challenges of
inter-generational succession, family firms are distinguished by their
governance structures, stakeholders, planning time horizons, capital structures, motives of founders and top managers, risk proclivity, compensation systems, and measures of success (Klein and Bell, 2007; Sirmon and
Hitt, 2003). Further, family businesses are fertile fields for psychodynamics
such as sibling rivalry, marital discord, and identity conflict among family
members – where family issues affect business issues and vice versa. These
characteristics suggest the founder is assimilating a diverse range of experiences distinguishing the family venture from its non-family counterparts.

The experience of the family business founder might also be expected
to vary from that of non-family managers within the same firm. Non-
family members play a significant role in family businesses, and their
influence tends to grow as the firm evolves (Mitchell et al., 2003).
They are attracted to the firm for a variety reasons, including the
ability to exert greater influence, realize individualized visions and goals,
achieve more independence, enjoy more collegiality and entrepreneurial

tolerance, and deal with less bureaucracy than they might in a public company (Aronoff and Ward, 2000). While compensation tends to be less in such firms, evidence suggests that emotional and social compensation, as well as psychological ownership, can be relevant incentives for non-family managers (Adams et al., 2005). Non-family managers may become disaffected and leave where they perceive fewer opportunities for personal development, career opportunities, or personal wealth, are given limited levels of responsibility, and participate only nominally in strategic decision-making. Disagreement between non-family executives and the owner regarding the need for innovation and growth is not uncommon (Poza, 2004). These issues may be exacerbated depending on how nepotism issues are handled, and when non-family managers are caught in the middle of family conflicts or taken advantage of as family members pursue personal interests.

THEORETICAL FOUNDATION

The relevant theoretical lens employed in work on experience varies among disciplines and is based on context (see Chapters 2, 3, and 4). In a family firm context, an especially relevant foundation can be found in social capital theory (Burt, 1992). Social capital represents the ability to attain advantages through membership in identifiable social groups, such as the family unit. Family firms are rooted in the household unit. As Steier (2001) notes, conventional perspectives on the entrepreneur emphasize solo actors or lone wolves, while the family business founder, embedded within the family social structure, is more typically engaged in collective action, leveraging relations within and around the family unit. The household can serve as opportunity platform and incubator. Moreover, particular household configurations can contribute to a more positive or negative experience, as the family itself fosters or hinders the venture.

Sorenson and Bierman (2009) posit that social capital (as opposed to human or financial capital) is a primary factor differentiating family and non-family businesses, as it cannot be hired or imported. Social capital is embodied in relations among family members, and is manifested in goodwill within the family and between family and others in the community, mutual support, reciprocal commitment, collaborative community, affective ties, and behavioral guidelines. It is a source of information and access to resources, and can serve to uphold social norms (Olson et al., 2003). As such, the stock of social capital is a factor explaining the tendency to start a family firm, while growth in the stock over time affects survival of the family and sustainability of the firm (Rodriguez et al., 2009).

The experience of creating a family firm includes not only the way the founder processes such events as the first sale or an inability to meet payroll, but also developments at the firm–family interface. These developments can encompass family demands, goal conflicts, values and integrity levels, and varying amounts of emotional support from family members. Families can be a source of resiliency and adaptability, store of trust and creativity, and type of stress buffer. They can also act as a source of friction, doubt, escalating conflict, and resource drain, resulting in higher stress levels. Not surprisingly, management of this family interface can impact firm performance (Olson et al., 2003).

As we discussed in earlier chapters, the launch of a business generates streams of events that, as they are experienced by the founder, ultimately influence the kind of entrepreneur and venture that emerge. Processing of events includes cognitive, affective, and physiological components. However, with a family firm, social capital and its corollary mix of family variables (e.g., resiliency, conflict, etc.) likely impacts this processing and the entrepreneur's ongoing affective state. While it is recognized that family involvement can materially impact venture development (Chua et al., 2004), one possible explanation of this influence is that founders of family firms experience venture creation differently than do non-family managers or founders of non-family firms. The experience is different because of the impact of family social capital on the processing of events as they occur. Hence, the tendency to experience venture creation as more stressful, lonely, exhilarating or ambiguous may be influenced by these family variables. Lack of trust or commitment in the family might exacerbate stress experienced when the founder is rejected for a loan, or fails to win a customer contract. Alternatively, shared norms and mutual support within the family could lead the founder to process events in such a way that the experience is less overwhelming, or frightening. The business also affects the family, and where such impacts are adverse it would seem plausible that there would be some effect on how the founder interprets events as they unfold in the firm.

Based on social capital theory, then, we would expect the family business founder to experience emergence of the venture in unique ways compared to other entrepreneurs, as the stock of social capital serves to moderate how events are processed and interpreted. Further, given that non-family managers are participants in many of the same events and activities as the founder, but cannot draw on the same reservoir of family social capital, they can also be expected to experience these events differently than do the founders.

THE RESEARCH STUDY

How do those involved in the early stages of a family business experience myriad events that unfold as a sustainable venture is established? Is it possible to capture the underlying dimensionality of the venture creation experience? Once captured, are there identifiable differences in the experiences of founders versus managers in family businesses, or of founders of family versus non-family businesses? To address these questions, a three-stage exploratory study was undertaken.

Consistent with earlier work by Mano and Oliver (1993) and Feldman (1995), affective experiences can be captured by giving subjects a set of semantic differential scales that they use to describe some phenomenon they have lived through (e.g., being a freshman in college, living with cancer). As such, we first needed an inventory of affective terms that describe the venture creation experience. This inventory was introduced earlier in Chapter 6 (see Box 6.1), and consisted of 48 descriptors of the entrepreneurial experience (e.g., stressful, boring, exhilarating, lonely). Based on it, we conducted a cross-sectional survey of family-owned firms.

The survey instrument centered on asking respondents to indicate the extent to which each of the 48 descriptors was applicable to their personal experience during the first three years of the family business. While acknowledging the limitations in cognitive retrieval with the use of self-reports of emotional experiences, Mano and Oliver (1993) argue this to be an effective and efficient method of assessment. A four-point response scale was employed (1 = very strong part of my experience, 2 = somewhat a part of my experience, 3 = a minor part, 4 = definitely not part of my experience). In addition, respondents indicated the extent to which the overall experience was positive/negative, intense/not intense, and satisfying/dissatisfying on five-point scales with a neutral mid-point. A pre-test was performed using 20 firms not part of the final sample.

The survey was sent to a sample of businesses from the Dun & Bradstreet's Million Dollar database. Firms that were less than four years old, employed more than 50 people, and were non-subsidiaries were used to construct the initial list. From this list, 1500 firms were randomly selected as our sample. A large sample was needed because Dun & Bradstreet does not designate family ownership status and a portion of the sample would not meet eligibility as a family business. A family firm was defined as one where members of a family have legal control and are involved in managing the firm (Mitchell et al., 2003). Respondents were asked to complete the survey if they met this definition.

Another sample constraint was the need to compare the start-up experiences of a dyad comprised of the family owner/CEO and a non-family manager. This required two complete responses per firm and several follow-up contacts were made with firms that had one response. Other efforts were conducted to improve survey response including a respondent-friendly questionnaire, multiple contacts with recipients, inclusion of a stamped return envelope and personalized correspondence. One hundred and three firms provided complete dyads of surveys (206 total surveys) and indicated they were family businesses employing a non-family manager.

A separate survey was employed to investigate affective experiences of founders of non-family-owned ventures, or independent entrepreneurs who had created growth-oriented ventures. Using Hoover's database, a mail survey was sent to 700 randomly selected non-subsidiary New York-based firms that were started four years prior to the survey. In this case, only the founder was surveyed. A total of 129 surveys were returned, for a response rate of 18.5 percent, of which 92 were useable and qualified as non-family firm entrepreneurs. No family members shared ownership or control of the business.

RESULTS: FAMILY BUSINESS FOUNDERS VS. MANAGERS

Exploratory factor analysis was performed on the 48 affect-related adjectives describing experiences of founders and managers during the first three years of venture operation. Bartlett's test of sphericity and the Kaiser-Meyer-Olkin (KMO) measure of sampling adequacy were computed to assess the appropriateness of the correlation matrix prior to factoring. Bartlett's test led to a clear rejection of the hypothesis of independence ($p < 0.001$) and the KMO measure of sampling adequacy was in the meritorious range (0.85) indicating that the matrix is appropriate for principal component analysis.

Criteria for factor selection consisted of eigenvalues > 1 and items that loaded > 0.50 on a factor. In all, 11 factors meeting the above criteria were revealed explaining 63 percent of the variance. The first four factors were composed of multiple items; the remaining seven factors consisted of single items. Factor loadings for a varimax rotation are displayed in Table 11.1. The factors labeled as (1) Exciting, (2) Threatening, (3) Exhausting, (4) Complex, (5) Ambiguous, (6) Empty, (7) Passionate, (8) No Rules to follow, (9) Hopeful, (10) Tedious, and (11) a sense of having to Outwork Others, were extracted in that order.

Thirteen items, Invigorating, Energizing, Joyful, Revitalizing, Adventurous, Exciting, Motivating, Exhilarating, Fun, Empowering, Creative, Dynamic, and Self-fulfilling loaded on the first factor (labeled

Table 11.1 *Exploratory factor analysis results (family founders and managers)*

Item	Factors										
	Exciting 1	Threatening 2	Exhausting 3	Complex 4	Ambiguous 5	Empty 6	Passionate 7	No rules 8	Hopeful 9	Tedious 10	Outwork 11
Invigorating	0.52	–	–	–	–	–	–	–	–	–	–
Energizing	0.72	–	–	–	–	–	–	–	–	–	–
Joyful	0.66	–	–	–	–	–	–	–	–	–	–
Revitalizing	0.73	–	–	–	–	–	–	–	–	–	–
Adventurous	0.61	–	–	–	–	–	–	–	–	–	–
Motivating	0.61	–	–	–	–	–	–	–	–	–	–
Exciting	0.65	–	–	–	–	–	–	–	–	–	–
Exhilarating	0.76	–	–	–	–	–	–	–	–	–	–
Fun	0.73	–	–	–	–	–	–	–	–	–	–
Empowering	0.70	–	–	–	–	–	–	–	–	–	–
Creative	0.51	–	–	–	–	–	–	–	–	–	–
Dynamic	0.68	–	–	–	–	–	–	–	–	–	–
Self-fulfilling	0.57	–	–	–	–	–	–	–	–	–	–
Inadequacy	–	0.55	–	–	–	–	–	–	–	–	–
Humiliating	–	0.66	–	–	–	–	–	–	–	–	–
Lonely	–	0.69	–	–	–	–	–	–	–	–	–
Insignificance	–	0.54	–	–	–	–	–	–	–	–	–
Frightening	–	0.57	–	–	–	–	–	–	–	–	–
Alienating	–	0.61	–	–	–	–	–	–	–	–	–
Strange	–	0.52	–	–	–	–	–	–	–	–	–

	6.37	5.90	5.68	1.84	1.80	1.73	1.73	1.55	1.47	1.40	1.36
Threatening	—	0.72	—	—	—	—	—	—	—	—	—
Being Lost	—	0.66	—	—	—	—	—	—	—	—	—
Exhausting	—	—	0.70	—	—	—	—	—	—	—	—
Demanding	—	—	0.63	—	—	—	—	—	—	—	—
Uncertain	—	—	0.51	—	—	—	—	—	—	—	—
Overwhelming	—	—	0.68	—	—	—	—	—	—	—	—
All-consuming	—	—	0.64	—	—	—	—	—	—	—	—
Stressful	—	—	0.72	—	—	—	—	—	—	—	—
Burdensome	—	—	0.53	—	—	—	—	—	—	—	—
Chaotic	—	—	0.67	—	—	—	—	—	—	—	—
Difficult	—	—	0.66	—	—	—	—	—	—	—	—
Complex	—	—	—	0.67	—	—	—	—	—	—	—
Novel	—	—	—	0.62	—	—	—	—	—	—	—
Ambiguous	—	—	—	—	0.73	—	—	—	—	—	—
Empty	—	—	—	—	—	0.68	—	—	—	—	—
Passionate	—	—	—	—	—	—	0.67	—	—	—	—
No Rules	—	—	—	—	—	—	—	0.84	—	—	—
Hopeful	—	—	—	—	—	—	—	—	0.71	—	—
Tedious	—	—	—	—	—	—	—	—	—	0.76	—
Outwork Others	—	—	—	—	—	—	—	—	—	—	0.62
Eigenvalue	6.37	5.90	5.68	1.84	1.80	1.73	1.73	1.55	1.47	1.40	1.36
% of variance explained	13.00	12.04	11.60	3.76	3.68	3.53	3.52	3.16	2.99	2.86	2.78

Exciting). Nine items loaded on the second factor (Threatening) including Inadequacy, Humiliating, Lonely, a feeling of Insignificance, Frightening, Alienating, Strange, Threatening, and a Sense of Being Lost. The following items made up the third factor (Exhausting): Exhausting, Demanding, Uncertain, Overwhelming, All-consuming, Stressful, Burdensome, Chaotic, and Difficult. The fourth factor (Complex) consisted of two items: Complex and Novel. Items for each of these multi-item factors were summed to form composite scales; the remaining scales were labeled according to the item that comprised that factor. Coefficient alpha for each of the composite scales was 0.90 for Exciting, 0.83 for Threatening, 0.86 for Exhausting, and 0.59 for Complex.

Multi-samples Analysis

Correlations between the 11 affect scales were computed for the family business founder and non-family manager samples. A multi-samples analysis was used to simultaneously test for invariance in the set of correlation coefficients taken as a whole. Assuming the correlation matrices for both samples are the same, a good fit indicates invariance. The test result ($\chi^2(110, n = 206) = 216.03$, $p < 0.001$) was a chi-square statistic large enough to reject the invariance hypothesis. Other fit (goodness-of-fit = 0.80; root mean square error of approximation = 0.10) and comparative fit indices (normed fit index = 0.55; non-normed fit index, comparative fit index, incremental fit index = 0.70) also indicate a poor fit. Based on this result, the samples were treated separately in the analyses that follow.

Correlation Analysis: Angles within the MDS

To further investigate variation in affective expression within samples, correlations between affect scales were examined. A large number of significant correlations ($p \geq 0.05$) emerged. As examples, with the founders, Exciting was positively correlated with Passionate ($r = 0.27$) and Hopeful ($r = 0.25$), while Threatening was correlated with scales for Exhausting ($r = 0.65$), Ambiguous ($r = 0.39$), Empty ($r = 0.45$), Tedious ($r = 0.38$), and having to Outwork Others ($r = 0.21$). For non-family managers, Exciting was positively correlated with the Complex ($r = 0.40$), Passionate ($r = 0.68$), and Hopeful ($r = 0.24$) scales. Similar to the founders sample, Threatening was correlated with measures of Exhausting ($r = 0.68$), Ambiguous ($r = 0.38$), Empty ($r = 0.41$), having to Outwork Others ($r = 0.41$), and Tedious ($r = 0.35$). Unlike the founders sample, Threatening was correlated with a sense of having No Rules to follow ($r = 0.42$).

Dimensional Analysis

As discussed in Chapter 7, affective self-reports frequently array in a circumplex structure around two primary dimensions: valence and arousal. The valence dimension refers to the hedonic quality or positive–negative aspects, whereas arousal refers to activation or attentive aspects of emotional experience (Feldman, 1995). Watson and Tellegen (1985) propose similar independent dimensions labeled positive and negative affectivity (PA, NA) positioned by a 45-degree rotation of the valence–arousal dimensions. Essentially, PA and NA are combinations of valence tone and arousal. High PA is a positively valenced state of strong engagement, and low PA is a negatively valenced state of weak engagement. Conversely, high NA is a negatively valenced engaging state and low NA is a positively valenced disengaging state.

Multi-dimensional scaling (MDS) of the scale intercorrelations was used to visually approximate patterns of similarities among measures of family business founders' and managers' affective experience. In MDS, the number of dimensions to be included is determined by a stress coefficient indicating the extent of the model's departure from the data. Generally, values ≤ 0.15 are considered acceptable, and ≤ 0.01 as excellent. It is seldom necessary to add dimensions over the number required to reduce stress below 0.05 (Kruskal and Wish, 1978). The proportion of variance of the scaled data accounted for by the MDS procedure is represented by R-square (RSQ), with 0.60 regarded as the minimum level (Green et al., 1989). Stress coefficients for a two-dimensional solution met acceptable criteria for both samples (founders: stress = 0.04, RSQ = 0.96; managers: stress = 0.02, RSQ = 0.98). Similarity patterns among the affect scales are shown in Figures 11.1a and b. Scales with higher positive correlations are positioned nearer together and scales with larger negative correlations farther apart.

Spatial analysis of the figures suggests a circumplex configuration that shows both structural similarity and difference between the samples. To measure the affect domain of the family business experience, a broad set of affect-related adjectives was accumulated for study. No attempt was made to include only high-end adjectives that would limit the range of scale scores, or adjectives that would equally represent each dimension. Rather than fall around the perimeter or cluster near the axes, scales positioned between and along the entire length of each dimension are spread out more or less evenly in regions of the two-dimensional space, thus providing a more complete picture of the full range of emotions associated with the experience.

Inspection of the affective structures clearly suggests that Dimension 1

Entrepreneurship as experience

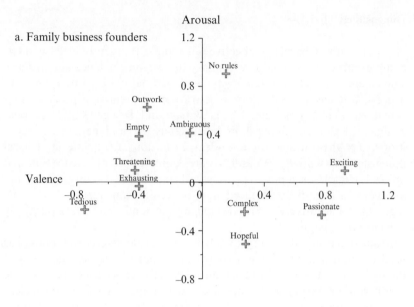

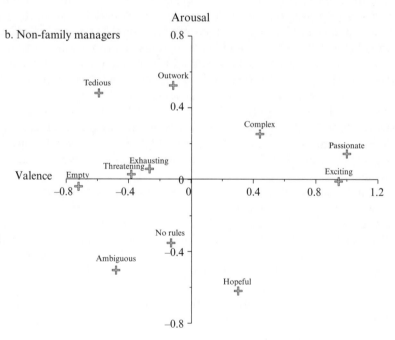

Figures 11.1a, b   Two-dimensional MDS maps for affect scales of family business founders and non-family business managers

on the horizontal axis represents valence. For founders, Tedious is located toward the negative extreme and Exciting and Passionate are located at the positive extreme, with other states in between. Working outwardly from the mid-point, Ambiguous, having to Outwork Others, Exhausting, Empty, and Threatening are negatively valenced, whereas No Rules to follow, Hopeful, and Complex emotions are positively valenced states. Although there is some reordering of the scales, the pattern of affect for non-family managers is comparable. Passionate and Exciting feelings are closely positioned at the positive extreme and Empty and Tedious are moderately positioned at its negative end. Hopeful and Complex are moderately positive while No Rules to follow, Outwork Others, Exhausting, Threatening, and Ambiguous are negatively valenced states.

Dimension 2 on the vertical axis represents perceived arousal and engagement associated with the experience. Firm founders perceive No Rules to follow as very high and having to Outwork Others, Ambiguous, and Empty as moderately high states of arousal. Tedious and Exhausting reflect negative affect but moderate levels of arousal, while complex and passionate are positive but also moderate on arousal. In contrast, Hopeful feelings are relatively low in arousal. For non-family managers, having to Outwork Others is associated with higher arousal. Managers perceive a Tedious state to be negative but more arousing than did founders. Complexity also generated higher arousal among managers. Experiences that were Ambiguous, and those with No Rules were relatively low in arousal. Only one emotion, Tedious, placed in the low NA space for managers, an area where more positively valenced states of disengagement are typical.

When we compare founders with the non-family managers, some interesting differences emerge. An experience where it feels like there are No Rules is more positive and intense for founders, and quite negative and less engaging for managers. The ambiguity that founders associate with more intensity and fairly neutral affect is experienced more negatively and less intensely by managers. Complexity is experienced as positive affect by managers, meaning it is positive and highly engaging, while founders find complexity to be less engaging. Tediousness is a more intense or engaging negative aspect of the experience of managers, and emptiness is a more engaging negative aspect of the experience of founders.

RESULTS: FAMILY VS. NON-FAMILY FOUNDERS

Similar analytic procedures and criteria were used to analyze the emotional experiences of founders of non-family businesses over a three-year operational time frame.[1] Prior to factoring, Bartlett's test (p < 0.001) and a KMO measure in the meritorious range (0.80) indicated that the matrix was appropriate for principal component analysis. An exploratory factor analysis of the 48 affect-related adjectives measured in the same metric revealed 12 factors explaining slightly over 68 percent of the variance. Of these factors, the first four consisted of multiple items and the remaining eight single items. Factor loadings are presented in Table 11.2. In order of extraction, the factors were labeled: (1) Exhausting, (2) Exciting, (3) Threatening, (4) Revitalizing, (5) Challenging, (6) Humiliating, (7) Powerful, (8) Demanding, (9) Ambiguous, (10) Hopeful, (11) Tedious, and (12) a sense of having to Outwork Others. As before, items for each of the multi-item factors were summed to form composite scales and the remaining scales were labeled by the single item that loaded ≥ 0.50 on that factor. Coefficient alphas (α) for the composite scales (α = 0.90 for Exhausting, 0.87 for Exciting, 0.77 for Threatening, and 0.72 for Revitalizing) indicate acceptable internal consistency.

Although the order of extraction and magnitude of item loadings differ somewhat, comparison of the first few components shows enough item congruence to justify receiving the same label as used with the family business founders. Eight items (Exhausting, Uncertain, Overwhelming, All-consuming, Stressful, Burdensome, Chaotic, Difficult) load on the Exhausting factor, four items (Inadequate, Threatening, Insignificance, Alienating) on the Threatening factor, and seven items (Energizing, Adventurous, Motivating, Exciting, Exhilarating, Empowering, Self-fulfilling) on the Exciting factor in both studies. Also note that the three items that loaded on the Exciting factor in Study I (Invigorating, Joyful, and Revitalizing) form a separate factor (i.e., Revitalizing). The last three single-item factors extracted in each study (i.e., Hopeful, Tedious, and sense of having to Outwork Others) are identical.

Similarity in item composition suggests that measurement of these affects is partially invariant across studies (Anderson and Engledow, 1977). Partial invariance in this subset of measures is insufficient for quantitatively comparing correlations across studies, but sufficient for qualitative comparison by means of multi-dimensional scaling (Steenkamp and Baumgartner, 1998). The first three composites, with similar scale reliabilities, as well as the last three single-item measures can be compared between founders of family and non-family businesses by visually matching their locations in conceptual space. The remaining measures (Challenging, Humiliating, Powerful, Demanding, and Ambiguous) are unique to the study of non-family firms.

Table 11.2   Exploratory factor analysis results (founders of non-family businesses)

Item	Factors											
	Exhausting 1	Exciting 2	Threatening 3	Revitalizing 4	Challenging 5	Humiliating 6	Powerful 7	Demanding 8	Ambiguous 9	Hopeful 10	Tedious 11	Out-work 12
Exhausting	0.55	–	–	–	–	–	–	–	–	–	–	–
Complex	0.50	–	–	–	–	–	–	–	–	–	–	–
Uncertain	0.52	–	–	–	–	–	–	–	–	–	–	–
Overwhelming	0.72	–	–	–	–	–	–	–	–	–	–	–
All-consuming	0.65	–	–	–	–	–	–	–	–	–	–	–
Frightening	0.66	–	–	–	–	–	–	–	–	–	–	–
Stressful	0.70	–	–	–	–	–	–	–	–	–	–	–
Burdensome	0.64	–	–	–	–	–	–	–	–	–	–	–
Chaotic	0.75	–	–	–	–	–	–	–	–	–	–	–
Intimidating	0.72	–	–	–	–	–	–	–	–	–	–	–
Unstable	0.52	–	–	–	–	–	–	–	–	–	–	–
Difficult	0.55	–	–	–	–	–	–	–	–	–	–	–
Terrifying	0.72	–	–	–	–	–	–	–	–	–	–	–
Energizing	–	0.50	–	–	–	–	–	–	–	–	–	–
Adventurous	–	0.78	–	–	–	–	–	–	–	–	–	–
Motivating	–	0.73	–	–	–	–	–	–	–	–	–	–
Passionate	–	0.68	–	–	–	–	–	–	–	–	–	–
Exciting	–	0.79	–	–	–	–	–	–	–	–	–	–
Exhilarating	–	0.70	–	–	–	–	–	–	–	–	–	–
Novel	–	0.51	–	–	–	–	–	–	–	–	–	–
Empowering	–	0.64	–	–	–	–	–	–	–	–	–	–
Feeling Free	–	0.57	–	–	–	–	–	–	–	–	–	–
Self-fulfilling	–	0.69	–	–	–	–	–	–	–	–	–	–

Table 11.2 (continued)

Item	Factors											
	Exhaust-ing 1	Excit-ing 2	Threat-ening 3	Revital-izing 4	Challen-ging 5	Humili-ating 6	Power-ful 7	Deman-ding 8	Ambig-uous 9	Hope-ful 10	Tedi-ous 11	Out-work 12
Inadequacy	–	–	0.56	–	–	–	–	–	–	–	–	–
No Rules	–	–	0.63	–	–	–	–	–	–	–	–	–
Insignificance	–	–	0.63	–	–	–	–	–	–	–	–	–
Empty	–	–	0.76	–	–	–	–	–	–	–	–	–
Alienating	–	–	0.52	–	–	–	–	–	–	–	–	–
Threatening	–	–	0.56	–	–	–	–	–	–	–	–	–
Invigorating	–	–	–	0.71	–	–	–	–	–	–	–	–
Joyful	–	–	–	0.70	–	–	–	–	–	–	–	–
Revitalizing	–	–	–	0.65	–	–	–	–	–	–	–	–
Challenging	–	–	–	–	0.81	–	–	–	–	–	–	–
Humiliating	–	–	–	–	–	0.80	–	–	–	–	–	–
Powerful	–	–	–	–	–	–	0.65	–	–	–	–	–
Demanding	–	–	–	–	–	–	–	0.74	–	–	–	–
Ambiguous	–	–	–	–	–	–	–	–	0.77	–	–	–
Hopeful	–	–	–	–	–	–	–	–	–	0.76	–	–
Tedious	–	–	–	–	–	–	–	–	–	–	0.76	–
Outwork	–	–	–	–	–	–	–	–	–	–	–	0.60
Others	–	–	–	–	–	–	–	–	–	–	–	–
Eigenvalue	7.49	6.16	3.54	2.45	1.99	1.97	1.76	1.74	1.73	1.69	1.51	1.17
% variance explained	15.28	12.57	7.22	4.99	4.70	4.20	3.6	3.55	3.53	3.45	3.7	2.39

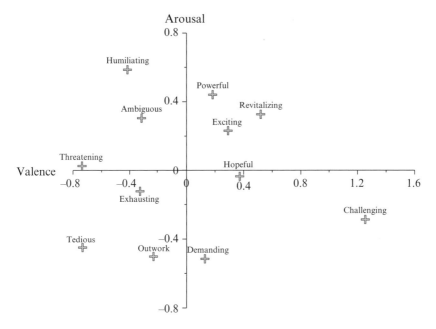

Figure 11.2   Two-dimensional MDS map for affect scales of founders of non-family businesses

Correlational Analysis

In assessing relationships among affect scales for non-family entrepreneurs, the Exhausting scale was positively correlated ($p \geq 0.05$) with all scales except Revitalizing and negatively correlated with Challenging ($r = -0.44$). Exciting was correlated with Revitalizing ($r = 0.54$), Powerful ($r = 0.51$), Demanding ($r = 0.32$), and Hopeful ($r = 0.42$). Threatening was associated with Humiliating ($r = 0.36$), Tedious ($r = 0.27$), and Outwork Others ($r = 0.29$), but negatively related to Challenging ($r = -0.41$). Revitalizing was correlated with Powerful ($r = 0.33$) and Hopeful ($r = 0.40$). Positive correlations were found between Demanding and both Hopeful ($r = 0.23$) and Outwork Others ($r = 0.37$), and Powerful and Outwork Others ($r = 0.30$). Challenging and Humiliating were negatively correlated ($r = -0.25$).

Dimensional Analysis

Figure 11.2 presents an MDS model that illustrates similarity patterns among the affect scales for non-family business founders in two-dimensional space (stress = 0.01, RSQ = 0.99). Inspection of the solution suggests that Dimension 1 (the horizontal) corresponds to positive–negative valence with Threatening and Challenging at the negative and positive ends respectively. A sense of having to Outwork Others, Ambiguous, Tedious, Exhausting, and Humiliating are also positioned on the negative side, with Demanding, Powerful, Exciting, Hopeful, and Revitalizing emotions on the positive side. On the vertical dimension, we see higher arousal where the experience is Powerful but also where it is Humiliating, and lower arousal where it is perceived to be Demanding and requires one to continually Outwork Others, perhaps reflecting a sense of tedium. It is instructive to consider the diagonals, which conform to positive and negative affectivity. Revitalizing, Powerful, and Exciting are engaging emotions located moderately high on the PA dimension, with Tedious, having to Outwork Others, and Exhausting emotions located on its low end. High NA consists of Humiliating, Ambiguous, and Threatening emotions.

A comparison of family and non-family founder experiences suggests strong affective responses to the streams of events occurring in a venture's founding years. Yet, meaningful differences emerge if we compare Figures 11.1a and 11.2. If one considers the 45-degree diagonals that produce high positive and negative affect spaces, results from non-family founders suggest considerable high engagement positive affect centering on experiences that are Powerful, Revitalizing, and Exciting. Where they found the experience to be one of high engagement but unpleasant, they indicated it was Humiliating, Ambiguous, and Threatening. Alternatively, for family business entrepreneurs, a number of aspects of their experience reflected high engagement negative effect, including the extent to which it was Ambiguous, Threatening, Empty, and required them to Outwork Others. Where it was a more positive and high-engagement experience for this sample, it was characterized in terms of having No Rules and being Exciting. The samples of founders also differed in how some factors were perceived. Compared to non-family entrepreneurs, family business founders viewed Exciting experiences more positively, and Threatening experiences less negatively. Finding the experience to be Hopeful was more engaging for non-family founders, while having to continually Outwork Others reflected a less engaging experience. The two groups tended to see the Tedious, Exhausting, and Ambiguous nature of the experience similarly.

Finally, for validity purposes, affect scales were correlated with three external variables: positivity, intensity, and satisfaction associated with the venture experience. Measures of positivity and satisfaction should relate to scales on the positive/negative halves of the valence dimension and intensity to levels of arousal in a meaningful way. A fairly consistent pattern of relations with the positivity and satisfaction measures was common across samples in both studies. Variable relations tend to follow the ordering of affects along the valence dimension and nearly all scales at the extremes are significantly correlated. For example, correlations with the positivity variable ranged from 0.53 ($p < 0.001$) for Exciting to −0.31 ($p < 0.01$) for the Threatening, Exhausting, and Empty emotions of family members. For non-family managers, emotions correlated with the satisfaction variable, r from 0.61 and 0.45 ($p < 0.001$) for Exciting and Passionate to −0.20 ($p < 0.05$) for Threatening. Relations with positivity and satisfaction variables, r of 0.31 and 0.34 ($p < 0.01$) for Revitalizing to −0.31 ($p < 0.01$) and −0.13 ($p > 0.05$) for Threatening, also demonstrate this tendency in the non-family firm sample.

The results for the intensity measure and engagement were mixed. Having No Rules to follow marks high arousal for founders, but falls in the lower range for managers. Corresponding correlations with Intensity are 0.02 ($p > 0.05$) and 0.23 ($p < 0.05$). Even though Powerful and Demanding emotions locate on opposite extremes of the arousal dimension for the non-family firm sample, correlations with the intensity variable are positive (r of 0.36 and 0.37, $p < 0.001$). Of the two primary dimensions, self-reported emotion generally reflects valence to a greater extent than arousal (Watson and Tellegen, 1985). Additionally, the reported three-year time frame makes arousal difficult to judge. Entrepreneurs' level of arousal fluctuates over time and may change systematically depending on stages of venture development. While validity variables such as intensity may correlate with arousal in momentary experiences, they are not as amenable to studying longer-term structures of affect (Larsen and Diener, 1992).

DISCUSSION

The findings suggest it is possible to visually capture venture creation in a circumplex, with a two-dimensional representation best reflecting the data. Consistent with work in psychology, a positive–negative valence dimension and an arousal–engagement dimension emerged.

With the valence dimension, factors such as Exciting and Passionate reflected a strongly positive experience, while Exhausting, Threatening, and Tedious were indicative of a negative experience. These findings were consistent across the samples. For the arousal dimension, family business founders were more engaged where experiences were perceived to have No Rules to follow, and more Ambiguous, and when one had to continually Outwork Others. Alternatively, arousal was higher among managers not in the family when the experience was one of having to Outwork Others or was more Tedious, while they were less aroused by Ambiguous, Hopeful experiences with No Rules. Founders of non-family businesses were aroused more by Humiliating, Powerful, Ambiguous, Revitalizing, and Exciting experiences.

The experiences of family business founders somewhat diverge from those of non-family managers and founders of non-family firms. The multi-samples and correlation analyses indicate patterns of variation in affective expression. When reflecting on similar contexts over the same period of time, differences exist for family business founders, particularly with regard to the lack of Rules, Ambiguity, Tediousness, and sense of Complexity (compared to non-family managers), and both the sense of having to Outwork Others and Hopefulness (compared to founders of non-family ventures). In further examining particular items underlying the scales, non-family entrepreneurs differed significantly from family business founders in reporting experiences that were more Exhausting, Demanding, All-consuming, Stressful, Terrifying, and Creative.

Also worth noting is the extent to which entrepreneurial experiences produce negative affect, especially in family firms. Two of three factors on which the greatest number of items loaded and that explained the largest percentage of variance reflected a negative valence. The factor labeled Threatening captured a sense of being Lonely and Lost, Humiliated, Inadequate and Frightened. The Exhausting factor reflected the Stressful, All-consuming and Difficult nature of the experience. Other manifestations of negative affect included a sense of having to Outwork Others and feelings of Ambiguity. While more attention has been devoted by scholars to the impact of positive affect, evidence suggests negative affect can result in more competitive behavior during episodes of social conflict (Baron, 2008), and a lower concern for others combined with a higher concern for self (Rhoades et al., 2001).

Examination of the intensity of affective experiences has historically proven to be more challenging (Larsen and Diener, 1992). Intensity reflects the strength, degree of reality, and relevance of an experienced event, and is highest when events are unexpected and result from the individual's own behavior. The early-stage venture context appears to be especially conducive to more intense experiences, with Ambiguity and No Rules serving to heighten intensity for family entrepreneurs and lessen it for managers. For non-family firm founders, intensity is captured in Humiliating, Powerful, Ambiguous, Exciting and Revitalizing experiences. This finding reinforces our discussion of peak experiences in Chapter 9.

Additional analysis demonstrated that satisfaction with the family business experience was correlated with nine of 11 affective factors. In general, satisfaction is heavily influenced by the frequency of positive emotional experiences (Diener and Lucas, 2000). Most notable were positive correlations between satisfaction and the sense that it was an Exciting ($r = 0.55$, $p < 0.01$) and Passionate experience ($r = 0.29$, $p < 0.01$), and negative correlations between satisfaction and the sense that the experience was Empty ($r = -0.27$, $p < -0.01$), Threatening ($r = -0.23$, $p < 0.01$), and Exhausting ($r = -0.21$, $p < 0.01$). Family entrepreneurs found the experience to be more positive ($t = 1.99$, $p < 0.05$), intense ($t = 3.38$, $p < 0.01$) and satisfactory ($t = 2.13$, $p < 0.05$) than did non-family managers. These results are consistent with Shane's (2008) argument that, compared to others, the self-employed work harder and earn relatively less, but experience higher job satisfaction.

Existence of general differences between family business founders and the other samples reinforces the contention that another variable may be at work as an individual processes events and streams containing peaks and valleys, uncertainty, ambiguity, stress, or other characteristics innate to the start-up context. Family social capital may play a role in moderating the cognitive, affective, and physiological processing that determines how experiences are interpreted, generate learning, and influence behavior. Yet, the impact would appear to be both positive and negative. To the extent that family business founders associated the experience with Emptiness or having to Outwork Others, the strong negative affect might reflect family conditions where there is more conflict, personal demands or lack of support. Yet, the strong positive affect associated with experiences where there were No Rules might be due to a higher stock of social capital available to the entrepreneur in the form of trust, encouragement, and moral stability, enabling him or her to be invigorated by a more free-form context. The tendency for non-family business founders to report experiences that are more Stressful, Exhausting or Terrifying when individual scale items were examined supports the net positive impact of social capital in the family context.

Some of the most emphasized issues in the family business literature, such as family dynamics, succession decisions, and willingness of the founder to eventually let go include an emotional component (Chrisman et al., 2009). It would seem that experiences that are higher versus lower in intensity and valence would have important implications for these issues. For instance, where the entrepreneur is more strongly engaged with an experience that is negative, this negativity might be expected to spill over to family relationships, result in less succession planning, and find the entrepreneur more willing to let go. While hypothetical, there is evidence that emotionally significant events such as those encountered in the early stages of the venture can be re-experienced and recollected years later, and also influence emotion-inducing action tendencies and behaviors well into the future (Sonnemans and Frijda, 1994).

Individuals might also be expected to differ in their propensities to experience positive affect. Baron (2008) raises this possibility, placing our findings in a different light. He suggests that such personal variables as optimism, extraversion, and self-efficacy may contribute to the tendency to experience positive affect. In a family business context, this might explain differences between family business entrepreneurs and non-family managers in terms of their evaluations of how positive and intense the experience was, and in terms of their mean scores on the dimensions most associated with positive affect.

CONCLUSIONS

In early venture stages, the founder is an actor in an unscripted temporal performance where novelty is continually encountered. Throughout this book, we have argued that these experiences take on properties rooted in affect. In this chapter we have provided an example of how the affective experiences of entrepreneurs can be captured. Building on the inventory of descriptors regarding what it is like to create a venture presented in Chapter 6, and consistent with earlier methodologies proposed by Mano and Oliver (1993) and Feldman (1995), empirical evidence has been provided of the rich, affective nature of the entrepreneurial experience. High mean scores on the descriptive adjectives that respondents were asked to assess serve to reinforce the importance of emotions in describing what it is like to be "in the moment" within an emerging venture. As a result, we get a sense of how entrepreneurs are affected by the peaks and valleys that arise as the firm takes form and becomes sustainable.

The study summarized in this chapter provides direction in terms of our ability to capture the underlying dimensionality of the venture creation experience. Specifically, both a positive–negative valence dimension and an arousal–engagement dimension were identified across the samples of individuals surveyed. Examining the entrepreneurial experience from the vantage point of different combinations of positive–negative affect and high–low engagement can be fruitful for gaining new insights into a wide range of variables that surround venture creation. In the present instance, we see how a social capital framework is useful for understanding differences in entrepreneurial experiences. Examples of other variables on which new light might be shed include entrepreneurial motives, entrepreneurial burnout, the need for control, the role of networks and alliances, partnerships, the impact of outside investors on a venture, and exit strategies, to name but a few.

Employing this dimensionality, the present chapter also demonstrates how differences in the experiences of various types of entrepreneurs and others involved in the early years of a venture can be identified. In this chapter, we saw meaningful differences in the experiences of founders versus managers in family businesses, and between founders of family versus non-family businesses. By focusing on such differences, it becomes possible to develop a richer understanding of the relative levels of satisfaction an individual realizes from the venture experience. Not only might experiences that are more engaging and those producing more positive affect lead to more satisfaction, but they might also help explain how long one stays with a venture and the tendency to start a second or third venture. Similarly, less engaging experiences or those filled with events that generate negative effect might have implications for the tendency for a venture to start small and stay small, and for the entrepreneur to engage in more dysfunctional personal behaviors.

NOTES

* This chapter is adapted from Morris, M.H., J.A. Allen, D.F. Kuratko and D. Brannon (2010), 'Experiencing family business creation: differences between founders, nonfamily managers, and founders of nonfamily firms', *Entrepreneurship Theory and Practice*, **34**(6): 1057–84.
1. Assumptions underlying the MDS procedure include comparability of the venture experience and representative samples of entrepreneurs (see Green et al., 1989). In the first data set, samples of family firm owners and managers were matched by venture to ensure their affective experiences were comparable. However, assuming the entrepreneurs' experience is comparable across separate samples of family and non-family firms is questionable (Hair et al., 2005). To test this assumption, a components analysis with varimax rotation was performed on the affect-related adjectives in aggregate. A dummy variable denoting non-family founders (compared to family firm founders and managers) was created to assess any effect sample membership might have on the experience. A multivariate regression model was estimated using the scales as simultaneous dependent variables and the dummy variable as a predictor. If the dummy variable is non-significant in the model, data from both studies can be pooled and separate analyses are unnecessary. The dummy variable was significantly related to several composite scales (Wilks' $\lambda = 0.93$, $p < 0.01$). As a result, the sample of non-family entrepreneurs was analyzed separately.

REFERENCES

Adams, A.F., J.H. Astrachan, G.E. Manners and P. Mazzola (2005), 'The importance of integrated goal setting', *Family Business Review*, **17**(4): 287–302.

Anderson, J.C. and J. Engledow (1977), 'A factor analytic comparison of U.S. and German information seekers', *Journal of Consumer Research*, **3**(2): 185–96.

Aronoff, C.E. and J.L. Ward (2000), 'More than family: non-family executives in the family business', *Family Business Leadership Series*. Marietta, GA: Business Ownership Resources.

Baron, R. (2008), 'Role of affect in the entrepreneurial process', *Academy of Management Review*, **33**(3): 328–40.

Burt, R.S. (1992), *Structural Holes*, Cambridge, MA: Harvard University Press.

Chrisman, J., J. Chua and F. Kellermanns (2009), 'Priorities, resource stocks, and performance in family and nonfamily firms', *Entrepreneurship Theory & Practice*, **33**(3): 739–60.

Chua, J., J. Chrisman and E. Chang (2004), 'Are family firms born or made? An exploratory investigation', *Family Business Review*, **17**(1): 37–54.

Diener, E. and R. E. Lucas (2000), 'Subjective emotional well-being', in M. Lewis and J.M. Haviland (eds), *Handbook of Emotions*, New York: Guilford.

Feldman, L. (1995), 'Valence focus and arousal focus: individual differences in the structure of affective experience', *Journal of Personality and Social Psychology*, **69**(2): 153–66.

Green, P., F. Carmone and S. Smith (1989), *Multidimensional Scaling*, Boston, MA: Allyn & Bacon.

Hair, J., R. Anderson, R. Tatham and W. Black (2005), *Multivariate Data Analysis*, Upper Saddle River, NJ: Prentice Hall.

Klein, S.B. and F.A. Bell (2007), 'Non-family executives in family businesses: a literature review', *Electronic Journal of Family Business Studies*, **1**(1): 19–37.

Kruskal, J.B. and M. Wish (1978), *Multidimensional Scaling*, Beverly Hills, CA: Sage.

Larsen, R.J. and E. Diener (1992), 'Problems and promises with the circumplex model of emotion', *Review of Personality and Social Psychology*, **13**(1): 25–59.

Mano, H. and R. Oliver (1993), 'Assessing the dimensionality and structure of the consumption experience', *Journal of Consumer Research*, **20**(3): 451–66.

Mitchell, R., E. Morse and P. Sharma (2003), 'The transacting cognitions of non-family employees in the family businesses setting', *Journal of Business Venturing*, **18**(4): 533–51.

Olson, P., V. Zuiker, S. Danes, K. Stafford, R. Heck, and K. Duncan (2003), 'Impact of family and business on family business sustainability', *Journal of Business Venturing*, **18**(5): 639–66.

Poza, E. (2004), *Family Business*, Mason, OH: Thompson/Southwest Publishing.

Rhoades, J., J. Arnold and J. Clifford (2001), 'The role of affective traits and affective states in disputants' motivation and behavior during episodes of organizational conflict', *Journal of Organizational Behavior*, **22**(3): 329–45.

Rodriguez, P., C. Tuggle and S. Hackett (2009), 'Examining ethnic entrepreneurship: an exploratory study of how "family capital" impacts venture start-up rates across ethnic groups', *Family Business Review*, **22**(3): 259–72.

Shane, S. (2008), *The Illusions of Entrepreneurship*, New Haven, CT: Yale University Press.

Sirmon, D.G. and M.A. Hitt (2003), 'Managing resources: linking unique resources, management and wealth creation in family firms', *Entrepreneurship Theory and Practice*, **27**(4): 339–58.

Sonnemans, J. and N. Frijda (1994), 'The structure of subjective emotional intensity', *Cognition & Emotion*, **8**(4): 329–50.

Sorenson, Ritch L. and L. Bierman (2009), 'Family capital, family business, and free enterprise', *Family Business Review*, **22**(2): 193.

Steenkamp, J.B. and H. Baumgartner (1998), 'Assessing measurement invariance in cross-national consumer research', *Journal of Consumer Research*, **25**(1): 78–90.

Steir, L. (2001), 'Next generation entrepreneurs and succession: modes and means of managing social capital', *Family Business Review*, **14**(2): 259–76.

Watson, D. and A. Tellegen (1985), 'Toward a consensual structure of mood', *Psychological Bulletin*, **98**(2): 219–35.

12. Conducting research on the entrepreneurial experience

> It is often recognized that entrepreneurship is to a great extent a form of art, a practice-oriented endeavor that requires a sensitive and committed engagement with a range of phenomena in the surrounding world. Still, much of the research and theory development favors large studies and positivist epistemology, where the liveliness of entrepreneurship tends to be suspended in favor of scientific rigor.
>
> (Henrik Berglund, 2007)

INTRODUCTION

George Berkeley (1685–1753) was an Irish clergyman and philosopher who famously wrote, "*esse est percipi* [to be is to be perceived]." Berkeley's theory, called immaterialism or subjective idealism, stated that material objects do not exist except as ideas embedded in the minds of perceivers. While the specifics of Berkeley's theory are not important to our present discussion, the reaction of Samuel Johnson, one of his contemporaries, to this theory is nevertheless illuminating. Johnson's biographer writes:

> After we came out of the church, we stood talking for some time together of Bishop Berkeley's ingenious sophistry to prove the non-existence of matter, and that everything in the universe is merely ideal. I observed that, though we are satisfied his doctrine is not true, it is impossible to refute it. I never shall forget the alacrity with which Johnson answered, striking his foot with mighty force against a large stone, till he rebounded from it, "I refute it *thus*." (Boswell, 1953, p. 333)

Researchers interested in the experience underlying entrepreneurship cannot help but think that Johnson won the debate, decisively. In today's empiricist and positivist world, unless a phenomenon is easy to understand, easy to see, and easy to measure, it is not quite worthy of study. At one end of the ontological spectrum, we find Johnson's rock. On the other, experience and subjective meaning. The passage of a second can change the meaning a person ascribes to a particular experience. How an individual comes to understand one experience depends on her experiences leading up to the moment in question as well as the experiences that come after. Even the action of recalling an experience and assigning meaning to the experience can influence how that experience is understood. Rocks can be easily measured: they tend to stay put. Experience and meaning simply does not. Even more, the methodologies used to get at the more ephemeral constructs and objects are frequently derided and relegated, though this is changing. Quantitative methodologies, empirics, and sophisticated statistical analysis are still de rigueur for the top journals publishing entrepreneurship research. Case studies, interviews, and ethnomethodological analyses are published less frequently, though journal editors claim to be doing their best to solicit better qualitative efforts (Gartner and Birley, 2002; Gephart, 2004).

Thus, researchers interested in experience and meaning face a two-fold problem: (1) the object of their study is simply difficult to capture; and (2) the methodologies they use to capture experience are themselves open to some degree of skepticism and doubt. In this chapter, we will describe some of the difficulties associated not only with researching experience within the entrepreneurship discipline, but review some of the criticisms of the methodologies deployed to study experience. The purpose of this chapter is not to provide a step-by-step instruction guide for pursuing a study of experience, nor is it an epistemology of qualitative research methods. Instead, our intent is to: (1) illustrate some of the difficulties that researchers may encounter in their pursuit of understanding experience and meaning; (2) review how quality might be achieved in the methodologies used in this pursuit; and (3) provide examples of studies of experience and entrepreneurship that have employed various methodological approaches.

This chapter will proceed as follows. First, we will review the current critiques of entrepreneurship as a field of research and describe how a greater emphasis on experience and meaning through an interpretivist research philosophy can help overcome these criticisms. Second, we will discuss more generally critiques leveled at methodologies used to understand experience within the organizational and management literature, and describe some guidelines for increasing the quality of such studies. Finally, we will provide some illustrative examples of studies within the entrepreneurship literature and broader organizational literature that have tackled methodological criticisms and succeeded in being published in the field's top journals.

EXPERIENCE IN ENTREPRENEURSHIP: PHILOSOPHY AND METHODOLOGY

Entrepreneurship is still a hodgepodge field characterized by balkanization – if only evidenced by the number of papers from scholars bemoaning the lack of theoretical or methodological coherence and direction (Bygrave, 2007; Davidsson et al., 2001; Gartner and Birley, 2002; Howorth et al., 2005; Leitch et al., 2010). Critical themes common to these papers are the lack of longitudinal studies, overemphasis on statistical analysis, excessive focus on process theories, and the domination of functionalist or positivist perspectives. Howarth and colleagues (2005) note that as the emphasis in entrepreneurship moves from the entrepreneur to the entrepreneurship process, these shortcomings have only been exacerbated. In an effort to keep up with their colleagues in the management fields, entrepreneurship scholars have adopted a functionalist perspective, with its assumptions of objective and universal truths (Grant and Perren, 2002; Howarth et al., 2005). The functionalism that dominates and influences the study of entrepreneurship is the same strain that led early American scholars away from the philosophies of Dewey and James (Bradley, 2005; Pollio et al., 1997) – the rise of hard science, economics, and psychology left little room for the interpretivist or phenomenological methodologies (Leitch et al., 2010). Lawson (2008) writes that the social sciences have adopted the methodologies of natural sciences because they have been characterized as "proper science."

The question underlying this particular critique of entrepreneurship research is not qualitative methods vs. quantitative methods, but rather positivist philosophy vs. interpretive philosophy. Positivism assumes that individuals, behavior, and social objects can be understood through grasping relationships between variables (Leitch et al., 2010). Here, the world exists in an objective state and truth is discoverable, general, and verifiable (Gephart, 2004). Interpretivist philosophies trace their roots to James, Dilthey, and especially Max Weber, and involve a search for *Verstehen*, or understanding the meanings that individuals attach to their experiences (Johnson et al., 2006; Leitch et al., 2010). Where research rooted in a positivist philosophy seeks commonalities, shared meaning, and generalizability, research rooted in an interpretivist philosophy accounts for the subjectivity of meaning. For interpretivists, meaning changes from person to person, time to time, and even researcher to researcher. The purpose, Gephart (2004, p. 457) explains, is to "[describe] how different meanings held by different persons or groups produce and sustain a sense of truth, particularly in the face of competing definitions of reality." Thus, positivism assumes that concepts and constructs remain constant over time; interpretivism eschews this notion and instead assumes that concepts and constructs are dependent entirely on the meanings and experiences of the individuals being measured.

These philosophies provide the superstructure on which research methodologies are built, and they are not necessarily exclusive. Positivism provides certain insights – truth certainly lies in the causal relationships discovered between variables. However, positivism is ill equipped to answer other questions. As Bygrave (2007) notes, positivism (and the methodologies employed to pursue positivist research agendas) is a study of averages and predictability, while much of entrepreneurship takes place in the edges of legitimacy (Zimmerman and Zeitz, 2002). Entrepreneurship often entails behavior that is *not* predictable. Although scholars have theorized processes of entrepreneurship that are relatively linear (Shane, 2003), the activity of venture creation is anything *but* linear or predictable.

Many of the critiques of entrepreneurship research – such as the use of self-response surveys, lack of longitudinal studies, an excessive focus on non-Schumpeterian entrepreneurship (Bygrave, 2007), as well as an over-reliance on empiricism and neglect of theory (Davidsson et al., 2001) – can be addressed by adopting an interpretivist philosophy. Importantly for our purposes, interpretivist philosophy can address the problems associated with studying experience and meaning in entrepreneurship. Positivism suffers in its limited ability to deal with such aspects of experiencing as: (1) its highly idiosyncratic and personal nature, (2) complex temporal boundaries, (3) differences between how one perceives and processes an event when it is happening and how one recalls that event upon reflection, (4) aspects of experience that occur at the subconscious level, and (5) the fact that a given experience occurs within the larger context of a life's worth of accumulated experience. Using positivist methodologies to study something as slippery as experience would be similar to using hedge clippers to cut someone's hair – the finesse and subjectivity inherent in studying a person's life and experiences would be smudged out with the heavy thumb of either positivist assumptions or methodologies based on statistical analysis. The problem with the positivist perspective is exacerbated in the entrepreneurship field, where study focuses on the "ephemeral, the indefinite and the irregular" (Law, 2004, p.4; also see Gartner and Birley, 2002; Neergaard and Ulhøi, 2007). Interpretivist research, in recognizing that meaning is relative and constantly changing, is thus better equipped to explain how the individual experiences new venture creation. It also shows promise for advancing the entrepreneurship field in general; where other social sciences have embraced interpretivist research agendas, entrepreneurship has not, which threatens the credibility (Low, 2001), usefulness (Hindle, 2004), and comprehensiveness (Van Maanen, 1979) of the field.

Importantly, while some methodologies are more commonly used in the positivist perspective and some methodologies are more commonly used in the interpretivist perspective, the philosophical perspective does not constitute a line between qualitative and quantitative methodologies

(Chandler and Lyon, 2001; Gephart, 2004). In fact, qualitative methodologies for data collection and data analysis can be used to pursue a positivist research agenda just as quantitative methods can be used to pursue an interpretivist research agenda. The interpretivist perspective is most interested in describing the construction of social meanings, either at the social level (e.g., ethnomethodological studies) or at the individual level (e.g., phenomenology). Therefore, methods focus on collecting and interpreting expressions of experience, most commonly through verbal descriptions from individuals.

With specific regard to entrepreneurship research, the interpretivist perspective has been manifested in both qualitative and quantitative efforts. Qualitative studies draw on ethnographic traditions in anthropology and sociology, where the researcher lives with or gets close to a given group, such as members of indigenous tribes, people in homeless shelters or entrepreneurs operating a business (Turner and Bruner, 1986). While we provide some more in-depth examples later of interpretivist research in entrepreneurship, one notable example is Rae and Carswell's (2000) study of how individuals learn to create high-performing ventures. They asked a purposefully selected group of entrepreneurs to tell their stories, eliciting their narrative processes of recollection and sense-making, and encouraging them to disclose insights about significant events and periods, which are then recorded and subjected to discourse analysis. The story lines and narrative structuring provide each entrepreneur with a personal theory that can give meanings to actions and events. Another example of a useful method includes the critical incidents approach, such as that employed by Cope and Watts (2000) to study entrepreneurial learning. In six case studies, entrepreneurs elaborated on the best and worst times in describing how their businesses developed. Following a narrative, the interviewer plays an active role in helping participants reflect upon and make sense of their experiences. Berglund (2007) describes a similar approach in an examination of how risk is experienced and enacted, where relatively unstructured interviews produced protocols that were systematically analyzed to create categories capturing homogeneous qualities of what was said. And finally, Sarasvathy (2001) uses verbal think-aloud protocols and analyzes semantic chunks relevant to her research question to develop a theory of effectuation in entrepreneurship.

Quantitative methods can also be employed to address questions of meaning and experience. For example, Cantor and colleagues (1991) examine the experience of being on one's own at college by first collecting baseline data on life tasks and perceived daily life stress through surveys, then employing event sampling and diary techniques to capture the fabric of daily life, and finally conducting a follow-up survey on life satisfaction and a reassessment of stress. Event sampling was accomplished with pagers or programmed watches and, when signaled, the student would record the activities and feelings of that moment's experience and record it on a formatted sheet. Such an approach could be adapted with a sample of entrepreneurs in their first month to determine how prior experience impacts the saliency attached to events as they occur and the affective reaction to key events, with the follow-up survey assessing satisfaction. A variation can be found in Feldman (1995), who also used pre- and post-experience surveys, which included daily mood measures taken at different times of day submitted daily over a period of three months. Most recently, Uy et al. (2010) have explored the application of experience sampling in entrepreneurship research, demonstrating a six-step, event-contingent protocol that utilizes cell phones, which they write is effective at studying affective states at multiple points in time, especially when events occur at irregular intervals.

Gephart (2004) writes that the line between qualitative and quantitative methodologies is often drawn overly bright: data collection *and* data analysis are the constituent parts of any methodology, and nothing precludes a qualitative method for data collection to join a quantitative method for data analysis. Whether this particular example constitutes qualitative or quantitative methods is debatable; nevertheless, the point remains that the qualitative method can include as rigorous a statistical or mathematical element as a method labeled quantitative. The more important distinction, as Gephart notes, is the purpose for which the method is employed. Positivist, quantitative research aims to falsify hypotheses of causal relationships between variables. Interpretive, qualitative research "[explains] how [societal members] directly experience everyday life realities" through collecting and analyzing the meanings they use (ibid., p.455). The other truly important distinction Gephart draws is that quantitative research starts and ends with mathematics while qualitative research, which starts and ends with the spoken or written word, is more literary and humanistic. Researching experience and meaning, especially as it emerges through the experience of venture creation, and as it manifests in the different disciplinary perspectives of an experience-based perspective on entrepreneurship, clearly falls within the interpretivist, qualitative paradigm. In the next section, we will discuss what it means, exactly, to be an interpretivist researcher and how to do high-quality interpretivist research.

INTERPRETIVISM: FOUNDATIONS AND PRACTICE

Interpretivist research involves the study of social reality (Leitch et al., 2010). As Van Maanen (1979, p.539) notes, interpretivist research seeks to explain "the meaning, not the frequency, of certain more or less naturally occurring phenomena in the social world." Interpretive research has exploded in recent years, partly as a reaction to the over-representation of positivist research with its reliance on methods commonly found in natural science (Prasad and Prasad, 2002; Sandberg, 2005). Positivist organizational researchers have confused the methodologies and research philosophies of natural scientists with those of the social and cultural sciences. This confusion has also obscured crucial assumptions underlying the study of society, culture, and human action, such as issues related to objectivity (both the researcher's and the subject's) and assumptions that generalizable facts exist in the social and human domain (Bohman, 1991; Prasad and Prasad, 2002). Sandberg (2005) describes three positivist assumptions that interpretivist research, which is based on phenomenology, rejects: (1) a dualist ontology; (2) an objectivist epistemology; and (3) the assumption that language is directly related to an objective reality as opposed to being socially defined and ever-changing.

Phenomenologists since Husserl have rejected dualist ontology, which is an assumption that treats an object and the environment in which the object is embedded as totally separate entities. Instead, Husserl, Schütz, and others have argued that an individual's consciousness and self-identity are created through meaningful experience, which can only occur and accumulate through an interaction with the outside, social world. Likewise, phenomenology rejects an objectivist epistemology, or the notion that there is an objective reality that can be objectively perceived and described. Instead, the descriptions individuals give about their experiences are subjective, dependent on the individual's accumulated experiences, and that social meaning is constructed through interaction with others (Blumer, 1969; Sandberg, 2005). Finally, phenomenology rejects the notion that language has objective meaning. Instead, language is a social object whose definition is constructed through social interaction and whose meaning is entirely dependent on the setting in which it is used (Charon, 1995; Goffman, 1974).

Obviously, the rejection of these assumptions causes particular problems for interpretivist research within an organizational, management and entrepreneurship setting:

- Objective reality cannot be objectively described.
- The language in which individuals provide their descriptions of experience is itself subjectively defined.
- Multiple, even infinite, layers of context affect how the experience is remembered, described, and even interpreted (Sandberg, 2005). First, one's affective sense of the experience differs when fully

engaged in the experience compared to when one later reflects on the experience. Pribram (1991) notes two modes of experience: (1) an "objective me," who uniquely experiences the contents or objects of an experience as it occurs; and (2) a "monitoring, narrative I," who subsequently reconstructs the experience in the form of a self-composed narrative; content can change between these modes). Second, the researcher's own subjectivity comes into play: (1) the researcher has the experience of recording and reading her subject's described experience; and (2) the researcher attaches meaning to this experience. Again, the content changes between modes.

In this setting, how do the findings produced through interpretivist research ever have value or knowledge or truth? Sandberg (2005, p. 46) puts it this way: "At the same time as advocates of interpretive research deny the possibility of producing objective knowledge, they want to claim that the knowledge they generate is true in some way or another."

The interpretivist's answer is that truth and knowledge are iterative. Though unlikely to ever satisfy a positivist dedicated to statistical analysis, this answer deals with objectivity, knowledge, and truth on phenomenological terms – it makes little sense to apply one philosophy's standards to another, especially when the latter is in some ways opposed to the former. First, although phenomenological philosophy repudiates the possibility that objective reality can ever be objectively communicated, it does not repudiate the notion of objectivity itself. While reality is a product of an individual's experience with the world, individuals, in their interactions with each other, create shared, intersubjective meanings to construct social reality – these shared meanings are objective social facts (Sandberg, 2005). Second, even though individuals are intimately tied to the social world, the social world transcends the individual and is thus objective (Bengtsson, 1989).

For the interpretivist researcher, truth is the conjunction between what is expected and what is discovered – what Sandberg (2005) calls intentional fulfillment. One of Husserl's philosophical descendants, Martin Heidegger (1992, p. 42) explains:

> I can in an empty way now think of my desk at home simply in order to talk about it. I can fulfill this empty intention in a way by envisaging it to myself, and finally by going home and seeing it itself in an authentic and final experience. In such a demonstrative fulfillment the emptily intended and the originally intuited come into coincidence. This bringing-into-coincidence – the intended being experienced in the intuited as itself and selfsame – is an act of identification. The intended identifies itself in the intuited; selfsameness is experienced.

The implications of what Heidegger writes is that truth exists when the researcher's expectation (i.e., interpretation) matches with what is meant by the phenomenon being researched (Sandberg, 2005). Truth is an iterative process. Differences between the researcher's interpretation and the description of an experience she is reading means that she has not reached truth. The researcher adjusts her interpretation through subsequent read-throughs until her interpretation and the meaning communicated in the subject being examined join together, just as with Heidegger's intuition of a desk and the desk he actually encounters in his home. One implication of this "described intentional fulfillment as truth" is that the researcher must have some awareness of the subject she is researching. As discussed in Chapter 3, Giorgi (2009) argued that psychologists should adopt a "psychological perspective" when engaging in phenomenological research. Likewise, management or entrepreneurship scholars should adopt an appropriate perspective of their own. Without familiarity with the day-to-day content of venture creation or the experiences an entrepreneur has, the interpretivist researcher in entrepreneurship will be unable or at least at a severe disadvantage in attempting to interpret the experiences she encounters.

Sandberg (2005) describes several criteria interpretivist researchers can use to ensure the validity of their interpretations, and he provides a methodology for enacting these validity checks. He calls the checks communicative, pragmatic, and transgressive validity plus reliability as interpretive awareness. Communicative validity is constructed in three phases. First, in entering into interaction with research subjects, the researcher and subjects should be aware of and understand the purpose of the study, which creates a "community of interpretation" (Apel, 1972). Apel writes that the validity of knowledge generated through interpretivist research can only be obtained when individuals (i.e., researcher and participants) share meanings, which can be achieved through establishing a common framework. Second, communicative validity can be obtained though establishing coherence of the described experience. Sandberg draws on hermeneutics, which dictates that the parts of a text must fit with the whole, and the whole with the parts (Palmer, 1972): the greater the degree of fit between the parts of the described experience and whole description, the greater the coherence. Lastly, an interpretivist researcher can enhance communicative validity by sharing her claims with other researchers. Sandberg (2005) compares this tactic to the phenomenological process of reality construction – interaction between individuals gives rise to social reality; likewise, interaction between scholars over an interpretation is the only real way to determine whether the researcher has revealed truth.

Pragmatic validity arises when the researcher attempts to cut through biases and obfuscations in the described experience. Participants may deploy certain tactics, such as impression management, or use metaphors, which distance the expressed narrative from the participant's actual lived-through experience (Alvesson, 2003; Sandberg, 2005). Sandberg (2000) describes certain tactics he used in a study to enhance pragmatic validity – for example, during an interview with a research participant, he would occasionally deliberately mis-state or mischaracterize a statement made by the participant. The participant would then re-establish and verify the veracity of statements they had previously made. He also notes that observation of research participants while experiencing is another tactic useful in establishing pragmatic validity: it provided a way for him to double check his interpretations of described experience with what he observed actually occurring.

Lastly, transgressive validity accounts for and makes the researcher aware of the inconsistencies and confusions that are irreducible in an interpretation – it is the recognition that truth is iterative. Sandberg, drawing on Lather (1993), suggests four tactics for obtaining transgressive validity. First, one should search for irony in the interpretation to discover the codified frameworks used to interpret the experience. Second, instead of using hermeneutic techniques to search for consistencies between the parts and the whole of the experience, search instead for contradictions in the experience – this strengthens and clarifies the researcher's interpretation. Third, recognize that the current research paradigm is strongly Western and strongly masculine. This recognition should lead to the inclusion of alternative points of view, particularly feminine points of view, which might further serve to contradict the researcher's given interpretation of an experience while making the final truth claim more generalizable. Fourth, Sandberg recommends incorporating interpretive awareness to obtain reliability of the researcher's truth claim. Each researcher carries with them certain theoretical perspectives, experiences, and other biases that influence their interpretations of others' experience. Instead of trying to hide or simply ignoring these biases, the researcher should acknowledge them and explain their possible influences on the study.

Sandberg further lists five discrete steps a scholar can use to achieve validity in their research, steps based on Giorgi's (2009) concept of bracketing experience (Ihde, 1971). In other words, these steps are tools the researcher can use to ensure that (1) the particular experience, and only information relating to that experience, is considered in making an interpretation, and (2) that the researcher does not begin to interpret the experience before she has gathered all the relevant information.

The first step is simply to keep an open mind – going into any research setting with a preconceived notion of what the experience means prevents the researcher from considering other possibilities or even recognizing certain descriptions of the experience that may prove relevant. The second step focuses on the "how" of the experience instead of the "what" or "why" (Sandberg, 2005, p. 60). Asking "how" in an interview gets the subject to describe details of the experience; "why" diverts the conversation to unrelated issues, such as the subject's cognitive processes during an experience. Carefully focusing on the details of the experience through asking "how" is also another tool to prevent the researcher from drawing conclusions about the experience too quickly. The third step requires that the researcher treat all the described parts of experience equally. The tendency might be to relegate or diminish certain bits of a subject's described experience, thus ranking certain descriptions as more important than others, which introduces bias into the data collection process and finally skews the researcher's interpretation. The fourth step incorporates transgressive validity – the researcher should approach the described experience with several different interpretations. This cross-checking allows the major structural meanings of the described experience to emerge, and it produces a more stable interpretation. The last step accounts for the subjectivity of individual experience and is comprised of three stages: (1) identify how the experience appears to the subject as reality; (2) identify how individuals undergo the experience; and (3) combine the two views: the integration of the ontic lived-through experience and the meaning assignment constitutes the phenomenon of experience.

There are several guides for conducting interpretive, qualitative research. Denzin and Lincoln's *Handbook of Qualitative Research* (2000) is oft cited; in entrepreneurship, there is Neergaard and Ulhøi's *Handbook of Qualitative Research Methods in Entrepreneurship* (2007), many chapters of which draw on a phenomenological, experienced-based perspective. Nevertheless, establishing standards for interpretive research have proven elusive. Van Maanen (1998, p. xxv) writes: "There are probably rules for writing the persuasive, memorable and publishable qualitative research article, but, rest assured, no one knows what they are." Despite this uncertain state, interpretive entrepreneurship research is being published in top journals. We have already described a few specific techniques that can be deployed as part of an overall methodology to pursue interpretive studies in entrepreneurship. The next section outlines several studies in greater detail that use interpretive methodologies to examine questions related to meaning and experience in entrepreneurship.

METHODS OVERVIEW AND EXAMPLES OF THREE STUDIES

In this section, we turn from a philosophical examination of the methodology underlying a research agenda of experience and look to how this approach has manifested itself within the entrepreneurship literature. In Table 12.1, we outline the various methodologies used to study experience in the entrepreneurship domain as well as the foundational texts that describe each methodology. The table portrays a body of work that is as wide and varied as experience itself, though each approach is rooted or at least draws on the interpretive philosophy we outlined above. Experience is ever-shifting, iterative, and emergent – therefore the tools we use to examine it have to be just as adaptive. Moreover, these methodologies continue to develop and new methodologies are constantly emerging (e.g., Uy et al., 2010).

In this section, we first provide a brief overview of the different methodologies more commonly used in experience-based research in general and in entrepreneurship more specifically. In so doing, we hope to show that not only is an experience-based perspective a critical component to understanding entrepreneurship, but that it is also a perspective that is gaining momentum as more and more scholars find themselves turning to examine the entrepreneurial experience. The variety in this field is testament to its vitality.

Following this, we describe in greater depth several studies that have adopted an interpretive methodology and use them to explicate a few of the points we outlined above. High-quality research on the entrepreneurship experience is being performed and published in top management journals. We'll note a few exemplars, how they employed interpretivism and how they achieved quality based on Sandberg's (2005) prescriptions above.

An Overview of the Field

The research presented in Table 12.1 is in alphabetical order, by methodology. However, if it were possible to create a loose typology of the kinds of methodologies being used in the field, it would likely contain two components. The first component would be composed of research examining descriptions of experience and how these represent meaningful constructions for the entrepreneur. The second component contains studies of a more empirical nature and examines how experience affects how entrepreneurs think. Where the first component has long provided the foundation of work on experience, the second component

Table 12.1   Overview of methods for investigating "experience" (listed alphabetically)

Method	Description of method (with focus on what makes it relevant to study of experience)	Key source(s) on the method itself	Exemplars in entrepreneurship
Auto/biography	Auto/biography, with its focus on the "I," overcomes the barrier between subject and researcher – experience and meaning is described directly by the subject	Lee (1999); Stanley (1993)	Foss (2004)
Critical incident analysis	Turns focus from the subject to the events that constitute meaningful experience	Chell (2004)	Cope (2003); Cope and Watts (2000)
Discourse analysis	Accesses the symbolic construction of the world through linguistic communication	Aronowitz (1988); Stubbs (1983)	Rae (2000)
Experience sampling method (ESM)	Technique used to access a subject's affective state *during* an experience	Balogun et al. (2003)	Uy et al. (2010)
Ethnography: Auto-ethnography	Turns the focus inward; the subject is the researcher, who elicits his or her own descriptions of experience	Boufoy-Bastick (2004)	Johannisson (2002)
Ethnography: Ethnographic realism	Researcher's written description attempts to give reader a first-hand appreciation for the experience	Alsop (2005); Sherry and Schouten (2002)	
Ethnography: Confessional ethnography	Researcher's own biases and experiences become a major part of the study	Alsop (2005); Schultze (2000)	
Ethnography: Dramatic ethnography	Focuses on the roles people adopt in their interactions with others	Alsop (2005)	de Montoya (2000)

	Description		
Ethnography: Critical ethnography Frame analysis	Emphasizes creation of concrete concepts, which synthesize theory and practical reality Understanding how individuals construct schemas of meaning across situations	Alsop (2005); Hart (2004) Goffman (1974)	Bruni et al. (2005)
Metaphorical analysis	Understanding how individuals verbally describe meaning, generally where uncertainty is high	Palmer and Dunford (1996)	Cornelissen and Clarke (2010)
Narrative analysis	Interpretation of both content and form of stories people tell about themselves	Riessman (1993)	de Montoya (2004); Downing (2005); Hjorth and Steyaert (2004)
Neuro-imaging: MRI and PET scan	Examines physiological manifestations of experience-related phenomena	Breiter et al. (2001); Cabeza and Nyberg (2000)	Hayton et al. (2011); Krueger and Day (2010)
Phenomenology: Empirical vs. Hermeneutic	Research as interpretive iterations of a subject as opposed to quantifiable reality	Ehrich (2005); Hein and Austin (2001)	
Phenomenology: Transcendental (Husserl)	Understanding the relationship between experience and consciousness	McGovern (2007)	
Phenomenology: Hermeneutic (Heidegger)	Understanding the relationship between experience and humanness – that is, a human's place in the world	Laverty (2003)	Seymour (2006)
Phenomenology: Hermeneutic (Ricoeur)	Knowledge of the self is mediated by texts, which must be interpreted	Ihde (1971); Rasmussen (1971)	
Phenomenology: Interpretative	A double hermeneutic: individuals try to make sense of the world while researchers interpret these meanings	Osborn and Smith (2008)	Cope (2010)

Table 12.1 (*continued*)

Method	Description of method (with focus on what makes it relevant to study of experience)	Key source(s) on the method itself	Exemplars in entrepreneurship
Phenomenology: Neuroph- enomenology	Focus is on the physiology of consciousness	Lutz and Thompson (2003); Varela (1996)	Adler and Obstfeld (2007)
Rhythmanalysis	The study of rhythms in nature and culture; how these rhythms constitute meaningful existence	Lefebvre (2004)	Verduyn (2010)
Semiotics: Pictorial/visual analysis; newspaper analysis; textual analysis	The study of objects as meaningful and socially defined symbols	Barley (1983); Barry (1999); Earl et al. (2004); Osborn and Smith (2008)	Cardon et al. (2011); Pitt (1998); Smith and Anderson (2007)
Verbal protocol analysis	The use of "think-aloud" techniques to access individuals' cognition while in-the-moment	Ericsson (2006); Ericsson and Simon (1980)	Dew et al. (2009); Sarasvathy (2008)
Visual ethnographic study	Examines the use of non-linguistic symbolism to communicate meaning	Banks and Murphy (1997); Collier and Collier (1992)	Clarke (2011)

Note: Social scientists have been examining experience-based phenomena for more than a century. We present methodologies commonly used by scholars both in and out of the entrepreneurship field. While many of these approaches have been broadly applied within entrepreneurship scholarship, not all have been used. Darkened cells indicate where a methodology has yet to be employed in entrepreneurship scholarship.

is gaining momentum, especially as it is related to studies on effectual logic. Interestingly, both approaches can inform the other. For example, verbal protocols, or "think-aloud" methodologies, draw on the notion that expressed experience provides useful data and is based on strongly interpretive assumptions. However, such protocols have also been useful in examining experience from a more empirical, positivist approach, such as it has been applied to effectuation research (e.g., Dew et al., 2009; Wiltbank et al., 2006).

As we have outlined in previous chapters, *described experience* lies at the heart of research in the field. Descriptions can take the form of transcribed interviews or think-aloud sessions (i.e., protocol analysis), written or verbal descriptions of experience (e.g., discourse analysis), verbal communications with others based on symbols (e.g., metaphors), cultural descriptions of experience (e.g., plays, novels, music, or rituals), and the attachment of meaning to experiences that ultimately lead to intersubjective meaning and construction of the social world (e.g., phenomenology). Described experiences provide the material for interpretive study.

Protocol analysis is commonly used to study the effect of experience on patterns of how people think (Ericsson and Simon, 1980, 1993). These think-aloud techniques ask research participants to verbalize their thoughts during a task. These verbalizations are recorded, examined, and coded in order to yield data. Though verbal protocols are useful in understanding the thought processes of individuals while engaged in an activity (Simon and Kaplan, 1989), they are less useful for understanding other components of cognition (such as pre-existing knowledge or cognitive frameworks). To access these, researchers should include supplementary questions in their interviews examining subjects' knowledge and experience resources. Ericsson and Simon (1993) argue that verbalizing inner thoughts does not alter the process in which people think, though they note that it may take longer for an individual to complete a particular task while engaged in a think-aloud session. In the entrepreneurship literature, think-aloud protocols have been used regularly, especially as more and more researchers turn to examining the underlying cognitive processes of opportunity identification and exploitation. From an experience-based perspective, think-aloud methodologies have been used to examine effectuation as a type of logic entrepreneurs use to make sense of their environment and then exploit opportunity. Sarasvathy (2008) uses think-aloud techniques to establish the differences in effectual logic versus causal logic (e.g., the focus on alliances, reliance on already-possessed resources, etc.). Dew and his colleagues took this research one step further and, using think-aloud techniques, examined the specific cognitive differences between experienced and nascent entrepreneurs (2009).

Discourse analysis is a broad category that refers to the study of language. Moreover, discourse analysis is particularly interested in how language, and symbolic communication in general, represents individual consciousness and meaning, especially within an institutional context (Lee, 1999). As we've described elsewhere in this book, individuals, to a large extent, construct the environment in which they live. Discourse analysis is an effort to understand how individuals enact environments by soliciting from subjects' descriptions of their understanding of their own experiences as well as their environment. Discourse analysis can examine autobiographies and entrepreneurs' described heuristics or narratives. One example of such an approach is Rae's (2000) study on how entrepreneurs develop what he calls "practical theory," which is how the entrepreneur connects day-to-day pragmatic activities with generalizable principles or rules of thumb. Drawing on Shotter (1995), Rae describes practical theory as the entrepreneur's iterative accounts of the trials-and-error, successes, and reflection each entrepreneur experiences during venture creation and operation. Downing (2005) extends the argument and writes that entrepreneurial ventures themselves are the products of discourse.

Symbolic communication is a critical component of any understanding of experience, whether from a sociological perspective, which we've described in a previous chapter, or from an entrepreneurship perspective. The use of metaphors is a long-studied aspect of organizational and entrepreneurial reality (Cornelissen and Clarke, 2010; Crossan et al., 1999; Palmer and Dunford, 1996; Tsoukas, 1991). Metaphors and other types of symbolic action (e.g., Zott and Huy, 2007), represent efforts to communicate meaning to others. Whether deliberately deployed as resource-acquisition strategies or as a technique to garner legitimacy or even inadvertently used, symbols and metaphors are externalizations of meaningful experiences that entrepreneurs have accumulated and enacted in their environment. The stories entrepreneurs tell about themselves and their ventures aren't always communicated in words. Visual cues can also play a major a role in communicating meaning. For example, Clarke (2011) demonstrates that entrepreneurs use four types of visual cues – setting, props, dress, and expressiveness – in their interactions with others. Clarke video-recorded 60 hours of interactions that entrepreneurs in three sample companies had with potential stakeholders. Drawing on the impression management literature (e.g., Goffman, 1967), Clarke found that entrepreneurs deliberately deploy visual tactics – for example, entrepreneurs may conceal crumbling facilities or out-of-date equipment in order to communicate an image of their business as being cutting-edge; likewise, some entrepreneurs consciously dress more formally when engaging in interactions with stakeholders: "You've got to know who you're dealing with . . . if I turn up in my training gear I don't think I'll be taken seriously" (Clarke, 2011, p. 1377).

Besides the stories entrepreneurs tell of themselves, there are those stories that are told about entrepreneurs. Moreover, it is important to recognize that even the word "entrepreneur" is a social construction – a word whose definition shifts depending on time and space. These externalized, and culture-wide expressions of meanings are the subject of ethnographic and semiotic methodologies. Both traditions are multifaceted and find homes within both anthropology and sociology. Ethnography is the study of cultures; semiotics is the study of the symbols used to communicate meanings within a culture, though it is applied somewhat more broadly than that (Smith and Anderson, 2007). For example, semiotics can include any symbolic meaning embodied by any object – which means its subject of study can include just about anything (Gorny, 1995). These are strongly interpretivist approaches to methodology, and we have described the philosophical and practical implications above and in other chapters. Smith and Anderson (2007) provide some structure for conducting semiotic research, including types of questions to ask and points to remember regarding types of symbols – for example, while a photograph represents a complete work in and of itself, it can also be subdivided into units of individual meaning which can affect the overall meaning.

Lastly, experience-based research on entrepreneurship can be of a phenomenological character. We have gone into great depth about phenomenology as a philosophy and sociology in previous chapters. Phenomenology considers the relationship between experiences, experience, meaning, and consciousness. One example of the application of phenomenology to entrepreneurship research includes Seymour's (2006, p. 149) exhortation to consider the phenomenological aspects of venture creation: "(a) How is the entrepreneur attuned to their world? (b) What are the possibilities the entrepreneur projects? (c) How does the entrepreneur articulate and share their understandings? (d) How is the entrepreneur entangled in their present entities and routines?". He argues that while entrepreneurship scholars have taken an empiricist approach, which fosters generalizable theory, much rich detail is being left out of the picture, especially since the field is characterized by human behavior and social interaction. Another example of research that falls within phenomenology would be Cope's work (2003 and 2010) on non-routine events and how they affect entrepreneurial learning. Cope draws on Mezirow's (1991) description of transformative learning events, which "[involve] a sequence of learning activities that begins with a disorienting dilemma and concludes with a changed self-concept that enables a reintegration into one's life context" (Mezirow, 1991, p. 193). Individuals encounter experiences that differ so greatly from expectations that they are forced to confront them and create new meanings; these experiences lead to higher-level learning as opposed to lower-level learning, such as task familiarity or routinization. Moving from an overall description of various methodologies employed to study experience-based research questions, we now consider more closely three studies that drew on interpretivist methodologies.

Study I (Kisfalvi, 2002)

Explicitly drawing on a phenomenological perspective, Kisfalvi's study is an effort to examine how life experiences affect strategic management choices. She adopts a psychodynamic approach, which is the notion that an individual is shaped from birth by their interactions with the social world (Erikson, 1985). The behaviors, schemas, and personalities people develop over time as a consequence of this interaction are extremely stable, which Kisfalvi argues renders personality traits as highly linked to behavior, challenging the stance of earlier entrepreneurship scholars (e.g., Gartner, 1989) that personality traits are poor predictors of entrepreneurial action. Kisfalvi's argument is that strategic decisions within the firm evoke deep personal reactions based on previous meaningful experiences.

Her study focuses on a single case study: the life and venture of Ben Levitsky, a Polish chemist, born in the 1920s to a Jewish family. Levitsky survived a concentration camp during World War II, while his parents, sisters, and brother died in Auschwitz. He spent the next decade as a chemist in Soviet-controlled Poland until he was able to escape to the West in 1956. Once in the United States, Levitsky started his own chemical company in 1960. Kisfalvi notes that five issues, each a consequence of specific previous experiences, shape how Levitsky runs his firm: survival, freedom and autonomy, success and achievement, recognition, and action. Life as a Jew in prewar Poland was tough; life in the concentration camp was a nightmare, and survival was a day-to-day question. Levitsky describes life on a farm as extremely frugal: "everything had value, even if a nail fell down [we picked it up] . . . and I'm still like this today" (Kisfalvi, 2002, p.504). While in the concentration camp, guards would hand out pieces of bread – Levitsky would cut his in half, eating one piece and saving the other. Sometimes, he'd be able to accumulate these halves until he'd have ten at a time. He called this "working capital" with which he was able to make trades with other prisoners. Kisfalvi notes that Levitsky's focus on survival manifests in his strategic decisions, such as in his maintaining total control over the firm's finances and his desire to remain debt-free, both of which have held the firm back in various ways. The other life issues Kisfalvi identified similarly affected how Levitsky operated his company and made strategic decisions. Also, Levitsky described how certain experiences while operating his business came to affect later decisions. For example, in 1968, a vendor once refused to send him a $62 machine part he had ordered after calling his bank and finding he had no credit – Levitsky called the vendor and demanded his order anyway, saying: "I have no credit limit because I don't need it! I am working with my own capital" (Kisfalvi, 2002, p. 501). The experience, though it happened decades ago and was over an insignificant amount, carries meaning for Levitsky and has had major implications on how he runs his firm, particularly influencing his wary stance toward banks.

Kisfalvi recognizes and explicates the problems associated with using a single case study, and she also follows many of the recommendations that Sandberg would later advocate. For example, she triangulated her interviews with Levitsky by gathering corroborating information from data available at the firm and through interviews with Levitsky's co-workers and family members (i.e., transgressive validity). She also spent several days a week for nine months unobtrusively observing Levitsky while at his firm (i.e., pragmatic validity). And while she did not discuss possible biases she might have as a researcher, she was nevertheless explicit about the limitations of the study (i.e., reliability as interpretive awareness).

Study II (Dodd, 2002)

This study examines the metaphors entrepreneurs use to discuss their actions in an effort to construct a "cultural model" of entrepreneurship, which is similar to Goffman's frame analysis (1974). In other words, a cultural model is a socially shared schema of meaning. In many ways, this study can be understood as an ethnography of entrepreneurship, which takes spoken symbols (i.e., metaphors) and relates them to a socially constructed reality (i.e., entrepreneurship). Though some of the constructs are decidedly not phenomenological in nature – for example, cultural models are described as being "presupposed" and "taken-for-granted," which is far from an experience-based perspective of social objects – the study is nevertheless an exercise in interpretive methodology.

To gather data, Dodd collected profiles and interviews of entrepreneurs from secondary sources. She selected 24 articles based on certain criteria: the story had to focus on the life narrative of an entrepreneur as opposed to specific or niche aspects of entrepreneurship; the story had to include a significant amount of direct quotes from the entrepreneur; and the story had to contain a significant use of metaphorical language. She culled the metaphors used by entrepreneurs, placed them in a second document, and then for each metaphor identified a vehicle and an object. One such example of a vehicle is dice-throwing with the object as risk-taking (Dodd, 2002, p. 524). From these vehicles and objects, she parsed out seven general categories of metaphors: entrepreneurship as a journey, race, parenting, building, war, iconoclasm, and passion. Using overlaps between categories (e.g., vehicles that fit under "journey" might also fit under "race" or "building"), Dodd constructs a cultural model of entrepreneurship.

While she is a little less clear regarding her methodology than the Kisfalvi study, Dodd more clearly describes the biases possibly at play in her study. For example, the use of secondary sources from the media tends to skew the sample toward successful entrepreneurs since few people would likely write about entrepreneurs who failed. A second bias is found in the fact that journalists serve as an intermediary between the entrepreneur and the reader. Dodd writes that one of the particular strengths of qualitative research – that is, the researcher can take into consideration the context of data collection – is entirely eliminated by the use of secondary sources. This is a serious limitation of her study, but Dodd follows interpretivst protocol and notes it in the article. Whether this is a fatal flaw is left up to the reader, and the iterative process to discover the truth begins.

Study III (Zott and Huy, 2007)

What is the relationship between symbolic action and resource acquisition in entrepreneurial firms? Zott and Huy attempt to address this question by analyzing different types of symbolic action, their correlations to resource acquisition, as well as factors that moderate the relationship. Though the study has tinges of positivism – for example, the authors present a causal model – it is strongly interpretivist in methodology and heavily draws on sociological traditions rooted in symbolic interactionism and impression management. Zott and Huy argue that entrepreneurs are particularly capable at communicating through four symbolic categories: personal credibility, professional organizing, organizational achievement, and the quality of stakeholder relationships. Symbolic communication requires that the user intend a meaning beyond the intrinsic meaning of a message (e.g., e-mailing Christmas cards to customers intrinsically communicates a holiday spirit; the symbolic meaning is that the company cares about its customers).

Starting with a pool of 230 potential research subjects, the authors found 26 ventures that fit stated criteria. The interview process took two years and included face-to-face interviews and follow-ups with the lead entrepreneurs of the firms as well as with stakeholders of the firms. The researchers asked the interviewees to provide detailed accounts of the firm's activities from start-up to the present moment. From this process,

Zott and Huy found seven extreme cases of high and low uses of symbolic action, and at these seven firms, they conducted even further interviews with a wide range of stakeholders. Taking the transcripts and notes from these interviews, they coded symbolic language into eight initial categories, which they narrowed to four. They clearly state in the study the criteria they used to identify symbolic language: the user has to intend a symbolic meaning, the message recipient has to perceive the message as symbolic, or the researchers saw it as symbolic. Zott and Huy matched the four categories of symbolic action that emerged from the interviews to how often they originated from stakeholders or entrepreneurs of the seven firms and were able to connect successful resource acquisition with the competent deployment of symbolic communication.

This study, besides being an example of explicitly described methodology, is also an example of what Sandberg called intentional fulfillment, wherein the researcher adapts her interpretation until it fits the data. Zott and Huy note that they initiated the study expecting to find that impression management alone accounted for resource acquisition; however, after collecting data and reinterpreting the results, they found that only a specific subset of impression management – that is, symbolic action – was relevant.

CONCLUSION

The three studies presented at the end of this chapter do not nearly capture the range of interpretivist research being published today in top entrepreneurship and management journals. They merely show the wide variety and applications that an interpretivist perspective can bring to studying entrepreneurs and entrepreneurship. They also show that top journals are willing to publish non-empiricist research, as long as it maintains high standards of validity and reliability. In this chapter, we have discussed some of the shortcomings of entrepreneurship research as it stands today, and we argue that the adoption of an interpretivist approach can go a long way in addressing some of the concerns scholars have leveled at the field. We then turned to a discussion of interpretivist research, and we tried to describe what its aims are and how it can be as valid a source of knowledge as other methodological approaches. Finally, we provided an overview of the types of methodologies used by researchers today to study experience-based research questions in entrepreneurship as well as described in greater detail several studies within the entrepreneurship domain that typify interpretivist research approaches that also exemplify rigorous methodologies.

The process of venture creation and the experiences entrepreneurs undergo while engaged in shaping and planning and creating their ventures are unique to each entrepreneur. The pursuit of generalizable theory, therefore, to answer questions regarding the very nature of entrepreneurship itself seems to leave a vast range of questions unanswered. As Rae (2000, p. 148) notes:

> It is . . . too easy to lose the value of the specific human experience. In this way, the voice of the entrepreneur – whoever he or she may be – seems to have become disconnected from academic study through being lost in the statistical samples. The gulf between the lived reality, experience and history of entrepreneurial life and the production and application of academic theory seems wide.

We hope, in this chapter and in the work we present throughout this volume, to suggest that this understanding need not be left on the table. The tools presented here may prove useful to help us finally answer what it *means* to be an entrepreneur engaged in venture creation.

REFERENCES

Adler, P.S. and D. Obstfeld (2007), 'The role of affect in creative projects and exploratory research', *Industrial and Corporate Change*, **16**(1): 19–50.

Alsop, R. (2005), 'Ethnographic methods for English studies', in G. Griffin (ed.), *Research Methods for English Studies*, Edinburgh: Edinburgh UP, pp. 111–29.

Alvesson, M. (2003), 'Beyond neopositivists, romantics and localists: a reflexive approach to interviews in organizational research', *Academy of Management Review*, **28**(1): 1–13.

Apel, K.O. (1972), 'The a priori of communication and the foundation of the humanities', *Man and World*, **51**: 3–37.

Aronowitz, S. (1988), *Science as Power: Discourse and Ideology in Modern Society*, Minneapolis, MN: University of Minnesota Press.

Balogun, J., A.S. Huff and P. Johnson (2003), 'Three responses to the methodological challenges of studying strategizing', *Journal of Management Studies*, **40**(1): 197–224.

Banks, M. and H. Murphy (1997), *Rethinking Visual Anthropology*, New Haven, CT: Yale.

Barley, S.R. (1983), 'Semiotics and the study of occupational and organizational cultures', *Administrative Science Quarterly*, **28**(3): 393–413.

Barry, J. (1999), *Art, Culture and the Semiotics of Meaning: Culture's Changing Signs of Life in Poetry, Drama, Painting and Sculpture*, London: Macmillan.

Bengtsson, J. (1989), 'Phenomenology: everyday research, existential philosophy, hermeneutics', in P. Manson (ed.), *Moderna samhallsteorier: traditioner riktningar teoretiker*, Stockholm: Prisma, pp. 67–108.

Berglund, H. (2007), 'Entrepreneurship and phenomenology: researching entrepreneurship as lived experience', in H. Neergaard and J. Parm Ulhøi (eds)

Handbook of Qualitative Research Methods in Entrepreneurship, Cheltenham, UK and Northampton, MA, USA: Edward Elgar, pp. 75–96.

Blumer, H. (1969), *Symbolic Interactionism: Perspective and Method*, Berkeley, CA: University of California Press.

Bohman, J. (1991), *New Philosophy of Social Science*, Cambridge, MA: MIT Press.

Boswell, J. (1953), *The Life of Johnson*, London: Oxford University Press.

Boufoy-Bastick, B. (2004), 'Auto-interviewing, auto-ethnography, and critical incident methodology for eliciting a self-conceptualised worldview', *Forum: Qualitative Social Research*, **5**(1), article 37.

Bradley, B. (2005), *Psychology and Experience*, Cambridge: Cambridge University Press.

Breiter, H.C., I. Aharon, D. Kahneman, A. Dale and P. Shizgal (2001), 'Functional imaging of neural responses to expectancy and experience of monetary gains and losses', *Neuron*, **30**(2): 619–39.

Bruni, A., S. Gherardi and B. Poggio (2005), *Gender and Entrepreneurship: An Ethnographical Approach*, New York: Routledge.

Bygrave, W.D. (2007), 'The entrepreneurship paradigm (I) revisited', in H. Neergaard and J. Parm Ulhøi (eds), *Handbook of Qualitative Research Methods in Entrepreneurship*, Cheltenham, UK and Northampton, MA, USA: Edward Elgar, pp. 17–48.

Cabeza, R. and L. Nyberg (2000), 'Imaging cognition II. An empirical review of 275 PET and fMRI studies', *Journal of Cognitive Neuroscience*, **12**(1): 1–47.

Cantor, N., J. Norem, C. Langston, S. Zirkel, W. Fleeson and C. Cook-Flanagan (1991), 'Life tasks and daily life experience, *Journal of Personality*, **59**(3): 425–51.

Cardon, M.S., C.E. Stevens and D.R. Potter (2011), 'Misfortunes or mistakes?: Cultural sensemaking and entrepreneurial failure', *Journal of Business Venturing*, **26**(1): 79–92.

Chandler, G.N. and D.W. Lyon (2001), 'Issues of research design and construct measurement in entrepreneurship research: the past decade', *Entrepreneurship Theory and Practice*, **25**(4): 101–13.

Charon, J.M. (1995), *Symbolic Interactionism: An Introduction, and Interpretation, an Integration*, Englewood Cliffs, NJ: Prentice Hall.

Chell, E. (2004), 'Critical incident technique', in C. Cassell and G. Symon (eds), *Essential Guide to Qualitative Methods in Organization Studies*, London: Sage, pp. 45–60.

Clarke, J. (2011), 'Revitalizing entrepreneurship: how visual symbols are used in entrepreneurial performances', *Journal of Management Studies*, **48**(6): 1365–91.

Collier, J. and M. Collier (1986), *Visual Anthropology: Photography as a Research Method*, Albuquerque, NM: University of New Mexico Press.

Cope, J. (2003), 'Entrepreneurial learning and critical reflection: discontinuous events as triggers for "higher-level" learning', *Management Learning*, **34**(4): 429–50.

Cope, J. (2010), 'Entrepreneurial learning from failure: an interpretive phenomenological analysis', *Journal of Business Venturing*, **26**(6): 604–23.

Cope, J. and G. Watts (2000), 'Learning by doing: an exploration of experience, critical incidents and reflection in entrepreneurial learning', *International Journal of Entrepreneurial Behaviour & Research*, **6**(3): 104–19.

Cornelissen, J.P. and J.S. Clarke (2010), 'Imagining and rationalizing opportunities: inductive reasoning and the creation and justification of new ventures', *Academy of Management Review*, **35**(4): 539–57.

Crossan, M.M., H.W. Lane and R.E. White (1999), 'An organizational learning framework: from intuition to institution', *Academy of Management Review*, **24**(3): 522–37.
Davidsson, P., M.B. Low and M. Wright (2001), 'Editor's introduction: Low and MacMillan ten years on: achievements and future directions for entrepreneurship research', *Entrepreneurship Theory and Practice*, **25**(4): 81–100.
de Montoya, M.L. (2000), 'Entrepreneurship and culture: the case of Freddy the strawberry man', in R. Swedberg (ed.), *Entrepreneurship*, Oxford: Oxford University Press, pp. 333–55.
de Montoya, M.L. (2004), 'Driven entrepreneurs: a case study of taxi drivers in Caracas', in D. Hjorth and C. Steyaert (eds), *Narrative and Discursive Approaches in Entrepreneurship*, Cheltenham, UK and Northampton, MA, USA: Edward Elgar, pp. 57–79.
Denzin, N.K. and Y.S. Lincoln (2000), *Handbook of Qualitative Research*, Thousand Oaks, CA: Sage.
Dew, N., S. Read, S. Sarasvathy and R. Wiltbank (2009), 'Effectual versus predictive logics in entrepreneurial decision-making: differences between experts and novices', *Journal of Business Venturing*, **24**(4): 287–309.
Dodd, S.D. (2002), 'Metaphors and meaning: a grounded cultural model of U.S. entrepreneurship', *Journal of Business Venturing*, **17**(5): 519–35.
Downing, S. (2005), 'The social construction of entrepreneurship: narrative and dramatic processes in the coproduction of organizations and identities', *Entrepreneurship Theory and Practice*, **29**(2): 185–204.
Earl, J., A. Martin, J. McCarthy and S. Soule (2004), 'The use of newspaper data in the study of collective action', *Annual Review of Sociology*, **30**(1): 65–80.
Ehrich, L.C. (2005), 'Revisiting phenomenology: its potential for management research', in *Proceedings: Challenges of Organizations in Global Markets, British Academy for Management Conference*, Said Business School, Oxford University, pp. 1–13.
Ericsson, K.A. (2006), 'Protocol analysis and expert thought: concurrent verbalizations of thinking during experts' performance on representative task', in K.A. Ericsson, N. Charness, P. Feltovich and R.R. Hoffman (eds), *Cambridge Handbook of Expertise and Expert Performance*, Cambridge: Cambridge University Press, pp. 223–42.
Ericsson, K.A. and H.A. Simon (1980), 'Verbal reports as data', *Psychological Review*, **87**(3): 215–51.
Ericsson, K.A. and H.A. Simon (1993), *Protocal Analysis: Verbal Reports as Data*, Cambridge, MA: Bradford Books/MIT Press.
Erikson, E.H. (1985), *Childhood and Society*, New York: Norton.
Feldman, L.A. (1995), 'Valence focus and arousal focus: individual differences in the structure of affective experiences', *Journal of Personality and Social Psychology*, **69**(1): 153–66.
Foss, L. (2004), '"Going against the grain . . . " Construction of entrepreneurial identity though narratives', in D. Hjorth and C. Steyaert (eds), *Narrative and Discursive Approaches to Entrepreneurship*, Cheltenham, UK and Northampton, MA, USA: Edward Elgar, pp. 80–104.
Gartner, W.B. (1989), 'Some suggestions for research on entrepreneurial traits and characteristics', *Entrepreneurship Theory and Practice*, **14**(1): 27–38.
Gartner, W.B. and S. Birley (2002), 'Introduction to the special issue on qualitative

methods in entrepreneurship research', *Journal of Business Venturing*, **17**(5): 387–95.

Gephart, R.P. (2004), 'Qualitative research and the *Academy of Management Journal*', *Academy of Management Journal*, **47**(4): 454–62.

Giorgi, A. (2009), *The Descriptive Phenomenological Method in Psychology: A Modified Husserlian Approach*, Pittsburgh, PA: Duquesne University Press.

Goffman, E. (1967), *Interaction Ritual: Essays on Face-to-face Behavior*, Garden City, NY: Anchor Books.

Goffman, E. (1974), *Frame Analysis: An Essay on the Organization of Experience*, New York: Harper Colophon.

Gorny, E. (1995), 'What is semiotics?', *Creator Magazine No. 3*, London.

Grant, P. and L. Perren (2002), 'Small business and entrepreneurial research: meta-theories, paradigms and prejudices', *International Small Business Journal*, **20**(2): 185–211.

Hart, G. (2004), 'Geography and development: critical ethnographies', *Progress in Human Geography*, **28**(1): 91–100.

Hayton, J., G.N. Chandler and D.R. DeTienne (2011), 'Entrepreneurial opportunity identification and new firm development processes: a comparison of family and non-family ventures', *International Journal of Entrepreneurship and Innovation Management*, **13**(1): 12–31.

Heidegger, M. (1992), *History of the Concept of Time*, Bloomington, IN: Indiana University Press.

Hein, S.F. and W.J. Austin (2001), 'Empirical and hermeneutic approaches to phenomenological research in psychology: A comparison', *Psychological Methods*, **6**(1): 3–17.

Hindle, K. (2004), 'Choosing qualitative methods for entrepreneurial cognition research: a canonical development approach', *Entrepreneurship Theory and Practice*, **28**(6): 575–607.

Hjorth, D. and C. Steyaert (2004), *Narrative and Discursive Approaches in Entrepreneurship*, Cheltenham, UK and Northampton, MA, USA: Edward Elgar.

Howorth, C., S. Tempest and C. Coupland (2005), 'Rethinking entrepreneurship methodology and definitions of the entrepreneur', *Journal of Small Business and Enterprise Development*, **12**(1): 24–40.

Ihde, D. (1971), *Hermeneutic Phenomenology: The Philosophy of Paul Ricoeur*, Evanston, IL: Northwestern University Press.

Johannisson, B. (2002), 'Energising entrepreneurship: ideological tensions in the medium-sized family business', in D.E. Fletcher (ed.), *Understanding Small Family Business*, London: Routledge, pp. 46–57.

Johnson, P., A. Buehring, C. Cassell and G. Symon (2006), 'Evaluating qualitative management research: towards a contingent criteriology', *International Journal of Management Reviews*, **8**(3): 131–51.

Kisfalvi, V. (2002), 'The entrepreneur's character, life issues, and strategy making', *Journal of Business Venturing*, **17**(5): 489–518.

Krueger, N.F. and M. Day (2010), 'Looking forward, looking backward: from entrepreneurial cognition to neuroentrepreneurship', *Handbook of Entrepreneurship Research*, **5**(4): 321–57.

Lather, P. (1993), 'Fertile obsession: validity after poststructuralism', *Sociological Quarterly*, **34**(4): 673–93.

Laverty, S.M. (2003), 'Hermeneutic phenomenology and phenomenology: a comparison of historical and methodological considerations', *International Journal of Qualitative Methods*, **2**(3), article 3.

Law, J. (2004), *After Method: Mess in Social Science Research*, London: Routledge.

Lawson, T. (2008), 'What has realism got to do with it?', in D. Hausman (ed.), *The Philosophy of Economics: An Anthology*, Cambridge: Cambridge University Press, pp. 439–54.

Lee, J. (1999), 'The utility of strategic postmodernism', *Sociological Perspectives*, **42**(4): 739–53.

Lefebvre, H. (2004), *Rhythmanalysis: Space, Time, and Everyday Life*, London: Continuum.

Leitch, C.M., F.M. Hill and R.T. Harrison (2010), 'The philosophy and practice of interpretivist research in entrepreneurship: quality, validation, and trust', *Organizational Research Methods*, **13**(1): 67–84.

Low, M.B. (2001), 'The adolescence of entrepreneurship research: specification of purpose', *Entrepreneurship Theory and Practice*, **25**(4): 17–25.

Lutz, A. and E. Thompson (2003), 'Neurophenomenology: integrating subjective experience and brain dynamics in the neuroscience of consciousness', *Journal of Consciousness Studies*, **10**(9–10): 31–52.

McGovern, S. (2007), 'The being of intentionality', *Lyceum*, **9**(1): 44–61.

Mezirow, J. (1991), *Transformative Dimensions of Adult Learning*, San Francisco, CA: Jossey-Bass.

Neergaard, H. and J. Parm Ulhøi (eds) (2007), 'Introduction: methodological variety in entrepreneurship research', in *Handbook of Qualitative Research Methods in Entrepreneurship*, Cheltenham, UK and Northampton, MA, USA: Edward Elgar, pp. 1–14.

Osborn, M. and J. Smith (2008), 'The fearfulness of chronic pain and the centrality of the therapeutic relationship containing it: an interpretative phenomenological analysis', *Qualitative Research in Psychology*, **5**(4): 276–88.

Palmer, R. (1972), *Hermeneutics: Interpretation Theory in Schleiermacher, Dilthey, Heidegger and Gadamer*, Evanston, IL: Northwestern University Press.

Palmer, I. and R. Dunford (1996), 'Conflicting uses of metaphors: reconceptualizing their use in the field of organizational change', *Academy of Management Review*, **21**(3): 691–717.

Pitt, M. (1998), 'A tale of two gladiators: "Reading" entrepreneurs as texts', *Organization Studies*, **19**(3): 387–414.

Pollio, H.R., T.B. Henley and C.G. Thompson (1997), *The Phenomenology of Everyday Life*, Cambridge and New York: Cambridge University Press.

Prasad, A. and P. Prasad (2002), 'The coming of age of interpretive organizational research', *Organizational Research Methods*, **5**(1): 4–11.

Pribram, K.H. (1991), *Brain and Perception: Holonomy and Structure in Figural Processing*, Hillsdale, NJ: Lawrence Erlbaum.

Rae, D. (2000), 'Practical theories from entrepreneurs' stories: discursive approaches to entrepreneurial learning', *Journal of Small Business and Enterprise Development*, **11**(2): 195–202.

Rae, D. and M. Carswell (2000), 'Using a life-story approach in researching entrepreneurial learning', *Education and Training*, **42**(4/5): 220–27.

Rasmussen, D.M. (1971), *Mythic-symbolic Language and Philosophical Anthropology*, The Hague: Martinus Nijhoff.

Riessman, C.K. (1993), *Narrative Analysis*, Newbury Park, CA: Sage.

Sandberg, J. (2000), 'Understanding human competence at work: an interpretive approach', *Academy of Management Journal*, **43**(1): 9–25.

Sandberg, J. (2005), 'How do we justify knowledge produced in interpretive approaches?', *Organizational Research Methods*, **8**(1): 41–68.

Sarasvathy, S. (2001), 'Causation and effectuation: toward a theoretical shift from economic inevitability to entrepreneurial contingency', *Academy of Management Review*, **26**(2): 243–88.

Sarasvathy, S.D. (2008), *Effectuation: Elements of Entrepreneurial Expertise*, Cheltenham, UK and Northampton, MA, USA: Edward Elgar.

Schultze, U. (2000), 'A confessional account of an ethnography about knowledge work', *MIS Quarterly*, **24**(1): 3–41.

Seymour, R.G. (2006), 'Hermeneutic phenomenology and international entrepreneurship research', *Journal of International Entrepreneurship*, **4**(4): 137–55.

Shane, S. (2003), *A General Theory of Entrepreneurship*, Cheltenham, UK and Northampton, MA, USA: Edward Elgar.

Sherry, J.F. and J.W. Schouten (2002), 'A role for poetry in consumer research', *Journal of Consumer Research*, **29**(2): 218–34.

Shotter, J. (1995), 'The manager as a practical author: a rhetorical-responsive, social constructionist approach to social-organizational problems', in D.M. Hosking, H.P. Daschler and K.J. Gergen (eds), *Management and Organisation: Relational Alternatives to Individualism*, Aldershot: Avebury.

Simon, H.A. and C.A. Kaplan (1989), 'Foundations of cognitive science', in M.J. Posner (ed.), *Foundations of Cognitive Science*, Cambridge, MA: MIT Press, pp. 1–47.

Smith, R. and A.R. Anderson (2007), 'Recognizing meaning: semiotics in entrepreneurial research', in H. Neergaard and J.P. Ulhøi (eds), *Handbook of Qualitative Research Methods in Entrepreneurship*, Cheltenham, UK and Northampton, MA, USA: Edward Elgar, pp. 169–92.

Stanley, L. (1993), 'On auto/biography in sociology', *Sociology*, **27**(1): 41–52.

Stubbs, M. (1983), *Discourse Analysis: The Sociolinguistic Analysis of Natural Language*, Chicago, IL: University of Chicago Press.

Tsoukas, H. (1991), 'The missing link: a transformational view of metaphors in organizational science', *Academy of Management Review*, **16**(3): 566–85.

Turner, V. and E.M. Bruner (eds) (1986), *The Anthropology of Experience*, Chicago, IL: University of Illinois Press.

Uy, M.A., M. Foo and H. Aguinis (2010), 'Using experience sampling methodology to advance entrepreneurship theory and research', *Organizational Research Methods*, **13**(1): 31–54.

Van Maanen, J. (1979), 'The fact of fiction in organizational ethnography', *Administrative Science Quarterly*, **24**(4): 539–50.

Van Maanen, J. (1998), 'Different strokes: qualitative research in the *Administrative Science Quarterly* from 1956 to 1996', in J. Van Maanen (ed.), *Qualitative Studies of Organizations*, Thousand Oaks, CA: Sage, pp. ix–xxxii.

Verduyn, K. (2010), 'Rhythmanalyzing the mergence of *The Republic of Tea*', in W. Gartner (ed.), *Entrepreneurial Narrative Theory Ethnomethodology and Reflexivity*, Clemson, SC: Clemson University Digital Press, pp. 153–67.

Varela, F.J. (1996), 'Neurophenomenology: a methodological remedy to the hard problem', *Journal of Consciousness Studies*, **3**(4): 330–50.

Wiltbank, R., N. Dew, S. Read and S.D. Sarasvathy (2006), 'What to do next? The case for non-predictive strategy', *Strategic Management Journal*, **27**(10): 981–98.

Zimmerman, M.A. and G.J. Zeitz (2002), 'Beyond survival: achieving new venture growth by building legitimacy', *Academy of Management Review*, **27**(3): 414–31.

Zott, C. and Q. Huy (2007), 'How entrepreneurs use symbolic management to acquire resources', *Administrative Science Quarterly*, **52**(1): 70–105.

13. Toward new insights and new questions

> In the beginning is the deed . . . We wish, then, to consider the surrounding lifeworld concretely, in its neglected relativity . . . the world in which we live intuitively . . . with its real entities . . . as they give themselves to us at first in straightforward experience . . . . Our exclusive task shall be to comprehend precisely . . . this whole merely subjective and apparently incomprehensible "Heraclitean flux."
>
> (Edmund Husserl, 1936)

INTRODUCTION

The preceding chapters have addressed various aspects of *an* experience, *the* experience of entrepreneurship, and aspects of an *experiential* view of entrepreneurship (as opposed to an institutional, cognitive, behavioral, or other perspective). The term "experience" is tied to notions of immediacy, visibility, direct participation, and authenticity – it highlights the potential of the present and the everyday. The study of entrepreneurship as experience is situated within key concepts and trajectories of an interdisciplinary framework, where philosophy, anthropology, psychology, sociology, and phenomenology – both as a philosophy and a method – play key roles. Phenomenology is a form of philosophy that "emphasizes the attempt to get to the truth of matters, to describe phenomena, in the broadest sense as whatever appears in the manner in which it appears, that is as it manifests itself to consciousness, to the experience" (Moran, 2000, p. 4). Thus, phenomenology centers on the first-person experience – it entails intentionality, subjectivity, inter-subjectivity, consciousness, perception, awareness, and embodiment. Phenomenology is not simply introspection or inner experience. Rather, the Husserlian notion of intentionality endows experience with qualities of *mine-ness* and *about-ness* (Larkin et al., 2011) – it is *my* experience and it is directed *at* something.

Before continuing, two disclaimers are in order. First, "experience" is a broad topic that is covered in multiple disciplines, each of which ascribes to a different approach and theoretical foundation. The selection of disciplines and aspects of experience we discuss in this book therefore represents a potpourri of philosophical principles. Although there are at least three distinct streams of research related to experience – experience as embodiment (phenomenology), experience as interaction (pragmatism) and experience as praxis (critical theory and cultural studies) – we focus on phenomenology and pragmatism because of their relevance in the extant entrepreneurship literature. Second, our engagement with the literatures from the disciplines we cover is necessarily restricted. Rather than attempting to present a full review of either existing experience-based studies in the field of entrepreneurship, or concentrating on a key discipline's relevance for entrepreneurship as experience (e.g., anthropology), our intention has been to engage with influential thinkers (philosophers and theorists) on the topic of experience and entrepreneurship research that addresses particular aspects of experience.

With these clarifications in hand, we now proceed with an explication of possibilities for future research in the domain of entrepreneurship that arise from an "experience" lens. We ask: how does a shift from a philosophy of mind (and its closer association with theory) to a philosophy of experience (and its closer association with practice) change the way we research, theorize, practice, and teach entrepreneurship? In what follows, we look beyond current horizons and do so in seven separate discussions: (1) a view of entrepreneurship through the looking glass of experience; (2) experiential knowing and experiential learning; (3) "feeling" the future; (4) openness to experience; (5) encountering entrepreneurship as phenomenonal experience; (6) experience as the flesh and blood of entrepreneurship; and (7) experiencing and the senses. The chapter concludes with observations regarding the extent to which entrepreneurship as experience questions current taken-for-granted assumptions in the mainstream entrepreneurship literature, followed by closing thoughts on the implications of an experience lens for entrepreneurship's researchers, theorists, practitioners, and educators.

ENTREPRENEURSHIP THROUGH THE LOOKING GLASS OF "EXPERIENCE"

In this book, most of the lessons about experience have been derived from disciplines in the social sciences – anthropology, psychology, and sociology. In this section we turn to a related field – marketing – a research domain that has given attention to experience for a long time, specifically the consumption experience (Arnould and Price, 1993; Thompson et al., 1989) and the experience economy (e.g., Pine and Gilmore, 1999).

Although there is no clear demarcation in the literature, authors tend to distinguish between an *experiential view* (e.g., Arnould and Price, 1993) and an *experience-based view* (e.g., Schmitt, 1999). An experiential view is typically concerned with the ontology, axiology, epistemology, methodology, and interpretive research (phenomenology and hermeneutics). Yanow (2000, p. 248) notes:

> In contrast to the view that scientific theories are a mirrored reflection of their research subjects, an interpretive epistemological perspective posits that scientific perception is mediated by the theoretical constructs that researchers bring to their observations . . . This is the hallmark of cultural or symbolic anthropology, ethnomethodology, symbolic interaction, ethnography, participant-observation, and other modes of analysis informed by and/or consistent with interpretive philosophical positions.

By contrast, an experience-based view centers on the dimensions of the experience itself – the body, senses, affect, feelings, emotions, and others. For example, Lormand (1996, p. 243) points out that different modes of experience affect the properties of every moment of experiencing, including "perceptual experiences, such as tastings and seeing; bodily sensational experiences, such as those of pains, tickles and itches; imaginative experiences, such as those of one's own actions and perceptions; and streams of thought, as in the experience of thinking 'in words' or 'in images'." In a similar vein, Schmitt (1999) uses the term "experiential marketing" to capture five different types of customer experiences: (1) sensory experiences through sight, touch, sound, taste, and smell (*sense*); (2) affective experiences that range from mildly positive moods to strong emotions of joy and pride (*feel*); (3) cognitive, problem-solving experiences that involve creativity, intrigue, and provocation (*think*); (4) physical experiences, behaviors, and lifestyles that are inspirational and aspirational (*act*); and (5) relational experiences that result from social identity and involve a reference group, system or culture (*relate*). Schmitt asserts that the value derived from these five types supplements, and to some extent can replace, the feature–function–benefit emphasis of traditional marketing.

Several possibilities exist for research that examines the experiences of entrepreneurs in terms of their sensory, affective, cognitive, behavioral, and relational content. While work has appeared on particular dimensions such as affective experience (e.g., Baron, 2008; Cardon et al., 2009), to date no study has examined the interactive effects of different dimensions of the same experience, or the extent to which a relational experience both contains and presupposes sensory, affective, cognitive, and behavioral experiences (see Schmitt, 1999). In fact, the sensory dimension – that is, the body – has largely been absent in the entrepreneurship literature.

A related notion, that of the "production of experiences" in an experience economy, is becoming increasingly important for entrepreneurs and their business models. Staging experiences is not about entertaining customers, but rather, engaging them (Pine and Gilmore, 1999). This engagement has become a central challenge in a world where social media rule. Thus, the entrepreneur is not only experiencing the venture but must also become an experience producer, with the customer as a participant in the experience (through consumption or co-creation). Pine and Gilmore's (1999) experiential framework consists of four experience realms: (1) entertainment (*feel*); (2) education (*learn*); (3) escape (*do*); and (4) aesthetics (*be*). Customers are led up the value ladder from commodities toward transformational experiences that transcend product attributes – with the framework centering on the personally relevant and meaningful aspects of the individual's everyday experiences (e.g., self-actualization, belongingness, achievement of aspirations). To date, there has been little exploration of the relevance of the experience economy for entrepreneurship, with an edited book by Hjorth and Kostera (2007) being a notable exception. They note (pp. 19–21) that:

> entrepreneurial qualities emphasize the most vital characteristics of experience: *immediacy* [the concrete situatedness of experience in time and space], *playfulness* [openness to the emerging event], *subjectivity* [the connection of experience to the experiencing subject], and *performativity* [the quality of being enacted, its inherent actualization]. [Emphasis added]

EXPERIENTIAL LEARNING AND EXPERIENTIAL KNOWING

In studies on entrepreneurial learning, researchers tend to highlight differences between experiential learning, learning from prior experience, learning by doing, and learning from failure, among others. Hence, where Corbett (2007) focuses on Kolb's (1984) experiential learning cycle – that is, experiencing, thinking, knowing, acting – Westhead and colleagues (2005) focus on novice serial and portfolio entrepreneurs who learn from previous start-up experiences. Authors who study entrepreneurial failure have focused on managing the cost of failure (McGrath, 1999), failure as a grieving experience (Shepherd, 2003), and learning as a grief recovery process (Cope, 2011). This raises the question: what is the difference between perceiving, experiencing, thinking, knowing, acting (doing), and learning? Elkjaer (2004) notes that learning and knowing are often construed as being synonymous, and it is worth drawing attention to the experiential aspects of these two terms.

To distinguish between experiential learning and experiential knowing, it is useful to consider two German words – *Erfahrung* and *Erlebnis* – which refer to two sides of experience. On the one hand, *Erfahrung* (reflective experience or reflection) involves post-experience reflection – it is associated with experiential learning. On the other hand, *Erlebnis* (perceptive experience or perception) involves pre-reflective experience – it entails experiential knowing. Jackson (1996, p.42) points out that there are "significant differences between the way the world appears to our consciousness when we are fully engaged in activity [*Erlebnis*] and the way it appears to us when we subject it to reflection and retrospective analysis [*Erfahrung*]." Let us examine these differences between experiential learning (learning from experience and *Erfahrung*) and experiential knowing (conscious, lived experience and *Erlebnis*) in order to reveal new research opportunities for entrepreneurship scholars.

Experiential Learning and *Erfahrung*

Several scholars have conducted phenomenological analysis of work-related learning. In their chapter on experiential learning as lived experience, Cunliffe and Easterby-Smith (2004, p.38) assert that "experience-based approaches ground learning in the experience of the student by encouraging him or her to develop a process of reflective action." They note that experiential learning typically occurs in one of two ways: (1) reflection on experiences created by instructors (team-building, outdoor development activities), or (2) reflection on work experience (using self-diagnostic instruments, diaries). They distinguish between social constructionist (learning as a relational, dialogical conversation; constructing reflexive accounts from within experience; learning as an ontological activity) and traditional experiential learning (learning as a cognitive thought process; reflective theorizing about experience; learning as a purely epistemological activity) – and argue in favor of the social constructionist approach to learning which incorporates "practical reflexivity" – that is, "a way of interacting that focuses on inquiry and critical dialogue . . . an ongoing questioning of how we construct a shared sense with others" (p.39). In a slightly different approach, Yanow and Tsoukas (2009) critique Donald Schön's work for its cognitivist bias and propose a reinterpreted version that entails a phenomenologically-oriented reflection-in-action perspective of practice. Drawing on pragmatism – particularly Dewey – Elkjaer (2004) proposes three positions on learning: (1) learning as knowledge acquisition (individual, cognitive process); (2) learning as participation (relational, context-dependent, practice-based); and (3) learning as emerging or becoming (pragmatic, interactive, growth-focused).

Not surprisingly, much of the work on learning by entrepreneurship scholars mirrors that of organizational scholars – both in terms of theory and method. As a result, entrepreneurial learning mostly addresses only *Erfahrung* (and centers on cognitive aspects). Despite its claims of the centrality of direct experience, Kolb's learning cycle explicitly focuses on the meta-cognitive aspects of experiential learning (see Vince, 1998 for a critique). Similarly, Cope (2011, p.605) suggests that failure represents a learning journey for entrepreneurs that depends on the person's orientations to grief recovery and their individual learning processes, including critical reflection and reflective action.

Experiential Knowing and *Erlebnis*

In the management and entrepreneurship literatures, scholars have mostly relied on Polanyi's (1962) distinction between analytical, digital, conscious modes of knowing and tacit, analogic, unconscious knowing. However, Heron and Reason (2001) point to four different ways of knowing (all involving consciousness), and they lie on a continuum (there is no dichotomy): (1) *experiential*; (2) *presentational*; (3) *propositional*; and (4) *practical*. They note (p.183):

> *Experiential knowing* is through direct face-to-face encounter with person, place or thing; it is knowing through the immediacy of perceiving, through empathy and resonance. *Presentational knowing* emerges from experiential knowing, and provides the first form of expressing meaning and significance through drawing on expressive forms of imagery through movement, dance, sound, music, drawing, painting, sculpture, poetry, poetry, story, drama, and so on. *Propositional knowing* "about" something, is knowing through ideas and theories, expressed in informative statements. *Practical knowing* is knowing "how to" do something and is expressed in a skill, knack or competence. [Original emphasis]

These various ways of knowing the world form a continuum as shown in Figure 13.1, and correspond with the primary modes of functioning associated with the psyche: (1) *affective*; (2) *imaginal*; (3) *conceptual*; and (4) *practical* (Heron, 1992). A number of aspects of Figure 13.1 become pertinent for our discussion. In terms of modes of the psyche, the experience of emotion (an individuating process) and the experience of feeling (a participatory process) are primary – they occur first. Further, "the concept drives a wedge between the psyche and its world" (Heron, 1992, p.146) – the language we use to classify and label reinforces the subject–object duality. Thus, presentational knowledge is an important bridge between experiential knowledge and propositional knowledge. And finally, Heron and Reason (2001) suggest that different ways of knowing require different

WAYS OF KNOWING

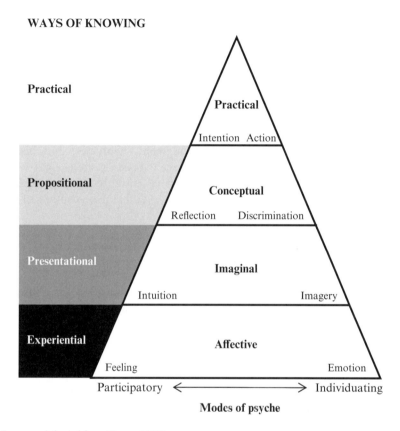

Source: Adapted from Heron (1992).

Figure 13.1   A conceptualization of modes of psyche and ways of knowing

forms of representation – and importantly, embodied, tacit knowledge requires presentational (aesthetic, artistic) forms of representation to avoid the split between subject and object.

New research questions arise from each of these points. With the first point, in the entrepreneurship literature affect is typically considered to be auxiliary, not primary. For example, sense-making is emotion-less. Weick et al. (2005, p.419) point out that "further exploration of emotion and sensemaking is crucial to clear up questions such as whether intra-organizational institutions are better portrayed as cold cognitive scripts built around rules, or as hot emotional attitudes built around values". In entrepreneurship research, sense-making is construed as a cognitive process with little attention given to the role of emotions. When affect is considered, it is construed as affective priming, supplementary to entrepreneurial cognition, or interfering with cognition.

In terms of the second point, studies on reflection and action (or reflection-in-action) only examine propositional and practical ways of knowing and neglect experiential and presentational ways. For example, in their subjectivist theory of entrepreneurship, Kor et al. (2007, p. 1192) discuss "the subjectively perceived multiple uses of a specific resource and the heterogeneous subjectively envisioned combinations of resources," and they link these perceptions to judgment, heuristics, and biases. Casson (1982, p. 14) notes, "the entrepreneur believes she is right while everyone else is wrong. Thus, the essence of entrepreneurship is being different – being different because one has a different perception of the situation."

Finally, in terms of the third point, there has been a growing recognition of the importance of aesthetic and art-based research in both organization studies (Warren, 2002) and entrepreneurship (e.g., Hjorth and Steyaert, 2009).

As a final observation, where Berglund (2006) draws parallels between phenomenology and Weickian enactment via social constructionism (e.g., Downing, 2005) and pragmatism (e.g., Sarasvathyan effectuation and Simonian science of the artificial), we believe there is merit in keeping the interpretive turn (social constructionism and phenomenology as method) and experience as interaction (American pragmatism as philosophy), separate from experience as embodiment (phenomenology as philosophy and method). Although social constructionism (e.g., the work of Gartner or Fletcher) pays attention to history, culture and community, it does not allow for embodiment. Although pragmatism pays attention to embodiment, it does so through language, metaphors and sense-making (that is, through primarily cognitive means).

"FEELING" THE FUTURE

We now turn our attention to time, and specifically, the role of time in so-called entrepreneurial resources. Mosakowski (1998, p. 625) refers to entrepreneurial resources as the individual's propensity to behave creatively, act with foresight, use intuition, and remain alert to emerging opportunities. Entrepreneurial resources also include effectuation (Sarasvathy, 2001) and contingency (Harmeling, 2010), among others. Due to space constraints, and because of their interconnections in a subjectivist theory of entrepreneurship (see Kor et al., 2007), we limit our discussion of future research options to two of these entrepreneurial resources (intuition and effectuation), with the aim of specifically highlighting an experience-based alternative to current conceptualizations.

Intuition is "the capacity of seeing things in a way which afterwards proves to be true, even though it cannot be established at the moment, and of grasping the essential fact, discarding the unessential, even though one can give no account of the principles by which this is done" (Schumpeter, 1934, p.85). Dane and Pratt (2009, p.3) note that "the 'outcome' of intuiting is an intuitive judgment. With regard to the process of intuition, most conceptualizations include the following features: (a) nonconscious information processing, (b) holistic associations, (c) affect, and (d) speed." In their review of intuition, Dane and Pratt (2009) distinguish between problem-based intuition, which includes intuition-as-expertise; moral intuition, with which the entrepreneur confronts ethical dilemmas; and creative intuition, which is the fusion of elements to create newness. More recent and controversial conceptions of intuition include phenomena such as clairvoyance, telepathy, or other forms of premonition and precognition, which are called *psi* (Bem, 2011, p.1):

> The term *psi* denotes anomalous processes of information or energy transfer that are currently unexplained in terms of known physical or biological mechanisms. Two variants of psi are *precognition* (conscious cognitive awareness) and *premonition* (affective apprehension) of a future event that could not otherwise be anticipated through any known inferential process. Precognition and premonition are themselves special cases of a more general phenomenon: the anomalous retroactive influence of some future event on an individual's current responses, whether those responses are conscious or nonconscious, cognitive or affective. [Original emphasis]

These psi phenomena influence cognition and affect retroactively by "time-reversing" psychological effects – that is, "the individual's responses are obtained before the putatively causal stimulus events occur" (ibid.). But in thinking about both psi phenomena and our more traditional conceptualizations, intuition consistently represents a link between information processing and decision-making. Salas and colleagues (2010) assert that intuition plays a critical role in expert decision-making, which we discuss next.

Turning to Saravathy's effectuation, we are interested in linkages not to controlling the future, but instead to "feeling the future" (Bem, 2011). Where Sarasvathy (2001) talks about economics with imagination, boundedly rational choice, affordable loss, thought experiments and verbal protocols, Bem (2011) focuses on extrasensory perception, emotional arousal (implicit, indirect, or physiological responses), precognitive approach/avoidance, visual images, and non-verbal fMRI experiments that monitor brain activity. While Haynie and colleagues (2010) examine meta-cognition (i.e., thinking about thinking), Bem (2011, p. 3) focuses on individuals' ability to detect a future event (i.e., a test of precognition). The notion of feeling the future presents a contrast to Sarasvathy's (2001) suggestion that entrepreneurs control the future.

Regardless of whether one endorses the validity of parapsychology or believes in the existence of paranormal phenomena, entrepreneurship researchers are prone to ascribe a certain clairvoyance or precognition to entrepreneurs, whether that is attributed to intuition, foresight, imagination or some other means for anomalous access to information (psi or "psychic ability") (Bem, 2011). In the end, entrepreneurs believe in "impossible" things. As a result, the mind–body problem comes back into the picture – specifically, how consciousness, precognition (knowing what is going to happen), and intuition (knowing the right thing to do in an uncertain situation) interact in explaining entrepreneurial decision-making and actions in uncertain environments.

Alertness is the perceptive interface between the individual and the world they experience, and it is how the entrepreneur ultimately comes to know their world. Unfortunately, mainstream studies emphasize propositional and practical ways of knowing while neglecting experiential and presentational ways of knowing – even though they use the lexicon that is associated with the latter. For example, in their conceptualization of a subjectivist theory of entrepreneurship, Kor and colleagues (2007, p. 1188) "embrace the Austrian economics (and existentialist) proposition that the future is not merely unknown, but unknowable." They link subjectivism variously to subjectivity in entrepreneurial discovery, creativity, perceptions, experiences, insight, imagination, intuition, and decision-making (cognitive biases and heuristics) – all of which constitutes knowledge-based resources. Noting that "[o]ne can distinguish between experiences leading to tacit knowledge versus experiences leading to explicit/codified knowledge" (p. 1201), their subjectivist theory focuses on learning and "personal (i.e. experiential) knowledge" (p. 1193), which is tacit, distributed, and subjective. However, as noted in Figure 13.1, the reference Kor and colleagues (2007) make to perceptions, intuition, and subjectivity places their argument inside the realm of *Erlebnis* and outside the realm of *Erfahrung* that they claim as their focus (i.e., non-theoretical, experience-based, knowledge).

More critically, subjectivists in entrepreneurship (e.g., Kor et al., 2007; Witt, 1989) have not yet considered the ontological and epistemological implications of their subjectivist ideas, particularly not insofar as the differences between subjectivity and subjectivism are concerned. Entrepreneurship researchers who use the term *subjective* often confuse its ontological sense with its epistemological sense. To explain what we mean, we refer to Hanly and Hanly (2001, pp. 517–19; emphasis added) who differentiate the concepts of subjectivity and subjectivism in terms of their respective *ontological, moral, psychological,* and *epistemological* aspects. They note, "*Ontologically,* subjectivity refers to the interiority of the psychic life of human beings and poses the question of the nature of its existence: is mind a substance in its own right, or is brain activity the substance of the human mind" (p. 517). At the same time, however, ontological subjectivists among philosophers (e.g., Plato, Berkeley, and Kant) have espoused epistemological realism (i.e., objectivism). Hanly and Hanly (ibid.) continue:

> *Morally,* subjectivity has to do with the value we attach to persons and other sentient creatures, our respect for their freedom, their claims on our care, and the obligation to treat others as we would wish ourselves to be treated by them . . . The ability to differentiate ourselves from others depends in turn on an ability to objectify ourselves. In this sense, moral experience and moral intersubjectivity depend on a capacity for some measure of epistemic objectivity in the sphere of individual psychology and relationships.

Finally, they note (p. 518):

> *Psychological* subjectivity refers to the interiority of a person's feelings, memories, imagination, thoughts, and sensory experience . . . Recognition of the subjectivity of psychological life does not imply subjectivism. As an *epistemological* position, subjectivism is a theory of knowledge based on the premise that observers must always significantly alter the nature of what is observed.

According to Horwitz (1994), the fundamental point of a subjectivist approach is that explanations in social sciences must start with the subjective mental states of those being studied. Social scientists must take seriously the roles of context and interpretation and recognize that the subjective perceptions of actors drive their actions, not the objective reality underlying the situation. Thus, an experience-based approach highlights the absence of (and a need for) a clear distinction between subjectivity and subjectivism in the subjectivist theory (Kor et al., 2007). The need for an appropriate interpretation of subjectivity and objectivity – as mutually exclusive categories – also affects other economics-based research streams in entrepreneurship that center on dichotomies such as subjective versus objective opportunities (McMullen and Shepherd, 2006) and the individual–opportunity nexus (Shane, 2003). Future work in these areas can be enhanced by adopting an experience-based, phenomenology-inspired approach to entrepreneurship where subjectivity, intentionality, and consciousness are primary concerns, and where *Erlebnis* rather than *Erfahrung* is center stage.

OPENNESS TO EXPERIENCE

The notion of the individual–opportunity nexus (Shane, 2003) has sparked renewed interest in the relevance of traits in entrepreneurship research, specifically the "Five Factor Model" of personality traits (extraversion, emotional stability, agreeableness, openness to experience, and conscientiousness) (Zhao and Seibert, 2006). One of the traits has proven consistently relevant in scholarly work – openness to experience – which describes someone who is intellectually curious and tends to seek new experiences and explore novel ideas. Someone high on openness can be described as creative, innovative, imaginative, reflective, and untraditional. Someone low on openness can be characterized as conventional, narrow in interests, and unanalytical (ibid.). Openness to experience has been associated with entrepreneurial motivation (Shane et al., 2003), the tendency to be self-employed (Shane et al., 2010), risk aversion (Fairlie and Holleran, 2011), entrepreneurial intentions (Zhao et al., 2010), innovativeness (Marcati et al., 2008) and venture survival (Ciavarella et al., 2004), among others.

Important developments in work on the traits of entrepreneurs present opportunities for further research related to the experience-based perspective. For instance, the renewed interest in the interface between biology and psychology in entrepreneurship research leads to new questions related to the psychopathology and psychobiology of the entrepreneur. A number of studies examine biology as a central factor in entrepreneurial behavior, venture creation, and the decision to become self-employed. These studies have found explanations in behavioral genetics (e.g., Nicolaou et al., 2008) and evolutionary biology (White et al., 2006), among others, which raise the old question of nature versus nurture – are entrepreneurs born or made? Whereas Nicolaou and colleagues (2008, 2011) claim that the tendency to engage in entrepreneurship is genetic (biological determinism), White and colleagues (2007) argue in favor of a biosocial model that combines nature and nurture (both biological and sociological factors). It also draws attention to two recent developments in developmental science – probabilistic epigenesis (Gottlieb, 2007) and neuroconstructivism (Westermann et al., 2007) – both of which present mounting evidence that oppose notions of biological determinism, and instead propose alternatives in which genes do not act in a predetermined manner; rather, behavior is dynamically shaped by interactions between nature and nurture (see Rutter, 2007; Shonkoff and Phillips, 2002). First, Gottlieb's (2007) meta-theoretical model of development – probabilistic epigenesis (PE) – centers on interactions between experience and gene expressions and "emphasizes the reciprocity of influences within and between levels of an organism's developmental manifold (genetic activity, neural activity, behavior, and the physical, social, and cultural influences of the external environment) and the ubiquity of gene–environment interaction in the realization of all phenotypes" (p. 1). Second, in neuroconstructivism, gene/brain/cognition/behavior/environment interactions take place through the encellment-embrainment-embodiment-ensocialment of genes, experience-dependent mechanisms, and sensory experience. Westermann and colleagues (2007, p. 79) note:

> The brain is closely linked to its body and the environment. Body use, constrained by the body's morphology, can generate novel sensory experiences through altering the experienced environment. This can be achieved either by moving the sensory organs (e.g. the eyes) without changing the external environment, or by manipulating the environment itself. The experienced environment generates neural activity which, through encellment, leads to changes in the underlying (and, through embrainment, in other) brain systems.

Thus, these new developments (and others) suggest that future research should move beyond considerations of biological and contextual factors in isolation, and instead examine interactions between biology, the body, the mind, and social/situational/environmental factors. Future studies that consider the extent to which situational factors facilitate or constrain the expression of biological factors may be able to put to rest arguments that entrepreneurial behavior is genetically determined and clarify the role of biological determinism in explaining entrepreneurial outcomes (e.g., Nicolaou et al., 2011).

In a related vein, the availability of new technologies, sophisticated instrumentation, and imaging methods such as fMRI, ERP, MEG, and NIRS (e.g., Casey and de Haan, 2002) may also prompt a shift in interest in entrepreneurship research from current perspectives that focus solely on psychological (intentions, attitudes, motivation, affect, emotion, passion), cognitive (heuristics, biases), behavioral (choice, decision-making), and biological (hormones, genes) factors to an examination of the physiological and neurological basis of entrepreneurship (consciousness, perception, intentionality, awareness, precognition, emotion).

Another noteworthy development is both theoretical and methodological, and involves the neuroscience of consciousness, that is, "neurophenomenology" (Varela, 1996). Lutz and Thompson (2003, p. 31) note:

> At a theoretical level, neurophenomenology pursues an embodied and large-scale dynamical approach to the neurophysiology of consciousness . . . At a methodological level, the neurophenomenological strategy is to make rigorous and extensive use of first-person data about subjective experience as a heuristic to describe and quantify the large-scale neurodynamics of consciousness.

They note that a number of challenging methodological issues surround the incorporation of first-person data into cognitive neuroscience, including: (1) the potential for first-person reports to be biased or inaccurate; (2) the possibility that the process of generating first-person reports about an experience can modify that experience; and (3) the "explanatory gap" in our understanding of how to relate first-person, phenomenological data to third-person, biobehavioral data. Neurophenomenology opens the door to some exciting possibilities for future research – most of which are related to the role of time and temporal perception. Examples include the individual's temporal cognition and openness to new venture experiences; the phenomenology of time or the individual's perception of the passage of time (e.g., the "cognitive-timer" model for time estimation versus the subjective experience of apparent duration) (Glicksohn, 2001); and connections between time, imagination, imagery, and emotion when creating a venture (D'Argembeau and Van der Linden, 2006).

ENCOUNTERING ENTREPRENEURSHIP AS PHENOMENAL EXPERIENCE

In this section we examine the "reality" of experience, that is, its ontology, and focus specifically on the prevailing mind–body duality in entrepreneurship research. Encountering entrepreneurship as phenomenal experience entails a study of phenomena, that is, the "appearances of things, or things as they appear in our experience, or the ways we experience things, thus the meanings things have in our experience" (Smith, 2011). This approach to entrepreneurship research brings us closer to an understanding of the structure of phenomena such as perception, consciousness, thought, emotion, intuition, memory, and imagination.

It is worth stressing that the notion of a *point of view* ("seeing" entrepreneurship) differs in significant ways from the notion of *the site of experience* ("experiencing" entrepreneurship). On the one hand, a point of view (seeing entrepreneurship) results from Western occularcentrism, where "accounts of reality have been based on Descartes' idea of a disembodied and rational eye as an instrument of order and control" (Belova, 2006, p. 93). Vision is privileged over the other senses and primarily resides in language. Entrepreneurship – as a science of the imagination (Gartner, 2007) – entails "seeing" with the mind's eye. Gartner notes, "The narrative of entrepreneurship is the generation of hypotheses about how the world might be: how the future might look and act . . . how entrepreneurs generate and modify their visions of the future, [as well as how scholars] generate and modify alternative visions of the future" (p. 614). Thus, both entrepreneurs and entrepreneurship scholars are looking, envisioning, seeing. Referring to Klein's (2008) notion of opportunities as imagined and Shackle's (1955) idea of entrepreneurship as action in pursuit of imagination, Dimov (2011, p. 62) stresses that "from the point of view of the individual entrepreneurs, the future is not known or predetermined, and so they act on what at the moment are their beliefs about what the future might be."

Entrepreneurship (and its behaviors, actions, opportunities, and so forth) depends on the worldview or the point of view of the individual, that is, the mainstream stresses the primacy of perception. Sandelands and Srivatsan (1993, p. 14) point out that Galileo's telescope and other scientific advances brought new insights – "literally, new 'seeing intos'" – which is similar to the Cartesian vision-centered rationality of "seeing" that is present in pattern detection or ways to connect the dots in entrepreneurial cognition (Baron, 2006), as well as sense-making through symbols and metaphors in opportunity recognition (Cornelissen and Clarke, 2010). Here, experience is epistemology grounded in vision that is "fixating," "atemporal," "objectifying," "appropriating," "controlling" (Belova, 2006, p. 105).

On the other hand, a notion of the site of experience (experiencing entrepreneurship) centers on the "lived experience," the interpreted and meaningfully lived part of being-in-the-world – a Heideggerian relatedness to the world – which highlights the importance of context. The word "experience," according to Dewey (1958, p. 8), "recognizes in its primary integrity no division between act and material, subject and object, but contains them both in an unanalyzed totality." Thus, a notion of the site of experience overcomes the mind–body, subject–object, agency–structure, and other dualities that dominate mainstream entrepreneurship research.

Although several researchers have considered the problem of ontology, these studies have maintained the problematic status of ontology in entrepreneurship research. Some scholars collapse ontology into epistemology (e.g., Alvarez and Barney, 2007; Sarasvathy, 2001). Others have preferred to simply elude the problem of ontology. For example, Klein (2008, p. 182) notes that:

> [b]y treating opportunities as a latent construct, this approach sidesteps the problem of defining opportunities as objective or subjective, real or imagined, and so on. The formation of entrepreneurial beliefs is treated as a potentially interesting psychological problem, but not part of the economic analysis of entrepreneurship.

Still others deny the relevance of ontology. According to Dimov (2011, p. 63):

> Some scholars have argued that the two featured streams of thought about entrepreneurial behavior, i.e., formal and substantive, offer alternative onto-logical accounts of opportunities, with the former representing a realist view [opportunities exist objectively] and the latter representing a constructivist view [opportunities are created endogenously] . . . the point of contention between the two streams is not the ontological status of opportunities but what constitutes an appropriate conception of entrepreneurial behavior. The ques-tion of ontology can be safely laid aside as it has no bearing on our analyses, whether these analyses are carried out from logical postulates or from empirical observations.

Here Dimov makes three points: (1) ontology is irrelevant – that is, only epistemology matters; (2) there are dualities at play (e.g., objective–subjec-tive, formal–substantive, realist–constructivist, mind–body, and so forth); and (3) opportunities are not distinct from entrepreneurial behavior.

Contrary to Dimov's (2011) assertions, an experience-based view of entrepreneurship centers on ontology. In his study on entrepreneurship as lived experience, Berglund (2006, pp. 80–81) draws distinctions between two phenomenologists: Husserl with an epistemological approach and Heidegger with an ontological approach to experience. Based on Husserl's transcendental phenomenology, a person lives in a world of objects with transcendental essences, and lived experiences can be reduced to their pure essences through bracketing (knowledge is ahistorical). According to Heidegger's hermeneutic phenomenology, a person exists as being in and of the world. The ontological human condition (*Dasein*) consti-tutes a "throwness," which implies both a situatedness and a relatedness (knowing is historical and grounded in cultural interpretation). Thus there is ample room for consideration of ontological implications in future entrepreneurship research where experience is the focus – whether this entails a rational means–ends choice of the formalist (e.g., Klein, 2008) or a substantive approach (Dimov, 2011).

EXPERIENCE: THE FLESH AND BLOOD OF ENTREPRENEURSHIP

By and large, entrepreneurship has been theorized based on quantita-tive data (statistics) and abstract concepts – and therefore it has tran-scended bodily and embodied experience. In this section, we first highlight the problem of disembodiment in entrepreneurship research and then explain what we mean with corporeality, followed by suggestions for future research that propose embodied alternatives to current approaches (e.g., entrepreneurial cognition, improvisational behavior, entrepreneurial action).

The corporeal turn in cultural studies presents a particularly fruitful area for future investigation because entrepreneurship research is mostly disembodied and acontextual. Authors subscribe to mind–body duality and often do not consider history, culture or community as part of the body's situatedness or psychological processes. For example, the lived experience has been the focus of attention in phenomenological descriptions of various experiential aspects of entrepreneurship (e.g., Berglund, 2006; Cope, 2011). However, these studies tend to focus on the "lived experience" and (inter)subjectivity, and often do not take into account the "lived body," bodily ways of knowing and bodily practices. Similarly, authors often talk about embodied metaphors (e.g., Heracleous and Jacobs, 2008) or artifacts and their embodied meanings (Yanow, 2000) – these approaches center on seeing, metaphors, and a point of view, that is, the interpretive turn. This is consistent with Weick and colleagues' (2005, p. 409) assertion that "[s]ensemaking is about the interplay of action and interpretation rather than the influence of evaluation on choice. When action is the central focus, interpretation, not choice, is the core phenomenon." As a result, subjectivity, intentionality, and consciousness are associated either with the mind or with the senses that are deemed to be located in the head (somehow separate from the body). Thus, the body that sleeps, works, gets stressed out, and interacts with other people, objects, and the world – that body is not part of the person we study in entrepreneurship.

Merleau-Ponty's phenomenology is central to discussions of corporeality, materiality (physicality), and embodiment. He stresses that the body is not "a collection of adjacent organs but a synergic system, all of the functions of which are exercised and linked together in the general action of being in the world" (Merleau-Ponty, 1962, p. 234). Moreover, the body acts as mediator of the world, that is, "the thickness of flesh between the seer and the thing is constitutive for the thing of its visibility as for the seer of his corporeity; it is not an obstacle between them, it is their means of communication" (Merleau-Ponty, 1968, p. 135). Thus, the notion of being-in-the-world is intimately tied to intentionality (consciousness), embodiment, and situatedness. Gendlin (1992, p. 345) explains how a pre-reflective, bodily sense of the situation comes about:

> What the word "perception" says cannot usually include how the living body consists of interactions with the world. "Perception" is usually something that appears before or to a body. But the body is an interaction also in that it breathes, not only in that it senses the cold of the air. It feeds; it does not only

see and smell food. It grows and sweats. It walks; it does not only perceive the hard resistance of the ground. And it walks not just as a displacement between two points in empty space, rather to go somewhere – to answer "the call of the things", as Merleau-Ponty said. The body senses the whole situation, and it urges, it implicitly shapes our next action. It senses itself living-in its whole context – the situation.

Overall:

> Merleau-Ponty brings together the various planes on which embodied being takes place: in the moment of perceiving "here and now", in the inter-involvement of self and other as bodies that share the common ground of flesh, and a profound sociality of interaction where understanding hinges on the frontier of an intermingling of subjects, consciousnesses, and corporalities. (Belova, 2006, p. 95)

Clearly the body is central in entrepreneurship research with its person-centric foci – entrepreneurs experience grief (Cope, 2011), stress and exhaustion (Hmieleski and Corbett, 2008), passion (Cardon et al., 2009), trauma (Haynie and Shepherd, 2011), and self-compassion (Shepherd and Cardon, 2009), among others. For example, Hmieleski and Corbett (2008, pp. 482–3) note that "we do not know if improvisational behavior [the ability of entrepreneurs to extemporaneously compose and execute novel plans] tends to energize versus exhaust entrepreneurs . . . because improvisation can be very risky and highly stressful" (p. 483), which suggests the body is somehow involved. However, they ascribe this exhaustion to cognitive overload during improvisational episodes and suggest that self-efficacy should help reduce the degree of psychological strain. Contrary to their expectations, they found that entrepreneurs high in self-efficacy could be burning themselves out by over-working and improvising to a greater extent than is good for their well-being. Overall, Hmieleski and Corbett (like many other entrepreneurship scholars) discount the role of the body in entrepreneurship, an omission that is less prevalent in other disciplines that study improvisation such as music.

A number of entrepreneurship studies have started to acknowledge and even accommodate the role of the body. In a recent study, Mitchell and colleagues (2011) propose socially situated cognition as a broad framework for entrepreneurial cognition that is more embodied, [en]active, situated and distributed. Others have focused on biology, specifically the role of genes (Nicolaou et al., 2008; Shane et al., 2010) and testosterone (White et al., 2006). We can distinguish between corporeality (biological determinism) and embodiment (social determinism), and discuss the relevance of each for an understanding of entrepreneurship that is deeply embodied, social, situated, and enactive. Deeper insights from psychology and phenomenology enable us to revisit the biological roots – the flesh and blood – of entrepreneurship. Importantly, the embodied condition of entrepreneurship challenges the prevailing ontological grounds of disembodied individuals that rely exclusively on their minds. Whereas entrepreneurship researchers tend to focus on the computational mind – that is, cognitive structures, heuristics, biases, beliefs, and so forth that are solely located in the head – examination of the phenomenological mind (see Gallagher and Zahavi, 2007) holds considerable promise for future research. Thus, there is considerable scope for research that focuses on a phenomenological reconceptualization of current disembodied perspectives on affect (Baron, 2008), improvisational behavior (Hmieleski and Corbett, 2008), entrepreneurial action (McMullen and Shepherd, 2006), entrepreneurial passion (Cardon et al., 2009), entrepreneurial motivation (Shane et al., 2003), entrepreneurial cognition (Gregoire et al., 2010a), and other constructs in the extant literature.

This raises the question: what does body-aware entrepreneurship research look like? A recent study that combines embodied, [en]active, situated cognition (EASC) and interpretative phenomenological analysis (IPA) (Larkin et al., 2011) offers some useful insights that overcome both the strong empiricist approach as well as limitations in the approach to embodiment in current research. Larkin and colleagues (ibid., pp. 319–20) conceptualize EASC as a conscious, intersubjective process of sense-making that:

> is to be understood as: situated (i.e., context-sensitive); temporal (i.e., varying according to time available); distributed (i.e., persons "off-load" certain cognitive work onto the environment, and thus the environment co-constitutes the cognitive system); engaged in the world, and thus action-orientated (i.e., intentional in the phenomenological sense); and embodied (i.e., at the very least, the body defines our perceptual involvement in the world).

They further stress that "IPA aims to understand how people make sense of events, relationships, and processes in the context of their particular lifeworlds. Whatever phenomenon is being studied, the aim is to understand 'what it is like to be experiencing this, for this particular person, in this context'." Thus, the ontological and epistemological underpinnings of EASC offers connections to and between research areas with diverse approaches to knowledge construction – such as phenomenology (philosophy of Husserl, Merleau-Ponty, Heidegger, and others), psychology (descriptive, empirical phenomenology of Giorgi) and cognitive science (experimental science and analytical philosophy of Searle and Dennett) – all of which are relevant fields for entrepreneurship research.

EXPERIENCING AND THE SENSES

Experience is considered the province of a phenomenology of sense perception. Csordas (1990, pp. 8–9) notes that "Merleau-Ponty's phenomenology involves a rejection of the empiricist model that suggests external objects stimulate our internal organs such that we register sensory data and instead embraces the idea that perception begins in the body and ends in objects." Thus, we do not *have* bodies – rather we *are* our bodies. We perceive the world bodily (through the senses) to construct meaning (make sense) and situate (a sense of direction) ourselves in the world. Thus, not only affect (as complement to cognition) but also the senses (as part of the body) play an important (albeit neglected) role in experience. According to Howes (2003, p. xi), "Sensation is not just a matter of physiological response and personal experience. It is the most fundamental domain of cultural expression, the medium through which all the values and practices of society are enacted."

Some entrepreneurs have started to capitalize on the sensory turn. For example, Apple's iPad involves tactile, embodied, and visuo-haptic interactions (Dourish, 2001) – vision and touch are intricately intertwined. Deeper insights about the role of culture and the senses come from anthropology. The body and its experiences in the world take a central place in emplaced and materialized meaning-making because:

> meanings are made in situ through the full spectrum of sensory phenomena with which actors engage – from what can be seen with the eye to what can be heard, touched, smelled, tasted – but also reverberate within webs of signifiers (e.g. the connotations of colors and plastics in the domain of children's toys) beyond the immediacy of unfolding interactions. (Hurdley and Dicks, 2011, p. 278)

The sensory turn draws attention to the "sensoriality" of experience (Pink, 2011, p. 271) and sensorial experiences (e.g., olfactory, tactile, kinaesthetic and auditory experiences). This "sensoriality" is associated with "a shift between *looking at* and collecting data on to *being in* and engaging in ways of knowing about the worlds and actions of other people" and thus two different forms of ethnography. The first approach to ethnography – *looking at* the world – centers on culture as it is represented in material forms and visual artifacts such as documents and architecture, that is, it depends on an "observational and culture-as-readable-text approach to ethnography, and its emphasis on the differences between different senses, different modes and different media" (ibid., p. 270; original emphasis). One such example in entrepreneurship research is Dodd's (2002) study examining descriptive narratives of entrepreneurs (see Chapter 12).

The second approach to ethnography – *being in* – involves:

> learning in and as part of the world, and seeking routes through which to share or imaginatively empathize with the actions of people in it . . . the idea of ethnography as a practice that seeks routes to understanding the experiences and meanings of other people's lives through different variations of being with, and doing things with them. (Ibid.)

Pink notes (p. 272) that it involves two key issues: "the idea of ethnography as producing knowledge with others, in movement and through engagement with/in a material, sensory (and) social environment. Second, the use of (audio) visual recording as a way of representing elements of this experience and the memories and imaginaries related to it." This anthropology-inspired type of sensory ethnography focuses on everyday practices, such as Michel de Certeau's *The Practice of Everyday Life* (1984), which has also received attention in entrepreneurship research.

Sensory experience in entrepreneurship can represent a phenomenological reconceptualization of mainstream (classical) views. Nicolaou et al. (2008) propose that sensation-seeking is a heritable factor in entrepreneurship – that is, they posit (p. 8) that:

> the personality trait of *sensation seeking* increases the likelihood that a person will choose an occupation that causes them to bear risk in the pursuit of novelty. This is because their genetic composition gives them higher arousal thresholds [related to the dopamine and norepinephrine levels in their systems] for experiencing physiological sensations from undertaking these activities. [Original emphasis]

Bem (2011) in turn suggests that sensation-seeking is a motivational factor that begins with the senses – *not* with genes – which presents an interesting challenge to Nicolaou and colleagues' (2008) argument that genes determine arousal and discomfort associated with novelty-pursuit and risk-taking, respectively, and thus determine the extent to which people decide to become self-employed. Bem posits a different possibility, namely, that entrepreneurs experience bodily sensations differently because they are less aware of sensory experiences other than visual perception because they are more alert to cognitive experiences. This is in line with our earlier discussion of the occularcentrism in entrepreneurship research. Another possibility is that there is no increase in their dopamine and norepine-phrine levels because of interference due to emotional experiences or pre-cognition in anticipation of future events.

An experiential perspective can help address whether an entrepreneur's sensorial experience is hard-wired in DNA or is actually the product of ongoing and anticipated events. Work such as that by Nicolaou et al. (2008) tends to focus on biology, such as the role of genetics and hormones. Our concern is that the experiential, physiological sensations of venture creation are overlooked, and the interaction between lived-through dura-tion, physiology, cognition and emotion is ignored. Researchers must further open the door to these biosocial examinations of entrepreneurship, and particularly develop insights into the role of emotions (e.g., Shepherd and Cardon, 2009).

Future research on the sensory aspects of the experience also suggests the need for different theories and methods. For example, Cromby (2002, p. 5) notes:

> discourse theory seems to leave little space for embodied subjectivity, for the body as body. Instead, the body is, on the one hand, a metaphor, trope or symbol and, on the other hand, a surface for the inscription of social forces, experience, and discourse. We need to go beyond this abraded, fleshless, ephemeral person to a view of the subject prey to physiological, anatomical and hormonal influences which act back upon the subjectivity they support, and also – through feedback generated within the brain/body system – may enter into the very core of subjectivity and agency.

CONCLUSIONS

In the present chapter, we noted a number of recent developments in various literatures that open up new avenues for entrepreneurship research. Some of the important developments include the shift from:

- a study of the exceptional, expertise and heroic feats of entrepre-neurs to the study of the everyday, lived experiences, life histories and cultures of people in their entrepreneurial pursuits and the practice of entrepreneurship (anthropology);
- text-based, linguistic representations to sensory (multi-modal), dialogic encounters of bodies that experience the world (sociology);
- experiential learning (knowledge and expertise) to experiential ways of knowing (psychology);
- disembodied, asocial, non-local sense-making to embodied, partici-pative, emplaced meaning-making;

- detached, unitary, third-person experience to participatory, multi-dimensional, first-person experience (marketing);
- a point of view to site of experience (corporeal turn); from a focus on (inter)subjectivity of "lived experience" – a cognitive perspective – to an approach that includes the bodily ways of knowing and bodily practices of the "lived body" – a phenomenological perspective (sensory turn);
- embodied cognition to embodied experience (empirical turn);
- ways of knowing to ways of being (ontological turn);
- an overt focus on sense-making to emplaced (situated and materialized) meaning-making, particularly the role of the senses in this process;
- the role of affect in cognition to the politics of experience (practice turn); from controlling the future to feeling the future (extrasensory perception); and
- cross-cultural factors that impact entrepreneurship to transnational entrepreneurship.

These shifts confirm the assertion of Sandelands and Srivatsan (1993, p. 14) that "it is a mistake to envisage sharp lines between theoretical concepts and experiences, [and] we must insist that all concepts be part theoretical and part experiential. Although lines between the two can be drawn, they come at the cost of neglecting experience as the mainspring of theoretical insight."

Importantly, the implications of an experience-based view that offers a more embodied, sensorial, practical, situated, and historical understanding of entrepreneurship are complex and multifold. First, the experiential facts of entrepreneurship do not fit with a philosophy of science that has evolved out of considerations that pertain to the laboratory sciences. These research methods (e.g., Gregoire et al., 2010b) are devoid of the social and cultural frame in which entrepreneurs live and work, and cannot account for the role of the body. Shifting our focus from the object or subject (involving third-person or second-person lab work) to the experience (often involving field work and first-person perspectives) has epistemological and methodological implications, and indeed suggests a need for back-and-forth interactions between research on the mind and disciplined phenomenology of lived experience (Thompson, 2004). Recently, entrepreneurship scholars have started to pay more attention to qualitative research methods – and insofar as "experience" is concerned, particularly, to narrative and discursive approaches (e.g., Gartner, 2007; Hjorth and Steyaert, 2004), ethnography (Van Manen, 1997) and phenomenology as method (e.g., Berglund, 2006; Cope, 2011). In addition to the need for more reflexive research practice, more qualitative studies and more mixed methods studies:

> what participants say and do needs to be interpreted alongside the material and sensorial settings in which they say and do it, and which play an active role in the shaping of emergent situations and encounters. Nevertheless, insufficient attention is often paid to the extent to which this emplaced and materialized meaning-making also mobilizes qualities that are displaced from our immediate sensory perceptions, in that they inhere in signifiers (objects and materials) embroiled in wider organizations of cultural value and meaning. (Hurdley and Dicks, 2011, p. 278)

They note further that in the "multidimensional character of social worlds, the 'sensory turn' centers the sensuous, bodied person – participant, researcher and audience/reader – as the 'place' for intimate, affective forms of knowing." Our musings regarding future research prospects on an experience-based view of entrepreneurship requires access to this experiential knowing and sensory experience where corporeal, multisensory, and culturally specific knowledge are put front and center (Hurdley, 2010). Examining this sensoriality of "ways of knowing" requires going beyond language and the spoken word. It also goes beyond visual methods that center on the relationship between images and words. Thus, innovative and unconventional methods (see Dicks and Hurdley, 2009) such as multisensory methods – tactile, acoustic, kinesthetic, and visual (e.g., art, photography, video, drama, film) – that combine "multimodality and anthropologically informed sensory ethnographic methodologies" (Pink, 2011, p. 261) are becoming increasingly important. Pink stresses the importance of intersensoriality (as in sensory anthropology), rather than an artificial binary of the senses and sensory knowledge-making (as in anthropology of the sense). Consequently, open-mindedness, researcher reflexivity, and intersubjectivity are core principles in the research process. Others have stressed that more attention must be given to philosophy when developing theories (Tsoukas and Chia, 2011).

Second, the implications of an experience-based view for theory development in entrepreneurship are threefold: (1) the need for more productive research questions, specifically through problematization as a useful alternative to gap-spotting when generating research questions (Sandberg and Alveson, 2011); (2) the need to pay more attention to philosophy (epistemology *and* ontology); and (3) the need for constructive interplay of theory concepts and experience concepts (Sandelands and Srivatsan, 1993), which implies the use of theories grounded in experience, action research, and middle-range theories. Sandelands and Srivatsan (ibid.)

point out that science risks the danger of losing touch with concrete experience. They note (p. 19) that "a science is fully alive and creative when wide-eyed and involved; when it sees, touches, hears, tastes, and feels. Intellectual celibacy, cut off from sensuous involvement, is a shame not a virtue." Thus, the epistemological-ontological grounding of "experience" makes several connections to disciplines and theories that have hitherto remained unexplored and underappreciated. We concur with Hjorth (2008, p. 329) and:

> see entrepreneurship research flourishing when conducted in the spirit of those hot-wiring thinkers like Gilles Deleuze, Michel Serres, Bruno Latour, and Michel Foucault (here limited to the French) who have become entrepreneurial researchers through curiously grasping (-prendre) those topics that belonged to no one. In such in-betweens (entre-), they have invented (with) concepts that enhances possibilities for thinking, living, and creating.

Third, an experience-based view has important implications for entrepreneurship practice, particularly insofar as the emotional side of improving personal performance is concerned. Dane (2011) highlights the value of contemplation and mindfulness (paying attention to what is happening in real time) in efforts to improve one's performance and behavior. He defines mindfulness "as a state of consciousness in which attention is focused on present-moment phenomena occurring both externally and internally." This kind of non-judgmental attention paid to the present moment requires attentional breadth, expertise, and intuition. Mindfulness also has beneficial effects on psychological well-being, mental as well as physical health, behavioral regulation, and interpersonal relationships (Brown et al., 2007).

Fourth, an experience-based view has implications for entrepreneurship education. Experiential learning is often interpreted as learning by doing which involves an internship, a start-up experience, or Kolb's (1984) experiential learning cycle. However, not every student wants (or even needs) to start a venture. Options for future research related to entrepreneurship as experience suggests that a more broad-based approach to entrepreneurship education is possible, that is, education as "interpretation." For example, Tilden (1957, p. 8) describes interpretation as "an educational activity which aims to reveal meanings and relationships through the use of original objects, by firsthand experience, and by illustrative media, rather than simply to communicate factual information." This notion of education as interpretation requires an approach in which every class session is conducted as a memorable and meaningful *experience* with sensory, cognitive, emotional, behavioral, and relational objectives to facilitate transformation and change (in addition to learning skills that can be transferred to multiple contexts). Notably, this type of learning is qualitative and individualized, which presents interesting challenges to the entrepreneurship educator in terms of quantification through the formal grading process.

Much has been said about future directions of entrepreneurship research (e.g., Ireland et al., 2005; Sorenson and Stuart, 2008; Wiklund et al., 2011), but these insights into where things are going largely ignore the focal topics in this book. Perhaps this is due to less familiarity with literatures residing outside that cited in mainstream published work within entrepreneurship, especially when these literatures often span several centuries. This book is a first attempt at sorting through the "critical mess" (Gartner, 2006) that is not restricted to entrepreneurship research, but that is also part of experience-based research. For example, Hjorth and Kostera (2007, p. 259) discuss an aesthetic experience in terms of "three things: 1) the experimental aspect, the act of trying; 2) the social aspect of participating; and 3) the affective aspect of being moved by participation. . . . They are all taken for the descriptions of the meanings of the Latin *experientia*." Similarly, the term "experiential" is often associated with the empirical or pragmatic. As we indicated in different chapters, several other terms are also intimately tied to the term "experience," including conscious individual experience (both past and present), lessons from experience (entrepreneurship-related learning), experiment (tied to improvisation), and practice (as enactment), which leads to confusion and conflicting results.

A key aim of this book has been to clarify the term "experience" and to promote an appreciation of its relevance – and indeed all related variants of the term such as *experiencing, experience-based* and *experiential* – for a more embodied, situated, and contextualized understanding of entrepreneurship, and the new connections it forges with other interdisciplinary fields. Where others have argued in favor of a reconciliation of entrepreneurship theory and strategic management research (and, by implication, economics), we believe a stronger connection between entrepreneurship and the humanities and cultural studies – and by extension, an experienced-based view of entrepreneurship – represents a more exciting and potentially fruitful future for our discipline. It is a path that is more likely to overcome efforts to subsume or merge entrepreneurship with some other discipline. As Merleau-Ponty (1962, p. 3) notes:

> Everything I know about the world, even if through science, I know as from a vision of mine or as from an experience of the world without which the symbols of science could not say anything. Science's whole universe is built over the lived world, and if we intend to think science with rigor, appreciate its full meaning and its scope, we need first to awake this experience of the world from which it is a second expression.

REFERENCES

Alvarez, S. and J. Barney (2007), 'Discovery and creation: alternative theories of entrepreneurial action', *Strategic Entrepreneurship Journal*, **1**(1): 11–26.

Arnould, E. and L. Price (1993), 'River magic: extraordinary experience and the extended service encounter', *Journal of Consumer Research*, **20**(1): 24–45.

Baron, R. (2006), 'Opportunity recognition as pattern recognition: how entrepreneurs "connect the dots" to identify new business opportunities', *Academy of Management Review*, **20**(1): 104–19.

Baron, R. (2008), 'The role of affect in the entrepreneurial process', *Academy of Management Review*, **33**(2): 328–40.

Belova, O. (2006), 'The event of seeing: a phenomenological perspective on visual sense-making', *Culture and Organization*, **12**(2): 93–107.

Bem, D.J. (2011), 'Feeling the future: experimental evidence for anomalous retroactive influences on cognition and affect', *Journal of Personality and Social Psychology*, **100**(3): 407–25.

Berglund, H. (2006), 'Researching entrepreneurship as lived experience', in H. Neergaard and J. Ulhøi (eds), *Handbook of Qualitative Research Methods*, Cheltenham, UK and Northampton, MA, USA: Edward Elgar, pp. 75–93.

Brown, K.W., R.M. Ryan and J.D. Creswell (2007), 'Mindfulness: theoretical foundations and evidence for its salutary effects', *Psychological Inquiry*, **18**(4): 211–37.

Cardon, M., J. Wincent, J. Singh and M. Drnovsek (2009), 'The nature and experience of entrepreneurial passion', *Academy of Management Review*, **34**(3): 511–32.

Casey, B. and M. de Haan (2002), 'Introduction: new methods in developmental science', *Developmental Science*, **5**(3): 265–7.

Casson, M. (1982), *The entrepreneur*, Totawa, NJ: Barnes & Noble Books.

Ciavarella, M., A. Buchholtz, C. Riordan, R. Gatewood and G.S. Stokes (2004), 'The Big Five and venture survival: is there a linkage?', *Journal of Business Venturing*, **19**(4): 465–83.

Cope, J. (2011), 'Entrepreneurial learning from failure: an interpretative phenomenological analysis', *Journal of Business Venturing*, **26**(6): 604–23.

Corbett, A. (2007), 'Learning asymmetries and the discovery of entrepreneurial opportunities', *Journal of Business Venturing*, **22**(1): 97–118.

Cornelissen, J. and J. Clarke (2010), 'Imagining and rationalizing opportunities: inductive reasoning and the creation and justification of new ventures', *Academy of Management Review*, **35**(4): 539–57.

Cromby, J. (2002), 'Review: David Howarth, discourse', *Forum: Qualitative Social Research*, **3**(2): article 6 available at http://www.qualitative-research.net/index.php/fqs/article/viewArticle/870/1892; accessed 22 November 2011.

Csordas, T.J. (1990), 'Embodiment as a paradigm for anthropology', *Ethos*, **18**(1): 5–47.

Cunliffe, A. and M. Easterby-Smith (2004), 'From reflection to practical reflexivity: experiential learning as lived experience', in M. Reynolds and R. Vince (eds), *Organization Reflection*, London: Ashgate, pp. 30–46.

Dane, E. (2011), 'Paying attention to mindfulness and its effects on task performance in the workplace', *Journal of Management*, **37**(4): 997–1018.

Dane, E. and M. Pratt (2009), 'Conceptualizing and measuring intuition: a review of recent trends', in G. Hodgkinson and J. Ford (eds), *International Review of Industrial and Organizational Psychology, Vol. 24*, Chichester, UK: Wiley, pp. 1–49.

D'Argembeau, A. and M. Van der Linden (2006), 'Individual differences in the phenomenology of mental time travel: the effect of vivid visual imagery and emotion regulation strategies', *Consciousness and Cognition*, **15**(2): 342–50.

De Certeau, M. (1984), *The Practice of Everyday Life*, Berkeley/Los Angeles: University of California Press.

Dewey, J. (1958), *Experience and Nature*, New York: Dover.

Dicks, B. and R. Hurdley (2009), 'Using unconventional media to disseminate qualitative research', *Qualitative Researcher*, **10**: 2–5.

Dimov, D. (2011), 'Grappling with the unbearable elusiveness of entrepreneurial opportunities', *Entrepreneurship Theory and Practice*, **35**(1): 57–81.

Dodd, S.D. (2002), 'Metaphors and meaning: a grounded cultural model of U.S. entrepreneurship', *Journal of Business Venturing*, **17**(5): 519–35.

Dourish, P. (2001), Where the Action is: the Foundations of Embodied Interaction, Cambridge, MA: MIT Press.

Downing, S. (2005), 'The social construction of entrepreneurship: narrative and dramatic processes in the coproduction of organizations and identities', *Entrepreneurship Theory and Practice*, **29**(2): 185–204.

Elkjaer, B. (2004), 'Organizational learning: the "third way"', *Management Learning*, **35**(4): 419–34.

Fairlie, R., and W. Holleran (2011), 'Entrepreneurship training, risk aversion and other personality traits: evidence from a random experiment', *Journal of Business Venturing*, accessed 22 November at www.sciencedirect.com.science/article/p::/s016748701100016x.

Gallagher, S. and D. Zahavi (2007), *The Phenomenological Mind: An Introduction to Philosophy of Mind and Cognitive Science*, London: Routledge.

Gartner, W.B. (2006), 'A "critical mess" approach to entrepreneurship scholarship', in A. Lundstrom and S. Halversson (eds), *Entrepreneurship Research: Past Perspectives and Future Prospects, Vol. 2(3)*, Hanover, MA: Now, pp. 73–82.

Gartner, W.B. (2007), 'Entrepreneurial narrative and a science of the imagination', *Journal of Business Venturing*, **22**(5): 613–27.

Gendlin, E. (1992), 'The primacy of the body, not the primacy of perception: how the body knows the situation and philosophy', *Man and World*, **25**(3–4): 341–53.

Glicksohn, J. (2001), 'Temporal cognition and the phenomenology of time: a multiplicative function for apparent duration', *Consciousness and Cognition*, **10**(1): 1–25.

Gottlieb, G. (2007), 'Probabilistic epigenesis', *Developmental Science*, **10**(1): 1–11.

Gregoire, D.A., P.S. Barr and D.A. Shepherd (2010a), 'Cognitive processes of opportunity recognition: the role of structural alignment', *Organization Science*, **21**(2): 413–31.

Gregoire, D.A., D.A. Shepherd and L.S. Lambert (2010b), 'Measuring opportunity-recognition beliefs: illustrating and validating an experimental approach', *Organizational Research Methods*, **13**(1): 114–45.

Hanly, C. and M. Hanly (2001), 'Critical realism: distinguishing the psychological subjectivity of the analyst from epistemological subjectivism', *Journal of the American Psychoanalytic Association*, **49**(2): 515–32.

Harmeling, S. (2010), 'Entrepreneurship and human progress: contingency as a resource', *International Journal of Entrepreneurship and Innovation*, **11**(3): 181–8.

Haynie, J. and D. Shepherd (2011), 'Toward a theory of discontinuous career transition: investigating career transitions necessitated by traumatic life events', *Journal of Applied Psychology*, **96**(3): 501–24.

Haynie, J., D. Shepherd, E. Mosakowski and P. Earley (2010), 'A situated metacognitive model of the entrepreneurial mindset', *Journal of Business Venturing*, **25**(2): 217–29.

Heracleous, L. and C.D. Jacobs (2008), 'Crafting strategy: the role of embodied metaphors', *Long Range Planning*, **41**(3): 309–25.

Heron, J. (1992), *Feeling and Personhood: Psychology in Another Key*, London: Sage.

Heron, J. and P. Reason (2001), 'The practice of co-operative inquiry: research "with" rather than "on" people', in P. Reason and H. Bradbury (eds), *Handbook of Action Research: Participative Inquiry and Practice*, London: Sage, pp. 179–88.

Hjorth, D. (2008), 'Nordic entrepreneurship research', *Entrepreneurship Theory and Practice*, **32**(2): 313–38.

Hjorth, D. and M. Kostera (2007), *Entrepreneurship and the Experience Economy*, Copenhagen: Copenhagen Business School Press.

Hjorth, D. and C. Steyaert (eds) (2004), *Narrative and Discursive Approaches in Entrepreneurship*, Cheltenham, UK and Northampton, MA, USA: Edward Elgar.

Hjorth, D. and C. Steyaert (eds) (2009), *The Politics and Aesthetics of Entrepreneurship. A Fourth Movements in Entrepreneurship Book*, Cheltenham, UK and Northampton, MA, USA: Edward Elgar.

Hmieleski, K. and A. Corbett (2008), 'The contrasting interaction effects of improvisational behavior with entrepreneurial self-efficacy on new venture performance and entrepreneur work satisfaction', *Journal of Business Venturing*, **23**(4): 482–96.

Horwitz, S. (1994), 'Subjectivism', in P.J. Boettke (ed.), *The Elgar Companion to Austrian Economics*, Cheltenham, UK and Northampton, MA, USA: Edward Elgar, pp. 17–22.

Howes, D. (2003), *Sensual Relations: Engaging the Senses in Culture and Social Theory*, Ann Arbor, MI: University of Michigan Press.

Hurdley, R. (2010), 'Book review: Sarah Pink, *Doing Sensory Ethnography*', *Qualitative Research*, **10**(3): 392–4.

Hurdley, R. and B. Dicks (2011), 'In-between practice: working in the "third space" of sensory and multimodal methodology', *Qualitative Research*, **11**(3): 277–92.

Husserl, E. (1936), *The Crisis of European Science and Transendental Phenomenology: An Introduction to Phenomenological Philosophy*, Dordrecht, Netherlands: Kluwer, p. 156.

Ireland, D.R., C.R. Reutzel and J.W. Webb (2005), 'From the editors. Entrepreneurship research in AMJ: what has been published, and what might the future hold?', *Academy of Management Journal*, **48**(4): 556–64.

Jackson, M. (1996), *Things as They Are: New Directions in Phenomenological Anthropology*, Bloomington, IN: Indiana University Press.

Klein, P.G. (2008), 'Opportunity discovery, entrepreneurial action, and economic organization', *Strategic Entrepreneurship Journal*, **2**(3): 175–90.

Kolb, D.A. (1984), *Experiential Learning: Experience as the Source of Learning and Development*, Englewood Cliffs: Prentice-Hall Inc.

Kor, Y., J. Mahoney and S. Michael (2007), 'Resources, capabilities and entrepre-neurial perceptions', *Journal of Management Studies*, **44**(7): 1187–212.

Larkin, M., V. Eatough and M. Osborn (2011), 'Interpretive phenomenological analysis and embodied, active, situated cognition', *Theory and Psychology*, **21**(3): 318–37.

Lormand, E. (1996), 'Nonphenomenal consciousness', *Noûs*, **30**(2): 242–61.

Lutz, A. and E. Thompson (2003), 'Neurophenomenology: integrating subjective experience and brain dynamics in the neuroscience of consciousness', *Journal of Consciousness Studies*, **10**: 31–52.

Marcati, A., G. Guido and A.M. Peluso (2008), 'The role of SME entrepreneurs' innovativeness and personality in the adoption of innovations', *Research Policy*, **37**(9): 1579–90.

McGrath, R.G. (1999), 'Falling forward: real options reasoning and entrepre-neurial failure', *Academy of Management Review*, **24**(1): 13–30.

McMullen, J.S. and D.A. Shepherd (2006), 'Entrepreneurial action and the role of uncertainty in the theory of the entrepreneur', *Academy of Management Review*, **31**(1): 132–52.

Merleau-Ponty, M. (1962), *Phenomenology of Perception*, translated by C. Smith, London: Routledge, originally published 1945.

Merleau-Ponty, M. (1968), *The Visible and the Invisible*, Evanston, IL: Northwestern University.

Mitchell, R.K., K. Brigham, H. Walker and R. Dino (2011), 'In search of entre-preneurship excellence: a person–environment fit approach', in R.K. Mitchell and R.N. Dino (eds), *In Search of Research Excellence*, Cheltenham, UK and Northampton, MA, USA: Edward Elgar, pp. 3–28.

Moran, D. (2000), *Introduction to Phenomenology*, London: Routledge.

Mosakowksi, E. (1998), 'Entrepreneurial resources, organizational choices, and competitive outcomes', *Organization Science*, **9**(5): 625–43.

Nicolaou, N., S. Shane, L. Cherkas and T.D. Spector (2008), 'The influ-ence of sensation seeking in the heritability of entrepreneurship', *Strategic Entrepreneurship Journal*, **2**(1): 7–21.

Nicolaou, N., S. Shane, G. Adi, M. Mangino and J. Harris (2011), 'A polymor-phism associated with entrepreneurship: evidence from dopamine receptor can-didate genes', *Small Business Economics*, **36**(2): 151–5.

Pine, J.B. and J.H. Gilmore (1999), *The Experience Economy: Work is Theatre and Every Business a Stage*, Boston, MA: Harvard Business School Press.

Pink, S. (2011), 'Multimodality, multisensoriality and ethnographic knowing: social semiotics and the phenomenology of perception', *Qualitative Research*, **11**(3): 261–76.

Polanyi, M. (1962), *Personal Knowledge: Towards a Post-critical Philosophy*, Chicago, IL: University of Chicago Press.

Rutter, M. (2007), 'Gene–environment interdependence', *Developmental Science*, **10**(1): 12–18.

Salas, E., M.A. Rosen and D. DiazGranados (2010), 'Expertise-based intuition and decision making in organizations', *Journal of Management*, **36**(4): 941–73.

Sandberg, J. and M. Alveson (2011), 'Ways of constructing research questions: gap-spotting or problematization', *Organization*, **18**(1): 23–44.

Sandelands, L.E. and V. Srivatsan (1993), 'The problem of experience in the study of organizations', *Organization Studies*, **14**(1): 1–22.

Sarasvathy, S.D. (2001), 'Causation and effectuation: toward a theoretical shift from economic inevitability to entrepreneurial contingency', *Academy of Management Review*, **26**(2): 243–63.

Schmitt, B.H. (1999), *Experiential Marketing: How to get Customers to Sense, Feel, Think, Act, and Relate to Your Company and Brands*, New York: The Free Press.

Schumpeter, J. (1934), *The Theory of Economic Development*, Cambridge, MA: Harvard University Press.

Shackle, G.L.S. (1955), *Uncertainty in Economics and Other Reflections*, New York: Cambridge University Press.

Shane, S. (2003), *A General Theory of Entrepreneurship: The Individual–opportunity Nexus*, Cheltenham, UK and Northampton, MA, USA: Edward Elgar.

Shane, S., E.A. Locke and C. Collins (2003), 'Entrepreneurial motivation', *Human Resource Management Review*, **13**(2): 257–79.

Shane, S., N. Nicolaou, L. Cherkas and T.D. Spector (2010), 'Genetics, the Big Five, and the tendency to be self-employed', *Journal of Applied Psychology*, **95**(6): 1154–62.

Shepherd, D.A. (2003), 'Learning from business failure: propositions of grief recovery for the self-employed', *Academy of Management Review*, **28**(2): 318–28.

Shepherd, D.A. and M. Cardon (2009), 'Negative emotional reactions to project failure and the self-compassion to learn from the experience', *Journal of Management Studies*, **46**(6): 923–49.

Shonkoff, J.P. and D.A. Phillips (2002), 'Rethinking nature and nurture', in J.P. Shonkoff and D.A. Williams (eds), *From Neurons to Neighborhoods*, Washington, DC: National Academy Press, pp. 39–56.

Smith, D. (2011), 'Phenomenology', in E. Zalta (ed.), *The Stanford Encyclopedia of Philosophy*, accessed 22 November at http://plato.stanford.edu/archives/fall2011/entries/phenomenology.

Sorenson, O. and T.E. Stuart (2008), 'Entrepreneurship: a field of dreams?', *Academy of Management Annals*, **2**(1): 517–43.

Tilden, F. (1957), *Interpreting Our Heritage*, Chapel Hill, NC: University of North Carolina.

Thompson, E. (2004), 'Life and mind: from autopoiesis to neurophenomenology. A tribute to Francisco Varela', *Phenomenology and the Cognitive Sciences*, **3**(4): 381–98.

Thompson, C.J., W.B. Locander and H.R. Pollio (1989), 'Putting consumer experience back into consumer research: the philosophy and method of existential phenomenology', *Journal of Consumer Research*, **16**(2):133–46.

Tsoukas, H. and R. Chia (ed.) (2011), *Philosophy and Organization Theory, Research in the Sociology of Organizations, vol. 32*, Emerald Group Publishing Ltd.

Van Manen, M. (1997), *Researching Lived Experience: Human Science for an Action Sensitive Pedagogy*, 2nd edn, London, ON: Althouse Press.

Varela, F.J. (1996), 'Neurophenomenology: a methodological remedy to the hard problem', *Journal of Consciousness Studies*, **3**(2): 330–50.

Vince, R. (1998), 'Behind and beyond Kolb's learning cycle', *Journal of Management Education*, **22**(3): 304–19.

Warren, S. (2002), 'Show me how it feels to work here: using photography to research organizational aesthetics', *Ephemera: Critical Dialogues on Organization*, **2**(3): 224–45.

Weick, K, K. Sutcliffe and D. Obstfeld (2005), 'Organizing and the process of sensemaking', *Organization Science*, **16**(4): 409–21.
Westhead, P., D. Ucbasaran and M. Wright (2005), 'Decisions, actions and performance: do novice, serial and portfolio entrepreneurs differ?', *Journal of Small Business Management*, **43**(4): 393–17.
Westermann, G., D. Mareschal, M.H. Johnson, S. Sirois, M.W. Spratling and M.S.C. Thomas (2007), 'Neuroconstructivism', *Developmental Science*, **10**(1): 75–83.
Wiklund, J., P. Davidsson, D.B. Audretsch and C. Karlsson (2011), 'The future of entrepreneurship research', *Entrepreneurship Theory and Practice*, **35**(1): 1–9.
White, R., S. Thornhill and E. Hampson (2006), 'Entrepreneurs and evolutionary biology: the relationship between testosterone and new venture creation', *Organizational Behavior and Human Decision Processes*, **100**(1): 21–34.
White, R., S. Thornhill and E. Hampson (2007), 'A biosocial model of entrepreneurship: the combined effects of nurture and nature', *Journal of Organizational Behavior*, **28**(4): 451–66.
Witt, U. (1989), 'Subjectivismin economics – a suggested reorientation', in K.G. Grunert and F. Olander (eds), *Understanding Economic Behaviour*, Boston, MA, and Dordrecht, Netherlands: Kluwer, pp. 409–31.
Yanow, D. (2000), 'Seeing organizational learning: a "cultural" view', *Organization*, **7**(2): 247–68.
Yanow, D. and H. Tsoukas (2009), 'What is reflection-in-action? A phenomenological account', *Journal of Management Studies*, **46**(2): 1339–64.
Zhao, H. and S.E. Seibert (2006), 'The Big-Five personality dimensions and entrepreneurial status: a meta-analytical review', *Journal of Applied Psychology*, **91**(2): 259–71.
Zhao, H., S.E. Seibert and G.T. Lumpkin (2010), 'The relationship of personality to entrepreneurial intentions and performance: a meta-analytic review', *Journal of Management*, **36**(2): 381–404.

Index

gestalt structure 13
temporal structure 10, 15, 21
structure of experience, *see*
    experience
structure of memory 67
subjective
    subjective creations 47
    subjective experience 58, 190, 295–6
    subjective meaning 47–8, 77, 82–5,
        87–8, 92–3, 98, 254
    subjective opportunities 293, 297
subjectivism 292, 293
subjectivity 43, 47, 50, 58, 70, 77–8, 81,
    257, 261, 264, 283, 286, 292–3, 299
    embodied subjectivity 304
    social subjectivity 47
    subjectivity of experienced reality 77
    subjectivity of meaning 78, 256
succession
    inter-generational succession 231
    succession decisions 249
    succession experience 28
    succession planning 249
symbolic action 88, 97, 279, 274–5
symbolic interactionism 77–81, 83–6,
    88–91, 95, 97–8
symbols 50, 77, 80, 81, 83, 87–91, 98,
    268–71, 273, 287, 308
sunk costs 170
systems 19, 66, 104–6, 165, 181, 304
    action system 105
    action-perception matching system
        105
    behavior-generation systems 105
    brain system 9, 295
    complex systems 164–5
    connectionist systems 103
    experiential system 106–7, 118,
        123
    motor system 106
    rational system 106–7, 118
    representation system 107
    processing systems 106–7, 114
    sensory system 106
    social system 46
    systems theory 164

task(s)
    cognitive tasks 112, 115, 135
    entrepreneurial tasks 150, 180, 194

task at hand 160, 203, 205, 223,
    227
task familiarity 59, 112, 272
team 28, 198–9, 223
    entrepreneurial team 28, 222
    founding team 28
    team-building 143, 171, 287
    team member 8, 225
    top management team 28
temporal
    atemporal 297
    temporal boundaries 16, 257
    temporal cognition 296
    temporal constraints 112
    temporal depth 11
    temporal dynamics 4, 133
    temporal event 14
    temporal experience 1, 15, 129, 144,
        163, 180
    temporal flux 8
    temporal focus 126
    temporal nature 5, 21, 132, 145
    temporal perception 296
    temporal performance 154, 250
    temporal relation 59
    temporal sequence 102, 155
    temporal series 4
    temporal space 37, 38
    temporal streams 11
    temporal structure 10, 15, 21
    temporal succession 10, 41
temporality 8, 11, 37, 38
temporalization 37
texts 44, 47, 267
theory
    activity theory 115
    affective events theory (AET) 142
    arousal theory 6
    attribution theory 6
    cognitive-experiential self-theory
        (CEST) 106
    connectionist theory 104, 118
    critical theory 9, 284
    expectancy theory 6
    flow theory 6
    identity theory 98, 215, 225
    institutional theory 51
    middle-range theory 306
    network theory 6
    Newman's theory 7